P9-BYQ-112

# THE CONCEPT OF MIND

*the text of this book is printed
on 100% recycled paper*

# THE CONCEPT OF MIND

### GILBERT RYLE

*Waynflete Professor of Metaphysical Philosophy*
*in the University of Oxford*

BARNES & NOBLE BOOKS

A DIVISION OF HARPER & ROW, PUBLISHERS

New York, Evanston, San Francisco, London

Copyright, 1949, by Gilbert Ryle
in the United Kingdom

©

Copyright, 1949, by Gilbert Ryle

*All rights reserved*

Published by special arrangements with
Hutchinson & Company, Ltd., 78 Great
Portland Street, London, W. 1, England

L. C. catalogue card number: 59-14155


SBN 389 00232 1

Printed in the United States of America

# CONTENTS

# INTRODUCTION

THIS book offers what may with reservations be described as a theory of the mind. But it does not give new information about minds. We possess already a wealth of information about minds, information which is neither derived from, nor upset by, the arguments of philosophers. The philosophical arguments which constitute this book are intended not to increase what we know about minds, but to rectify the logical geography of the knowledge which we already possess.

Teachers and examiners, magistrates and critics, historians and novelists, confessors and non-commissioned officers, employers, employees and partners, parents, lovers, friends and enemies all know well enough how to settle their daily questions about the qualities of character and intellect of the individual with whom they have to do. They can appraise his performances, assess his progress, understand his words and actions, discern his motives and see his jokes. If they go wrong, they know how to correct their mistakes. More, they can deliberately influence the minds of those with whom they deal by criticism, example, teaching, punishment, bribery, mockery and persuasion, and then modify their treatments in the light of the results produced.

Both in describing the minds of others and in prescribing for them, they are wielding with greater or less efficiency concepts of mental powers and operations. They have learned how to apply in concrete situations such mental-conduct epithets as 'careful', 'stupid', 'logical', 'unobservant', 'ingenious', 'vain', 'methodical', 'credulous', 'witty', 'self-controlled' and a thousand others.

It is, however, one thing to know how to apply such concepts, quite another to know how to correlate them with one another and with concepts of other sorts. Many people can talk sense with concepts but cannot talk sense about them; they know by practice how to operate with concepts, anyhow inside familiar fields, but they cannot state the logical regulations governing their use. They are like people who know their way about their own parish, but cannot construct or read a map of it, much less a map of the region or continent in which their parish lies.

For certain purposes it is necessary to determine the logical cross-bearings of the concepts which we know quite well how to apply. The attempt to perform this operation upon the concepts of the powers, operations and states of minds has always been a big part of the task of philosophers. Theories of knowledge, logic, ethics, political theory and æsthetics are the products of their inquiries in this field. Some of these inquiries have made considerable regional progress, but it is part of the thesis of this book that during the three centuries of the epoch of natural science the logical categories in terms of which the concepts of mental powers and operations have been co-ordinated have been wrongly selected. Descartes left as one of his main philosophical legacies a myth which continues to distort the continental geography of the subject.

A myth is, of course, not a fairy story. It is the presentation of facts belonging to one category in the idioms appropriate to another. To explode a myth is accordingly not to deny the facts but to re-allocate them. And this is what I am trying to do.

To determine the logical geography of concepts is to reveal the logic of the propositions in which they are wielded, that is to say, to show with what other propositions they are consistent and inconsistent, what propositions follow from them and from what propositions they follow. The logical type or category to which a concept belongs is the set of ways in which it is logically legitimate to operate with it. The key arguments employed in this book are therefore intended to show why certain sorts of operations with the concepts of mental powers and processes are breaches of logical rules. I try to use *reductio ad absurdum* arguments both to disallow operations implicitly recommended by the Cartesian myth and to indicate to what logical types the concepts under investigation ought to be allocated. I do not, however, think it improper to use from time to time arguments of a less rigorous sort, especially when it seems expedient to mollify or acclimatise. Philosophy is the replacement of category-habits by category-disciplines, and if persuasions of conciliatory kinds ease the pains of relinquishing inveterate intellectual habits, they do not indeed reinforce the rigorous arguments, but they do weaken resistances to them.

Some readers may think that my tone of voice in this book is excessively polemical. It may comfort them to know that the assumptions against which I exhibit most heat are assumptions of which I myself have been a victim. Primarily I am trying to get some disorders out of my own system. Only secondarily do I hope to help other theorists to recognise our malady and to benefit from my medicine.

# CHAPTER I

# DESCARTES' MYTH

## (1) *The Official Doctrine.*

THERE is a doctrine about the nature and place of minds which is so prevalent among theorists and even among laymen that it deserves to be described as the official theory. Most philosophers, psychologists and religious teachers subscribe, with minor reservations, to its main articles and, although they admit certain theoretical difficulties in it, they tend to assume that these can be overcome without serious modifications being made to the architecture of the theory. It will be argued here that the central principles of the doctrine are unsound and conflict with the whole body of what we know about minds when we are not speculating about them.

The official doctrine, which hails chiefly from Descartes, is something like this. With the doubtful exceptions of idiots and infants in arms every human being has both a body and a mind. Some would prefer to say that every human being is both a body and a mind. His body and his mind are ordinarily harnessed together, but after the death of the body his mind may continue to exist and function.

Human bodies are in space and are subject to the mechanical laws which govern all other bodies in space. Bodily processes and states can be inspected by external observers. So a man's bodily life is as much a public affair as are the lives of animals and reptiles and even as the careers of trees, crystals and planets.

But minds are not in space, nor are their operations subject to mechanical laws. The workings of one mind are not witnessable by other observers; its career is private. Only I can take direct cognisance of the states and processes of my own mind. A person therefore lives through two collateral histories, one consisting of what happens in and to his body, the other consisting of what happens in and to his mind. The first is public, the second private. The events in the first history are events in the physical world, those in the second are events in the mental world.

It has been disputed whether a person does or can directly monitor all or only some of the episodes of his own private history; but, according to the official doctrine, of at least some of these episodes he has direct and unchallengeable cognisance. In consciousness, self-consciousness and introspection he is directly and authentically apprised of the present states and operations of his mind. He may have great or small uncertainties about concurrent and adjacent episodes in the physical world, but he can have none about at least part of what is momentarily occupying his mind.

It is customary to express this bifurcation of his two lives and of his two worlds by saying that the things and events which belong to the physical world, including his own body, are external, while the workings of his own mind are internal. This antithesis of outer and inner is of course meant to be construed as a metaphor, since minds, not being in space, could not be described as being spatially inside anything else, or as having things going on spatially inside themselves. But relapses from this good intention are common and theorists are found speculating how stimuli, the physical sources of which are yards or miles outside a person's skin, can generate mental responses inside his skull, or how decisions framed inside his cranium can set going movements of his extremities.

Even when 'inner' and 'outer' are construed as metaphors, the problem how a person's mind and body influence one another is notoriously charged with theoretical difficulties. What the mind wills, the legs, arms and the tongue execute; what affects the ear and the eye has something to do with what the mind perceives; grimaces and smiles betray the mind's moods and bodily castigations lead, it is hoped, to moral improvement. But the actual transactions between the episodes of the private history and those of the public history remain mysterious, since by definition they can belong to neither series. They could not be reported among the happenings described in a person's autobiography of his inner life, but nor could they be reported among those described in some one else's biography of that person's overt career. They can be inspected neither by introspection nor by laboratory experiment. They are theoretical shuttlecocks which are forever being bandied from the physiologist back to the psychologist and from the psychologist back to the physiologist

Underlying this partly metaphorical representation of the bifurcation of a person's two lives there is a seemingly more profound and philosophical assumption. It is assumed that there are two different kinds of existence or status. What exists or happens may have the status of physical existence, or it may have the status of mental existence. Somewhat as the faces of coins are either heads or tails, or somewhat as living creatures are either male or female, so, it is supposed, some existing is physical existing, other existing is mental existing. It is a necessary feature of what has physical existence that it is in space and time, it is a necessary feature of what has mental existence that it is in time but not in space. What has physical existence is composed of matter, or else is a function of matter; what has mental existence consists of consciousness, or else is a function of consciousness.

There is thus a polar opposition between mind and matter, an opposition which is often brought out as follows. Material objects are situated in a common field, known as 'space', and what happens to one body in one part of space is mechanically connected with what happens to other bodies in other parts of space. But mental happenings occur in insulated fields, known as 'minds', and there is, apart maybe from telepathy, no direct causal connection between what happens in one mind and what happens in another. Only through the medium of the public physical world can the mind of one person make a difference to the mind of another. The mind is its own place and in his inner life each of us lives the life of a ghostly Robinson Crusoe. People can see, hear and jolt one another's bodies, but they are irremediably blind and deaf to the workings of one another's minds and inoperative upon them.

What sort of knowledge can be secured of the workings of a mind? On the one side, according to the official theory, a person has direct knowledge of the best imaginable kind of the workings of his own mind. Mental states and processes are (or are normally) conscious states and processes, and the consciousness which irradiates them can engender no illusions and leaves the door open for no doubts. A person's present thinkings, feelings and willings, his perceivings, rememberings and imaginings are intrinsically 'phosphorescent'; their existence and their nature are inevitably betrayed to their owner. The inner life is a stream of consciousness of such a sort that it would be absurd to suggest that the mind whose life is that stream might be unaware of what is passing down it.

True, the evidence adduced recently by Freud seems to show that there exist channels tributary to this stream, which run hidden from their owner. People are actuated by impulses the existence of which they vigorously disavow; some of their thoughts differ from the thoughts which they acknowledge; and some of the actions which they think they will to perform they do not really will. They are thoroughly gulled by some of their own hypocrisies and they successfully ignore facts about their mental lives which on the official theory ought to be patent to them. Holders of the official theory tend, however, to maintain that anyhow in normal circumstances a person must be directly and authentically seized of the present state and workings of his own mind.

Besides being currently supplied with these alleged immediate data of consciousness, a person is also generally supposed to be able to exercise from time to time a special kind of perception, namely inner perception, or introspection. He can take a (non-optical) 'look' at what is passing in his mind. Not only can he view and scrutinize a flower through his sense of sight and listen to and discriminate the notes of a bell through his sense of hearing; he can also reflectively or introspectively watch, without any bodily organ of sense, the current episodes of his inner life. This self-observation is also commonly supposed to be immune from illusion, confusion or doubt. A mind's reports of its own affairs have a certainty superior to the best that is possessed by its reports of matters in the physical world. Sense-perceptions can, but consciousness and introspection cannot, be mistaken or confused.

On the other side, one person has no direct access of any sort to the events of the inner life of another. He cannot do better than make problematic inferences from the observed behaviour of the other person's body to the states of mind which, by analogy from his own conduct, he supposes to be signalised by that behaviour. Direct access to the workings of a mind is the privilege of that mind itself; in default of such privileged access, the workings of one mind are inevitably occult to everyone else. For the supposed arguments from bodily movements similar to their own to mental workings similar to their own would lack any possibility of observational corroboration. Not unnaturally, therefore, an adherent of the official theory finds it difficult to resist this consequence of his premisses, that he has no good reason to believe that there do exist minds other than his own. Even if he prefers to believe that to other human bodies there are harnessed minds not unlike his own, he cannot claim to be able to discover their individual characteristics, or the particular things that they undergo and do. Absolute solitude is on this showing the ineluctable destiny of the soul. Only our bodies can meet.

As a necessary corollary of this general scheme there is implicitly prescribed a special way of construing our ordinary concepts of mental powers and operations. The verbs, nouns and adjectives, with which in ordinary life we describe the wits, characters and higher-grade performances of the people with whom we have do, are required to be construed as signifying special episodes in their secret histories, or else as signifying tendencies for such episodes to occur. When someone is described as knowing, believing or guessing something, as hoping, dreading, intending or shirking something, as designing this or being amused at that, these verbs are supposed to denote the occurrence of specific modifications in his (to us) occult stream of consciousness. Only his own privileged access to this stream in direct awareness and introspection could provide authentic testimony that these mental-conduct verbs were correctly or incorrectly applied. The onlooker, be he teacher, critic, biographer or friend, can never assure himself that his comments have any vestige of truth. Yet it was just because we do in fact all know how to make such comments, make them with general correctness and correct them when they turn out to be confused or mistaken, that philosophers found it necessary to construct their theories of the nature and place of minds. Finding mental-conduct concepts being regularly and effectively used, they properly sought to fix their logical geography. But the logical geography officially recommended would entail that there could be no regular or effective use of these mental-conduct concepts in our descriptions of, and prescriptions for, other people's minds.

## (2) The Absurdity of the Official Doctrine.

Such in outline is the official theory. I shall often speak of it, with deliberate abusiveness, as 'the dogma of the Ghost in the

Machine'. I hope to prove that it is entirely false, and false not in detail but in principle. It is not merely an assemblage of particular mistakes. It is one big mistake and a mistake of a special kind. It is, namely, a category-mistake. It represents the facts of mental life as if they belonged to one logical type or category (or range of types or categories), when they actually belong to another. The dogma is therefore a philosopher's myth. In attempting to explode the myth I shall probably be taken to be denying well-known facts about the mental life of human beings, and my plea that I aim at doing nothing more than rectify the logic of mental-conduct concepts will probably be disallowed as mere subterfuge.

I must first indicate what is meant by the phrase 'Category-mistake'. This I do in a series of illustrations.

A foreigner visiting Oxford or Cambridge for the first time is shown a number of colleges, libraries, playing fields, museums, scientific departments and administrative offices. He then asks 'But where is the University? I have seen where the members of the Colleges live, where the Registrar works, where the scientists experiment and the rest. But I have not yet seen the University in which reside and work the members of your University.' It has then to be explained to him that the University is not another collateral institution, some ulterior counterpart to the colleges, laboratories and offices which he has seen. The University is just the way in which all that he has already seen is organized. When they are seen and when their co-ordination is understood, the University has been seen. His mistake lay in his innocent assumption that it was correct to speak of Christ Church, the Bodleian Library, the Ashmolean Museum *and* the University, to speak, that is, as if 'the University' stood for an extra member of the class of which these other units are members. He was mistakenly allocating the University to the same category as that to which the other institutions belong.

The same mistake would be made by a child witnessing the march-past of a division, who, having had pointed out to him such and such battalions, batteries, squadrons, etc., asked when the division was going to appear. He would be supposing that a division was a counterpart to the units already seen, partly similar to them and partly unlike them. He would be shown his mistake by being told that in watching the battalions, batteries and squadrons marching past he had been watching the division marching past. The march-past was not a parade of battalions, batteries, squadrons *and* a division; it was a parade of the battalions, batteries and squadrons *of* a division.

One more illustration. A foreigner watching his first game of cricket learns what are the functions of the bowlers, the batsmen, the fielders, the umpires and the scorers. He then says 'But there is no one left on the field to contribute the famous element of team-spirit. I see who does the bowling, the batting and the wicket-keeping; but I do not see whose role it is to exercise *esprit de corps*.' Once more, it would have to be explained that he was looking for the wrong type of thing. Team-spirit is not another cricketing-operation supplementary to all of the other special tasks. It is, roughly, the keenness with which each of the special tasks is performed, and performing a task keenly is not performing two tasks. Certainly exhibiting team-spirit is not the same thing as bowling or catching, but nor is it a third thing such that we can say that the bowler first bowls *and* then exhibits team-spirit or that a fielder is at a given moment *either* catching *or* displaying *esprit de corps*.

These illustrations of category-mistakes have a common feature which must be noticed. The mistakes were made by people who did not know how to wield the concepts *University*, *division* and *team-spirit*. Their puzzles arose from inability to use certain items in the English vocabulary.

The theoretically interesting category-mistakes are those made by people who are perfectly competent to apply concepts, at least in the situations with which they are familiar, but are still liable in their abstract thinking to allocate those concepts to logical types to which they do not belong. An instance of a mistake of this sort would be the following story. A student of politics has learned the main differences between the British, the French and the American Constitutions, and has learned also the differences and connections between the Cabinet, Parliament, the various Ministries, the Judicature and the Church of England. But he still becomes embarrassed when asked questions about the connections between the Church of England, the Home Office and the British Constitution. For while the Church and the Home Office are institutions, the British Constitution is not another institution in the same sense of that noun. So inter-institutional relations which can be asserted or denied to hold between the Church and the Home Office cannot be asserted or denied to hold between either of them and the British Constitution. 'The British Constitution' is not a term of the same logical type as 'the Home Office' and 'the Church of England'. In a partially similar way, John Doe may be a relative, a friend, an enemy or a stranger to Richard Roe; but he cannot be any of these things to the Average Taxpayer. He knows how to talk sense in certain sorts of discussions about the Average Taxpayer, but he is baffled to say why he could not come across him in the street as he can come across Richard Roe.

It is pertinent to our main subject to notice that, so long as the student of politics continues to think of the British Constitution as a counterpart to the other institutions, he will tend to describe it as a mysteriously occult institution; and so long as John Doe continues to think of the Average Taxpayer as a fellow-citizen, he will tend to think of him as an elusive insubstantial man, a ghost who is everywhere yet nowhere.

My destructive purpose is to show that a family of radical category-mistakes is the source of the double-life theory. The representation of a person as a ghost mysteriously ensconced in a machine derives from this argument. Because, as is true, a person's thinking, feeling and purposive doing cannot be described solely in the idioms of physics, chemistry and physiology, therefore they must be described in counterpart idioms. As the human body is a complex organised unit, so the human mind must be another complex organised unit, though one made of a different sort of stuff and with a different sort of structure. Or, again, as the human body, like any other parcel of matter, is a field of causes and effects, so the mind must be another field of causes and effects, though not (Heaven be praised) mechanical causes and effects.

(3) *The Origin of the Category-mistake.*

One of the chief intellectual origins of what I have yet to prove to be the Cartesian category-mistake seems to be this. When Galileo showed that his methods of scientific discovery were competent to provide a mechanical theory which should cover every occupant of space, Descartes found in himself two conflicting motives. As a man of scientific genius he could not but endorse the claims of mechanics, yet as a religious and moral man he could not accept, as Hobbes accepted, the discouraging rider to those claims, namely that human nature differs only in degree of complexity from clockwork. The mental could not be just a variety of the mechanical.

He and subsequent philosophers naturally but erroneously availed themselves of the following escape-route. Since mental-conduct words are not to be construed as signifying the occurrence of mechanical processes, they must be construed as signifying the occurrence of non-mechanical processes; since mechanical laws explain movements in space as the effects of other movements in space, other laws must explain some of the non-spatial workings of minds as the effects of other non-spatial workings of minds. The difference between the human behaviours which we describe as intelligent and those which we describe as unintelligent must be a difference in their causation; so, while some movements of human tongues and limbs are the effects of mechanical causes, others must be the effects of non-mechanical causes, i.e. some issue from movements of particles of matter, others from workings of the mind.

The differences between the physical and the mental were thus represented as differences inside the common framework of the categories of 'thing', 'stuff', 'attribute', 'state', 'process', 'change', 'cause' and 'effect'. Minds are things, but different sorts of things from bodies; mental processes are causes and effects, but different sorts of causes and effects from bodily movements. And so on. Somewhat as the foreigner expected the University to be an extra edifice, rather like a college but also considerably different, so the repudiators of mechanism represented minds as extra centres of causal processes, rather like machines but also considerably different from them. Their theory was a para-mechanical hypothesis.

That this assumption was at the heart of the doctrine is shown by the fact that there was from the beginning felt to be a major theoretical difficulty in explaining how minds can influence and be influenced by bodies. How can a mental process, such as willing, cause spatial movements like the movements of the tongue? How can a physical change in the optic nerve have among its effects a mind's perception of a flash of light? This notorious crux by itself shows the logical mould into which Descartes pressed his theory of the mind. It was the self-same mould into which he and Galileo set their mechanics. Still unwittingly adhering to the grammar of mechanics, he tried to avert disaster by describing minds in what was merely an obverse vocabulary. The workings of minds had to be described by the mere negatives of the specific descriptions given to bodies; they are not in space, they are not motions, they are not modifications of matter, they are not accessible to public observation. Minds are not bits of clockwork, they are just bits of not-clockwork.

As thus represented, minds are not merely ghosts harnessed to machines, they are themselves just spectral machines. Though the human body is an engine, it is not quite an ordinary engine, since some of its workings are governed by another engine inside it—this interior governor-engine being one of a very special sort. It is invisible, inaudible and it has no size or weight. It cannot be taken to bits and the laws it obeys are not those known to ordinary engineers. Nothing is known of how it governs the bodily engine.

A second major crux points the same moral. Since, according to the doctrine, minds belong to the same category as bodies and since bodies are rigidly governed by mechanical laws, it seemed to many theorists to follow that minds must be similarly governed by rigid non-mechanical laws. The physical world is a deterministic system, so the mental world must be a deterministic system. Bodies cannot help the modifications that they undergo, so minds cannot help pursuing the careers fixed for them. *Responsibility, choice, merit* and *demerit* are therefore inapplicable concepts—unless the compromise solution is adopted of saying that the laws governing mental processes, unlike those governing physical processes, have the congenial attribute of being only rather rigid. The problem of the Freedom of the Will was the problem how to reconcile the hypothesis that minds are to be described in terms drawn from the categories of mechanics with the knowledge that higher-grade human conduct is not of a piece with the behaviour of machines.

It is an historical curiosity that it was not noticed that the entire argument was broken-backed. Theorists correctly assumed that any sane man could already recognise the differences between, say, rational and non-rational utterances or between purposive and automatic behaviour. Else there would have been nothing requiring to be salved from mechanism. Yet the explanation given presupposed that one person could in principle never recognise the difference between the rational and the irrational utterances issuing from other human bodies, since he could never get access to the postulated immaterial causes of some of their utterances. Save for the doubtful exception of himself, he could never tell the difference between a man and a Robot. It would have to be conceded, for example, that, for all that we can tell, the inner lives of persons who are classed as idiots or lunatics are as rational as those of anyone else. Perhaps only their overt behaviour is disappointing; that is to say, perhaps 'idiots' are not really idiotic, or 'lunatics' lunatic. Perhaps, too, some of those who are classed as sane are really idiots. According to the theory, external observers could never know how the overt behaviour of others is correlated with their mental powers and processes and so they could never know or even plausibly conjecture whether their applications of mental-conduct concepts to these other people were correct or incorrect. It would then be hazardous or impossible for a man to claim sanity or logical consistency even for himself, since he would be debarred from comparing his own performances with those of others. In short, our characterisations of persons and their performances as intelligent, prudent and virtuous or as stupid, hypocritical and cowardly could never have been made, so the problem of providing a special causal hypothesis to serve as the basis of such diagnoses would never have arisen. The question, 'How do persons differ from machines?' arose just because everyone already knew how to apply mental-conduct concepts before the new causal hypothesis was introduced. This causal hypothesis could not therefore be the source of the criteria used in those applications. Nor, of course, has the causal hypothesis in any degree improved our handling of those criteria. We still distinguish good from bad arithmetic, politic from impolitic conduct and fertile from infertile imaginations in the ways in which Descartes himself distinguished them before and after he speculated how the applicability of these criteria was compatible with the principle of mechanical causation.

He had mistaken the logic of his problem. Instead of asking by what criteria intelligent behaviour is actually distinguished from non-intelligent behaviour, he asked 'Given that the principle of mechanical causation does not tell us the difference, what other causal principle will tell it us?' He realised that the problem was not one of mechanics and assumed that it must therefore be one of some counterpart to mechanics. Not unnaturally psychology is often cast for just this role.

When two terms belong to the same category, it is proper to construct conjunctive propositions embodying them. Thus a purchaser may say that he bought a left-hand glove and a right-hand glove, but not that he bought a left-hand glove, a right-hand glove and a pair of gloves. 'She came home in a flood of tears and a sedan-chair' is a well-known joke based on the absurdity of conjoining terms of different types. It would have been equally ridiculous to construct the disjunction 'She came home either in a flood of tears or else in a sedan-chair'. Now the dogma of the Ghost in the Machine does just this. It maintains that there exist both bodies and minds; that there occur physical processes and mental processes; that there are mechanical causes of corporeal movements and mental causes of corporeal movements. I shall argue that these and other analogous conjunctions are absurd; but, it must be noticed, the argument will not show that either of the illegitimately conjoined propositions is absurd in itself. I am not, for example, denying that there occur mental processes. Doing long division is a mental process and so is making a joke. But I am saying that the phrase 'there occur mental processes' does not mean the same sort of thing as 'there occur physical processes', and, therefore, that it makes no sense to conjoin or disjoin the two.

If my argument is successful, there will follow some interesting consequences. First, the hallowed contrast between Mind and Matter will be dissipated, but dissipated not by either of the equally hallowed absorptions of Mind by Matter or of Matter by Mind, but in quite a different way. For the seeming contrast of the two will be shown to be as illegitimate as would be the contrast of 'she came home in a flood of tears' and 'she came home in a sedan-chair'. The belief that there is a polar opposition between Mind and Matter is the belief that they are terms of the same logical type.

It will also follow that both Idealism and Materialism are answers to an improper question. The 'reduction' of the material world to mental states and processes, as well as the 'reduction' of mental states and processes to physical states and processes, pre-suppose the legitimacy of the disjunction 'Either there exist minds or there exist bodies (but not both)'. It would be like saying,

'Either she bought a left-hand and a right-hand glove or she bought a pair of gloves (but not both)'.

It is perfectly proper to say, in one logical tone of voice, that there exist minds and to say, in another logical tone of voice, that there exist bodies. But these expressions do not indicate two different species of existence, for 'existence' is not a generic word like 'coloured' or 'sexed'. They indicate two different senses of 'exist', somewhat as 'rising' has different senses in 'the tide is rising', 'hopes are rising', and 'the average age of death is rising'. A man would be thought to be making a poor joke who said that three things are now rising, namely the tide, hopes and the average age of death. It would be just as good or bad a joke to say that there exist prime numbers and Wednesdays and public opinions and navies; or that there exist both minds and bodies. In the succeeding chapters I try to prove that the official theory does rest on a batch of category-mistakes by showing that logically absurd corollaries follow from it. The exhibition of these absurdities will have the constructive effect of bringing out part of the correct logic of mental-conduct concepts.

(4) *Historical Note.*

It would not be true to say that the official theory derives solely from Descartes' theories, or even from a more widespread anxiety about the implications of seventeenth century mechanics. Scholastic and Reformation theology had schooled the intellects of the scientists as well as of the laymen, philosophers and clerics of that age. Stoic-Augustinian theories of the will were embedded in the Calvinist doctrines of sin and grace; Platonic and Aristotelian theories of the intellect shaped the orthodox doctrines of the immortality of the soul. Descartes was reformulating already prevalent theological doctrines of the soul in the new syntax of Galileo. The theologian's privacy of conscience became the philosopher's privacy of consciousness, and what had been the bogy of Predestination reappeared as the bogy of Determinism.

It would also not be true to say that the two-worlds myth did no theoretical good. Myths often do a lot of theoretical good, while they are still new. One benefit bestowed by the para-mechanical myth was that it partly superannuated the then prevalent para-political myth. Minds and their Faculties had previously been described by analogies with political superiors and political subordinates. The idioms used were those of ruling, obeying, collaborating and rebelling. They survived and still survive in many ethical and some epistemological discussions. As, in physics, the new myth of occult Forces was a scientific improvement on the old myth of Final Causes, so, in anthropological and psychological theory, the new myth of hidden operations, impulses and agencies was an improvement on the old myth of dictations, deferences and disobediences.

# KNOWING HOW AND KNOWING THAT

(1) *Foreword.*

IN this chapter I try to show that when we describe people as exercising qualities of mind, we are not referring to occult episodes of which their overt acts and utterances are effects; we are referring to those overt acts and uttterances themselves. There are, of course, differences, crucial for our inquiry, between describing an action as performed absent-mindedly and describing a physiologically similar action as done on purpose, with care or with cunning. But such differences of description do not consist in the absence or presence of an implicit reference to some shadow-action covertly prefacing the overt action. They consist, on the contrary, in the absence or presence of certain sorts of testable explanatory-cum-predictive assertions.

(2) *Intelligence and Intellect.*

The mental-conduct concepts that I choose to examine first are those which belong to that family of concepts ordinarily surnamed 'intelligence'. Here are a few of the more determinate adjectives of this family: 'clever', 'sensible', 'careful', 'methodical', 'inventive', 'prudent', 'acute', 'logical', 'witty', 'observant', 'critical', 'experimental', 'quick-witted', 'cunning', 'wise', 'judicious' and 'scrupulous'. When a person is deficient in intelligence he is described as 'stupid' or else by more determinate epithets such as 'dull', 'silly', 'careless', 'unmethodical', 'uninventive', 'rash', 'dense', 'illogical', 'humourless', 'unobservant', 'uncritical', 'unexperimental', 'slow,' 'simple', 'unwise' and 'injudicious'.

It is of first-rate importance to notice from the start that stupidity is not the same thing, or the same sort of thing, as ignorance. There is no incompatibility between being well-informed and being silly, and a person who has a good nose for arguments or jokes may have a bad head for facts.

Part of the importance of this distinction between being intelligent and possessing knowledge lies in the fact that both philosophers and laymen tend to treat intellectual operations as the core of mental conduct; that is to say, they tend to define all other mental-conduct concepts in terms of concepts of cognition. They suppose that the primary exercise of minds consists in finding the answers to questions and that their other occupations are merely applications of considered truths or even regrettable distractions from their consideration. The Greek idea that immortality is reserved for the theorising part of the soul was discredited, but not dispelled, by Christianity.

When we speak of the intellect or, better, of the intellectual powers and performances of persons, we are referring primarily to that special class of operations which constitute theorising. The goal of these operations is the knowledge of true propositions or facts. Mathematics and the established natural sciences are the model accomplishments of human intellects. The early theorists naturally speculated upon what constituted the peculiar excellences of the theoretical sciences and disciplines, the growth of which they had witnessed and assisted. They were predisposed to find that it was in the capacity for rigorous theory that lay the superiority of men over animals, of civilised men over barbarians and even of the divine mind over human minds. They thus bequeathed the idea that the capacity to attain knowledge of truths was the defining property of a mind. Other human powers could be classed as mental only if they could be shown to be somehow piloted by the intellectual grasp of true propositions. To be rational was to be able to recognise truths and the connections between them. To act rationally was, therefore, to have one's non-theoretical propensities controlled by one's apprehension of truths about the conduct of life.

The main object of this chapter is to show that there are many activities which directly display qualities of mind, yet are neither themselves intellectual operations nor yet effects of intellectual operations. Intelligent practice is not a step-child of theory. On the contrary theorising is one practice amongst others and is itself intelligently or stupidly conducted.

There is another reason why it is important to correct from the start the intellectualist doctrine which tries to define intelligence in terms of the apprehension of truths, instead of the apprehension of truths in terms of intelligence. Theorising is an activity which most people can and normally do conduct in silence. They articulate in sentences the theories that they construct, but they do not most of the time speak these sentences out loud. They say them to themselves. Or they formulate their thoughts in diagrams and pictures, but they do not always set these out on paper. They 'see them in their minds' eyes'. Much of our ordinary thinking is conducted in internal monologue or silent soliloquy, usually accompanied by an internal cinematograph-show of visual imagery.

This trick of talking to oneself in silence is acquired neither quickly nor without effort; and it is a necessary condition of our acquiring it that we should have previously learned to talk intelligently aloud and have heard and understood other people doing so. Keeping our thoughts to ourselves is a sophisticated accomplishment. It was not until the Middle Ages that people learned to read without reading aloud. Similarly a boy has to learn to read aloud before he learns to read under his breath, and to prattle aloud before he prattles to himself. Yet many theorists have supposed that the silence in which most of us have learned to think is a defining property of thought. Plato said that in thinking the soul is talking to itself. But silence, though often convenient, is inessential, as is the restriction of the audience to one recipient.

The combination of the two assumptions that theorising is the primary activity of minds and that theorising is intrinsically a private, silent or internal operation remains one of the main supports of the dogma of the ghost in the machine. People tend to identify their minds with the 'place' where they conduct their secret thoughts. They even come to suppose that there is a special mystery about how we publish our thoughts instead of realising that we employ a special artifice to keep them to ourselves.

(3) *Knowing How and Knowing That.*

When a person is described by one or other of the intelligence-epithets such as 'shrewd' or 'silly', 'prudent' or 'imprudent', the description imputes to him not the knowledge, or ignorance, of this or that truth, but the ability, or inability, to do certain sorts of things.

Theorists have been so preoccupied with the task of investigating the nature, the source and the credentials of the theories that we adopt that they have for the most part ignored the question what it is for someone to know how to perform tasks. In ordinary life, on the contrary, as well as in the special business of teaching, we are much more concerned with people's competences than with their cognitive repertoires, with the operations than with the truths that they learn. Indeed even when we are concerned with their intellectual excellences and deficiencies, we are interested less in the stocks of truths that they acquire and retain than in their capacities to find out truths for themselves and their ability to organise and exploit them, when discovered. Often we deplore a person's ignorance of some fact only because we deplore the stupidity of which his ignorance is a consequence.

There are certain parallelisms between knowing *how* and knowing *that*, as well as certain divergences. We speak of learning how to play an instrument as well as of learning that something is the case; of finding out how to prune trees as well as of finding out that the Romans had a camp in a certain place; of forgetting how to tie a reef-knot as well as of forgetting that the German for 'knife' is '*Messer*'. We can wonder *how* as well as wonder *whether*.

On the other hand we never speak of a person believing or opining *how*, and though it is proper to ask for the grounds or reasons for someone's acceptance of a proposition, this question cannot be asked of someone's skill at cards or prudence in investments.

What is involved in our descriptions of people as knowing how to make and appreciate jokes, to talk grammatically, to play chess, to fish, or to argue? Part of what is meant is that, when they perform these operations, they tend to perform them well, i.e. correctly or efficiently or successfully. Their performances come up to certain standards, or satisfy certain criteria. But this is not enough. The well-regulated clock keeps good time and the well-drilled circus seal performs its tricks flawlessly, yet we do not call them 'intelligent'. We reserve this title for the persons responsible for their performances. To be intelligent is not merely to satisfy criteria, but to apply them; to regulate one's actions and not merely to be well-regulated. A person's performance is described as careful or skilful, if in his operations he is ready to detect and correct lapses, to repeat and improve upon successes, to profit from the examples of others and so forth. He applies criteria in performing critically, that is, in trying to get things right.

This point is commonly expressed in the vernacular by saying that an action exhibits intelligence, if, and only if, the agent is thinking what he is doing while he is doing it, and thinking what he is doing in such a manner that he would not do the action so well if he were not thinking what he is doing. This popular idiom is sometimes appealed to as evidence in favour of the intellectualist legend. Champions of this legend are apt to try to reassimilate knowing *how* to knowing *that* by arguing that intelligent performance involves the observance of rules, or the application of criteria. It follows that the operation which is characterised as intelligent must be preceded by an intellectual acknowledgment of these rules or criteria; that is, the agent must first go through the internal process of avowing to himself certain propositions about what is to be done ('maxims', 'imperatives' or 'regulative propositions' as they are sometimes called); only then can he execute his performance in accordance with those dictates. He must preach to himself before he can practise. The chef must recite his recipes to himself before he can cook according to them; the hero must lend his inner ear to some appropriate moral imperative before swimming out to save the drowning man; the chess-player must run over in his head all the relevant rules and tactical maxims of the game before he can make correct and skilful moves. To do something thinking what one is doing is, according to this legend, always to do two things; namely, to consider certain appropriate propositions, or prescriptions, and to put into practice what these propositions or prescriptions enjoin. It is to do a bit of theory and then to do a bit of practice.

Certainly we often do not only reflect before we act but reflect in order to act properly. The chess-player may require some time in which to plan his moves before he makes them. Yet the general assertion that all intelligent performance requires to be prefaced by the consideration of appropriate propositions rings unplausibly, even when it is apologetically conceded that the required consideration is often very swift and may go quite unmarked by the agent. I shall argue that the intellectualist legend is false and that when we describe a performance as intelligent, this does not entail the double operation of considering and executing.

First, there are many classes of performances in which intelligence is displayed, but the rules or criteria of which are unformulated. The wit, when challenged to cite the maxims, or canons, by which he constructs and appreciates jokes, is unable to answer. He knows how to make good jokes and how to detect bad ones, but he cannot tell us or himself any recipes for them. So the practice of humour is not a client of its theory. The canons of aesthetic taste, of tactful manners and of inventive technique similarly remain unpropounded without impediment to the intelligent exercise of those gifts.

Rules of correct reasoning were first extracted by Aristotle, yet men knew how to avoid and detect fallacies before they learned his lessons, just as men since Aristotle, and including Aristotle, ordinarily conduct their arguments without making any internal reference to his formulae. They do not plan their arguments before constructing them. Indeed if they had to plan what to think before thinking it they would never think at all; for this planning would itself be unplanned.

Efficient practice precedes the theory of it; methodologies presuppose the application of the methods, of the critical investigation of which they are the products. It was because Aristotle found himself and others reasoning now intelligently and now stupidly and it was because Izaak Walton found himself and others angling sometimes effectively and sometimes ineffectively that both were able to give to their pupils the maxims and prescriptions of their arts. It is therefore possible for people intelligently to perform some sorts of operations when they are not yet able to consider any propositions enjoining how they should be performed. Some intelligent performances are not controlled by any anterior acknowledgments of the principles applied in them.

The crucial objection to the intellectualist legend is this. The consideration of propositions is itself an operation the execution of which can be more or less intelligent, less or more stupid. But if, for any operation to be intelligently executed, a prior theoretical operation had first to be performed and performed intelligently, it would be a logical impossibility for anyone ever to break into the circle.

Let us consider some salient points at which this regress would arise. According to the legend, whenever an agent does anything intelligently, his act is preceded and steered by another internal act of considering a regulative proposition appropriate to his practical problem. But what makes him consider the one maxim which is appropriate rather than any of the thousands which are not? Why does the hero not find himself calling to mind a cooking-recipe, or a rule of Formal Logic? Perhaps he does, but then his intellectual process is silly and not sensible. Intelligently reflecting how to act is, among other things, considering what is pertinent and disregarding what is inappropriate. Must we then say that for the hero's reflections how to act to be intelligent he must first reflect how best to reflect how to act? The endlessness of this implied regress shows that the application of the criterion of appropriateness does not entail the occurrence of a process of considering this criterion.

Next, supposing still that to act reasonably I must first perpend the reason for so acting, how am I led to make a suitable application of the reason to the particular situation which my action is to meet? For the reason, or maxim, is inevitably a proposition of some generality. It cannot embody specifications to fit every detail of the particular state of affairs. Clearly, once more, I must be sensible and not stupid, and this good sense cannot itself be a product of the intellectual acknowledgment of any general principle. A soldier does not become a shrewd general merely by endorsing the strategic principles of Clausewitz; he must also be competent to apply them. Knowing how to apply maxims cannot be reduced to, or derived from, the acceptance of those or any other maxims.

To put it quite generally, the absurd assumption made by the intellectualist legend is this, that a performance of any sort inherits all its title to intelligence from some anterior internal operation of planning what to do. Now very often we do go through such a process of planning what to do, and, if we are silly, our planning is silly, if shrewd, our planning is shrewd. It is also notoriously possible for us to plan shrewdly and perform stupidly, i.e. to flout our precepts in our practice. By the original argument, therefore, our intellectual planning process must inherit its title to shrewdness from yet another interior process of planning to plan, and this process could in its turn be silly or shrewd. The regress is infinite, and this reduces to absurdity the theory that for an operation to be

intelligent it must be steered by a prior intellectual operation. What
distinguishes sensible from silly operations is not their parentage but
their procedure, and this holds no less for intellectual than for
practical performances. 'Intelligent' cannot be defined in terms of
'intellectual' or 'knowing *how*' in terms of 'knowing *that*';
'thinking what I am doing' does not connote 'both thinking what to
do and doing it'. When I do something intelligently, i.e. thinking
what I am doing, I am doing one thing and not two. My performance has a special procedure or manner, not special antecedents.

(4) *The Motives of the Intellectualist Legend.*
    Why are people so strongly drawn to believe, in the face of their
own daily experience, that the intelligent execution of an operation
must embody two processes, one of doing and another of theorising?
Part of the answer is that they are wedded to the dogma of the ghost
in the machine. Since doing is often an overt muscular affair, it
is written off as a merely physical process. On the assumption of
the antithesis between 'physical' and 'mental', it follows that muscular
doing cannot itself be a mental operation. To earn the title 'skilful',
'cunning', or 'humorous', it must therefore get it by transfer from
another counterpart act occurring not 'in the machine' but 'in the
ghost'; for 'skilful', 'cunning' and 'humorous' are certainly mental
predicates.
    It is, of course, perfectly true that when we characterise as
witty or tactful some piece of overt behaviour, we are not considering only the muscular movements which we witness. A parrot
might have made the same remark in the same situation without
our crediting it with a sense of humour, or a lout might have done
precisely what the tactful man did, without our thinking him
tactful. But if one and the same vocal utterance is a stroke of humour
from the humorist, but a mere noise-response, when issuing from
the parrot, it is tempting to say that we are ascribing wit not to
something that we hear but to something else that we do not hear.
We are accordingly tempted to say that what makes one audible
or visible action witty, while another audibly or visibly similar
action was not, is that the former was attended by another inaudible
and invisible action which was the real exercise of wit. But to
admit, as we must, that there may be no visible or audible difference
between a tactful or witty act and a tactless or humourless one is

not to admit that the difference is constituted by the performance or non-performance of some extra secret acts.

The cleverness of the clown may be exhibited in his tripping and tumbling. He trips and tumbles just as clumsy people do, except that he trips and tumbles on purpose and after much rehearsal and at the golden moment and where the children can see him and so as not to hurt himself. The spectators applaud his skill at seeming clumsy, but what they applaud is not some extra hidden performance executed 'in his head'. It is his visible performance that they admire, but they admire it not for being an effect of any hidden internal causes but for being an exercise of a skill. Now a skill is not an act. It is therefore neither a witnessable nor an unwitnessable act. To recognise that a performance is an exercise of a skill is indeed to appreciate it in the light of a factor which could not be separately recorded by a camera. But the reason why the skill exercised in a performance cannot be separately recorded by a camera is not that it is an occult or ghostly happening, but that it is not a happening at all. It is a disposition, or complex of dispositions, and a disposition is a factor of the wrong logical type to be seen or unseen, recorded or unrecorded. Just as the habit of talking loudly is not itself loud or quiet, since it is not the sort of term of which 'loud' and 'quiet' can be predicated, or just as a susceptibility to headaches is for the same reason not itself unendurable or endurable, so the skills, tastes and bents which are exercised in overt or internal operations are not themselves overt or internal, witnessable or unwitnessable. The traditional theory of the mind has misconstrued the type-distinction between disposition and exercise into its mythical bifurcation of unwitnessable mental causes and their witnessable physical effects.

The clown's trippings and tumblings are the workings of his mind, for they are his jokes; but the visibly similar trippings and tumblings of a clumsy man are not the workings of that man's mind. For he does not trip on purpose. Tripping on purpose is both a bodily and a mental process, but it is not two processes, such as one process of purposing to trip and, as an effect, another process of tripping. Yet the old myth dies hard. We are still tempted to argue that if the clown's antics exhibit carefulness, judgment, wit, and appreciation of the moods of his spectators, there must be occurring in the clown's head a counterpart performance to that which is taking place on the sawdust. If he is thinking what he is doing, there must be occurring behind his painted face a cogitative shadow-operation which we do not witness, tallying with, and controlling, the bodily contortions which we do witness. Surely the thinking of thoughts is the basic activity of minds and surely, too, the process of thinking is an invisible and inaudible process. So how can the clown's visible and audible performance be his mind at work?

To do justice to this objection it is necessary to make a verbal concession. There has fairly recently come into general use a certain special sense of the words 'mental' and 'mind'. We speak of 'mental arithmetic', of 'mind-reading' and of debates going on 'in the mind', and it certainly is the case that what is in this sense mental is unwitnessable. A boy is said to be doing 'mental arithmetic' when instead of writing down, or reciting aloud, the numerical symbols with which he is operating, he says them to himself, performing his calculations in silent soliloquy. Similarly a person is said to be reading the mind of another when he describes truly what the other is saying or picturing to himself in auditory or visual images. That these are special uses of 'mental' and 'mind' is easily shown. For a boy who does his calculating aloud, or on paper, may be reasoning correctly and organising his steps methodically; his reckoning is not the less a careful intellectual operation for being conducted in public instead of in private. His performance is therefore an exercise of a mental faculty in the normal sense of 'mental'.

Now calculating does not first acquire the rank of proper thinking when its author begins to do it with his lips closed and his hands in his pockets. The sealing of the lips is no part of the definition of thinking. A man may think aloud or half under his breath; he may think silently, yet with lip-movements conspicuous enough to be read by a lip-reader; or he may, as most of us have done since nursery-days, think in silence and with motionless lips. The differences are differences of social and personal convenience, of celerity and of facility. They need import no more differences into the coherence, cogency or appropriateness of the intellectual operations performed than is imported into them by a writer's preference for pencils over pens, or for invisible ink over ordinary ink. A deaf and dumb person talks in manual signs. Perhaps, when he wants to keep his thoughts to himself, he makes these signs with his hands kept behind his back or under the table. The fact that these signs might happen to be observed by a Paul Pry would not lead us or their maker to say that he was not thinking.

This special use of 'mental' and 'mind' in which they signify what is done 'in one's head' cannot be used as evidence for the dogma of the ghost in the machine. It is nothing but a contagion from that dogma. The technical trick of conducting our thinking in auditory word-images, instead of in spoken words, does indeed secure secrecy for our thinking, since the auditory imaginings of one person are not seen or heard by another (or, as we shall see, by their owner either). But this secrecy is not the secrecy ascribed to the postulated episodes of the ghostly shadow-world. It is merely the convenient privacy which characterises the tunes that run in my head and the things that I see in my mind's eye.

Moreover the fact that a person says things to himself in his head does not entail that he is thinking. He can babble deliriously, or repeat jingles in inner speech, just as he can in talking aloud. The distinction between talking sense and babbling, or between thinking what one is saying and merely saying, cuts across the distinction between talking aloud and talking to oneself. What makes a verbal operation an exercise of intellect is independent of what makes it public or private. Arithmetic done with pencil and paper may be more intelligent than mental arithmetic, and the public tumblings of the clown may be more intelligent than the tumblings which he merely 'sees' in his mind's eye or 'feels' in his mind's legs, if, as may or may not be the case, any such imaginings of antics occur.

(5) 'In my head'.

It is convenient to say something here about our everyday use of the phrase 'in my head'. When I do mental arithmetic, I am likely to say that I have had the numbers with which I have been working 'in my head' and not on paper; and if I have been listening to a catchy air or a verbal jingle, I am likely to describe myself later on as still having the tune or jingle 'running in my head'. It is 'in my head' that I go over the Kings of England, solve anagrams and compose limericks. Why is this felt to be an appropriate and expressive metaphor? For a metaphor it certainly is. No one thinks that when a tune is running in my head, a surgeon could unearth a little orchestra buried inside my skull or that a doctor by applying a stethoscope to my cranium could hear a muffled tune, in the way in which I hear the muffled whistling of my neighbour when I put my ear to the wall between our rooms.

It is sometimes suggested that the phrase derives from theories about the relations between brains and intellectual processes. It probably is from such theories that we derive such expressions as 'racking one's brains to solve a problem'; yet no one boasts of having solved an anagram 'in his brains'. A schoolboy would sometimes be ready to say that he had done an easy piece of arithmetic in his head, though he did not have to use his brains over it; and no intellectual effort or acumen is required in order to have a tune running in one's head. Conversely, arithmetic done with paper and pencil may tax one's brains, although it is not done 'in the head'.

It appears to be primarily of imagined *noises* that we find it natural to say that they take place 'inside our heads'; and of these imagined noises it is primarily those that we imagine ourselves both uttering and hearing. It is the words which I fancy myself saying to myself and the tunes which I fancy myself humming or whistling to myself which are first thought of as droning through this corporeal studio. With a little violence the phrase 'in my head' is then sometimes, by some people, extended to all fancied noises and even transferred to the description of the things that I fancy I see; but we shall come back to this extension later on.

What then tempts us to describe our imaginations of ourselves saying or humming things to ourselves by saying that the things are said or hummed in our heads? First, the idiom has an indispensable negative function. When the wheel-noises of the train make 'Rule Britannia' run in my head, the wheel-noises are audible to my fellow-passengers, but my 'Rule Britannia' is not. The rhythmic rattle fills the whole carriage; my 'Rule Britannia' does not fill that compartment or any part of it, so it is tempting to say that it fills instead another compartment, namely one that is a part of me. The rattle-noises have their source in the wheels and the rails; my 'Rule Britannia' does not have its source in any orchestra outside me, so it is tempting to state this negative fact by saying that it has its source inside me. But this by itself would not explain why I find it a natural metaphor to say that 'Rule Britannia' is running in my head rather than in my throat, chest or stomach.

When I hear the words that you utter or the tunes that the band plays, I ordinarily have an idea, sometimes a wrong one, from which direction the noises come and at what distance from me their source is. But when I hear the words that I myself utter aloud, the tunes that I myself hum, the sounds of my own chewing, breathing and coughing, the situation is quite different, since here there is no question of the noises coming from a source which is in any direction or at any distance from me. I do not have to turn my head about in order to hear better, nor can I advance my ear nearer to the source of the noise. Furthermore, though I can shut out, or muffle, your voice and the band's tunes by stopping up my ears, this action, so far from decreasing, increases the loudness and resonance of my own voice. My own utterances, as well as other head-noises like throbbings, sneezes, sniffs and the rest, are not airborne noises coming from a more or less remote source; they are made in the head and are heard through the head, though some of them are also heard as airborne noises. If I make noises of a very resonant or hacking kind, I can feel the vibrations or jerks in my head in the same sense of 'feel in' as I feel the vibrations of the tuning-fork in my hand.

Now these noises are literally and not metaphorically in the head. They are real head-borne noises, which the doctor could hear through his stethoscope. But the sense in which we say that the schoolboy doing mental arithmetic has his numbers not on paper but in his head is not this literal sense but a metaphorical sense borrowed from it. That his numbers are not really being heard in his head in the way in which he really hears his own coughing in his head is easily shown. For if he whistles or yells loudly with his ears stopped up, he can half-deafen himself or set his ears singing. But if in doing his mental arithmetic, he 'sings' his numbers to himself as if in a very shrill voice, nothing half-deafening occurs. He makes and hears no shrill noises, for he is merely imagining himself making and hearing shrill noises, and an imagined shriek is not a shriek, and it is not a whisper either. But he describes his numbers as being in his head, just as I describe my 'Rule Britannia' as running in my head, because this is a lively way of expressing the fact that the imagination of the production-cum-audition is a vivid one. Our phrase 'in my head' is meant to be understood as inside inverted commas, like the verb 'see' in such expressions as "I 'see' the incident now, though it took place forty years ago". If we were really doing what we imagine ourselves doing, namely hearing ourselves saying or humming things, then these noises would be in our heads in the literal usage of the phrase. However since we are not producing or hearing noises, but only fancying ourselves doing so, when we say that the numbers and the tunes that we imagine ourselves droning to ourselves are 'in our heads', we say it in the knowing tone of voice reserved for expressing things which are not to be taken literally.

I have said that there is some inclination to expand the employment of the idiom 'in my head', to cover not only imagined self-made and head-borne noises but also imagined noises in general and, even wider, imagined sights as well. I suspect that this inclination, if I am right in thinking that it exists, derives from the following familiar set of facts. In the case of all the specifically head-senses, either we are endowed with a natural set of shutters or we can easily provide an artificial set. We can shut out the view with our eyelids or with our hands; our lips shield our tongues; our fingers can be used to stop our ears and nostrils. So what is there for you and me to see, hear, taste and smell can be excluded by putting up these shutters. But the things that I see in my mind's eye are not excluded when I close my eyes. Indeed sometimes I 'see' them more vividly than ever when I do so. To dismiss the ghastly vision of yesterday's road-accident, I may even have to open my eyes. This makes it tempting to describe the difference between imaginary and real views by saying that while the objects of the latter are on the far side of the shutters, the objects of the former are on the near side of them; the latter are well outside my head, so the former are well inside it. But this point needs a certain elaboration.

Sight and hearing are distance-senses, while touch, taste and smell are not; that is to say, when we make our ordinary uses of the verbs 'see', 'hear', 'watch', 'listen', 'espy', 'overhear' and the rest, the things we speak of as 'seen' and 'listened to' are things at a distance from us. We hear a train far away to the south and we get a peep at a planet up in the sky. Hence we find a difficulty in talking about the whereabouts of the spots that float 'before the eye'. For though seen they are not out there. But we do not speak of feeling or tasting things in the distance, and if asked how far off and in which direction a thing lies, we do not reply 'Let me have a sniff or a taste'. Of course we may explore tactually and kinaesthetically, but when we find out in these ways where the electric light switch is, we are finding that it is where the finger-tips are. An object handled is where the hand is, but an object seen or heard is not, usually, anywhere near where the eye or ear is.

So when we want to emphasise the fact that something is not really being seen or heard, but is only being imagined as seen or heard, we tend to assert its imaginariness by denying its distance, and, by a convenient impropriety, we deny its distance by asserting its metaphorical nearness. 'Not out there, but in here; not outside the shutters and real, but inside the shutters and unreal', 'not an external reality, but an internal phantasm'. We have no such linguistic trick for describing what we imagine ourselves feeling, smelling, or tasting. A passenger on a ship feels the deck rolling beneath him chiefly in his feet and calves; and when he gets ashore, he still 'feels' the pavement rolling beneath him 'in his feet and calves'; but as kinaesthetic feeling is not a distance-sense, he cannot pillory his imaginary leg-feelings as illusions by saying that the rolling is in his legs and not in the street, for the rolling that he had felt when aboard has equally been felt in his legs. He could not have said 'I feel the other end of the ship rolling'. Nor does he describe the illusory rolling of the pavements as being 'felt in his head', but only as 'felt in his legs'.

I suggest, then, that the phrase 'in the head' is felt to be an appropriate and expressive metaphor in the first instance for vividly imagined self-voiced noises, and secondarily for any imaginary noises and even for imaginary sights, because in these latter cases a denial of distance, by assertion of metaphorical nearness, is intended to be construed as an assertion of imaginariness; and the nearness is relative, not so much to the head-organs of sight and hearing themselves, as to the places where their shutters are put up. It is an interesting verbal point that people sometimes use 'mental' and 'merely mental' as synonyms for 'imaginary'.

But it does not matter for my general argument whether this excursus into philology is correct or not. It will serve to draw attention to the sorts of things which we say are 'in our heads', namely, such things as imagined words, tunes and, perhaps, vistas.

When people employ the idiom 'in the mind', they are usually expressing over-sophisticatedly what we ordinarily express by the less misleading metaphorical use of 'in the head'. The phrase 'in the mind' can and should always be dispensed with. Its use habituates its employers to the view that minds are queer 'places', the occupants of which are special-status phantasms. It is part of the function of this book to show that exercises of qualities of mind do not, save *per accidens*, take place 'in the head', in the ordinary sense of the phrase, and those which do so have no special priority over those which do not.

(6) *The positive account of Knowing How*.

So far I hope to have shown that the exercise of intelligence in practice cannot be analysed into a tandem operation of first considering prescriptions and then executing them. We have also examined some of the motives which incline theorists to adopt this analysis.

But if to perform intelligently is to do one thing and not two things, and if to perform intelligently is to apply criteria in the conduct of the performance itself, it remains to show how this factor does characterise those operations which we recognise as skilful, prudent, tasteful or logical. For there need be no visible or audible differences between an action done with skill and one done from sheer habit, blind impulse, or in a fit of absence of mind. A parrot may squawk out 'Socrates is mortal' immediately after someone has uttered premisses from which this conclusion follows. One boy may, while thinking about cricket, give by rote the same correct answer to a multiplication problem which another boy gives who is thinking what he is doing. Yet we do not call the parrot 'logical', or describe the inattentive boy as working out the problem.

Consider first a boy learning to play chess. Clearly before he has yet heard of the rules of the game he might by accident make a move with his knight which the rules permit. The fact that he makes a permitted move does not entail that he knows the rule which permits it. Nor need the spectator be able to discover in the way the boy makes this move any visible feature which shows whether the move is a random one, or one made in knowledge of the rules. However, the boy now begins to learn the game properly, and this generally involves his receiving explicit instruction in the rules. He probably gets them by heart and is then ready to cite them on demand. During his first few games he probably has to go over the rules aloud or in his head, and to ask now and then how they should be applied to this or that particular situation. But very soon he comes to observe the rules without thinking of them. He makes the permitted moves and avoids the forbidden ones; he notices and protests when his opponent breaks the rules. But he no longer cites to himself or to the room the formulae in which the bans and permissions are declared. It has become second nature to him to do what is allowed and to avoid what is forbidden. At this stage he might even have lost his former ability to cite the rules. If asked to instruct another beginner, he might have forgotten how to state the rules and he would show the beginner how to play only by himself making the correct moves and cancelling the beginner's false moves.

But it would be quite possible for a boy to learn chess without ever hearing or reading the rules at all. By watching the moves made by others and by noticing which of his own moves were conceded and which were rejected, he could pick up the art of playing correctly while still quite unable to propound the regulations in terms of which 'correct' and 'incorrect' are defined. We all learned the rules of hunt-the-thimble and hide-and-seek and the elementary rules of grammar and logic in this way. We learn *how* by practice, schooled indeed by criticism and example, but often quite unaided by any lessons in the theory.

It should be noticed that the boy is not said to know how to play, if all that he can do is to recite the rules accurately. He must be able to make the required moves. But he is said to know how to play if, although he cannot cite the rules, he normally does make the permitted moves, avoid the forbidden moves and protest if his opponent makes forbidden moves. His knowledge *how* is exercised primarily in the moves that he makes, or concedes, and in the moves that he avoids or vetoes. So long as he can observe the rules, we do not care if he cannot also formulate them. It is not what he does in his head or with his tongue, but what he does on the board that shows whether or not he knows the rules in the executive way of being able to apply them. Similarly a foreign scholar might not know how to speak grammatical English as well as an English child, for all that he had mastered the theory of English grammar.

## (7) *Intelligent Capacities versus Habits.*

The ability to apply rules is the product of practice. It is therefore tempting to argue that competences and skills are just habits. They are certainly second natures or acquired dispositions, but it does not follow from this that they are mere habits. Habits are one sort, but not the only sort, of second nature, and it will be argued later that the common assumption that all second natures are mere habits obliterates distinctions which are of cardinal importance for the inquiries in which we are engaged.

The ability to give by rote the correct solutions of multiplication problems differs in certain important respects from the ability to solve them by calculating. When we describe someone as doing something by pure or blind habit, we mean that he does it automatically and without having to mind what he is doing. He does not exercise care, vigilance, or criticism. After the toddling-age we walk on pavements without minding our steps. But a mountaineer walking over ice-covered rocks in a high wind in the dark does not move his limbs by blind habit; he thinks what he is doing, he is ready for emergencies, he economises in effort, he makes tests and experiments; in short he walks with some degree of skill and judgment. If he makes a mistake, he is inclined not to repeat it, and if he finds a new trick effective he is inclined to continue to use it and to improve on it. He is concomitantly walking and teaching himself how to walk in conditions of this sort. It is of the essence of merely habitual practices that one performance is a replica of its predecessors. It is of the essence of intelligent practices that one performance is modified by its predecessors. The agent is still learning.

This distinction between habits and intelligent capacities can be illustrated by reference to the parallel distinction between the methods used for inculcating the two sorts of second nature. We build up habits by drill, but we build up intelligent capacities by training. Drill (or conditioning) consists in the imposition of repetitions. The recruit learns to slope arms by repeatedly going through just the same motions by numbers. The child learns the alphabet and the multiplication tables in the same way. The practices are not learned until the pupil's responses to his cues are automatic, until he can 'do them in his sleep', as it is revealingly put. Training, on the other hand, though it embodies plenty of sheer drill, does not consist of drill. It involves the stimulation by criticism and example of the pupil's own judgment. He learns how to do things thinking what he is doing, so that every operation performed is itself a new lesson to him how to perform better. The soldier who was merely drilled to slope arms correctly has to be trained to be proficient in marksmanship and map-reading. Drill dispenses with intelligence, training develops it. We do not expect the soldier to be able to read maps 'in his sleep'.

There is a further important difference between habits and intelligent capacities, to bring out which it is necessary to say a few words about the logic of dispositional concepts in general.

When we describe glass as brittle, or sugar as soluble, we are using dispositional concepts, the logical force of which is this. The brittleness of glass does not consist in the fact that it is at a given moment actually being shivered. It may be brittle without ever being shivered. To say that it is brittle is to say that if it ever is, or ever had been, struck or strained, it would fly, or have flown, into fragments. To say that sugar is soluble is to say that it would dissolve, or would have dissolved, if immersed in water.

A statement ascribing a dispositional property to a thing has much, though not everything, in common with a statement subsuming the thing under a law. To possess a dispositional property is not to be in a particular state, or to undergo a particular change; it is to be bound or liable to be in a particular state, or to undergo a particular change, when a particular condition is realised. The same is true about specifically human dispositions such as qualities of character. My being an habitual smoker does not entail that I am at this or that moment smoking; it is my permanent proneness to smoke when I am not eating, sleeping, lecturing or attending funerals, and have not quite recently been smoking.

In discussing dispositions it is initially helpful to fasten on the simplest models, such as the brittleness of glass or the smoking habit of a man. For in describing these dispositions it is easy to unpack the hypothetical proposition implicitly conveyed in the ascription of the dispositional properties. To be brittle is just to be bound or likely to fly into fragments in such and such conditions; to be a smoker is just to be bound or likely to fill, light and draw on a pipe in such and such conditions. These are simple, single-track dispositions, the actualisations of which are nearly uniform.

But the practice of considering such simple models of dispositions, though initially helpful, leads at a later stage to erroneous assumptions. There are many dispositions the actualisations of which can take a wide and perhaps unlimited variety of shapes; many disposition-concepts are determinable concepts. When an object is described as hard, we do not mean only that it would resist deformation; we mean also that it would, for example, give out a sharp sound if struck, that it would cause us pain if we came into sharp contact with it, that resilient objects would bounce off it, and so on indefinitely. If we wished to unpack all that is conveyed in describing an animal as gregarious, we should similarly have to produce an infinite series of different hypothetical propositions.

Now the higher-grade dispositions of people with which this inquiry is largely concerned are, in general, not single-track dispositions, but dispositions the exercises of which are indefinitely heterogeneous. When Jane Austen wished to show the specific kind of pride which characterised the heroine of 'Pride and Prejudice', she had to represent her actions, words, thoughts and feelings in a thousand different situations. There is no one standard type of action or reaction such that Jane Austen could say 'My heroine's kind of pride was just the tendency to do this, whenever a situation of that sort arose'.

Epistemologists, among others, often fall into the trap or expecting dispositions to have uniform exercises. For instance, when they recognise that the verbs 'know' and 'believe' are ordinarily used dispositionally, they assume that there must therefore exist one-pattern intellectual processes in which these cognitive dispositions are actualised. Flouting the testimony of experience, they postulate that, for example, a man who believes that the earth is round must from time to time be going through some unique proceeding of cognising, 'judging', or internally re-asserting, with a feeling of confidence, 'The earth is round'. In fact, of course, people do not harp on statements in this way, and even if they did do so and even if we knew that they did, we still should not be satisfied that they believed that the earth was round, unless we also found them inferring, imagining, saying and doing a great number of other things as well. If we found them inferring, imagining, saying and doing these other things, we should be satisfied that they believed the earth to be round, even if we had the best reasons for thinking that they never internally harped on the original statement at all. However often and stoutly a skater avers to us or to himself, that the ice will bear, he shows that he has his qualms, if he keeps to the edge of the pond, calls his children away from the middle, keeps his eye on the life-belts or continually speculates what would happen, if the ice broke.

## (8) *The exercise of intelligence.*

In judging that someone's performance is or is not intelligent, we have, as has been said, in a certain manner to look beyond the performance itself. For there is no particular overt or inner performance which could not have been accidentally or 'mechanically' executed by an idiot, a sleepwalker, a man in panic, absence of mind or delirium or even, sometimes, by a parrot. But in looking beyond the performance itself, we are not trying to pry into some hidden counterpart performance enacted on the supposed secret stage of the agent's inner life. We are considering his abilities and propensities of which this performance was an actualisation. Our inquiry is not into causes (and *a fortiori* not into occult causes), but into capacities, skills, habits, liabilities and bents. We observe, for example, a soldier scoring a bull's eye. Was it luck or was it skill? If he has the skill, then he can get on or near the bull's eye again, even if the wind strengthens, the range alters and the target moves. Or if his second shot is an outer, his third, fourth and fifth shots will probably creep nearer and nearer to the bull's eye. He generally checks his breathing before pulling the trigger, as he did on this occasion; he is ready to advise his neighbour what allowances to make for refraction, wind, etc. Marksmanship is a complex of skills, and the question whether he hit the bull's eye by luck or from good marksmanship is the question whether or not he has the skills, and, if he has, whether he used them by making his shot with care, self-control, attention to the conditions and thought of his instructions.

To decide whether his bull's eye was a fluke or a good shot, we need and he himself might need to take into account more than this one success. Namely, we should take into account his subsequent shots, his past record, his explanations or excuses, the advice he gave to his neighbour and a host of other clues of various sorts. There is no one signal of a man's knowing how to shoot, but a modest assemblage of heterogeneous performances generally suffices to establish beyond reasonable doubt whether he knows how to shoot or not. Only then, if at all, can it be decided whether he hit the bull's eye because he was lucky, or whether he hit it because he was marksman enough to succeed when he tried.

A drunkard at the chessboard makes the one move which upsets his opponent's plan of campaign. The spectators are satisfied that this was due not to cleverness but to luck, if they are satisfied that most of his moves made in this state break the rules of chess, or have no tactical connection with the position of the game, that he would not be likely to repeat this move if the tactical situation were to recur, that he would not applaud such a move if made by another player in a similar situation, that he could not explain why he had done it or even describe the threat under which his King had been.

Their problem is not one of the occurrence or non-occurrence of ghostly processes, but one of the truth or falsehood of certain 'could' and 'would' propositions and certain other particular applications of them. For, roughly, the mind is not the topic of sets of untestable categorical propositions, but the topic of sets of testable hypo-thetical and semi-hypothetical propositions. The difference between a normal person and an idiot is not that the normal person is really two persons while the idiot is only one, but that the normal person can do a lot of things which the idiot cannot do; and 'can' and 'cannot' are not occurrence words but modal words. Of course, in describing the moves actually made by the drunk and the sober players, or the noises actually uttered by the idiotic and the sane men, we have to use not only 'could' and 'would' expressions, but also 'did' and 'did not' expressions. The drunkard's move was made recklessly and the sane man was minding what he was saying. In Chapter V I shall try to show that the crucial differences between such occurrence reports as 'he did it recklessly' and 'he did it on purpose' have to be elucidated not as differences between simple and composite occurrence reports, but in quite another way.

Knowing *how*, then, is a disposition, but not a single-track disposition like a reflex or a habit. Its exercises are observances of rules or canons or the applications of criteria, but they are not tandem operations of theoretically avowing maxims and then putting them into practice. Further, its exercises can be overt or covert, deeds performed or deeds imagined, words spoken aloud or words heard in one's head, pictures painted on canvas or pictures in the mind's eye. Or they can be amalgamations of the two.

These points may be jointly illustrated by describing what happens when a person argues intelligently. There is a special point in selecting this example, since so much has been made of the rationality of man; and part, though only part, of what people understand by 'rational' is 'capable of reasoning cogently'.

First, it makes no important difference whether we think of the reasoner as arguing to himself or arguing aloud, pleading, perhaps, before an imagined court or pleading before a real court. The criteria by which his arguments are to be adjudged as cogent, clear, relevant and well organised are the same for silent as for declaimed or written ratiocinations. Silent argumentation has the practical advantages of being relatively speedy, socially undisturbing and secret; audible and written argumentation has the advantage of being less slap-dash, through being subjected to the criticisms of the audience and readers. But the same qualities of intellect are exercised in both, save that special schooling is required to inculcate the trick of reasoning in silent soliloquy.

Next, although there may occur a few stages in his argument which are so trite that he can go through them by rote, much of his argument is likely never to have been constructed before. He has to meet new objections, interpret new evidence and make connections between elements in the situation which had not previously been co-ordinated. In short he has to innovate, and where he innovates he is not operating from habit. He is not repeating hackneyed moves. That he is now thinking what he is doing is shown not only by this fact that he is operating without precedents, but also by the fact that he is ready to recast his expression of obscurely put points, on guard against ambiguities or else on the look out for chances to exploit them, taking care not to rely on easily refutable inferences, alert in meeting objections and resolute in steering the general course of his reasoning in the direction of his final goal. It will be argued later that all these words 'ready', 'on guard', 'careful', 'on the look out' and 'resolute' are semi-dispositional, semi-episodic words. They do not signify the concomitant occurrence of extra but internal operations, nor mere capacities and tendencies to perform further operations if the need for them should arise, but something between the two. The careful driver is not actually imagining or planning for all of the countless contingencies that might crop up; nor is he merely competent to recognise and cope with any one of them, if it should arise. He has not foreseen the runaway donkey, yet he is not unprepared for it. His readiness to cope with such emergencies would show itself in the operations he would perform, if they were to occur. But it also actually does show itself by the ways in which he converses and handles his controls even when nothing critical is taking place.

Underlying all the other features of the operations executed by the intelligent reasoner there is the cardinal feature that he reasons logically, that is, that he avoids fallacies and produces valid proofs and inferences, pertinent to the case he is making. He observes the rules of logic, as well as those of style, forensic strategy, professional etiquette and the rest. But he probably observes the rules of logic without thinking about them. He does not cite Aristotle's formulae to himself or to the court. He applies in his practice what Aristotle abstracted in his theory of such practices. He reasons with a correct method, but without considering the prescriptions of a methodology. The rules that he observes have become his way of thinking, when he is taking care; they are not external rubrics with which he has to square his thoughts. In a word, he conducts his operation efficiently, and to operate efficiently is not to perform two operations. It is to perform one operation in a certain manner or with a certain style or procedure, and the description of this *modus operandi* has to be in terms of such semi-dispositional, semi-episodic epithets as 'alert', 'careful', 'critical', 'ingenious', 'logical', etc.

What is true of arguing intelligently is, with appropriate modifications, true of other intelligent operations. The boxer, the surgeon, the poet and the salesman apply their special criteria in the performance of their special tasks, for they are trying to get things right; and they are appraised as clever, skilful, inspired or shrewd not for the ways in which they consider, if they consider at all, prescriptions for conducting their special performances, but for the ways in which they conduct those performances themselves. Whether or not the boxer plans his manoeuvres before executing them, his cleverness at boxing is decided in the light of how he fights. If he is a Hamlet of the ring, he will be condemned as an inferior fighter, though perhaps a brilliant theorist or critic. Cleverness at fighting is exhibited in the giving and parrying of blows, not in the acceptance or rejection of propositions about blows, just as ability at reasoning is exhibited in the construction of valid arguments and the detection of fallacies, not in the avowal of logicians' formulae. Nor does the surgeon's skill function in his tongue uttering medical truths but only in his hands making the correct movements.

All this is meant not to deny or depreciate the value of intellectual operations, but only to deny that the execution of intelligent performances entails the additional execution of intellectual operations. It will be shown later (in Chapter IX), that the learning of all but the most unsophisticated knacks requires some intellectual capacity. The ability to do things in accordance with instructions necessitates understanding those instructions. So some propositional competence is a condition of acquiring any of these competences. But it does not follow that exercises of these competences require to be accompanied by exercises of propositional competences. I could not have learned to swim the breast stroke, if I had not been able to understand the lessons given me in that stroke; but I do not have to recite those lessons, when I now swim the breast stroke.

A man knowing little or nothing of medical science could not be a good surgeon, but excellence at surgery is not the same thing as knowledge of medical science; nor is it a simple product of it. The surgeon must indeed have learned from instruction, or by his own inductions and observations, a great number of truths; but he must also have learned by practice a great number of aptitudes. Even where efficient practice is the deliberate application of considered prescriptions, the intelligence involved in putting the prescriptions into practice is not identical with that involved in intellectually grasping the prescriptions. There is no contradiction, or even paradox, in describing someone as bad at practising what he is good at preaching. There have been thoughtful and original literary critics who have formulated admirable canons of prose style in execrable prose. There have been others who have employed brilliant English in the expression of the silliest theories of what constitutes good writing.

The central point that is being laboured in this chapter is of considerable importance. It is an attack from one flank upon the category-mistake which underlies the dogma of the ghost in the machine. In unconscious reliance upon this dogma theorists and laymen alike constantly construe the adjectives by which we characterise performances as ingenious, wise, methodical, careful, witty, etc. as signalising the occurrence in someone's hidden stream of consciousness of special processes functioning as ghostly harbingers or more specifically as occult causes of the performances so characterised. They postulate an internal shadow-performance to be the real carrier of the intelligence ordinarily ascribed to the overt act, and think that in this way they explain what makes the overt act a manifestation of intelligence. They have described the overt act as an effect of a mental happening, though they stop short, of course, before raising the next question—what makes the postulated mental happenings manifestations of intelligence and not mental deficiency.

In opposition to this entire dogma, I am arguing that in describing the workings of a person's mind we are not describing a second set of shadowy operations. We are describing certain phases of his one career; namely we are describing the ways in which parts of his conduct are managed. The sense in which we 'explain' his actions is not that we infer to occult causes, but that we subsume under hypothetical and semi-hypothetical propositions. The explanation is not of the type 'the glass broke because a stone hit it', but more nearly of the different type 'the glass broke when the stone hit it, because it was brittle'. It makes no difference in theory if the performances we are appraising are operations executed silently in the agent's head, such as what he does, when duly schooled to it, in theorising, composing limericks or solving anagrams. Of course it makes a lot of difference in practice, for the examiner cannot award marks to operations which the candidate successfully keeps to himself.

But when a person talks sense aloud, ties knots, feints or sculpts, the actions which we witness are themselves the things which he is intelligently doing, though the concepts in terms of which the physicist or physiologist would describe his actions do not exhaust those which would be used by his pupils or his teachers in appraising their logic, style or technique. He is bodily active and he is mentally active, but he is not being synchronously active in two different 'places', or with two different 'engines'. There is the one activity, but it is one susceptible of and requiring more than one kind of explanatory description. Somewhat as there is no aerodynamical or physiological difference between the description of one bird as 'flying south' and of another as 'migrating', though there is a big biological difference between these descriptions, so there need be no physical or physiological differences between the descriptions of one man as gabbling and another talking sense, though the rhetorical and logical differences are enormous.

The statement 'the mind is its own place', as theorists might construe it, is not true, for the mind is not even a metaphorical 'place'. On the contrary, the chessboard, the platform, the scholar's desk, the judge's bench, the lorry-driver's seat, the studio and the football field are among its places. These are where people work and play stupidly or intelligently. 'Mind' is not the name of another person, working or frolicking behind an impenetrable screen; it is not the name of another place where work is done or games are played; and it is not the name of another tool with which work is done, or another appliance with which games are played.

(9) *Understanding and Misunderstanding*

It is being maintained throughout this book that when we characterise people by mental predicates, we are not making untestable inferences to any ghostly processes occurring in streams of consciousness which we are debarred from visiting; we are describing the ways in which those people conduct parts of their predominantly public behaviour. True, we go beyond what we see them do and hear them say, but this going beyond is not a going behind, in the sense of making inferences to occult causes; it is going beyond in the sense of considering, in the first instance, the powers and propensities of which their actions are exercises. But this point requires expansion.

A person who cannot play chess can still watch games of chess. He sees the moves being made as clearly as does his neighbour who knows the game. But the spectator who does not know the game cannot do what his neighbour does—appreciate the stupidity or cleverness of the players. What is this difference between merely witnessing a performance and understanding what is witnessed? What, to take another example, is the difference between hearing what a speaker says and making sense of what he is heard to say?

Advocates of the double-life legend will answer that understanding the chess-player's moves consists in inferring from the visible moves made on the board to unwitnessable operations taking place on the player's private stage. It is a process of inference analogous to that by which we infer from the seen movements of the railway-signals to the unseen manipulations of the levers in the signal-box. Yet this answer promises something that could never be fulfilled. For since, according to the theory, one person cannot in principle visit another person's mind as he can visit signal-boxes, there could be no way of establishing the necessary correlation between the overt moves and their hidden causal counterparts. The analogy of the signal-box breaks down in another place. The connections between levers and signal-arms are easy to discover. The mechanical principles of the fulcrum and the pulley, and the behaviour of metals in tension and compression are, at least in outline, familiar to us all. We know well enough how the machinery inside the signal-box works, how that outside the signal-box works and how the two are mechanically coupled. But it is admitted by those who believe in the legend of the ghost in the machine that no one yet knows much about the laws governing the supposed workings of the mind, while the postulated interactions between the workings of the mind and the movements of the hand are acknowledged to be completely mysterious. Enjoying neither the supposed status of the mental, nor the supposed status of the physical, these interactions cannot be expected to obey either the known laws of physics, or the still to be discovered laws of psychology.

It would follow that no one has ever yet had the slightest understanding of what anyone else has ever said or done. We read the words which Euclid wrote and we are familiar with the things which Napoleon did, but we have not the slightest idea what they had in their minds. Nor has any spectator of a chess tournament or a football match ever yet had an inkling of what the players were after.

But this is patently absurd. Anybody who can play chess already understands a good deal of what other players do, and a brief study of geometry enables an ordinary boy to follow a good deal of Euclid's reasoning. Nor does this understanding require a prolonged grounding in the not yet established laws of psychology. Following the moves made by a chess-player is not doing anything remotely resembling problematic psychological diagnosis. Indeed, supposing that one person could understand another's words or actions only in so far as he made causal inferences in accordance with psychological laws, the queer consequence would follow that if any psychologist had discovered these laws, he could never have conveyed his discoveries to his fellow men. For *ex hypothesi* they could not follow his exposition of them without inferring in accordance with them from his words to his thoughts.

No one feels happy with the view that for one person to follow what another person says or does is to make inferences somewhat like those made by a water-diviner from the perceived twitching of the twig to the subterranean flow of water. So the consolatory amendment is sometimes made that, since a person is directly aware of the correlations between his own private experiences and his own overt actions, he can understand the performances of others by imputing to them a similar correlation. Understanding is still psychological divining, but it is divination reinforced by analogies from the diviner's direct observation of the correlations between his own inner and outer lives. But this amendment does not abolish the difficulty.

It will be argued later that a person's appraisals of his own performances do not differ in kind from his appraisals of those of others, but for the present purpose it is enough to say that, even if a person did enjoy a privileged illumination in the ascription of mental-conduct concepts to his own performances, his supposed analogical argument to the mental processes of others would be completely fallacious.

If someone has inspected a number of railway-signals and signal-boxes, he can then in a new case make a good probable inference from observed signal-movements to unobserved lever-movements. But if he had examined only one signal-box and knew nothing about the standardisation-methods of large corporations, his inference would be pitiably weak, for it would be a wide generalisation based on a single instance. Further, one signal-arm is closely similar to another in appearance and movements, so the inference to a correspondingly close similarity between the mechanisms housed in different signal-boxes has some strength. But the observed appearances and actions of people differ very markedly, so the imputation to them of inner processes closely matching one another would be actually contrary to the evidence.

Understanding a person's deeds and words is not, therefore, any kind of problematic divination of occult processes. For this divination does not and cannot occur, whereas understanding does occur. Of course it is part of my general thesis that the supposed occult processes are themselves mythical; there exists nothing to be the object of the postulated diagnoses. But for the present purpose it is enough to prove that, if there were such inner states and operations, one person would not be able to make probable inferences to their occurrence in the inner life of another.

If understanding does not consist in inferring, or guessing, the alleged inner-life precursors of overt actions, what is it? If it does not require mastery of psychological theory together with the ability to apply it, what knowledge does it require? We saw that a spectator who cannot play chess also cannot follow the play of others; a person who cannot read or speak Swedish cannot understand what is spoken or written in Swedish; and a person whose reasoning powers are weak is bad at following and retaining the arguments of others. Understanding is a part of knowing *how*. The knowledge that is required for understanding intelligent performances of a specific kind is some degree of competence in performances of that kind. The competent critic of prose-style, experimental technique, or embroidery, must at least know how to write, experiment or sew. Whether or not he has also learned some psychology matters about as much as whether he has learned any chemistry, neurology or economics. These studies may in certain circumstances assist his appreciation of what he is criticising; but the one necessary condition is that he has some mastery of the art or procedure, examples of which he is to appraise. For one person to see the jokes that another makes, the one thing he must have is a sense of humour and even that special brand of sense of humour of which those jokes are exercises.

Of course, to execute an operation intelligently is not exactly the same thing as to follow its execution intelligently. The agent is originating, the spectator is only contemplating. But the rules which the agent observes and the criteria which he applies are one with those which govern the spectator's applause and jeers. The commentator on Plato's philosophy need not possess much philosophic originality, but if he cannot, as too many commentators cannot, appreciate the force, drift or motive of a philosophical argument, his comments will be worthless. If he can appreciate them, then he knows how to do part of what Plato knew how to do.

If I am competent to judge your performance, then in witnessing it I am on the alert to detect mistakes and muddles in it, but so are you in executing it; I am ready to notice the advantages you might take of pieces of luck, but so are you. You learn as you proceed, and I too learn as you proceed. The intelligent performer operates critically, the intelligent spectator follows critically. Roughly, execution and understanding are merely different exercises of knowledge of the tricks of the same trade. You exercise your knowledge how to tie a clove-hitch not only in acts of tying clove-hitches and in correcting your mistakes, but also in imagining tying them correctly, in instructing pupils, in criticising the incorrect or clumsy movements and applauding the correct movements that they make, in inferring from a faulty result to the error which produced it, in predicting the outcomes of observed lapses, and so on indefinitely. The words 'understanding' and 'following' designate certain of those exercises of your knowledge *how*, which you execute without having, for example, any string in your hand.

It should by now be otiose to point out that this does not imply that the spectator or reader, in following what is done or written, is making analogical inferences from internal processes of his own to corresponding internal processes in the author of the actions or writings. Nor need he, though he may, imaginatively represent himself as being in the shoes, the situation and the skin of the author. He is merely thinking what the author is doing along the same lines as those on which the author is thinking what he is doing, save that the spectator is finding what the author is inventing. The author is leading and the spectator is following, but their path is the same. Nor, again, does this account of understanding require or encourage us to postulate any mysterious electric sympathies between kindred souls. Whether or not the hearts of two chess-players beat as one, which they will not do if they are opponents, their ability to follow one another's play depends not on this valvular coincidence but upon their competence at chess, their interest in this game and their acquired familiarity with one another's methods of playing.

This point, that the capacity to appreciate a performance is one in type with the capacity to execute it, illustrates a contention previously argued, namely that intelligent capacities are not single-track dispositions, but are dispositions admitting of a wide variety of more or less dissimilar exercises. It is however necessary to make two provisos. First, the capacity to perform and to appreciate an operation does not necessarily involve the ability to formulate criticisms or lessons. A well-trained sailor boy can both tie complex knots and discern whether someone else is tying them correctly or incorrectly, deftly or clumsily. But he is probably incapable of the difficult task of describing in words how the knots should be tied. And, second, the ability to appreciate a performance does not involve the same degree of competence as the ability to execute it. It does not take genius to recognise genius, and a good dramatic critic may be indifferent as an actor or playwright. There would be no teachers or pupils if the ability to understand operations required complete ability to perform them. Pupils are taught how to do things by people who know better than they how to do them. Euclid's Elements are neither a sealed, nor an open, book to the schoolboy.

One feature in this account of understanding has been grasped, though from the wrong end, by certain philosophers who have tried to explain how an historian, scholar or literary critic can understand the deeds or words of his subjects. Adhering without question to the dogma of the ghost in the machine, these philosophers were naturally perplexed by the pretensions of historians to interpret the actions and words of historic personages as expressions of their actual thoughts, feelings and intentions. For if minds are impenetrable to one another, how can historians penetrate the minds of their heroes? Yet if such penetration is impossible, the labours of all scholars, critics and historians must be vain; they may describe the signals, but they can never begin to interpret them as effects of operations in the eternally sealed signal-boxes.

These philosophers have put forward the following solution of their spurious puzzle. Though I cannot witness the workings of your mind or Plato's mind, but only the overt actions and written words which I take to be outward 'expressions' of those inner workings, I can, with due effort and practice, deliberately enact such ' operations in my own private theatre as would naturally originate just such actions and words. I can think private thoughts of my own which would be well expressed by the sentences ascribed to Plato's hand, and I can, in fact or in fancy, execute volitions of my own which originate or would originate actions like those which I have witnessed you performing. Having put myself into a frame of mind in which I act like you, or write like Plato, I can then impute to you and to him similar frames of mind. If this imputation is correct, then, from knowing what it is like for me to be in the frame of mind which issues in these actions and words, I can also know what it was like to be Plato writing his Dialogues and what it is like to be you, tying, perhaps, a clove-hitch. By re-enacting your overt actions I re-live your private experiences. In a fashion, the student of Plato makes himself a second Plato, a sort of re-author of his Dialogues, and thus and only thus he understands those Dialogues.

Unfortunately this programme of mimicking Plato's mental processes can never be wholly successful. I am, after all, a twentieth-century English student of Plato, a thing which Plato never was. My culture, schooling, language, habits and interests are different from his and this must impair the fidelity of my mimicry of his frame of mind and therefore the success of my attempts to understand him. Still, it is argued, this is, in the nature of the case, the best that I can do. Understanding must be imperfect. Only by really being Plato could I really understand him.

Some holders of theories of this type add extra comforts to it. Though minds are inaccessible to one another, they may be said to resonate, like tuning-forks, in harmony with one another, though unfortunately they would never know it. I cannot literally share your experiences, but some of our experiences may somehow chime together, though we cannot be aware of their doing so, in a manner which almost amounts to genuine communion. In the most fortunate cases we may resemble two incurably deaf men singing in tune and in time with one another. But we need not dwell on such embellishments to a theory which is radically false.

For this theory is just another unsuccessful attempt to wriggle out of a perfectly mythical dilemma. It assumes that understanding would have to consist in contemplating the unknowable workings of insulated ghosts and tries to remedy this trouble by saying that, in default of such knowledge, I can do nearly as well by contemplating such ghostly operations of my own as would naturally issue in overt 'expressions' similar to those of the persons whom I wish to understand. But this involves a further unwarrantable but interesting assumption, namely that to similar overt deeds and words there always correspond similar internal processes, an assumption which is, according to the theory itself, completely untestable. It assumes, also quite improperly, that it follows from the fact that I go through certain internal processes that I must perfectly appreciate them for what they are, i.e. that I cannot misconstrue, or be puzzled by, anything that goes on in my own stream of consciousness. In short, this whole theory is a variant of the doctrine that understanding consists in problematic causal divination, reinforced by a weak analogical argument.

What makes the theory worth discussing is that it partly avoids equating understanding with psychological diagnosis, i.e. with causal inferences from overt behaviour to mental process in accordance with laws yet to be discovered by psychologists; and it avoids this equation by making an assumption to which it is not entitled but which is on the edge of the truth. It assumes that the qualities of people's minds are reflected in the things that they overtly say and do. So historians and scholars in studying the styles and procedures of literary and practical activities are on the right track; it is, according to the theory, just their inescapable misfortune that this track terminates in the chasm separating the 'physical' from the 'mental', the 'overt' from the 'inner'. Now, had the holders of this theory seen that the styles and procedures of people's activities *are* the way their minds work and are not merely imperfect reflections of the postulated secret processes which were supposed to be the workings of minds, their dilemma would have evaporated. The claims of historians and scholars to be able in principle to understand what their subjects did and wrote would have been automatically vindicated. It is not they who have been studying shadows.

Overt intelligent performances are not clues to the workings of minds; they are those workings. Boswell described Johnson's mind when he described how he wrote, talked, ate, fidgeted and fumed. His description was, of course, incomplete, since there were notoriously some thoughts which Johnson kept carefully to himself and there must have been many dreams, daydreams and silent babblings

which only Johnson could have recorded and only a James Joyce
would wish him to have recorded.

Before we conclude this inquiry into understanding, something
must be said about partial understanding and misunderstanding.

Attention has already been drawn to certain parallelisms and
certain non-parallelisms between the concept of knowing *that* and
the concept of knowing *how*. A further non-parallelism must now
be noticed. We never speak of a person having partial knowledge
of a fact or truth, save in the special sense of his having knowledge
of a part of a body of facts or truths. A boy can be said to have
partial knowledge of the counties of England, if he knows some of
them and does not know others. But he could not be said to have
incomplete knowledge of Sussex being an English county. Either
he knows this fact or he does not know it. On the other hand, it
is proper and normal to speak of a person knowing in part how
to do something, i.e. of his having a particular capacity in a
limited degree. An ordinary chess-player knows the game pretty
well but a champion knows it better, and even the champion has
still much to learn.

This holds too, as we should now expect, of understanding. An
ordinary chess-player can partly follow the tactics and strategy of a
champion; perhaps after much study he will completely understand
the methods used by the champion in certain particular matches.
But he can never wholly anticipate how the champion will fight
his next contest and he is never as quick or sure in his interpretations
of the champion's moves as the champion is in making or, perhaps,
in explaining them.

Learning *how* or improving in ability is not like learning *that*
or acquiring information. Truths can be imparted, procedures can
only be inculcated, and while inculcation is a gradual process,
imparting is relatively sudden. It makes sense to ask at what moment
someone became apprised of a truth, but not to ask at what moment
someone acquired a skill. 'Part-trained' is a significant phrase,
'part-informed' is not. Training is the art of setting tasks which
the pupils have not yet accomplished but are not any longer quite
incapable of accomplishing.

The notion of misunderstanding raises no general theoretical
difficulties. When the card-player's tactics are misconstrued by his
opponents, the manoeuvre they think they discern is indeed a

possible manoeuvre of the game, though it happens not to be his manoeuvre. Only someone who knew the game could interpret the play as part of the execution of the supposed manoeuvre. Misunderstanding is a by-product of knowing *how*. Only a person who is at least a partial master of the Russian tongue can make the wrong sense of a Russian expression. Mistakes are exercises of competences.

Misinterpretations are not always due to the inexpertness or carelessness of the spectator; they are due sometimes to the carelessness and sometimes to the cunning of the agent or speaker. Sometimes, again, both are exercising all due skill and care, but it happens that the operations performed, or the words spoken, could actually be constituents of two or more different undertakings. The first ten motions made in tying one knot might be identical with the first ten motions required for tying another, or a set of premisses suitable for establishing one conclusion might be equally suitable for establishing another. The onlooker's misinterpretation may then be acute and well-grounded. It is careless only in being premature. Feinting is the art of exploiting this possibility.

It is obvious that where misunderstanding is possible, understanding is possible. It would be absurd to suggest that perhaps we always misconstrue the performances that we witness, for we could not even learn to misconstrue save in learning to construe, a learning process which involves learning not to misconstrue. Misinterpretations are in principle corrigible, which is part of the value of controversy.

### (10) *Solipsism*

Contemporary philosophers have exercised themselves with the problem of our knowledge of other minds. Enmeshed in the dogma of the ghost in the machine, they have found it impossible to discover any logically satisfactory evidence warranting one person in believing that there exist minds other than his own. I can witness what your body does, but I cannot witness what your mind does, and my pretensions to infer from what your body does to what your mind does all collapse, since the premisses for such inferences are either inadequate or unknowable.

We can now see our way out of the supposed difficulty. I discover that there are other minds in understanding what other people say and do. In making sense of what you say, in appreciating your jokes, in unmasking your chess-stratagems, in following your arguments and in hearing you pick holes in my arguments, I am not inferring to the workings of your mind, I am following them. Of course, I am not merely hearing the noises that you make, or merely seeing the movements that you perform. I am understanding what I hear and see. But this understanding is not inferring to occult causes. It is appreciating how the operations are conducted. To find that most people have minds (though idiots and infants in arms do not) is simply to find that they are able and prone to do certain sorts of things, and this we do by witnessing the sorts of things they do. Indeed we do not merely discover that there are other minds; we discover what specific qualities of intellect and character particular people have. In fact we are familiar with such specific matters long before we can comprehend such general propositions as that John Doe has a mind, or that there exist minds other than our own; just as we know that stones are hard and sponges are soft, kittens are warm and active, potatoes are cold and inert, long before we can grasp the proposition that kittens are material objects, or that matter exists.

Certainly there are some things which I can find out about you only, or best, through being told of them by you. The oculist has to ask his client what letters he sees with his right and left eyes and how clearly he sees them; the doctor has to ask the sufferer where the pain is and what sort of a pain it is; and the psycho-analyst has to ask his patient about his dreams and daydreams. If you do not divulge the contents of your silent soliloquies and other imaginings, I have no other sure way of finding out what you have been saying or picturing to yourself. But the sequence of your sensations and imaginings is not the sole field in which your wits and character are shown; perhaps only for lunatics is it more than a small corner of that field. I find out most of what I want to know about your capacities, interests, likes, dislikes, methods and convictions by observing how you conduct your overt doings, of which by far the most important are your sayings and writings. It is a subsidiary question how you conduct your imaginings, including your imagined monologues.

CHAPTER III

# THE WILL

**(1) *Foreword*.**

MOST of the mental-conduct concepts whose logical behaviour
we examine in this book, are familiar and everyday concepts. We
all know how to apply them and we understand other people when
they apply them. What is in dispute is not how to apply them,
but how to classify them, or in what categories to put them.

The concept of volition is in a different case. We do not know
in daily life how to use it, for we do not use it in daily life and do
not, consequently, learn by practice how to apply it, and how not to
misapply it. It is an artificial concept. We have to study certain
specialist theories in order to find out how it is to be manipulated.
It does not, of course, follow from its being a technical concept
that it is an illegitimate or useless concept. 'Ionisation' and 'off-side'
are technical concepts, but both are legitimate and useful. 'Phlogiston'
and 'animal spirits' were technical concepts, though they have now
no utility.

I hope to show that the concept of volition belongs to the latter
tribe.

**(2) *The Myth of Volitions*.**

It has for a long time been taken for an indisputable axiom that
the Mind is in some important sense tripartite, that is, that there
are just three ultimate classes of mental processes. The Mind or
Soul, we are often told, has three parts, namely, Thought, Feeling
and Will; or, more solemnly, the Mind or Soul functions in three
irreducibly different modes, the Cognitive mode, the Emotional
mode and the Conative mode. This traditional dogma is not only
not self-evident, it is such a welter of confusions and false inferences
that it is best to give up any attempt to re-fashion it. It should be
treated as one of the curios of theory.

62

The main object of this chapter is not, however, to discuss the whole trinitarian theory of mind but to discuss, and discuss destructively, one of its ingredients. I hope to refute the doctrine that there exists a Faculty, immaterial Organ, or Ministry, corresponding to the theory's description of the 'Will' and, accordingly, that there occur processes, or operations, corresponding to what it describes as 'volitions'. I must however make it clear from the start that this refutation will not invalidate the distinctions which we all quite properly draw between voluntary and involuntary actions and between strong-willed and weak-willed persons. It will, on the contrary, make clearer what is meant by 'voluntary' and 'involuntary', by 'strong-willed' and 'weak-willed', by emancipating these ideas from bondage to an absurd hypothesis.

Volitions have been postulated as special acts, or operations, 'in the mind', by means of which a mind gets its ideas translated into facts. I think of some state of affairs which I wish to come into existence in the physical world, but, as my thinking and wishing are unexecutive, they require the mediation of a further executive mental process. So I perform a volition which somehow puts my muscles into action. Only when a bodily movement has issued from such a volition can I merit praise or blame for what my hand or tongue has done.

It will be clear why I reject this story. It is just an inevitable extension of the myth of the ghost in the machine. It assumes that there are mental states and processes enjoying one sort of existence, and bodily states and processes enjoying another. An occurrence on the one stage is never numerically identical with an occurrence on the other. So, to say that a person pulled the trigger intentionally is to express at least a conjunctive proposition, asserting the occurrence of one act on the physical stage and another on the mental stage; and, according to most versions of the myth, it is to express a causal proposition, asserting that the bodily act of pulling the trigger was the effect of a mental act of willing to pull the trigger.

According to the theory, the workings of the body are motions of matter in space. The causes of these motions must then be *either* other motions of matter in space *or*, in the privileged case of human beings, thrusts of another kind. In some way which must forever remain a mystery, mental thrusts, which are not movements of matter in space, can cause muscles to contract. To describe a man as intentionally pulling the trigger is to state that such a mental thrust did cause the contraction of the muscles of his finger. So the language of 'volitions' is the language of the para-mechanical theory of the mind. If a theorist speaks without qualms of 'volitions', or 'acts of will', no further evidence is needed to show that he swallows whole the dogma that a mind is a secondary field of special causes. It can be predicted that he will correspondingly speak of bodily actions as 'expressions' of mental processes. He is likely also to speak glibly of 'experiences', a plural noun commonly used to denote the postulated non-physical episodes which constitute the shadow-drama on the ghostly boards of the mental stage.

The first objection to the doctrine that overt actions, to which we ascribe intelligence-predicates, are results of counterpart hidden operations of willing is this. Despite the fact that theorists have, since the Stoics and Saint Augustine, recommended us to describe our conduct in this way, no one, save to endorse the theory, ever describes his own conduct, or that of his acquaintances, in the recommended idioms. No one ever says such things as that at 10 a.m. he was occupied in willing this or that, or that he performed five quick and easy volitions and two slow and difficult volitions between midday and lunch-time. An accused person may admit or deny that he did something, or that he did it on purpose, but he never admits or denies having willed. Nor do the judge and jury require to be satisfied by evidence, which in the nature of the case could never be adduced, that a volition preceded the pulling of the trigger. Novelists describe the actions, remarks, gestures and grimaces, the daydreams, deliberations, qualms and embarrassments of their characters; but they never mention their volitions. They would not know what to say about them.

By what sorts of predicates should they be described? Can they be sudden or gradual, strong or weak, difficult or easy, enjoyable or disagreeable? Can they be accelerated, decelerated, interrupted, or suspended? Can people be efficient or inefficient at them? Can we take lessons in executing them? Are they fatiguing or distracting? Can I do two or seven of them synchronously? Can I remember executing them? Can I execute them, while thinking of other things, or while dreaming? Can they become habitual? Can I forget how to do them? Can I mistakenly believe that I have

executed one, when I have not, or that I have not executed one, when
I have? At which moment was the boy going through a volition
to take the high dive? When he set foot on the ladder? When he
took his first deep breath? When he counted off 'One, two, three
—Go', but did not go? Very, very shortly before he sprang? What
would his own answer be to those questions?

Champions of the doctrine maintain, of course, that the
enactment of volitions is asserted by implication, whenever an overt
act is described as intentional, voluntary, culpable or meritorious;
they assert too that any person is not merely able but bound to
know that he is willing when he is doing so, since volitions are
defined as a species of conscious process. So if ordinary men and
women fail to mention their volitions in their descriptions of their
own behaviour, this must be due to their being untrained in the
dictions appropriate to the description of their inner, as distinct from
their overt, behaviour. However, when a champion of the doctrine
is himself asked how long ago he executed his last volition, or how
many acts of will he executes in, say, reciting 'Little Miss Muffet'
backwards, he is apt to confess to finding difficulties in giving the
answer, though these difficulties should not, according to his own
theory, exist.

If ordinary men never report the occurrence of these acts, for
all that, according to the theory, they should be encountered vastly
more frequently than headaches, or feelings of boredom; if ordinary
vocabulary has no non-academic names for them; if we do not know
how to settle simple questions about their frequency, duration or
strength, then it is fair to conclude that their existence is not asserted
on empirical grounds. The fact that Plato and Aristotle never
mentioned them in their frequent and elaborate discussions of the
nature of the soul and the springs of conduct is due not to any
perverse neglect by them of notorious ingredients of daily life but
to the historical circumstance that they were not acquainted with a
special hypothesis the acceptance of which rests not on the discovery
but on the postulation, of these ghostly thrusts.

The second objection is this. It is admitted that one person can
never witness the volitions of another; he can only infer from an
observed overt action to the volition from which it resulted, and
then only if he has any good reason to believe that the overt action
was a voluntary action, and not a reflex or habitual action, or one

resulting from some external cause. It follows that no judge, schoolmaster, or parent ever knows that the actions which he judges merit praise or blame; for he cannot do better than guess that the action was willed. Even a confession by the agent, if such confessions were ever made, that he had executed a volition before his hand did the deed would not settle the question. The pronouncement of the confession is only another overt muscular action. The curious conclusion results that though volitions were called in to explain our appraisals of actions, this explanation is just what they fail to provide. If we had no other antecedent grounds for applying appraisal-concepts to the actions of others, we should have no reasons at all for inferring from those actions to the volitions alleged to give rise to them.

Nor could it be maintained that the agent himself can know that any overt action of his own is the effect of a given volition. Supposing, what is not the case, that he could know for certain, either from the alleged direct deliverances of consciousness, or from the alleged direct findings of introspection, that he had executed an act of will to pull the trigger just before he pulled it, this would not prove that the pulling was the effect of that willing. The connection between volitions and movements is allowed to be mysterious, so, for all he knows, his volition may have had some other movement as its effect and the pulling of the trigger may have had some other event for its cause.

Thirdly, it would be improper to burke the point that the connection between volition and movement is admitted to be a mystery. It is a mystery not of the unsolved but soluble type, like the problem of the cause of cancer, but of quite another type. The episodes supposed to constitute the careers of minds are assumed to have one sort of existence, while those constituting the careers of bodies have another sort; and no bridge-status is allowed. Transactions between minds and bodies involve links where no links can be. That there should be any causal transactions between minds and matter conflicts with one part, that there should be none conflicts with another part of the theory. Minds, as the whole legend describes them, are what must exist if there is to be a causal explanation of the intelligent behaviour of human bodies; and minds, as the legend describes them, live on a floor of existence defined as being outside the causal system to which bodies belong

Fourthly, although the prime function of volitions, the task for the performance of which they were postulated, is to originate bodily movements, the argument, such as it is, for their existence entails that some mental happenings also must result from acts of will. Volitions were postulated to be that which makes actions voluntary, resolute, meritorious and wicked. But predicates of these sorts are ascribed not only to bodily movements but also to operations which, according to the theory, are mental and not physical operations. A thinker may ratiocinate resolutely, or imagine wickedly; he may try to compose a limerick and he may meritoriously concentrate on his algebra. Some mental processes then can, according to the theory, issue from volitions. So what of volitions themselves? Are they voluntary or involuntary acts of mind? Clearly either answer leads to absurdities. If I cannot help willing to pull the trigger, it would be absurd to describe my pulling it as 'voluntary'. But if my volition to pull the trigger is voluntary, in the sense assumed by the theory, then it must issue from a prior volition and that from another *ad infinitum*. It has been suggested, to avoid this difficulty, that volitions cannot be described as either voluntary or involuntary. 'Volition' is a term of the wrong type to accept either predicate. If so, it would seem to follow that it is also of the wrong type to accept such predicates as 'virtuous' and 'wicked', 'good' and 'bad', a conclusion which might embarrass those moralists who use volitions as the sheet-anchor of their systems.

In short, then, the doctrine of volitions is a causal hypothesis, adopted because it was wrongly supposed that the question, 'What makes a bodily movement voluntary?' was a causal question. This supposition is, in fact, only a special twist of the general supposition that the question, 'How are mental-conduct concepts applicable to human behaviour?' is a question about the causation of that behaviour.

Champions of the doctrine should have noticed the simple fact that they and all other sensible persons knew how to decide questions about the voluntariness and involuntariness of actions and about the resoluteness and irresoluteness of agents before they had ever heard of the hypothesis of the occult inner thrusts of actions. They might then have realised that they were not elucidating the criteria already in efficient use, but, tacitly assuming their validity, were trying to correlate them with hypothetical occurrences of a para-mechanical pattern. Yet this correlation could, on the one hand, never be scientifically established, since the thrusts postulated were screened from scientific observation; and, on the other hand, it would be of no practical or theoretical use, since it would not assist our appraisals of actions, depending as it would on the presupposed validity of those appraisals. Nor would it elucidate the logic of those appraisal-concepts, the intelligent employment of which antedated the invention of this causal hypothesis.

Before we bid farewell to the doctrine of volitions, it is expedient to consider certain quite familiar and authentic processes with which volitions are sometimes wrongly identified.

People are frequently in doubt what to do; having considered alternative courses of action, they then, sometimes, select or choose one of these courses. This process of opting for one of a set of alternative courses of action is sometimes said to be what is signified by 'volition'. But this identification will not do, for most voluntary actions do not issue out of conditions of indecision and are not therefore results of settlements of indecisions. Moreover it is notorious that a person may choose to do something but fail, from weakness of will, to do it; or he may fail to do it because some circumstance arises after the choice is made, preventing the execution of the act chosen. But the theory could not allow that volitions ever fail to result in action, else further executive operations would have to be postulated to account for the fact that sometimes voluntary actions are performed. And finally the process of deliberating between alternatives and opting for one of them is itself subject to appraisal-predicates. But if, for example, an act of choosing is describable as voluntary, then, on this suggested showing, it would have in its turn to be the result of a prior choice to choose, and that from a choice to choose to choose. . . .

The same objections forbid the identification with volitions of such other familiar processes as that of resolving or making up our minds to do something and that of nerving or bracing ourselves to do something. I may resolve to get out of bed or go to the dentist, and I may, clenching my fists and gritting my teeth, brace myself to do so, but I may still backslide. If the action is not done, then, according to the doctrine, the volition to do it is also unexecuted. Again, the operations of resolving and nerving ourselves are themselves members of the class of creditable or discreditable actions, so they cannot constitute the peculiar ingredient which, according to the doctrine, is the common condition of any performance being creditable or discreditable.

(3) *The Distinction between Voluntary and Involuntary.*

It should be noticed that while ordinary folk, magistrates, parents and teachers, generally apply the words 'voluntary' and 'involuntary' to actions in one way, philosophers often apply them in quite another way.

In their most ordinary employment 'voluntary' and 'involuntary' are used, with a few minor elasticities, as adjectives applying to actions which ought not to be done. We discuss whether someone's action was voluntary or not only when the action seems to have been his fault. He is accused of making a noise, and the guilt is his, if the action was voluntary, like laughing; he has successfully excused himself, if he satisfies us that it was involuntary, like a sneeze. In the same way in ordinary life we raise questions of responsibility only when someone is charged, justly or unjustly, with an offence. It makes sense, in this use, to ask whether a boy was responsible for breaking a window, but not whether he was responsible for finishing his homework in good time. We do not ask whether it was his fault that he got a long-division sum right, for to get a sum right is not a fault. If he gets it wrong, he may satisfy us that his failure was not his fault, perhaps because he had not yet been shown how to do such calculations.

In this ordinary use, then, it is absurd to discuss whether satisfactory, correct or admirable performances are voluntary or involuntary. Neither inculpation nor exculpation is in point. We neither confess to authorship nor adduce extenuating circumstances; neither plead 'guilty' nor plead 'not guilty'; for we are not accused.

But philosophers, in discussing what constitutes acts voluntary or involuntary, tend to describe as voluntary not only reprehensible but also meritorious actions, not only things that are someone's fault but also things that are to his credit. The motives underlying their unwitting extension of the ordinary sense of 'voluntary', 'involuntary' and 'responsible' will be considered later. For the moment it is worth while to consider certain consequences which follow from it. In the ordinary use, to say that a sneeze was involuntary is to say that the agent could not help doing it, and to say that a laugh was voluntary is to say that the agent could have helped doing it. (This is not to say that the laugh was intentional. We do not laugh on purpose.) The boy could have got the sum right which he actually got wrong; he knew how to behave, but he misbehaved; he was competent to tie a reef-knot, though what he unintentionally produced was a granny-knot. His failure or lapse was his fault. But when the word 'voluntary' is given its philosophically stretched use, so that correct as well as incorrect, admirable as well as contemptible acts are described as voluntary, it seems to follow by analogy with the ordinary use, that a boy who gets his sum right can also be described as having been 'able to help it'. It would then be proper to ask: Could you have helped solving the riddle? Could you have helped drawing the proper conclusion? Could you have helped tying a proper reef-knot? Could you have helped seeing the point of that joke? Could you have helped being kind to that child? In fact, however, no one could answer these questions, though it is not at first obvious why, if it is correct to say that someone could have avoided getting a sum wrong, it is incorrect to say that he could have avoided getting it right.

The solution is simple. When we say that someone could have avoided committing a lapse or error, or that it was his fault that he committed it, we mean that he knew how to do the right thing, or was competent to do so, but did not exercise his knowledge or competence. He was not trying, or not trying hard enough. But when a person has done the right thing, we cannot then say that he knew how to do the wrong thing, or that he was competent to make mistakes. For making mistakes is not an exercise of competence, nor is the commission of slips an exercise of knowledge *how*; it is a failure to exercise knowledge *how*. It is true in one sense of 'could' that a person who had done a sum correctly could have got it wrong; in the sense, namely, that he is not exempt from the liability to be careless. But in another sense of 'could', to ask, 'Could you have got it wrong?' means 'Were you sufficiently intelligent and well-trained and were you concentrating hard enough to make a miscalculation?', and this is as silly a question as to ask whether someone's teeth are strong enough to be broken by cracking nuts.

The tangle of largely spurious problems, known as the problem of the Freedom of the Will, partly derives from this unconsciously stretched use of 'voluntary' and these consequential misapplications of different senses of 'could' and 'could have helped'.

The first task is to elucidate what is meant in their ordinary, undistorted use by 'voluntary', 'involuntary', 'responsible', 'could not have helped' and 'his fault', as these expressions are used in deciding concrete questions of guilt and innocence.

If a boy has tied a granny-knot instead of a reef-knot, we satisfy ourselves that it was his fault by first establishing that he knew how to tie a reef-knot, and then by establishing that his hand was not forced by external coercion and that there were no other agencies at work preventing him from tying the correct knot. We establish that he could tie reef-knots by finding out that he had been taught, had had practice, usually got them right, or by finding that he could detect and correct knots tied by others, or by finding that he was ashamed of what he had done and, without help from others, put it right himself. That he was not acting under duress or in panic or high fever or with numb fingers, is discovered in the way in which we ordinarily discover that highly exceptional incidents have not taken place; for such incidents would have been too remarkable to have gone unremarked, at least by the boy himself.

The first question which we had to decide had nothing to do with the occurrence or non-occurrence of any occult episode in the boy's stream of consciousness; it was the question whether or not he had the required higher-level competence, that of knowing how to tie reef-knots. We were not, at this stage, inquiring whether he committed, or omitted, an extra public or private operation, but only whether he possessed or lacked a certain intelligent capacity. What satisfied us was not the (unattainable) knowledge of the truth or falsity of a particular covert cause-overt effect proposition, but the (attainable) knowledge of the truth or falsity of a complex and partially general hypothetical proposition—not, in short, that he did tie a shadowy reef- or granny-knot behind the scenes, but that he could have tied a real one with this rope and would have done so on this occasion, if he had paid more heed to what he was doing. The lapse was his fault because, knowing how to tie the knot, he still did not tie it correctly.

Consider next the case of an act which everyone would decide was not the agent's fault. A boy arrives late for school and on inquiry it turns out that he left home at the usual time, did not dally on his way to the omnibus halt and caught the usual omnibus. But the vehicle broke down and could not complete the journey. The boy ran as fast as he could the rest of the way, but was still late. Clearly all the steps taken by the boy were either the same as those which normally bring him to school in time, or were the only steps open to him for remedying the effects of the breakdown. There was nothing else that he could have done and his teacher properly recommends him to follow the same routine on future occasions. His late arrival was not the result of a failure to do what he was capable of doing. He was prevented by a circumstance which was not in his power to modify. Here again the teacher is judging an action with reference to the capacities and opportunities of the agent; his excuse is accepted that he could not have done better than he did. The whole question of the involuntariness of his late arrival is decided without the boy being asked to report any deliverances of consciousness or introspection about the execution or non-execution of any volitions.

It makes no difference if the actions with which an agent is charged either are or embody operations of silent soliloquy or other operations with verbal or non-verbal images. A slip in mental arithmetic is the pupil's fault on the same grounds as a slip made in written arithmetic; and an error committed in matching colours in the mind's eye may merit the reproach of carelessness in the same way as an error committed in matching colours on the draper's counter. If the agent could have done better than he did, then he could have helped doing it as badly as he did.

Besides considering the ordinary senses of 'voluntary', 'involuntary', 'responsible', 'my fault' and 'could' or 'could not help', we should notice as well the ordinary uses of such expressions as 'effort of will', 'strength of will' and 'irresolute'. A person is described as behaving resolutely when in the execution of difficult, protracted or disagreeable tasks he tends not to relax his efforts, not to let his attention be diverted, not to grumble and not to think much or often about his fatigue or fears. He does not shirk or drop things to which he has set his hand. A weak-willed person is one who is easily distracted or disheartened, apt to convince himself that another time will be more suitable or that the reasons for undertaking the task were not after all very strong. Note that it is no part of the definition of resoluteness or of irresoluteness that a resolution should actually have been formed. A resolute man may firmly resist temptations to abandon or postpone his task, though he never went through a prefatory ritual-process of making up his mind to complete it. But naturally such a man will also be disposed to perform any vows which he has made to others or to himself. Correspondingly the irresolute man will be likely to fail to carry out his often numerous good resolutions, but his lack of tenacity of purpose will be exhibited also in surrenders and slacknesses in courses of action which were unprefaced by any private or public undertakings to accomplish them.

Strength of will is a propensity the exercises of which consist in sticking to tasks; that is, in not being deterred or diverted. Weakness of will is having too little of this propensity. The performances in which strength of will is exerted may be performances of almost any sort, intellectual or manual, imaginative or administrative. It is not a single-track disposition or, for that and other reasons, a disposition to execute occult operations of one special kind.

By 'an effort of will' is meant a particular exercise of tenacity of purpose, occurring when the obstacles are notably great, or the counter-temptations notably strong. Such efforts may, but need not, be accompanied by special processes, often of a ritual character, of nerving or adjuring oneself to do what is required; but these processes are not so much ways in which resoluteness is shown as ways in which fear of irresoluteness manifests itself.

Before we leave the concept or concepts of voluntariness, two further points need to be made. (1) Very often we oppose things done voluntarily to things suffered under compulsion. Some soldiers are volunteers, others are conscripts; some yachtsmen go out to sea voluntarily, others are carried out to sea by the wind and tide. Here questions of inculpation and exculpation need not arise. In asking whether the soldier volunteered or was conscripted, we are asking whether he joined up because he wanted to do so, or whether he joined up because he had to do so, where 'had to' entails 'no matter what he wanted'. In asking whether the yachtsman went out to sea of his own accord or whether he was carried out, we are asking whether he went out on purpose, or whether he would still have gone out as he did, even if he had meant not to do so. Would bad news from home, or a warning from the coastguard, have stopped him?

What is involuntary, in this use, is not describable as an act. Being carried out to sea, or being called up, is something that happens to a person, not something which he does. In this respect, this antithesis between voluntary and involuntary differs from the antithesis we have in mind when we ask whether someone's tying of a granny-knot, or his knitting of his brows, is voluntary or involuntary. A person who frowns involuntarily is not forced to frown, as a yachtsman may be forced out to sea; nor is the careless boy forced to tie a granny-knot, as the conscript is forced to join the army. Even frowning is something that a person does. It is not done to him. So sometimes the question 'Voluntary or involuntary?' means 'Did the person do it, or was it done to him?'; sometimes it presupposes that he did it, but means 'Did he do it with or without heeding what he was doing?' or 'Did he do it on purpose or inadvertently, mechanically, or instinctively, etc.?'

(2) When a person does something voluntarily, in the sense that he does it on purpose or is trying to do it, his action certainly reflects some quality or qualities of mind, since (it is more than a verbal point to say) he is in some degree and in one fashion or another minding what he is doing. It follows also that, if linguistically equipped, he can then tell, without research or conjecture, what he has been trying to accomplish.   But, as will be argued in Chapter V, these implications of voluntariness do not carry with them the double-life corollaries often assumed. To frown intentionally is not to do one thing on one's forehead and another thing in a second metaphorical place; nor is it to do one thing with one's brow-muscles and another thing with some non-bodily organ. In particular, it is not to bring about a frown on one's forehead by first bringing about a frown-causing exertion of some occult non-muscle. 'He frowned intentionally' does not report the occurrence of two episodes. It reports the occurrence of one episode, but one of a very different character from that reported by 'he frowned involuntarily', though the frowns might be photographically as similar as you please.

(4) *Freedom of the Will.*

It has been pointed out that in some philosophers' discussions of the voluntariness of actions, the words 'voluntary', 'involuntary' and 'responsible' are used, not with their ordinary restriction to lapses or apparent lapses, but with a wider scope covering all performances which are to be adjudged favourably or unfavourably by any criteria of excellence or admissibility. In their use, a person is described as voluntarily doing the right thing and as voluntarily doing the wrong thing, or as being responsible not only for actions for which he is subject to accusation, but also for actions entitling him to kudos. It is used, that is, as a synonym of 'intentional'.

Now the philosophers who have worked with this stretched usage have had a strong intellectual motive for doing so. They felt the need for an apparatus of terms by which to demarcate those things and occurrences to which *either* plaudits *or* strictures are appropriate from those to which neither are appropriate. Without such an apparatus it would, they felt, be impossible to state what are the qualifications for membership of the realm of Spirit, the lack of which entails relegation to the realm of brute Nature.

The main source of this concern to discover some peculiar element present, wherever Spirit is present, and absent, where it is absent, was alarm at the bogy of Mechanism. It was believed that the physical sciences had established, or were on the way to establishing, that the things and events of the external world are rigidly governed by discoverable laws, laws the formulations of which admit no appraisal-words. It was felt that all external happenings are confined within the iron grooves of mechanical causation. The genesis, the properties and the courses of these happenings were, or would be, totally explained in terms of measurable and, it was supposed, therefore purposeless forces.

To salve our right to employ appraisal-concepts, the field of their proper application had to be shown to lie somewhere else than this external world, and an internal world of unmeasurable but purposeful forces was thought to do the trick. 'Volitions' being already nominated as the required outputs of internal forces, it was then natural to suppose that voluntariness, defined in terms of propagation by volitions, was the common and peculiar element which makes occurrences spiritual. Scientific propositions and appraisal-propositions were accordingly distinguished as being respectively descriptions of what takes place in the external world and descriptions of what takes place in the internal world—at least until psychologists claimed that their assertions were scientific descriptions of what takes place in the inner world.

The question whether human beings can merit praise or blame was consequently construed as the question whether volitions are effects.

### (5) *The Bogy of Mechanism.*

Whenever a new science achieves its first big successes, its enthusiastic acolytes always fancy that all questions are now soluble by extension of its methods of solving its questions. At one time theorists imagined that the whole world was nothing more than a complex of geometrical figures, at another that the whole world was describable and explicable in the propositions of pure arithmetic. Chemical, electrical, Darwinian and Freudian cosmogonies have also enjoyed their bright but brief days. 'At long last', the zealots always say, 'we can give, or at least indicate, a solution of all difficulties and one which is unquestionably a scientific solution'.

The physical sciences launched by Copernicus, Galileo, Newton and Boyle secured a longer and a stronger hold upon the cosmogony-builders than did either their forerunners or their successors. People still tend to treat laws of Mechanics not merely as the ideal type of scientific laws, but as, in some sense, the ultimate laws of Nature. They tend to hope or fear that biological, psychological and sociological laws will one day be 'reduced' to mechanical laws—though it is left unclear what sort of a transaction this 'reduction' would be.

I have spoken of Mechanism as a bogy. The fear that theoretically minded persons have felt lest everything should turn out to be explicable by mechanical laws is a baseless fear. And it is baseless not because the contingency which they dread happens not to be impending, but because it makes no sense to speak of such a contingency. Physicists may one day have found the answers to all physical questions, but not all questions are physical questions. The laws that they have found and will find may, in one sense of the metaphorical verb, govern everything that happens, but they do not ordain everything that happens. Indeed they do not ordain anything that happens. Laws of nature are not fiats.

An illustration may elucidate this point. A scientifically trained spectator, who is not acquainted with chess or any other game, is permitted to look at a chessboard in the intervals between the moves. He does not yet see the players making the moves. After a time he begins to notice certain regularities. The pieces known to us as 'pawns', normally move only one square at a time and then only forwards, save in certain special circumstances when they move diagonally. The pieces known to us as 'bishops' only move diagonally, though they can move any number of squares at a time. Knights always make dog-legged moves. And so on. After much research this spectator will have worked out all the rules of chess, and he is then allowed to see that the moves of the pieces are made by people whom we know as 'players'. He commiserates with them upon their bondage. "Every move that you make", he says, "is governed by unbreakable rules; from the moment that one of you puts his hand on a pawn, the move that he will make with it is, in most cases, accurately predictable. The whole course of what you tragically dub your 'game' is remorselessly pre-ordained; nothing in it takes place which cannot be shown to be governed by one or other of the iron rules. Heartless necessity dictates the play, leaving no room in it for intelligence or purpose. True, I am not yet competent to explain every move that I witness by the rules that I have so far discovered. But it would be unscientific to suppose that there are inexplicable moves. There must therefore be further rules, which I hope to discover and which will satisfactorily complete the explanations which I have inaugurated." The players, of course, laugh and explain to him that though every move is governed, not one of them is ordained by the rules. "True, given that I start to move my bishop, you can predict with certainty that it will end on a square of the same colour as that from which it started. That can be deduced from the rules. But that, or how far, I shall move my bishop at this or that stage of the game is not stated in, or deducible from, the rules. There is plenty of room for us to display cleverness and stupidity and to exercise deliberation and choice. Though nothing happens that is irregular, plenty happens that is surprising, ingenious and silly. The rules are the same for all the games of chess that have ever been played, yet nearly every game that has ever been played has taken a course for which the players can recall no close parallels. The rules are unalterable, but the games are not uniform. The rules prescribe what the players may not do; everything else is permitted, though many moves that are permitted would be bad tactics.

"There are no further rules of the game for you to discover and the 'explanations' which you hope to find for the particular moves that we make can, of course, be discovered, but they are not explanations in terms of rules but in terms of some quite different things, namely, such things as the player's consideration and application of tactical principles. Your notion of what constitutes an explanation was too narrow. The sense in which a rule 'explains' a move made in conformity with it is not the same as the sense in which a tactical principle explains a move, for all that every move that obeys a tactical principle also obeys a rule. Knowing how to apply tactical principles involves knowing the rules of the game, but there is no question of these principles being 'reducible' to rules of the game."

This illustration is not intended to suggest that the laws of physics are very much like the rules of chess; for the course of Nature is not a game and its laws are not human inventions or conventions. What the illustration is meant to bring out is the fact there is no contradiction in saying that one and the same process, such as the move of a bishop, is in accordance with two principles of completely different types and such that neither is 'reducible' to the other, though one of them presupposes the other.

Hence there derive two quite different sorts of 'explanation' of the moves, neither of which is incompatible with the other. Indeed the explanation in terms of tactical canons presupposes that in terms of the rules of chess, but it is not deducible from those rules. This point can be expressed in another way. A spectator might ask, in one sense of 'why', why the bishop always ends a move on a square of the same colour as that on which it began the game; he would be answered by being referred to the rules of chess, including those prescribing the design of the board. He might then ask, in another sense of 'why', why a player at a certain stage of the game moved one of his bishops (and not some other piece) to one square (and not to another); he might be answered that it was to force the opposing Queen to cease to threaten the player's King.

Words like 'explanation', 'law', 'rule', 'principle', 'why', 'because', 'cause', 'reason', 'govern', 'necessitate', etc., have a range of typically different senses. Mechanism seemed to be a menace because it was assumed that the use of these terms in mechanical theories is their sole use; that all 'why' questions are answerable in terms of laws of motion. In fact all 'why' questions of one type are perhaps answerable in those terms and no 'why' questions of other types are answerable merely in those terms.

It may well be that throughout the whole length of *The Decline and Fall of the Roman Empire* Gibbon never once infringes the rules of English grammar. They governed his entire writing, yet they did not ordain what he should write, or even the style in which he should write; they merely forbade certain ways of conjoining words. Knowing these rules and Gibbon's obedience to them, a reader can predict from the fact that a particular sentence has for its subject a plural noun that its verb will be a plural verb. His predictions will be uniformly correct, yet we feel no inclination to lament that Gibbon's pen ran in a fatal groove. Grammar tells the reader that the verb must be a plural verb, but not which verb it will be.

An argumentative passage from *The Decline and Fall* might be examined for the grammatical rules which its word-arrangements observe, the stylistic canons which its word-arrangements observe, and the logical rules which its word-arrangements observe. There is no conflict or competition between these different types of principles; all alike are applied in the same material; all alike can supply licenses for correct predictions; all alike may be referred to for answers to questions of the same verbal pattern 'Why did Gibbon write this and not something else?'

The discoveries of the physical sciences no more rule out life, sentience, purpose or intelligence from presence in the world than do the rules of grammar extrude style or logic from prose. Certainly the discoveries of the physical sciences say nothing of life, sentience, or purpose, but nor do the rules of grammar say anything about style or logic. For the laws of physics apply to what is animate as well as to what is inanimate, to intelligent people as well as to idiots, just as the rules of grammar apply to *Whitaker's Almanac* as well as to *The Decline and Fall*, to Mrs. Eddy's as well as to Hume's reasonings.

The favourite model to which the fancied mechanistic world is assimilated is that of billiard balls imparting their motion to one another by impact. Yet a game of billiards provides one of the simplest examples of a course of events for the description of which mechanical terms are necessary without being sufficient. Certainly from accurate knowledge of the weight, shape, elasticity and movements of the balls, the constitution of the table and the conditions of the atmosphere it is in principle possible, in accordance with known laws, to deduce from a momentary state of the balls what will be their later state. But it does not follow from this that the course of the game is predictable in accordance with those laws alone. A scientific forecaster, who was ignorant of the rules and tactics of the game and of the skill and plans of the players, could predict, perhaps, from the beginning of a single stroke, the positions in which the balls will come to rest before the next stroke is made; but he could predict no further. The player himself may be able to foresee with modest probability the sort of break that he will make, for he knows, perhaps, the best tactics to apply to situations like this and he knows a good deal about his own skill, endurance, patience, keenness and intentions.

It must be noticed that in so far as the player has any skill in getting the balls where he wishes, he must have knowledge, of a rule-of-thumb sort, of the mechanical principles which govern the accelerations and decelerations of the balls. His knowledge how to execute his intentions is not at loggerheads with his knowledge of mechanical laws; it depends on that knowledge. In applying appraisal-concepts to his play we are not worried by the fact that the motions imparted by him to the balls are governed by mechanical laws; for there could not be a game of skill at all if, *per impossibile*, the instruments of the game behaved randomly.

The modern interpretation of natural laws as statements not of necessities but of very, very long odds is sometimes acclaimed as providing a desiderated element of non-rigorousness in Nature. Now at last, it is sometimes felt, we can be scientific while reserving just a very few occasions in which appraisal-concepts can be properly applied. This silly view assumes that an action could not merit favourable or unfavourable criticism, unless it were an exception to scientific generalisations. But the billiards player asks for no special indulgences from the laws of physics any more than he does from the rules of billiards. Why should he? They do not force his hand. The fears expressed by some moral philosophers that the advance of the natural sciences diminishes the field within which the moral virtues can be exercised rests on the assumption that there is some contradiction in saying that one and the same occurrence is governed both by mechanical laws and by moral principles, an assumption as baseless as the assumption that a golfer cannot at once conform to the laws of ballistics *and* obey the rules of golf *and* play with elegance and skill. Not only is there plenty of room for purpose where everything is governed by mechanical laws, but there would be no place for purpose if things were not so governed. Predictability is a necessary condition of planning.

Mechanism then is a mere bogy and while there is much to be elucidated in the special concepts of biology, anthropology, sociology, ethics, logic, æsthetics, politics, economics, historiography, etc., there is no need for the desperate salvage-operation of withdrawing the applications of them out of the ordinary world to some postulated other world, or of setting up a partition between things that exist in Nature and things that exist in non-Nature. No occult precursors of overt acts are required to preserve for their agent his title to plaudits or strictures for performing them, nor would they be effective preservatives if they did exist.

Men are not machines, not even ghost-ridden machines. They are men—a tautology which is sometimes worth remembering. People often pose such questions as 'How does my mind get my hand to make the required movements?' and even 'What makes my hand do what my mind tells it to do?' Questions of these patterns are properly asked of certain chain-processes. The question 'What makes the bullet fly out of the barrel?' is properly answered by 'The expansion of gases in the cartridge'; the question 'What makes the cartridge explode?' is answered by reference to the percussion of the detonator; and the question 'How does my squeezing the trigger make the pin strike the detonator?' is answered by describing the mechanism of springs, levers and catches between the trigger and the pin. So when it is asked 'How does my mind get my finger to squeeze the trigger?' the form of the question presupposes that a further chain-process is involved, embodying still earlier tensions, releases and discharges, though this time 'mental' ones. But whatever is the act or operation adduced as the first step of this postulated chain-process, the performance of it has to be described in just the same way as in ordinary life we describe the squeezing of the trigger by the marksman. Namely we say simply 'He did it' and not 'He did or underwent something else which caused it'.

In conclusion, it is perhaps worth while giving a warning against a very popular fallacy. The hearsay knowledge that everything in Nature is subject to mechanical laws often tempts people to say that Nature is either one big machine, or else a conglomeration of machines. But in fact there are very few machines in Nature. The only machines that we find are the machines that human beings make, such as clocks, windmills and turbines. There are a very few natural systems which somewhat resemble such machines, namely, such things as solar systems. These do go on by themselves and repeat indefinitely the same series of movements. The do go, as few unmanufactured things go, 'like clock-work'. True, to make machines we have to know and apply Mechanics. But inventing machines is not copying things found in inanimate Nature.

Paradoxical though it may seem, we have to look rather to living organisms for examples in Nature of self-maintaining, routine-observing systems. The movements of the heavenly bodies provided one kind of 'clock'. It was the human pulse that provided the next. Nor is it merely primitive animism which makes native children think of engines as iron horses. There is very little else in Nature to which they are so closely analogous. Avalanches and games of billiards are subject to mechanical laws; but they are not at all like the workings of machines.

# CHAPTER IV

# EMOTION

## (1) Foreword.

IN this chapter I discuss certain of the concepts of emotion and feeling.

This scrutiny is necessary because adherents of the dogma of the ghost in the machine can adduce in support of it the consent of most philosophers and psychologists to the view that emotions are internal or private experiences. Emotions are described as turbulences in the stream of consciousness, the owner of which cannot help directly registering them; to external witnesses they are, in consequence, necessarily occult. They are occurrences which take place not in the public, physical world but in your or my secret, mental world.

I shall argue that the word 'emotion' is used to designate at least three or four different kinds of things, which I shall call 'inclinations' (or 'motives'), 'moods', 'agitations' (or 'commotions') and 'feelings'. Inclinations and moods, including agitations, are not occurrences and do not therefore take place either publicly or privately. They are propensities, not acts or states. They are, however, propensities of different kinds, and their differences arc important. Feelings, on the other hand, are occurrences, but the place that mention of them should take in descriptions of human behaviour is very different from that which the standard theories accord to it. Moods or frames of mind are, unlike motives, but like maladies and states of the weather, temporary conditions which in a certain way *collect* occurrences, but they are not themselves extra occurrences.

## (2) Feelings versus Inclinations.

By 'feelings' I refer to the sorts of things which people often describe as thrills, twinges, pangs, throbs, wrenches, itches, prickings, chills, glows, loads, qualms, hankerings, curdlings, sinkings, tensions, gnawings and shocks. Ordinarily, when people report the occurrence of a feeling, they do so in a phrase like 'a throb of compassion,' 'a shock of surprise' or 'a thrill of anticipation'.

It is an important linguistic fact that these names for specific feelings, such as 'itch', 'qualm' and 'pang' are also used as names of specific bodily sensations. If someone says that he has just felt a twinge, it is proper to ask whether it was a twinge of remorse or of rheumatism, though the word 'twinge' is not necessarily being used in quite the same sense in the alternative contexts.

There are further respects in which the ways in which we speak of, say, qualms of apprehension are analogous to the ways in which we speak of, say, qualms of sea-sickness. We are ready to characterise either as acute or faint, sudden or lingering, intermittent or steady. A man may wince from a pricking of his conscience or from a pricking in his finger. Moreover, we are in some cases ready to locate, say, the sinking feeling of despair in the pit of the stomach or the tense feeling of anger in the muscles of the jaw and fist. Other feelings which we are not prepared to locate in any particular part of the body, like glows of pride, seem to pervade the whole body in much the same way as do glows of warmth.

James boldly identified feelings with bodily sensations, but for our purposes it is enough to show that we talk of feelings very much as we talk of bodily sensations, though it is possible that there is a tinge of metaphor in our talk of the former which is absent from our talk of the latter.

On the other hand, it is necessary to do justice to the crucial fact that we do report feelings in such idioms as 'qualms of apprehension' and 'glows of pride'; we do, that is, distinguish a glow of pride from a glow of warmth, and I shall have to try to bring out the force of such distinctions. I hope to show that though it is quite proper to describe someone as feeling a throb of compassion, his compassion is not to be equated with a throb or a series of throbs, any more than his fatigue is his gasps; so no disillusioning consequences would follow from acknowledging that throbs, twinges and other feelings are bodily sensations.

In one sense, then, of 'emotion' the feelings are emotions. But there is quite another sense of 'emotion' in which theorists classify as emotions the motives by which people's higher-level behaviour is explained. When a man is described as vain, considerate, avaricious, patriotic or indolent, an explanation is being given of why he conducts his actions, daydreams and thoughts in the way he does, and, according to the standard terminology, vanity, kindliness, avarice, patriotism and laziness rank as species of emotion; they come thence to be spoken of as feelings.

But there is a great verbal muddle here, associated with a great logical muddle. To begin with, when someone is described as a vain or indolent man, the words 'vain' and 'indolent' are used to signify more or less lasting traits in his character. In this use he might be said to have been vain since childhood, or indolent during his entire half-holiday. His vanity and indolence are dispositional properties, which could be unpacked in such expressions as 'Whenever situations of certain sorts have arisen, he has always or usually tried to make himself prominent' or 'Whenever he was faced by an option between doing something difficult and not doing it, he shirked doing the difficult thing'. Sentences beginning with 'Whenever' are not singular occurrence reports. Motive words used in this way signify tendencies or propensities and therefore cannot signify the occurrence of feelings. They are elliptical expressions of general hypothetical propositions of a certain sort, and cannot be construed as expressing categorical narratives of episodes.

It will however be objected that, besides this dispositional use of motive words, there must also be a corresponding active use of them. For a man to be punctual in the dispositional sense of the adjective, he must tend to be punctual on particular occasions; and the sense in which he is said to be punctual for a particular rendezvous is not the dispositional but the active sense of 'punctual'. 'He tends to be at his rendezvous on time' expresses a general hypothetical proposition, the truth of which requires that there should also be corresponding true categorical propositions of the pattern 'he was at today's rendezvous in good time'. So, it will be argued, for a man to be a vain or indolent man there must be particular exercises of vanity and indolence occurring at particular moments, and these will be actual emotions or feelings.

This argument certainly establishes something, but it does not establish the point desired. While it is true that to describe a man as vain is to say that he is subject to a specific tendency, it is not true that the particular exercises of this tendency consist in his registering particular thrills or twinges. On the contrary, on hearing that a man is vain we expect him, in the first instance, to behave in certain ways, namely to talk a lot about himself, to cleave to the society of the eminent, to reject criticisms, to seek the footlights and to disengage himself from conversations about the merits of others. We expect him also to indulge in roseate daydreams about his own successes, to avoid recalling past failures and to plan for his own advancement. To be vain is to tend to act in these and innumerable other kindred ways. Certainly we also expect the vain man to feel certain pangs and flutters in certain situations; we expect him to have an acute sinking feeling, when an eminent person forgets his name, and to feel buoyant of heart and light of toe on hearing of the misfortunes of his rivals. But feelings of pique and buoyancy are not more directly indicative of vanity than are public acts of boasting or private acts of daydreaming. Indeed they are less directly indicative, for reasons which will shortly appear.

Some theorists will object that to speak of an act of boasting as one of the direct exercises of vanity is to leave out the cardinal factor in the situation. When we explain why a man boasts by saying that it is because he is vain, we are forgetting that a disposition is not an event and so cannot be a cause. The cause of his boasting must be an event antecedent to his beginning to boast. He must be moved to boast by some actual 'impulse', namely an impulse of vanity. So the immediate or direct actualisations of vanity are particular vanity impulses, and these are feelings. The vain man is a man who tends to register particular feelings of vanity; these cause or impel him to boast, or perhaps to will to boast, and to do all the other things which we say are done from vanity.

It should be noticed that this argument takes it for granted that to explain an act as done from a certain motive, in this case from vanity, is to give a causal explanation. This means that it assumes that a mind, in this case the boaster's mind, is a field of special causes; that is why a vanity feeling has been called in to be the inner cause of the overt boasting. I shall shortly argue that to explain an act as done from a certain motive is not analogous to saying that the glass broke, because a stone hit it, but to the quite different type of statement that the glass broke, when the stone hit it, because the glass was brittle. Just as there are no other momentary actualisations of brittleness than, for example, flying into fragments when struck, so no other momentary actualisations of chronic vanity need to be postulated than such things as boasting, day-dreaming about triumphs and avoiding conversations about the merits of others.

But before expanding this argument I want to show how intrinsically unplausible the view is that, on each occasion that a vain man behaves vaingloriously, he experiences a particular palpitation or pricking of vanity. To put it quite dogmatically, the vain man never feels vain. Certainly, when thwarted, he feels acute dudgeon and when unexpectedly successful, he feels buoyant. But there is no special thrill or pang which we call a 'feeling of vanity'. Indeed, if there were such a recognisable specific feeling, and the vain man was constantly experiencing it, he would be the first instead of the last person to recognise how vain he was.

Take another example. A man is interested in Symbolic Logic. He regularly reads books and articles on the subject, discusses it, works out problems in it and neglects lectures on other subjects. According to the view which is here contested, he must therefore constantly experience impulses of a peculiar kind, namely feelings of interest in Symbolic Logic, and if his interest is very strong these feelings must be very acute and very frequent. He must therefore be able to tell us whether these feelings are sudden, like twinges, or lasting, like aches; whether they succeed one another several times a minute or only a few times an hour; and whether he feels them in the small of his back or in his forehead. But clearly his only reply to such specific questions would be that he catches himself experiencing no peculiar throbs or qualms while he is attending to his hobby. He may report a feeling of vexation, when his studies are interrupted, and the feeling of a load off his chest, when distractions are removed; but there are no peculiar feelings of interest in Symbolic Logic for him to report. While undisturbedly pursuing his hobby, he feels no perturbations at all.

Suppose, however, that there were such feelings cropping up, maybe, about every two or twenty minutes. We should still expect to find him discussing and studying the subject in the intervals between these occurrences, and we should correctly say that he was still discussing and studying the subject from interest in it.

This point by itself establishes the conclusion that to do something from a motive is compatible with being free from any particular feelings while doing it.

Of course, the standard theories of motives do not speak so crudely of qualms, pangs and flutters. They speak more sedately of desires, impulses or promptings. Now there are feelings of wanting, namely those we call 'hankerings', 'cravings' and 'itchings'. So let us put our question in this way. Is being interested in Symbolic Logic equivalent to being liable or prone to feel certain special hankerings, gnawings or cravings? And does working at Symbolic Logic from interest in it involve feeling one such itching before each bit of the work is begun? If the affirmative answer is given, then there can be no answer to the question, 'From what motive does the student work at the subject in the intervals between the itchings?' And if to say that his interest was strong meant that the supposed feelings were frequent and acute, the absurd consequence would follow that the more strongly a man was interested in a subject, the more his attention would be distracted from it. To call a feeling or sensation 'acute' is to say that it is difficult not to attend to it, and to attend to a feeling is not the same thing as to attend to a problem in Symbolic Logic.

We must reject, then, the conclusion of the argument which tried to prove that motive words are the names of feelings or else of tendencies to have feelings. But what was wrong with the argument for this conclusion?

There are at least two quite different senses in which an occurrence is said to be 'explained'; and there are correspondingly at least two quite different senses in which we ask 'why' it occurred and two quite different senses in which we say that it happened 'because' so and so was the case. The first sense is the causal sense. To ask why the glass broke is to ask what caused it to break, and we explain, in this sense, the fracture of the glass when we report that a stone hit it. The 'because' clause in the explanation reports an event, namely the event which stood to the fracture of the glass as cause to effect.

But very frequently we look for and get explanations of occurrences in another sense of 'explanation'. We ask why the glass shivered when struck by the stone and we get the answer that it was because the glass was brittle. Now 'brittle' is a dispositional adjective;

that is to say, to describe the glass as brittle is to assert a general hypothetical proposition about the glass. So when we say that the glass broke when struck because it was brittle, the 'because' clause does not report a happening or a cause; it states a law-like proposition. People commonly say of explanations of this second kind that they give the 'reason' for the glass breaking when struck.

How does the law-like general hypothetical proposition work? It says, roughly, that the glass, *if* sharply struck or twisted, etc. *would* not dissolve or stretch or evaporate but fly into fragments. The matter of fact that the glass did at a particular moment fly into fragments, when struck by a particular stone, is explained, in this sense of 'explain', when the first happening, namely the impact of the stone, satisfies the protasis of the general hypothetical proposition, and when the second happening, namely the fragmentation of the glass, satisfies its apodosis.

This can now be applied to the explanation of actions as issuing from specified motives. When we ask 'Why did someone act in a certain way?' this question might, so far as its language goes, either be an inquiry into the cause of his acting in that way, or be an inquiry into the character of the agent which accounts for his having acted in that way on that occasion. I suggest, what I shall now try to prove, that explanations by motives are explanations of the second type and not of the first type. It is perhaps more than a merely linguistic fact that a man who reports the motive from which something is done is, in common parlance, said to be giving the 'reason' for the action. It should be also noticed that there are lots of different kinds of such explanations of human actions. A twitch may be explained by a reflex, the filling of a pipe by an inveterate habit; the answering of a letter by a motive. Some of the differences between reflexes, habits and motives will have to be described at a later stage.

The present issue is this. The statement 'he boasted from vanity' ought, on one view, to be construed as saying that 'he boasted and the cause of his boasting was the occurrence in him of a particular feeling or impulse of vanity'. On the other view, it is to be construed as saying 'he boasted on meeting the stranger and his doing so satisfies the law-like proposition that whenever he finds a chance of securing the admiration and envy of others, he does whatever he thinks will produce this admiration and envy'.

My first argument in favour of the second way of construing such statements is that no one could ever know or even, usually, reasonably conjecture that the cause of someone else's overt action was the occurrence in him of a feeling. Even if the agent reported, what people never do report, that he had experienced a vanity itch just before he boasted, this would be very weak evidence that the itch caused the action, since for all we know, the cause was any one of a thousand other synchronous happenings. On this view the imputation of motives would be incapable of any direct testing and no reasonable person would put any reliance on any such imputation. It would be like water-divining in places where well-sinking was forbidden.

In fact, however, we do discover the motives of other people. The process of discovering them is not immune from error, but nor are the errors incorrigible. It is or is like an inductive process, which results in the establishment of law-like propositions and the applications of them as the 'reasons' for particular actions. What is established in each case is or includes a general hypothetical proposition of a certain sort. The imputation of a motive for a particular action is not a causal inference to an unwitnessed event but the subsumption of an episode proposition under a law-like proposition. It is therefore analogous to the explanation of reactions and actions by reflexes and habits, or to the explanation of the fracture of the glass by reference to its brittleness.

The way in which a person discovers his own long-term motives is the same as the way in which he discovers those of others. The quantity and quality of the information accessible to him differ in the two inquiries, but its items are in general of the same sort. He has, it is true, a fund of recollections of his own past deeds, thoughts, fancies and feelings; and he can perform the experiments of fancying himself confronted by tasks and opportunities which have not actually occurred. He can thus base his appreciations of his own lasting inclinations on data which he lacks for his appreciations of the inclinations of others. On the other side, his appreciations of his own inclinations are unlikely to be unbiased and he is not in a favourable position to compare his own actions and reactions with those of others. In general we think that an impartial and discerning spectator is a better judge of a person's prevailing motives, as well as of his habits, abilities and weaknesses, than is that person himself, a view which is directly contrary to the theory which holds that an agent possesses a Privileged Access to the so-called springs of his own actions and is, because of that access, able and bound to discover, without inference or research, from what motives he tends to act and from what motive he acted on a particular occasion.

We shall see later on (Chapter V) that a person who does or undergoes something, heeding what he is doing or undergoing, can, commonly, answer questions about the incident without inference or research. But what gives him those ready-made answers can and often does give his companions also those same ready-made answers. He does not have to be a detective, but nor do they.

Another argument supports this thesis. A person replying to an interrogation might say that he was delving into a ditch in order to find the larvæ of a certain species of insect; that he was looking for these larvæ in order to find out on what fauna or flora they were parasitic; that he was trying to find out on what they were parasitic in order to test a certain ecological hypothesis; and that he wanted to test this hypothesis in order to test a certain hypothesis about Natural Selection. At each stage he declares his motive or reason for pursuing certain investigations. And each successive reason that he gives is of a higher level of generality than its predecessor. He is subsuming one interest under another, somewhat as more special laws are subsumed under more general laws. He is not recording a chronological series of earlier and earlier stages, though of course he could do this if asked the quite different questions What first aroused your interest in this problem? and in that?

In the case of every action, taken by itself, for which it is natural to ask 'From what motive was it done?' it is always possible that it was not done from a motive but from force of habit. Whatever I do or say, it is always conceivable, though nearly always false, that I did it, or said it, in complete absence of mind. The performance of an action from a motive is different from its performance out of habit; but the sorts of things which belong to the one class also belong to the other. Now to say that an action was done from force of habit is patently to say that a specific disposition explains the action. No one, I trust, thinks that 'habit' is the name of a peculiar internal event or class of events. To ask whether an action

was done from force of habit or from kindliness of heart is therefore
to ask which of two specified dispositions is the explanation of the
action.

Finally, we should consider by what tests we should try to decide
a dispute about the motive from which a person had done something; did he, for example, throw up a well-paid post for a relatively
humble Government job from patriotism or from a desire to be
exempt from military service? We begin, perhaps, by asking him;
but on this sort of matter his avowals, to us or to himself, would
very likely not be frank. We next try, not necessarily unsuccessfully, to settle the dispute by considering whether his words,
actions, embarrassments, etc., on this and other occasions square
with the hypothesis that he is physically timorous and averse from
regimentation, or whether they square with the hypothesis that he
is relatively indifferent to money and would sacrifice anything to
help win the war. We try, that is, to settle by induction the relevant
traits in his character. In applying, then, the results of our induction
to his particular decision, i.e. in explaining why he came to it, we
do not press him to recall the itches, pangs and throbs that he
registered in making it; nor, probably, do we trouble to infer to
their occurrence. And there is a special reason for not paying much
heed to the feelings had by a person whose motives are under
investigation, namely that we know that lively and frequent feelings
are felt by sentimentalists whose positive actions show quite
clearly that their patriotism, e.g. is a self-indulgent make-believe.
Their hearts duly sink when they hear that their country's plight is
desperate, but their appetites are unaffected and the routines of
their lives are unmodified. Their bosoms swell at a march-past, but
they avoid marching themselves. They are rather like theatregoers
and novel readers, who also feel genuine pangs, glows, flutters and
twinges of despair, indignation, exhilaration and disgust, with the
difference that the theatregoers and novel readers realise that they
are making-believe.

To say, then, that a certain motive is a trait in someone's
character is to say that he is inclined to do certain sorts of things,
make certain sorts of plans, indulge in certain sorts of daydreams
and also, of course, in certain situations to feel certain sorts of
feelings. To say that he did something from that motive is to say
that this action, done in its particular circumstances, was just the

sort of thing that that was an inclination to do. It is to say 'he *would* do that'.

## (3) *Inclinations versus Agitations.*

Quite different from inclinations are the states of mind or moods, persons in which are described as agitated, disturbed, distracted or upset. To be anxious, startled, shocked, excited, convulsed, flabbergasted, in suspense, flurried and irritated, arc familiar kinds of agitation. They are commotions, the degrees of upsettingness of which are ordinarily characterised as degrees of violence. In respect of any one of them it makes sense to say that a person is too much disturbed to think or act coherently, too much startled to utter a word, or too excited to be able to concentrate. When people are said to be speechless with amazement, or paralysed by horror, the specific agitation is, in effect, being described as extremely violent.

This point already indicates part of the difference between inclinations and agitations. It would be absurd to say that a person's interest in Symbolic Logic was so violent that he could not concentrate on Symbolic Logic, or that someone was too patriotic to be able to work for his country. Inclinations are not disturbances and so cannot be violent or mild disturbances. A man whose dominant motive is philanthropy or vanity cannot be described as distracted or upset by philanthropy or vanity; for he is not distracted or upset at all. He is entirely single-minded. Philanthropy and vanity are not gusts or storms.

As the words 'distraction' and 'agitation' themselves indicate, people in these conditions are, to use a hazardous metaphor, subject to opposing forces. The two radical kinds of such conflicts are these, namely when one inclination runs counter to another, and when an inclination is thwarted by the hard facts of the world. A man who wants a country life and wants to hold a position which requires his living in a town is inclined in opposing directions. A man who wants to live and is dying is precluded by the facts from doing what he wants. These instances show an important feature of agitations, namely that they presuppose the existence of inclinations which are not themselves agitations, much as eddies presuppose the existence of currents which are not themselves eddies. An eddy is an interference-condition which requires that there exist, say, two currents, or a current and a rock; an agitation requires that there exist two inclinations or an inclination and a factual impediment. Grief, of one sort, is affection blocked by death; suspense, of one sort, is hope interfered with by fear. To be torn between patriotism and ambition the victim must be both patriotic and ambitious.

Hume, following Hutcheson, was partially alive to this distinction between inclinations and agitations, when he noticed that some 'passions' are intrinsically calm, while others are violent. He noticed too that a calm passion might 'vanquish' a violent passion. But his antithesis of 'calm' and 'violent' suggests a mere difference of degree between two things of the same kind. In fact, inclinations and agitations are things of different kinds. Agitations can be violent or mild, inclinations cannot be either. Inclinations·can be relatively strong or relatively weak, but this difference is not a difference of degree of upsettingness; it is a difference of degree of operativeness, which is quite a different sort of difference. Hume's word 'passion' was being used to signify things of at least two disparate types.

When a man is described as being both very avaricious and rather fond of gardening, part of what is being said is that the former motive is stronger than the latter, in the sense that much more of his internal and external conduct is directed towards self-enrichment than is directed towards horticulture. Moreover, when situations arise in which a slight financial loss would be accompanied by a major improvement to his garden, he is likely to give up the orchids and to keep the cash. But more is being said than this. For a man to be describable as very avaricious, this propensity must in the same way be dominant over all or nearly all his other inclinations. Even to be described as rather fond of gardening indicates that this motive dominates a lot of other inclinations. The strengths of motives are their relative strengths *vis-à-vis* either some other specified motive, or every other motive, or most other motives. They are determined partly by the way in which the agent distributes his internal and external activities and, what is only a special case of this, partly by the outcomes of competitions between his inclinations, when circumstances bring about such competitions, i.e. when he cannot do two things, to both of which he is inclined. Indeed, to say that his motives have such and such strengths is simply to say that he tends to distribute his activities in such and such ways.

Sometimes a particular motive is so strong that it always, or nearly always, dominates every other motive. The miser or the saint would perhaps sacrifice everything, even life itself, rather than lose what he most prizes. Such a man would, if the world were kind, never be seriously agitated or distracted, since no other inclination is strong enough seriously to compete or conflict with his heart's desire. He could not be set at loggerheads with himself.

Now one of the most popular uses of 'emotion', 'emotional', 'moved', etc., is to describe the agitations, or other moods, in which people from time to time are, or to which they are liable. By a 'highly emotional person' is commonly meant a person who is frequently and violently distraught, thrilled or flustered. If, for any reason, this is chosen as the standard, or proper sense, of 'emotion', then motives or inclinations are not emotions at all. Vanity would not be an emotion, though chagrin would; being interested in Symbolic Logic would not be an emotion, though being bored by other topics would. But there is no point in trying to prune the ambiguities of the word 'emotion', so it is better to say that motives are, if you like, emotions, but not in the sense in which agitations are emotions.

We must distinguish between two different ways in which we use words like 'worried', 'excited' and 'embarrassed'. Sometimes we use them to signify temporary moods, as when we say that someone was embarrassed for some minutes, or worried for an hour. Sometimes we use them for susceptibilities to moods, as when we say that someone is embarrassed by praise, i.e. is regularly embarrassed, whenever he is praised. Similarly 'rheumatic' sometimes means 'having a bout of rheumatism', sometimes 'prone to have bouts of rheumatism'; and 'Ireland is rainy' may mean that there is a good deal of rain there now, or that there usually is a good deal of rain there. Clearly, susceptibilities to specific agitations are on the same general footing with inclinations, namely that both are general propensities and not occurrences. Anxiety about the issue of a war, or grief for a dead friend, may characterise a person for months or years. He keeps on relapsing into anxiety, or he keeps on grieving.

To say that a person has for days or weeks been vexed by someone's criticisms of him is not to say that at every moment of that time he has been in the mood to do pettish things, think resentful thoughts or register feelings of dudgeon. For he is also from time to time in the mood to eat, conduct his business and play his games. What it does mean is that he is prone to relapse into this mood; he keeps on getting into the frame of mind in which he cannot help harping on the injustice which he has suffered; cannot help intermittently daydreaming of self-vindications and retaliations; cannot even seriously try to impute creditable motives to his critic, or to recognise any substance in his criticisms. And to say that he keeps on relapsing into this mood is to describe him in dispositional terms. When susceptibilities to specific moods are chronic, they are traits of character.

But what sort of a description are we giving, when we say of someone that he is at a particular time and for a shortish or longish period in a particular mood? Part of the answer will be given in Section (4) of this chapter. Here it is enough to show that though moods, like maladies and states of the weather, are relatively short-term conditions; they are not determinate incidents, though they issue in determinate incidents.

From the fact that a person has been having indigestion for an hour it does not follow that he has had one long pain or a series of short pains during that hour; perhaps he had no pains at all. Nor does it follow that he has been feeling sick, or that he spurned his food, or that he looked pale. It is enough if some or other of these and further appropriate occurrences have taken place. There is no unique episode, the occurrence of which is a necessary or sufficient condition of having indigestion. 'Indigestion' does not, therefore, stand for any such unique episode. In the same way a sulky or hilarious person may or may not say certain things, talk in a certain tone of voice, grimace or gesticulate in certain ways, have certain daydreams or register certain feelings. Being sulky or hilarious requires some or other of these and further appropriate actions and reactions, but there is no one of them which is a necessary or sufficient condition of being sulky or hilarious. 'Sulkiness' and 'hilarity' do not, therefore, stand for any one specific action or reaction.

To be sulky is to be in the mood to act or react in some or other of certain vaguely describable, though easily recognisable, ways, whenever junctures of certain sorts arise. This shows that mood words like 'tranquil', and 'jovial', including words for agitations, like 'harassed' and 'homesick', stand for liabilities. Even to be for a brief moment scandalised or in a panic is, for that moment, to be liable to do some such things as stiffen or shriek, or to be unable to finish one's sentence, or to remember where the fire-escape is to be found.

Certainly a person is not to be described as being in a particular mood unless an adequate number of appropriate episodes actually occur. 'He is in a cynical mood', like 'he is nervous', does not merely say 'He would...' or 'He could not. ...' It alludes to actual behaviour as well as mentioning liabilities; or, rather, it alludes to actual behaviour as realising these liabilities. It conjointly explains what is actually going on and authorises predictions of what will go on, if . . . or of what would have gone on, if. . . . It is rather like saying 'the glass was brittle enough to crack, when that pebble struck it.'

But though agitations, like other moods, are liability conditions, they are not propensities to act intentionally in certain ways. A woman wrings her hands in anguish, but we do not say that anguish is the motive from which she wrings her hands. Nor do we inquire with what object an embarrassed man blushes, stammers, squirms or fidgets. A keen walker walks because he wants to walk, but a perplexed man does not wrinkle his brows because he wants or means to wrinkle them, though the actor or hypocrite may wrinkle his brows because he wants or means to appear perplexed. The reason for these differences is simple. To be distracted is not like being thirsty in the presence of drinking-water; it is like being thirsty in the absence of water, or in the presence of foul water. It is wanting to do something while not being able to do it, or wanting to do something and at the same time wanting not to do it. It is the conjunction of an inclination to behave in a certain way with an inhibition upon behaving in that way. The agitated person cannot think what to do, or what to think. Aimless and vacillating behaviour, as well as paralysis of behaviour, are symptoms of agitations in a way in which making a joke is not a symptom but an exercise of a sense of humour.

Motives then are not agitations, not even mild agitations, nor are agitations motives. But agitations presuppose motives, or rather they presuppose behaviour trends of which motives are for us the most interesting sort. Conflicts of habits with habits, or habits with unkind facts, or habits with motives are also commotion-conditions. An inveterate smoker on parade, or without any matches, or in Lent, is in this plight. There is however a linguistic matter which is the source of some confusion. There are some words which signify both inclinations and agitations, besides some which never signify anything but agitations, and others again which never signify anything but inclinations. Words like 'uneasy', 'anxious', 'distressed', 'excited', 'startled' always signify agitations. Phrases like 'fond of fishing', 'keen on gardening', 'bent on becoming a bishop' never signify agitations. But words like 'love', 'want', 'desire', 'proud', 'eager' and many others stand sometimes for simple inclinations and sometimes for agitations which are resultant upon those inclinations and interferences with the exercise of them. Thus 'hungry' in the sense of 'having a good appetite' means roughly 'is eating or would eat heartily and without sauces, etc.'; but this is different from the sense in which a person might be said to be 'too hungry to concentrate on his work'. Hunger in this second sense is a distress, and requires for its existence the conjunction of an appetite with the inability to eat. Similarly the sense in which a boy is proud of his school is different from the sense in which he is speechless with pride on being unexpectedly given a place in a school team.

To remove a possible misapprehension, it must be pointed out that not all agitations are disagreeable. People voluntarily subject themselves to suspense, fatigue, uncertainty, perplexity, fear and surprise in such practices as angling, rowing, travelling, crossword puzzles, rock-climbing and joking. That thrills, raptures, surprise, amusement and relief are agitations is shown by the fact that we can say that someone is too much thrilled, amused or relieved to act, think or talk coherently. We are then describing him as being moved in the sense of 'stirred' and not as being motivated in the sense of 'keen to do or get something'.

## (4) Moods.

We commonly describe people as being at particular times for shorter or longer periods in certain moods. We say, for example, that a person is depressed, happy, uncommunicative or restless, and has been so for minutes or for days. Only when a mood is chronic do we use such mood words as descriptions of character. A person may be melancholy today, though he is not a melancholic person.

In saying that he is in a certain mood we are saying something fairly general; not that he is all the time or frequently doing one unique thing, or having one unique feeling, but that he is in the frame of mind to say, do and feel a wide variety of loosely affiliated things. A person in a frivolous vein is in the mood to make more jokes than usual, to be more tickled than usual by the jokes of others, to polish off important matters of business without anxious consideration, to put heart and soul into childish games, and so on indefinitely.

A person's momentary mood is a different sort of thing from the motives which actuate him. We can say of a person that he is ambitious, loyal to his party, humane and interested in entomology, and that he is all of these things, in a certain sense, at the same time. Not that such inclinations are synchronous occurrences or states, since they are not occurrences or states at all. But if a situation were to arise in which he could both advance his career and help his party, he would do both rather than do either without the other.

Moods, on the contrary, monopolise. To say that he is in one mood is, with reservations for complex moods, to say that he is not in any other. To be in the mood to act and react in certain ways is also not to be in the mood to act or react in a lot of other ways. To be in a conversational mood is not to be in a reading, writing or lawn-mowing mood. We talk about moods in terms like those, and sometimes borrowed from those, in which we talk about the weather, and we sometimes talk about the weather in terms borrowed from the language of moods. We do not mention moods or the weather, unless they are changeable. If it is showery here today, then it is not a settled drizzle here today. If John Doe was sullen yesterday evening, then he was not hilarious, sad, serene or companionable yesterday evening. Further, somewhat as this morning's weather in a given locality made the same sort of difference to every section of that neighbourhood, so a person's mood during a given period colours all or most of his actions and reactions during that period. His work and his play, his talk and his grimaces, his appetite and his daydreams, all reflect his touchiness, his joviality or his depression. Any one of them may serve as a barometer for all the others.

Mood words are short-term tendency words, but they differ from motive words, not only in the short term of their application, but in their use in characterizing the total 'set' of a person during that short term. Somewhat as the entire ship is cruising south-east, rolling, or vibrating, so the entire person is nervous, serene or gloomy. His own corresponding inclination will be to describe the whole world as menacing, congenial, or grey. If he is jovial, he finds everything jollier than usual; and if he is sulky, not only his employer's tone of voice and his own knotted shoe-lace seem unjust to him, but everything seems to be doing him injustices.

Mood words are commonly classified as the names of feelings. But if the word 'feeling' is used with any strictness, this classification is quite erroneous. To say that a person is happy or discontented is not merely to say that he has frequent or continuous tingles or gnawings; indeed, it is not to say even this, for we should not withdraw our statement on hearing that the person had had no such feelings, and we should not be satisfied that he was happy or discontented merely by his avowal that he had them frequently and acutely. They might be symptoms of indigestion or intoxication.

Feelings, in any strict sense, are things that come and go or wax and wane in a few seconds; they stab or they grumble; we feel them all over us or else in a particular part. The victim may say that he keeps on having tweaks, or that they come only at fairly long intervals. No one would describe his happiness or discontentment in any such terms. He says that he feels happy or discontented, but not that he keeps on feeling, or that he steadily feels happy or discontented. If a person is too gay to brood over a rebuff, he is not undergoing so violent a feeling that he can think of nothing else, and therefore not of the rebuff; on the contrary, he enjoys much more than usual all the things he does and all the thoughts he thinks, including thoughts of the rebuff. He does not mind thinking of it as much as he would usually do.

The main motives for classifying moods as feelings seem to be twofold. (1) Theorists have felt constrained to put them into one of their three permitted pigeon-holes, Thought, Will and Feeling; and as moods will not fit either of the first two holes, they must be made to fit the third. We need not spend time on this motive. (2) A person in a lazy, frivolous or depressed mood may, with perfect idiomatic correctness, avow his frame of mind by saying 'I feel lazy', or 'I am beginning to feel frivolous', or 'I still feel depressed'. How can such expressions be idiomatically correct unless they report the occurrence of feelings? If 'I feel a tingle' announces a tingling feeling, how can 'I feel energetic' help announcing an energy feeling?

But this instance begins to make the argument ring unplausibly. Energy is obviously not a feeling. Similarly, if the patient says, 'I feel ill', or 'I feel better', no one will therefore classify illness or convalescence as feelings. 'He felt stupid', 'capable of climbing the tree', 'about to faint' are other uses of the verb 'to feel', where the accusatives to the verb are not the names of feelings.

Before coming back to the association of 'feel' with mood words, we should consider some differences between such avowals as 'I feel a tickle' and 'I feel ill'. If a person feels a tickle, he has a tickle, and if he has a tickle, he feels it. But if he feels ill, he may not be ill, and if he is ill, he may not feel ill. Doubtless a person's feeling ill is some evidence for his being ill; but feeling a tickle is not evidence for his having a tickle, any more than striking a blow is evidence for the occurrence of a blow. In 'feel a tickle' and 'strike a blow', 'tickle' and 'blow' are cognate accusatives to the verbs 'feel' and 'strike'. The verb and its accusative are two expressions for the same thing, as are the verbs and their accusatives in 'I dreamt a dream' and 'I asked a question'.

But 'ill' and 'capable of climbing the tree' are not cognate accusatives to the verb 'to feel'; so they are not in grammar bound to signify feelings, as 'tickle' is in grammar bound to signify a feeling. Another purely grammatical point shows the same thing. It is indifferent whether I say 'I feel a tickle' or 'I have a tickle'; but 'I have . . .' cannot be completed by '. . . ill', '. . . capable of climbing the tree', '. . . happy' or '. . . discontented'. If we try to restore the verbal parallel by bringing in the appropriate abstract nouns, we find a further incongruity; 'I feel happiness', 'I feel illness' or 'I feel ability to climb the tree', if they mean anything, do not mean at all what is meant by 'I feel happy, ill, or capable of climbing the tree'.

On the other hand, besides these differences between the different uses of 'I feel . . .' there are important analogies as well. If a person says that he has a tickle, we do not ask for his evidence, or require him to make quite sure. Announcing a tickle is not proclaiming the results of an investigation. A tickle is not something established by careful witnessing, or something inferred from clues, nor do we praise for their powers of observation or reasoning people who let us know that they feel tickles, tweaks and flutters. Just the same is true of avowals of moods. If a person says 'I feel bored', or 'I feel depressed', we do not ask him for his evidence, or request him to make sure. We may accuse him of shamming to us or to himself, but we do not accuse him of having been careless in his observations or rash in his inferences, since we do not think that his avowal was a report of observations or conclusions. He has not been a good or a bad detective; he has not been a detective at all. Nothing would surprise us more than to hear him say 'I feel depressed' in the alert and judicious tone of voice of a detective, a microscopist, or a diagnostician, though this tone of voice is perfectly congruous with 'I *was* feeling depressed' and '*he* feels depressed'. If the avowal is to do its job, it must be said in a depressed tone of voice; it must be blurted out to a sympathizer, not reported to an investigator. Avowing 'I feel depressed' is doing one of the things, namely one of the conversational things, that depression is the mood to do. It is not a piece of scientific premiss-providing, but a piece of conversational moping. That is why, if we are suspicious, we do not ask 'Fact or fiction?', 'True or false?', 'Reliable or unreliable?', but 'Sincere or shammed?' The conversational avowal of moods requires not acumen, but openness. It comes from the heart, not from the head. It is not discovery, but voluntary non-concealment.

Of course people have to learn how to use avowal expressions appropriately and they may not learn these lessons very well. They learn them from ordinary discussions of the moods of others and from such more fruitful sources as novels and the theatre. They learn from the same sources how to cheat both other people and themselves by making sham avowals in the proper tones of voice and with the other proper histrionic accompaniments.

If we now raise the epistemologist's question 'How does a person find out what mood he is in?' we can answer that if, as may not be the case, he finds it out at all, he finds it out very much as we find it out. As we have seen, he does not groan 'I feel bored' because he has found out that he is bored, any more than the sleepy man yawns because he has found out that he is sleepy.

Rather, somewhat as the sleepy man finds out that he is sleepy by finding, among other things, that he keeps on yawning, so the bored man finds out that he is bored, if he does find this out, by finding that among other things he glumly says to others and to himself 'I feel bored' and 'How bored I feel'. Such a blurted avowal is not merely one fairly reliable index among others. It is the first and the best index, since being worded and voluntarily uttered, it is meant to be heard and it is meant to be understood. It calls for no sleuth-work.

In some respects avowals of moods like 'I feel cheerful' more closely resemble announcements of sensations like 'I feel a tickle' than they resemble utterances like 'I feel better' or 'I feel capable of climbing the tree'. Just as it would be absurd to say 'I feel a tickle but maybe I haven't one', so, in ordinary cases, it would be absurd to say 'I feel cheerful but maybe I am not'. But there would be no absurdity in saying 'I feel better but perhaps I am worse', or 'I feel capable of climbing the tree but maybe I could not'.

This difference can be brought out in another way. Sometimes it is natural to say 'I feel as if I could eat a horse', or 'I feel as if my temperature has returned to normal'. But it would seldom if ever be natural to say 'I feel as if I were in the dumps', or 'I feel as if I were bored', any more than it would be natural to say 'I feel as if I had a pain'. Not much would be gained by discussing at length why we use the English verb 'to feel' in these different ways. There are hosts of other ways in which it is also used. I can say 'I felt a lump in the mattress', 'I felt cold', 'I felt queer', 'I felt my jaw-muscles stiffen', 'I felt my gorge rise', 'I felt my chin with my thumb', 'I felt in vain for the lever', 'I felt as if something important was about to happen', 'I felt that there was a flaw somewhere in the argument', 'I felt quite at home', 'I felt that he was angry'. A feature common to most of these uses is that the speaker does not want further questions to be put. They would be either unanswerable questions, or unaskable questions. That he felt it is enough to settle some debates; that he merely felt it is enough to show that debates should not even begin.

Names of moods, then, are not the names of feelings. But to be in a particular mood is to be in the mood, among other things, to feel certain sorts of feelings in certain sorts of situations. To be in a lazy mood, is, among other things, to tend to have sensations of lassitude in the limbs when jobs have to be done, to have cosy feelings of relaxation when the deck-chair is resumed, not to have electricity feelings when the game begins, and so forth. But we are not thinking primarily of these feelings when we say that we feel lazy; in fact, we seldom pay much heed to sensations of these kinds, save when they are abnormally acute.

Are names of moods names of emotions? The only tolerable reply is that of course they are, in the sense that some people some of the time use the word 'emotion'. But then we must add that in this sense an emotion is not something that can be segregated from thinking, daydreaming, voluntarily doing things, grimacing or feeling pangs and itches. To have the emotion, in this sense, which we ordinarily refer to as 'being bored', is to be in the mood to think certain sorts of thoughts, and not to think other sorts, to yawn and not to chuckle, to converse with stilted politeness, and not to talk with animation, to feel flaccid and not to feel resilient. Boredom is not some unique distinguishable ingredient, scene or feature of all that its victim is doing and undergoing; rather it is the temporary complexion of that totality. It is not like a gust, a sunbeam, a shower or the temperature; it is like the morning's weather.

(5) *Agitations and Feelings.*

In an early part of this chapter, I undertook to try to bring out what is meant by describing, for example, a certain glow as a glow of pride, or a qualm as a qualm of anxiety. It is helpful, to begin with, to notice that, anyhow commonly, the word which completes the phrase 'pang of . . .' or 'chill of . . .' is the name of an agitation. I shall now argue that feelings are intrinsically connected with agitations and are not intrinsically connected with inclinations, save in so far as inclinations are factors in agitations. But I am not trying to establish a novel psychological hypothesis; I am trying to show only that it is part of the logic of our descriptions of feelings that they are signs of agitations and are not exercises of inclinations.

We have seen that anyhow many of the words used to designate feelings are also used to designate bodily sensations. A flutter may be a flutter of anticipation or it may be a flutter of bodily exhaustion; a man may squirm either with embarrassment or with stomach-ache. A child sometimes does not know whether the lump he feels in his throat is a sign of misery, or a sign that he is sickening for something.

Before considering our special problem, 'By what criteria do we come to mark off some feelings as feelings 'of surprise' or 'of disgust'?', let us consider the prior question, 'By what criteria do we come to class certain bodily sensations as, for example, twinges of toothache or qualms of *mal de mer*?' Indeed, by what criteria do we come to locate or mis-locate sensations as being, in some sense of 'in', in the right knee or in the pit of the stomach? The answer is that we learn both to locate sensations and to give their crude physiological diagnoses from a rule-of-thumb experimental process, reinforced, normally, by lessons taught by others. The pain is in the finger in which I see the needle; it is in that finger by the sucking of which alone the pain is alleviated. Similarly the dull load which I feel, and locate in the stomach, comes to be recognised as a sign of indigestion, because it is correlated with loss of appetite, a liability to subsequent nausea, alleviation by certain medicines and hot-water bottles. Phrases like 'a twinge of toothache' already embody causal hypotheses, and the embodied hypotheses are sometimes wrong. A wounded soldier may say that he feels a twinge of rheumatism in his right leg, when he has no right leg, and when 'rheumatism' is the wrong diagnosis of the pain he feels.

Similarly, when a person reports a chill of disquiet or a tug of commiseration, he is not merely reporting a feeling; he is giving a diagnosis of it, but a diagnosis which is not in terms of a physiological disturbance. In some cases his diagnosis may be erroneous; he may diagnose as a twinge of remorse what is really a twinge of fear, and what he takes to be a sinking feeling of boredom may actually be a sinking feeling of inferiority. He may even ascribe to dyspepsia a feeling which is really a sign of anxiety, or ascribe to excitement fluttering sensations caused by over-smoking. Naturally such mis-diagnoses are more common in children than in grown-ups, and in persons in untried situations than in persons living their charted lives. But the point here being made is that whether we are attaching a sensation to a physiological condition or attaching a feeling to an emotional condition, we are applying a causal hypothesis. Pains do not arrive already hall-marked 'rheumatic', nor do throbs arrive already hall-marked 'compassionate'.

Next, it would be absurd to speak of someone having a sensation, or a feeling, on purpose; or to ask someone what he had a twinge *for*. Rather, the occurrence of a sensation or of a feeling is accounted for by saying, for example, that the electric current gave me a tingling sensation, or that the sound of the siren gave me a squirming feeling in my stomach, where no one would adduce a motive for feeling this tingle or that squirm. Feelings, in other words, are not among the sorts of things of which it makes sense to ask from what motives they issue. The same is true, for the same reasons, of the other signs of agitations. Neither my twinges nor my winces, neither my squirming feelings nor my bodily squirmings, neither my feelings of relief nor my sighs of relief, are things which I do for a reason; nor, in consequence, are they things which I can be said to do cleverly or stupidly, successfully or unsuccessfully, carefully or carelessly—or indeed do at all. They are neither well managed nor ill managed; they are not managed at all, though the actor's winces and the hypocrite's sighs are well or ill managed. It would be nonsense to say that someone tried to have a twinge, though not nonsense to say that he tried to induce one.

This point shows why we were right to suggest above that feelings do not belong directly to simple inclinations. An inclination is a certain sort of proneness or readiness to do certain sorts of things on purpose. These things are therefore describable as being done from that motive. They are the exercises of the disposition that we call 'a motive'. Feelings are not from motives and are therefore not among the possible exercises of such propensities. The widespread theory that a motive such as vanity, or affection, is in the first instance a disposition to experience certain specific feelings is therefore absurd. There are, of course, tendencies to have feelings; being vertiginous and rheumatic are such tendencies. But we do not try to modify tendencies of these kinds by sermons.

What feelings do causally belong to are agitations; they are signs of agitations in the same sort of way as stomach-aches are signs of indigestion. Roughly, we do not, as the prevalent theory holds, act purposively because we experience feelings; we experience feelings, as we wince and shudder, because we are inhibited from acting purposively.

It is worth remarking, before we leave this part of the subject that we can induce in ourselves genuine and acute feelings by merely imagining ourselves in agitating circumstances. Novel-readers and theatregoers feel real pangs and real liftings of the heart, just as they may shed real tears and scowl unfeigned scowls. But their distresses and indignations are feigned. They do not affect their owners' appetites for chocolates, or change the tones of voice of their conversations. Sentimentalists are people who indulge in induced feelings without acknowledging the fictitiousness of their agitations.

(6) *Enjoying and Wanting.*

The words 'pleasure' and 'desire' play a large role in the terminology of moral philosophers and of some schools of psychology. It is important briefly to indicate some of the differences between the supposed logic of their use and its actual logic.

First, it seems to be generally supposed that 'pleasure' and 'desire' are always used to signify feelings. And there certainly are feelings which can be described as feelings of pleasure and desire. Some thrills, shocks, glows and ticklings are feelings of delight, surprise, relief and amusement; and hankerings, itches, gnawings and yearnings are signs that something is both wanted and missed. But the transports, surprises, reliefs and distresses of which such feelings are diagnosed, or mis-diagnosed, as signs are not themselves feelings; they are agitations or moods, just as are the transports and distresses which a child betrays by his skips and his whimpers. Nostalgia is an agitation and one which can be called in one sense a 'desire'; but it is not merely a feeling or series of feelings. Besides experiencing these, the homesick person also cannot help thinking and dreaming of home, resisting sugges-tions that he should prolong his absence and being half-hearted about recreations of which he is ordinarily fond. If these and similar trends were not present, we should not call him homesick, whatever feelings were reported.

'Pleasure', then, is sometimes used to denote special kinds of moods, such as elation, joy and amusement. It is accordingly used to complete the descriptions of certain feelings, such as flutters, glows and thrills. But there is another sense in which we say that a person who is so absorbed in some activity, such as golf or argument, that he is reluctant to stop, or even to think of anything else, is 'taking pleasure in' or 'enjoying' doing what he is doing, though he is in no degree convulsed or beside himself, and though he is not, therefore, experiencing any particular feelings.

Doubtless the absorbed golfer experiences numerous flutters and glows of rapture, excitement and self-approbation in the course of his game. But when asked whether or not he had enjoyed the periods of the game between the occurrences of such feelings, he would obviously reply that he had, for he had enjoyed the whole game. He would at no moment of it have welcomed an interruption; he was never inclined to turn his thoughts or conversation from the circumstances of the game to other matters. He did not have to try to concentrate on the game. He concentrated on it without lecturing or adjuring himself to do so. It would have been, and perhaps was, an effort to concentrate on anything else.

In this sense, to enjoy doing something, to want to do it and not to want to do anything else are different ways of phrasing the same thing. And just this linguistic fact illustrates an important point. A hankering is not the same as, or at all similar to, a flutter or a glow. But that someone has an inclination to do something that he is doing and no inclination not to do it can be signified indifferently by 'he enjoys doing it' and by 'he is doing what he wants to do' and by 'he does not want to stop'. It is a fulfilled propensity to act or react, where these are heeded actions and reactions.

We see then that 'pleasure' can be used to signify at least two quite different types of things.

(1) There is the sense in which it is commonly replaced by the verbs 'enjoy' and 'like'. To say that a person has been enjoying digging is not to say that he has been both digging and doing or experiencing something else as a concomitant or effect of the digging; it is to say that he dug with his whole heart in his task, i.e. that he dug, wanting to dig and not wanting to do anything else (or nothing) instead. His digging was a propensity-fulfilment. His digging was his pleasure, and not a vehicle of his pleasure.

(2) There is the sense of 'pleasure' in which it is commonly replaced by such words as 'delight', 'transport', 'rapture', 'exultation' and 'joy'. These are names of moods signifying agitations. 'Too delighted to talk coherently' and 'crazy with joy' are

legitimate expressions. Connected with such moods, there exist certain feelings which are commonly described as 'thrills of pleasure', 'glows of pleasure' and so forth. It should be noticed that though we speak of thrills of pleasure coursing through us, or of glows of pleasure warming our hearts, we do not ordinarily speak of pleasures or of pleasure coursing through us or warming our hearts. Only theorists are misguided enough to classify either delight or enjoyment with feelings. That this classification is misguided is shown by the facts (1) that enjoying digging is not both digging and having a (pleasant) feeling; and (2) that delight, amusement, etc. are moods, and that moods are not feelings. It is also shown by the following considerations. It always makes sense to ask about any sensation or feeling whether its owner enjoyed having it, disliked having it or did not care one way or the other about it. Most sensations and feelings are neither enjoyed nor disliked. It is exceptional to heed them at all. Now this applies to thrills, flutters and glows just as much as to tingles. So, even though what a person has felt is properly described as a thrill of pleasure or, more specifically, as a tickle of amusement, it is still a proper question whether he not only enjoyed the joke but also enjoyed the tickled feeling that it gave him. Nor should we be much surprised to hear him reply that he was so much delighted by the joke that the 'tickled' feeling was quite uncomfortable; or to hear someone else, who has been crying from grief, admit that the crying itself had been slightly agreeable. I discuss in Section (4) of this chapter the two main motives for misclassifying moods as feelings. The motives for ranking 'enjoy' as a word for a feeling are parallel, though not identical, since enjoying is not a mood. One can be in the mood, or not in the mood, to enjoy something.

Similar considerations, which need not be developed, would show that 'dislike', 'want' and 'desire' do not denote pangs, itchings or gnawings. (It should be mentioned that 'pain', in the sense in which I have pains in my stomach, is not the opposite of 'pleasure'. In this sense, a pain is a sensation of a special sort, which we ordinarily dislike having.)

Liking and disliking, joy and grief, desire and aversion are, then, not 'internal' episodes which their owner witnesses, but his associates do not witness. They are not episodes and so are not the sorts of things which can be witnessed or unwitnessed. Certainly a person can usually, but not always, tell without research whether he enjoys something or not, and what his present mood is. But so can his associates, provided that he is conversationally open with them and does not wear a mask. If he is conversationally open neither with them nor with himself, both will have to do some research to find out these things, and they are more likely to succeed than he.

## (7) The criteria of motives.

So far it has been argued that to explain an action as done from a certain motive is not to correlate it with an occult cause, but to subsume it under a propensity or behaviour-trend. But this is not enough. To explain an action as due to habit, or as due to an instinct, or a reflex, squares with this formula, yet we distinguish actions done, say, from vanity or affection from those done automatically in one of these other ways. I shall restrict myself to trying to indicate some of the criteria by which we would ordinarily decide that an agent had done something not from force of habit but from a specified motive. But it must not be supposed that the two classes are demarcated from one another as an equatorial day from an equatorial night. They shade into one another as an English day shades into an English night. Kindliness shades into politeness through the twilight of considerateness, and politeness shades into drill through the twilight of etiquette. The drill of a keen soldier is not quite like the drill of a merely docile soldier.

When we say that someone acts in a certain way from sheer force of habit, part of what we have in mind is this, that in similar circumstances he always acts in just this way; that he acts in this way whether or not he is attending to what he is doing; that he is not exercising care or trying to correct or improve his performance; and that he may, after the act is over, be quite unaware that he has done it. Such actions are often given the metaphorical title 'automatic'. Automatic habits are often deliberately inculcated by sheer drill, and only by some counter-drill is a formed habit eradicated.

But when we say that someone acts in a certain way from ambition or sense of justice, we mean by implication to deny that the action was merely automatic. In particular we imply that the agent was in some way thinking or heeding what he was doing, and would not have acted in that way, if he had not been thinking what he was doing. But the precise force of this expression 'thinking what he was doing' is somewhat elusive. I certainly can run upstairs two stairs at a time from force of habit and at the same time notice that I am doing so and even consider how the act is done. I can be a spectator of my habitual and of my reflex actions and even a diagnostician of them, without these actions ceasing to be automatic. Notoriously such attention sometimes upsets the automatism.

Conversely, actions done from motives can still be naive, in the sense that the agent has not coupled, and perhaps cannot couple, his action with a secondary operation of telling himself or the company what he is doing, or why he is doing it. Indeed even when a person does pass internal or spoken comments upon his current action, this second operation of commenting is ordinarily itself naive. He cannot also be commenting on his commentaries *ad infinitum*. The sense in which a person is thinking what he is doing, when his action is to be classed not as automatic but as done from a motive, is that he is acting more or less carefully, critically, consistently and purposefully, adverbs which do not signify the prior or concomitant occurrence of extra operations of resolving, planning or cogitating, but only that the action taken is itself done not absent-mindedly but in a certain positive frame of mind. The description of this frame of mind need not mention any episodes other than this act itself, though it is not exhausted in that mention.

In short, the class of actions done from motives coincides with the class of actions describable as more or less intelligent. Any act done from a motive can be appraised as relatively sagacious or stupid, and *vice versa*. Actions done from sheer force of habit are not characterized as sensible or silly, though of course the agent may show sense or silliness in forming, or in not eradicating, the habit.

But this brings up a further point. Two actions done from the same motive may exhibit different degrees of competence, and two similar actions exhibiting the same degree of competence may be done from different motives. To be fond of rowing does not entail being accomplished or effective at it, and, of two people equally effective at it, one may be rowing for the sport and the other for the sake of health or glory. That is, the abilities with which things are done are personal characteristics of a different kind from the motives or inclinations which are the reasons why they are done; and we distinguish acts done from force of habit from non-automatic actions by the fact that the latter are exercises of both at once. Things done quite absent-mindedly are done neither with methods nor for reasons, though they may be efficacious and they may have complex procedures.

In ascribing a specific motive to a person we are describing the sorts of things that he tends to try to do or bring about, while in ascribing to him a specific competence we are describing the methods and the effectiveness of the methods by which he conducts these attempts. It is the distinction between aims and techniques. The more common idiom of 'ends and means' is often misleading. If a man makes a sarcastic joke, his performance cannot be split up into steps and landings, yet the judgment that it was made from hatred is still distinguishable from the judgment that it was made with ingenuity.

Aristotle realized that in talking about motives we are talking about dispositions of a certain sort, a sort different from competences; he realized too that any motive, unlike any competence, is a propensity of which it makes sense to say that in a given man in a given walk of life this motive is too strong, too weak, or neither too strong, nor too weak. He seems to suggest that in appraising the moral, as distinct from the technical, merits and demerits of actions we are commenting on the excessive, proper or inadequate strength of the inclinations of which they are the exercises. Now we are not concerned here with ethical questions, or with questions about the nature of ethical questions. What is relevant to our inquiry is the fact, recognised by Aristotle as cardinal, that the relative strengths of inclinations are alterable. Changes of environment, companionship, health and age, external criticisms and examples can all modify the balance of power between the inclinations which constitute one side of a person's character. But so can his own concern about this balance modify it. A person may find that he is too fond of gossip, or not attentive enough to other people's comfort, and he may, though he need not, develop a second order inclination to strengthen some of his weak, and weaken some of his strong propensities. He may become not merely academically critical, but executively corrective of his own character. Of course, his new second order motive for schooling his first order motives may still be a prudential or economic one. An ambitious hotel-proprietor might drill himself in equability, considerateness and probity solely from the desire to increase his income; and his techniques of self-regimentation might be more effective than those employed by a person whose ideal was loftier. In the case, however, of the hotel-proprietor there would be one inclination the relative strength of which *vis-à-vis* the others had been left uncriticized and unregulated, namely his desire to get rich. This motive might be, though it need not be, too strong in him. If so, we might call him 'shrewd', but we should not yet call him 'wise'. To generalize this point, a part of what is meant by saying of any inclination that it is too strong in a given agent is that the agent tends to act from that inclination even when he is also inclined to weaken that inclination by deliberately acting differently. He is a slave of nicotine, or of allegiance to a political party, if he can never bring himself to take enough of the serious steps by which alone the strength of these motives could be reduced, even though he has some second order inclination to reduce it. What is here being described is part of what is ordinarily called 'self-control', and when what is ordinarily miscalled an 'impulse' is irresistible and therefore uncontrollable, it is a tautology to say that it is too strong.

(8) *The Reasons and the Causes of Actions.*

I have argued that to explain an action as done from a specified motive or inclination is not to describe the action as the effect of a specified cause. Motives are not happenings and are not therefore of the right type to be causes. The expansion of a motive-expression is a law-like sentence and not a report of an event.

But the general fact that a person is disposed to act in such and such ways in such and such circumstances does not by itself account for his doing a particular thing at a particular moment; any more than the fact that the glass was brittle accounts for its fracture at 10 p.m. As the impact of the stone at 10 p.m. caused the glass to break, so some antecedent of an action causes or occasions the agent to perform it when and where he does so. For example, a man passes his neighbour the salt from politeness; but his politeness is merely his inclination to pass the salt when it is wanted, as well as to perform a thousand other courtesies of the same general kind. So besides the question 'for what reason did he pass the salt'? there is the quite different question 'what made him pass the salt at that moment to that neighbour'? This question is probably answered by 'he heard his neighbour ask for it', or 'he noticed his neighbour's eye wandering over the table', or something of the sort.

We are perfectly familiar with the sorts of happenings which induce or occasion people to do things. If we were not, we could not get them to do what we wish, and the ordinary dealings between people could not exist. Customers could not purchase, officers could not command, friends could not converse, or children play, unless they knew how to get other people and themselves to do things at particular junctures.

The object of mentioning these important trivialities is twofold; first, to show that an action's having a cause does not conflict with its having a motive, but is already prescribed for in the protasis of the hypothetical proposition which states the motive; and second, to show that, so far from our wanting to hear of occult or ghostly causes of actions, we already know just what sorts of familiar and usually public happenings are the things which get people to act in particular ways at particular times.

If the doctrine of the ghost in the machine were true, not only would people be absolute mysteries to one another, they would also be absolutely intractable. In fact they are relatively tractable and relatively easy to understand.

(9) *Conclusion*.

There are two quite different senses of 'emotion', in which we explain people's behaviour by reference to emotions. In the first sense we are referring to the motives or inclinations from which more or less intelligent actions are done. In the second sense we are referring to moods, including the agitations or perturbations of which some aimless movements are signs. In neither of these senses are we asserting or implying that the overt behaviour is the effect of a felt turbulence in the agent's stream of consciousness. In a third sense of 'emotion', pangs and twinges are feelings or emotions, but they are not, save *per accidens*, things by reference to which we explain behaviour. They are things for which diagnoses are required, not things required for the diagnoses of behaviour. Impulses, described as feelings which impel actions, are para-mechanical myths. This does not mean that people never act on the impulse of the moment, but only that we should not swallow the traditional stories about the occult antecedents of either deliberate or impulsive actions.

Consequently, though the description of the higher-level behaviour of people certainly requires mention of emotions in the first two senses, this mention does not entail inferences to occult inner states or processes. The discovery by me of your motives and moods is not analogous to uncheckable water-divining; it is partly analogous to my inductions to your habits, instincts and reflexes, partly to my inferences to your maladies and your tipsiness. But, in favourable circumstances, I find out your inclinations and your moods more directly than this. I hear and understand your conversational avowals, your interjections and your tones of voice; I see and understand your gestures and facial expressions. I say 'understand' in no metaphorical sense, for even interjections, tones of voice, gestures and grimaces are modes of communication. We learn to produce them, not indeed from schooling, but from imitation. We know how to sham by putting them on and we know, in some degree, how to avoid giving ourselves away by assuming masks. It is not only their vocabularies that make foreigners difficult to understand. My discovery of my own motives and moods is not different in kind, though I am ill placed to see my own grimaces and gestures, or to hear my own tones of voice. Motives and moods are not the sorts of things which could be among the direct intimations of consciousness, or among the objects of introspection, as these factitious forms of Privileged Access are ordinarily described. They are not 'experiences', any more than habits or maladies are 'experiences'.

# CHAPTER V

## DISPOSITIONS AND OCCURRENCES

(1) *Foreword.*

I HAVE already had occasion to argue that a number of the words which we commonly use to describe and explain people's behaviour signify dispositions and not episodes. To say that a person knows something, or aspires to be something, is not to say that he is at a particular moment in process of doing or undergoing anything, but that he is able to do certain things, when the need arises, or that he is prone to do and feel certain things in situations of certain sorts.

This is, in itself, hardly more than a dull fact (almost) of ordinary grammar. The verbs 'know', 'possess' and 'aspire' do not behave like the verbs 'run', 'wake up' or 'tingle'; we cannot say 'he knew so and so for two minutes, then stopped and started again after a breather', 'he gradually aspired to be a bishop', or 'he is now engaged in possessing a bicycle'. Nor is it a peculiarity of people that we describe them in dispositional terms. We use such terms just as much for describing animals, insects, crystals and atoms. We are constantly wanting to talk about what can be relied on to happen as well as to talk about what is actually happening; we are constantly wanting to give explanations of incidents as well as to report them; and we are constantly wanting to tell how things can be managed as well as to tell what is now going on in them. Moreover, merely to classify a word as signifying a disposition is not yet to say much more about it than to say that it is not used for an episode. There are lots of different kinds of dispositional words. Hobbies are not the same sort of thing as habits, and both are different from skills, from mannerisms, from fashions, from phobias and from trades. Nest-building is a different sort of property from being feathered, and being a conductor of electricity is a different sort of property from being elastic.

There is, however, a special point in drawing attention to the fact that many of the cardinal concepts in terms of which we describe specifically human behaviour are dispositional concepts, since the vogue of the para-mechanical legend has led many people to ignore the ways in which these concepts actually behave and to construe them instead as items in the descriptions of occult causes and effects. Sentences embodying these dispositional words have been interpreted as being categorical reports of particular but unwitness-able matters of fact instead of being testable, open hypothetical and what I shall call 'semi-hypothetical' statements. The old error of treating the term 'Force' as denoting an occult force-exerting agency has been given up in the physical sciences, but its relatives survive in many theories of mind and are perhaps only moribund in biology.

The scope of this point must not be exaggerated. The vocabulary we use for describing specifically human behaviour does not consist only of dispositional words. The judge, the teacher, the novelist, the psychologist and the man in the street are bound also to employ a large battery of episodic words when talking about how people do, or should, act and react. These episodic words, no less than dispositional words, belong to a variety of types, and we shall find that obliviousness to some of these differences of type has both fostered, and been fostered by, the identification of the mental with the ghostly. Later in this chapter I shall discuss two main types of mental episodic-words. I do not suggest that there are no others.

## (2) The Logic of Dispositional Statements

When a cow is said to be a ruminant, or a man is said to be a cigarette-smoker, it is not being said that the cow is ruminating now or that the man is smoking a cigarette now. To be a ruminant is to tend to ruminate from time to time, and to be a cigarette-smoker is to be in the habit of smoking cigarettes.

The tendency to ruminate and the habit of cigarette-smoking could not exist, unless there were such processes or episodes as ruminating and smoking cigarettes. 'He is smoking a cigarette now' does not say the same sort of thing as 'he is a cigarette-smoker', but unless statements like the first were sometimes true, statements like the second could not be true. The phrase 'smoke a cigarette' has both episodic uses and, derivative from them, tendency-stating uses. But this does not always occur. There are many tendency-stating and capacity-stating expressions which cannot also be employed in reports of episodes. We can say that something is elastic, but when required to say in what actual events this potentiality is realised, we have to change our vocabulary and say that the object is contracting after being stretched, is just going to expand after being compressed, or recently bounced on sudden impact. There is no active verb corresponding to 'elastic', in the way in which 'is ruminating' corresponds to 'is a ruminant'. Nor is the reason for this non-parallelism far to seek. There are several different reactions which we expect of an elastic object, while there is, roughly, only one sort of behaviour that we expect of a creature that is described to us as a ruminant. Similarly there is a wide range of different actions and reactions predictable from the description of someone as 'greedy', while there is, roughly, only one sort of action predictable from the description of someone as 'a cigarette-smoker'. In short, some dispositional words are highly generic or determinable, while others are highly specific or determinate; the verbs with which we report the different exercises of generic tendencies, capacities and liabilities are apt to differ from the verbs with which we name the dispositions, while the episodic verbs corresponding to the highly specific dispositional verbs are apt to be the same. A baker can be baking now, but a grocer is not described as 'grocing' now, but only as selling sugar now, or weighing tea now, or wrapping up butter now. There are halfway houses. With qualms we will speak of a doctor as engaged now in doctoring someone, though not of a solicitor as now solicitoring, but only as now drafting a will, or now defending a client.

Dispositional words like 'know', 'believe', 'aspire', 'clever' and 'humorous' are determinable dispositional words. They signify abilities, tendencies or pronenesses to do, not things of one unique kind, but things of lots of different kinds. Theorists who recognise that 'know' and 'believe' are commonly used as dispositional verbs are apt not to notice this point, but to assume that there must be corresponding acts of knowing or apprehending and states of believing; and the fact that one person can never find another person executing such wrongly postulated acts, or being in such states is apt to be accounted for by locating these acts and states inside the agent's secret grotto.

A similar assumption would lead to the conclusion that since being a solicitor is a profession, there must occur professional activities of solicitoring, and, as a solicitor is never found doing any such unique thing, but only lots of different things like drafting wills, defending clients and witnessing signatures, his unique professional activity of solicitoring must be one which he performs behind locked doors. The temptation to construe dispositional words as episodic words and this other temptation to postulate that any verb that has a dispositional use must also have a corresponding episodic use are two sources of one and the same myth. But they are not its only sources.

It is now necessary to discuss briefly a general objection that is sometimes made to the whole programme of talking about capacities, tendencies, liabilities and pronenesses. Potentialities, it is truistically said, are nothing actual. The world does not contain, over and above what exists and happens, some other things which are mere would-be things and could-be happenings. To say of a sleeping man that he can read French, or of a piece of dry sugar that it is soluble in water, seems to be pretending at once to accord an attribute and to put that attribute into cold storage. But an attribute either does, or does not, characterise something. It cannot be merely on deposit account. Or, to put it in another way, a significant affirmative indicative sentence must be either true or false. If it is true, it asserts that something has, or some things have, a certain character; if it is false, then its subject lacks that character. But there is no halfway house between a statement's being true and its being false, so there is no way in which the subject described by a statement can shirk the disjunction by being merely able or likely to have or lack the character. A clock can strike the hour that it is, or strike an hour that it is not; but it cannot strike an hour that might be the correct one but is neither the correct nor an incorrect one.

This is a valid objection to one kind of account of such statements as that the sugar is soluble, or the sleeper can read French, namely an account which construes such statements as asserting extra matters of fact. This was indeed the mistake of the old Faculty theories which construed dispositional words as denoting occult agencies or causes, i.e. things existing, or processes taking place, in a sort of limbo world. But the truth that sentences containing words like 'might', 'could' and 'would . . . if' do not report limbo facts does not entail that such sentences have not got proper jobs of their own to perform. The job of reporting matters of fact is only one of a wide range of sentence-jobs.

It needs no argument to show that interrogative, imperative and optative sentences are used for other ends than that of notifying their recipients of the existence or occurrence of things. It does, unfortunately, need some argument to show that there are lots of significant (affirmative and negative) indicative sentences which have functions other than that of reporting facts. There still survives the preposterous assumption that every true or false statement either asserts or denies that a mentioned object or set of objects possesses a specified attribute. In fact, some statements do this and most do not. Books of arithmetic, algebra, geometry, jurisprudence, philosophy, formal logic and economic theory contain few, if any, factual statements. That is why we call such subjects 'abstract'. Books on physics, meteorology, bacteriology and comparative philology contain very few such statements, though they may tell us where they are to be found. Technical manuals, works of criticism, sermons, political speeches and even railway-guides may be more or less instructive, and instructive in a variety of ways, but they teach us few singular, categorical, attributive or relational truths.

Leaving on one side most of the sorts of sentences which have other than fact-reporting jobs, let us come straight to laws. For though assertions that mentioned individuals have capacities, liabilities, tendencies and the rest are not themselves statements of laws, they have features which can best be brought out after some peculiarities of law sentences have been discussed.

Laws are often stated in grammatically uncomplex indicative sentences, but they can also be stated in, among other constructions, hypothetical sentences of such patterns as 'Whatever is so and so, is such and such' or 'If a body is left unsupported, it falls at such and such a rate of acceleration'. We do not call a hypothetical sentence a 'law', unless it is a 'variable' or 'open' hypothetical statement, i.e. one of which the protasis can embody at least one expression like 'any' or 'whenever'. It is in virtue of this feature that a law applies to instances, though its statement does not mention them. If I know that any pendulum that is longer by any amount than any other pendulum will swing slower than the shorter pendulum by an amount proportional to its excess length, then on finding a particular pendulum three inches longer than another particular pendulum, I can infer how much slower it will swing. Knowing the law does not involve already having found these two pendulums; the statement of the law does not embody a report of their existence. On the other hand, knowing or even understanding the law does involve knowing that there could be particular matters of fact satisfying the protasis and therefore also satisfying the apodosis of the law. We have to learn to use statements of particular matters of fact, before we can learn to use the law-statements which do or might apply to them. Law-statements belong to a different and more sophisticated level of discourse from that, or those, to which belong the statements of the facts that satisfy them. Algebraical statements are in a similar way on a different level of discourse from the arithmetical statements which satisfy them.

Law-statements are true or false but they do not state truths or falsehoods of the same type as those asserted by the statements of fact to which they apply or are supposed to apply. They have different jobs. The crucial difference can be brought out in this way. At least part of the point of trying to establish laws is to find out how to infer from particular matters of fact to other particular matters of fact, how to explain particular matters of fact by reference to other matters of fact, and how to bring about or prevent particular states of affairs. A law is used as, so to speak, an inference-ticket (a season ticket) which licenses its possessors to move from asserting factual statements to asserting other factual statements. It also licenses them to provide explanations of given facts and to bring about desired states of affairs by manipulating what is found existing or happening. Indeed we should not admit that a student has learned a law, if all he were prepared to do were to recite it. Just as a student, to qualify as knowing rules of grammar, multiplication, chess or etiquette, must be able and ready to apply these rules in concrete operations, so, to qualify as knowing a law, he must be able and ready to apply it in making concrete inferences from and to particular matters of fact, in explaining them and, perhaps also, in bringing them about, or preventing them. Teaching a law is, at least *inter alia*, teaching how to do new things, theoretical and practical, with particular matters of fact.

It is sometimes urged that if we discover a law, which enables us to infer from diseases of certain sorts to the existence of bacteria of certain sorts, then we have discovered a new existence, namely a causal connection between such bacteria and such diseases; and that consequently we now know, what we did not know before, that there exist not only diseased persons and bacteria, but also an invisible and intangible bond between them. As trains cannot travel, unless there exist rails for them to travel on, so, it is alleged, bacteriologists cannot move from the clinical observation of patients to the prediction of microscopic observations of bacteria, unless there exists, though it can never be observed, an actual tie between the objects of these observations.

Now there is no objection to employing the familiar idiom 'causal connection'. Bacteriologists do discover causal connections between bacteria and diseases, since this is only another way of saying that they do establish laws and so provide themselves with inference-tickets which enable them to infer from diseases to bacteria, explain diseases by assertions about bacteria, prevent and cure diseases by eliminating bacteria, and so forth. But to speak as if the discovery of a law were the finding of a third, unobservable existence is simply to fall back into the old habit of construing open hypothetical statements as singular categorical statements. It is like saying that a rule of grammar is a sort of extra but unspoken noun or verb, or that a rule of chess is a sort of extra but ir.visible chessman. It is to fall back into the old habit of assuming that all sorts of sentences do the same sort of job, the job, namely, of ascribing a predicate to a mentioned object.

The favourite metaphor 'the rails of inference' is misleading in just this way. Railway lines exist in just the same sense that trains exist, and we discover that rails exist in just the way that we discover that trains exist. The assertion that trains run from one place to another does imply that a set of observable rails exists between the two places. So to speak of the 'rails of inference' suggests that inferring from diseases to bacteria is really not inferring at all, but describing a third entity; not *arguing* 'because so and so, therefore such and such', but *reporting* 'there exists an unobserved bond between this observed so and so and that observed such and such'. But if we then ask 'What is this third, unobserved entity postulated for?' the only answer given is 'to warrant us in arguing from diseases to bacteria'. The legitimacy of the inference is assumed all the time. What is gratuitously desiderated is a story that shall seem to reduce 'therefore' sentences and 'if any . . .' sentences to sentences of the pattern 'Here is a . . .'; i.e. of obliterating the functional differences between arguments and narratives. But much as railway tickets cannot be 'reduced' to queer counterparts of the railway journeys that they make possible; and much as railway journeys cannot be 'reduced' to queer counterparts of the railway stations at which they start and finish, so law-statements cannot be 'reduced' to counterparts of the inferences and explanations that they license, and inferences and explanations cannot be 'reduced' to counterparts of the factual statements that constitute their termini. The sentence-job of stating facts is different from the job of stating an argument from factual statement to factual statement, and both are different from the job of giving warrants for such arguments. We have to learn to use sentences for the first job before we can learn to use them for the second, and we have to learn to use them for the first and the second jobs before we can learn to use them for the third. There are, of course, plenty of other sentence-jobs, which it is not our present business to consider. For example, the sentences which occupy these pages have not got any of the jobs which they have been describing.

We can now come back to consider dispositional statements, namely statements to the effect that a mentioned thing, beast or person, has a certain capacity, tendency or propensity, or is subject to a certain liability. It is clear that such statements are not laws, for they mention particular things or persons. On the other hand they resemble laws in being partly 'variable' or 'open'. To say that this lump of sugar is soluble is to say that it would dissolve, if submerged anywhere, at any time and in any parcel of water. To say that this sleeper knows French, is to say that if, for example, he is ever addressed in French, or shown any French newspaper, he responds pertinently in French, acts appropriately or translates it correctly into his own tongue. This is, of course, too precise. We should not withdraw our statement that he knows French on finding that he did not respond pertinently when asleep, absent-minded, drunk or in a panic; or on finding that he did not correctly translate highly technical treatises. We expect no more than that he will ordinarily cope pretty well with the majority of ordinary French-using and French-following tasks. 'Knows French' is a vague expression and, for most purposes, none the less useful for being vague.

The suggestion has been made that dispositional statements about mentioned individuals, while not themselves laws, are deductions from laws, so that we have to learn some perhaps crude and vague laws before we can make such dispositional statements. But in general the learning process goes the other way. We learn to make a number of dispositional statements about individuals before we learn laws stating general correlations between such statements. We find that some individuals are both oviparous and feathered, before we learn that any individual that is feathered is oviparous.

Dispositional statements about particular things and persons are also like law statements in the fact that we use them in a partly similar way. They apply to, or they are satisfied by, the actions, reactions and states of the object; they are inference-tickets, which license us to predict, retrodict, explain and modify these actions, reactions and states.

Naturally, the addicts of the superstition that all true indicative sentences either describe existents or report occurrences will demand that sentences such as 'this wire conducts electricity', or 'John Doe knows French', shall be construed as conveying factual information of the same type as that conveyed by 'this wire is conducting electricity' and 'John Doe is speaking French'. How could the statements be true unless there were something now going on, even though going on, unfortunately, behind the scenes? Yet they have to agree that we do often know that a wire conducts electricity and that individuals know French, without having first discovered any undiscoverable goings on. They have to concede, too, that the theoretical utility of discovering these hidden goings on would consist only in its entitling us to do just that predicting, explaining and modifying which we already do and often know that we are entitled to do. They would have to admit, finally, that these postulated processes are themselves, at the best, things the existence of which they themselves infer from the fact that we can predict, explain and modify the observable actions and reactions of individuals. But if they demand actual 'rails' where ordinary inferences are made, they will have to provide some further actual 'rails' to justify their own peculiar inference from the legitimacy of ordinary inferences to the 'rails' which they postulate to carry them. The postulation of such an endless hierarchy of 'rails' could hardly be attractive even to those who are attracted by its first step.

Dispositional statements are neither reports of observed or observable states of affairs, nor yet reports of unobserved or unobservable states of affairs. They narrate no incidents. But their jobs are intimately connected with narratives of incidents, for, if they are true, they are satisfied by narrated incidents. 'John Doe has just been telephoning in French' satisfies what is asserted by 'John Doe knows French', and a person who has found out that John Doe knows French perfectly needs no further ticket to enable him to argue from his having read a telegram in French to his having made sense of it. Knowing that John Doe knows French is being in possession of that ticket, and expecting him to understand this telegram is travelling with it.

It should be noticed that there is no incompatibility in saying that dispositional statements narrate no incidents and allowing the patent fact that dispositional statements can have tenses. 'He was a cigarette-smoker for a year' and 'the rubber began to lose its elasticity last summer' are perfectly legitimate dispositional statements; and if it were never true that an individual might be going to know something, there could exist no teaching profession. There can be short-term, long-term or termless inference-tickets. A rule of cricket might be in force only for an experimental period, and even the climate of a continent might change from epoch to epoch.

(3) *Mental Capacities and Tendencies.*

There is at our disposal an indefinitely wide range of dispositional terms for talking about things, living creatures and human beings. Some of these can be applied indifferently to all sorts of things; for example, some pieces of metal, some fishes and some human beings weigh 140 lb., are elastic and combustible, and all of them, if left unsupported, fall at the same rate of acceleration. Other dispositional terms can be applied only to certain kinds of things; 'hibernates', for example, can be applied with truth or falsity only to living creatures, and 'Tory' can be applied with truth or falsity only to non-idiotic, non-infantile, non-barbarous human beings. Our concern is with a restricted class of dispositional terms, namely those appropriate only to the characterisation of human beings. Indeed, the class we are concerned with is narrower than that, since we are concerned only with those which are appropriate to the characterisation of such stretches of human behaviour as exhibit qualities of intellect and character. We are not, for example, concerned with any mere reflexes which may happen to be peculiar to men, or with any pieces of physiological equipment which happen to be peculiar to human anatomy.

Of course, the edges of this restriction are blurred. Dogs as well as infants are drilled to respond to words of command, to pointing and to the ringing of dinner-bells; apes learn to use and even construct instruments; kittens are playful and parrots are imitative. If we like to say that the behaviour of animals is instinctive while part of the behaviour of human beings is rational, though we are drawing attention to an important difference or family of differences, it is a difference the edges of which are, in their turn, blurred. Exactly when does the instinctive imitativeness of the infant develop into rational histrionics? By which birthday has the child ceased ever to respond to the dinner-bell like a dog and begun always to respond to it like an angel? Exactly where is the boundary line between the suburb and the country?

Since this book as a whole is a discussion of the logical behaviour of some of the cardinal terms, dispositional and occurrent, in which we talk about minds, all that is necessary in this section is to indicate some general differences between the uses of some of our selected dispositional terms. No attempt is made to discuss all these terms, or even all of the types of these terms.

Many dispositional statements may be, though they need not be, and ordinarily are not, expressed with the help of the words 'can', 'could' and 'able'. 'He is a swimmer', when it does not signify that he is an expert, means merely that he can swim. But the words 'can' and 'able' are used in lots of different ways, as can be illustrated by the following examples. 'Stones can float (for pumice-stone floats)'; 'that fish can swim (for it is not disabled, although it is now inert in the mud)'; 'John Doe can swim (for he has learned and not forgotten)'; 'Richard Roe can swim (if he is willing to learn)'; 'you can swim (when you try hard)'; 'she can swim (for the doctor has withdrawn his veto)' and so on. The first example states that there is no license to infer that because this is a stone, it will not float; the second denies the existence of a physical impediment; the last asserts the cessation of a disciplinary impediment. The third, fourth and fifth statements are informative about personal qualities, and they give different sorts of information.

To bring out the different forces of some of these different uses of 'can' and 'able', it is convenient to make a brief disquisition on the logic of what are sometimes called the 'modal words', such as 'can', 'must', 'may', 'is necessarily', 'is not necessarily' and 'is not necessarily not'. A statement to the effect that something must be, or is necessarily, the case functions as what I have called an 'inference-ticket'; it licenses the inference to the thing's being the case from something else which may or may not be specified in the statement. When the statement is to the effect that something is necessarily not, or cannot be, the case, it functions as a license to infer to its not being the case. Now sometimes it is required to refuse such a license to infer that something is not the case, and we commonly word this refusal by saying that it can be the case, or that it is possibly the case. To say that something can be the case does not entail that it is the case, or that it is not the case, or, of course, that it is in suspense between being and not being the case, but only that there is no license to infer from something else, specified or unspecified, to its not being the case.

This general account also covers most 'if–then' sentences. An 'if–then' sentence can nearly always be paraphrased by a sentence containing a modal expression, and *vice versa*. Modal and hypothetical sentences have the same force. Take any ordinary 'if–then' sentence, such as 'if I walk under that ladder, I shall meet trouble during the day' and consider how we should colloquially express its contradictory. It will not do to attach a 'not' to the protasis verb, to the apodosis verb, or to both at once, for the results of all three operations would be equally superstitious statements. It would do, but it would not be convenient or colloquial to say 'No, it is not the case that if I walk under a ladder I shall have trouble'. We should ordinarily reject the superstition by saying 'No, I might walk under the ladder and not have trouble' or 'I could walk under it without having trouble' or, to generalise the rejection, 'trouble does not necessarily come to people who walk under ladders'. Conversely the original superstitious statement could have been worded 'I could not walk under a ladder without experiencing trouble during the day'. There is only a stylistic difference between the 'if-then' idiom and the modal idioms.

It must, however, not be forgotten that there are other uses of 'if', 'must' and 'can' where this equivalence does not hold. 'If' sometimes means 'even though'. It is also often used in giving conditional undertakings, threats and wagers. 'Can' and 'must' are sometimes used as vehicles of non-theoretical permissions, orders and vetoes. True, there are similarities between giving or refusing licenses to infer and giving or refusing licenses to do other things, but there `are big differences as well. We do not, for instance, naturally describe as true or false the doctor's ruling 'the patient must stay in bed, can dictate letters, but must not smoke'; whereas it is quite natural to describe as true or false such sentences as 'a syllogism can have two universal premisses', 'whales cannot live without surfacing from time to time', 'a freely falling body must be accelerating' and 'people who walk under ladders need not come to disaster during the day'. The ethical uses of 'must', 'may' and 'may not' have affinities with both. We are ready to discuss the truth of ethical statements embodying such words, but the point of making such statements is to regulate parts of people's conduct, other than their inferences. In having both these features they resemble the treatment recommendations given to doctors by their medical text-books, rather than the regimen-instructions given by doctors to their patients. Ethical statements, as distinct from particular *ad hominem* behests and reproaches, should be regarded as warrants addressed to any potential givers of behests and reproaches, and not to the actual addressees of such behests and reproaches, i.e. not as personal action-tickets but as impersonal injunction-tickets; not imperatives but 'laws' that only such things as imperatives and punishments can satisfy. Like statute laws they are to be construed not as orders, but as licences to give and enforce orders.

We may now return from this general discussion of the sorts of jobs performed by modal sentences to consider certain specific differences between a few selected 'can' sentences, used for describing personal qualities.

To say that John Doe can swim differs from saying of a puppy that it can swim. For to say that the puppy can swim is compatible with saying that it has never been taught to swim, or had practice in swimming, whereas to say that a person can swim implies that he has learned to swim and has not forgotten. The capacity to acquire capacities by being taught is not indeed a human peculiarity. The puppy can be taught or drilled to beg, much as infants are taught to walk and use spoons. But some kinds of learning, including the way in which most people learn to swim, involve the understanding and application either of spoken instructions or at least of staged demonstrations; and a creature that can learn things in these ways is unhesitatingly conceded to have a mind, where the teachability of the dog and infant leaves us hesitant whether or not to say that they yet qualify for this certificate.

To say that Richard Roe can swim (for he can learn to swim) is to say that he is competent to follow and apply such instructions and demonstrations, though he may not yet have begun to do so. It would be wrong to predict about him, what it would be right to predict about an idiot, that since he now flounders helplessly in the water, he will still flounder helplessly after he has been given tuition.

To say that you can swim (if you try) is to use an interesting intermediate sort of 'can'. Whereas John Doe does not now have to try to swim, and Richard Roe cannot yet swim, however hard he tries, you know what to do but only do it, when you apply your whole mind to the task. You have understood the instructions and demonstrations, but still have to give yourself practice in the application of them. This learning to apply instructions by deliberate and perhaps difficult and alarming practice is something else which we regard as peculiar to creatures with minds. It exhibits qualities of character, though qualities of a different order from those exhibited by the puppy that shows tenacity and courage even in its play, since the novice is making himself do something difficult and alarming with the intention to develop his capacities. To say that he can swim if he tries is, therefore, to say both that he can understand instructions and also that he can intentionally drill himself in applying them.

It is not difficult to think of many other uses of 'can' and 'able'. In 'John Doe has been able to swim since he was a boy, but now he can invent new strokes' we have one such use. 'Can invent' does not mean 'has learned and not forgotten how to invent'. Nor is it at all like the 'can' in 'can sneeze'. Again the 'can' in 'can defeat all but champion swimmers' does not have the same force as either that in 'can swim' or that in 'can invent'. It is a 'can' which applies to race-horses.

There is one further feature of 'can' which is of special pertinence to our central theme. We often say of a person, or of a performing animal, that he can do something, in the sense that he can do it correctly or well. To say that a child can spell a word is to say that he can give, not merely some collection or other of letters, but the right collection in the right order. To say that he can tie a reef-knot is to say not merely that when he plays with bits of string, sometimes reef-knots and sometimes granny-knots are produced, but that reef-knots are produced whenever, or nearly whenever, reef-knots are required, or at least that they are nearly always produced when required and when the child is trying. When we use, as we often do use, the phrase 'can tell' as a paraphrase of 'know', we mean by 'tell', 'tell correctly'. We do not say that a child can tell the time, when all that he does is deliver random time-of-day statements, but only when he regularly reports the time of day in conformity with the position of the hands of the clock, or with the position of the sun, whatever these positions may be.

Many of the performance-verbs with which we describe people and, sometimes with qualms, animals, signify the occurrence not just of actions but of suitable or correct actions. They signify achievements. Verbs like 'spell', 'catch', 'solve', 'find', 'win', 'cure', 'score', 'deceive', 'persuade', 'arrive' and countless others signify not merely that some performance has been gone through, but also that something has been brought off by the agent going through it. They are verbs of success. Now successes are sometimes due to luck; a cricketer may score a boundary by making a careless stroke. But when we say of a person that he can bring off things of a certain sort, such as solve anagrams or cure sciatica, we mean that he can be relied on to succeed reasonably often even without the aid of luck. He knows how to bring it off in normal situations.

We also use corresponding verbs of failure, like 'miss', 'misspell' 'drop', 'lose', 'foozle' and 'miscalculate'. It is an important fact that if a person can spell or calculate, it must also be possible for him to misspell and miscalculate; but the sense of 'can' in 'can spell' and 'can calculate' is quite different from its sense in 'can misspell' and 'can miscalculate'. The one is a competence, the other is not another competence but a liability. For certain purposes it is also necessary to notice the further difference between both these senses of 'can' and the sense in which it is true to say that a person cannot solve an anagram incorrectly, win a race unsuccessfully, find a treasure unavailingly, or prove a theorem invalidly. For this 'cannot' is a logical 'cannot'. It says nothing about people's competences or limitations, but only that, for instance, 'solve incorrectly' is a self-contradictory expression. We shall see later that the epistemologist's hankering for some incorrigible sort of observation derives partly from his failure to notice that in one of its senses 'observe' is a verb of success, so that in this sense, 'mistaken observation' is as self-contradictory an expression as 'invalid proof' or 'unsuccessful cure'. But just as 'invalid argument' and 'unsuccessful treatment' are logically permissible expressions, so 'inefficient' or 'unavailing observation' is a permissible expression, when 'observe' is used not as a 'find' verb but as a 'hunt' verb.

Enough has been said to show that there is a wide variety of types of 'can' words, and that within this class there is a wide variety of types of capacity-expressions and liability-expressions. Only some of these capacity-expressions and liability-expressions are peculiar to the description of human beings, but even of these there are various types.

Tendencies are different from capacities and liabilities. 'Would if . . .' differs from 'could'; and 'regularly does . . . when . . .' differs from 'can'. Roughly, to say 'can' is to say that it is not a certainty that something will not be the case, while, to say 'tends', 'keeps on' or 'is prone', is to say that it is a good bet that it will be, or was, the case. So 'tends to' implies 'can', but is not implied by it. 'Fido tends to howl when the moon shines' says more than 'it is not true that if the moon shines, Fido is silent'. It licenses the hearer not only not to rely on his silence, but positively to expect barking.

But there are lots of types of tendency. Fido's tendency to get mange in the summer (unless specially dieted) is not the same sort of thing as his tendency to bark when the moon shines (unless his master is gruff with him). A person's blinking at fairly regular intervals is a different sort of tendency from his way of flickering his eyelids when embarrassed. We might call the latter, what we should not call the former, a 'mannerism'.

We distinguish between some behaviour tendencies and some others by calling some of them 'pure habits', others of them 'tastes', 'interests', 'bents' and 'hobbies' and yet others of them 'jobs' and 'occupations'. It might be a pure habit to draw on the right sock before the left sock, a hobby to go fishing when work and weather permit, and a job to drive lorries. It is, of course, easy to think of borderline cases of regular behaviour which we might hesitate to classify; some people's jobs are their hobbies and some people's jobs and hobbies are nearly pure habits. But we are fairly clear about the distinctions between the concepts themselves. An action done from pure habit is one that is not done on purpose and is one that the agent need not be able to report having done even immediately after having done it; his mind may have been on something else. Actions performed as parts of a person's job may be done by pure habit; still, he does not perform them when not on the job. The soldier does not march, when home on leave, but only when he knows that he has got to march, or ought to march. He resumes and drops the habit when he puts on and takes off his uniform.

Exercises of hobbies, interests and tastes are performed, as we say, 'for pleasure'. But this phrase can be misleading, since it suggests that these exercises are performed as a sort of investment from which a dividend is anticipated. The truth is the reverse, namely that we do these things because we like doing them, or want to do them, and not because we like or want something accessory to them. We invest our capital reluctantly in the hope of getting dividends which will make the outlay worth while, and if we were offered the chance of getting the dividends without investing the capital, we should gladly abstain from making the outlay. But the angler would not accept or understand an offer of the pleasures without the activities of angling. It is angling that he enjoys, not something that angling engenders.

To say that someone is now enjoying or disliking something entails that he is paying heed to it. There would be a contradiction in saying that the music pleased him though he was paying no attention to what he heard. There would, of course, be no contradiction in saying that he was listening to the music but neither enjoying nor disliking it. Accordingly, to say that someone is fond of or keen on angling entails not merely that he tends to wield his rod by the river when he is not forced or obliged not to do so, but that he tends to do so with his mind on it, that he tends to be wrapped up in daydreams and memories of angling, and to be absorbed in conversations and books on the subject. But this is not the whole story. A conscientious reporter tends to listen intently to the words of public speakers, even though he would not do this, if he were not obliged to do it. He does not do it when off duty. In these hours he is, perhaps, wont to devote himself to angling. He does not have to try to concentrate on fishing as he has to try to concentrate on speeches. He concentrates without trying. This is a large part of what 'keen on' means.

Besides pure habits, jobs and interests there are many other types of higher level tendencies. Some behaviour regularities are adherences to resolutions or policies imposed by the agent on himself; some are adherences to codes or religions inculcated into him by others. Addictions, ambitions, missions, loyalties, devotions and chronic negligences are all behaviour tendencies, but they are tendencies of very different kinds.

Two illustrations may serve to bring out some of the differences between capacities and tendencies, or between competences and pronenesses. (a) Both skills and inclinations can be simulated, but we use abusive names like 'charlatan' and 'quack' for the frauds who pretend to be able to bring things off, while we use the abusive word 'hypocrite' for the frauds who affect motives and habits. (b) Epistemologists are apt to perplex themselves and their readers over the distinction between knowledge and belief. Some of them suggest that these differ only in degree of something or other, and some that they differ in the presence of some intro-spectible ingredient in knowing which is absent from believing, or vice versa. Part of this embarrassment is due to their supposing that 'know' and 'believe' signify occurrences, but even when it is seen that both are dispositional verbs, it has still to be seen that they are dispositional verbs of quite disparate types. 'Know' is a capacity verb, and a capacity verb of that special sort that is used for signifying that the person described can bring things off, or get things right. 'Believe', on the other hand, is a tendency verb and one which does not connote that anything is brought off or got right. 'Belief' can be qualified by such adjectives as 'obstinate', 'wavering', 'unswerving', 'unconquerable', 'stupid', 'fanatical', 'whole-hearted', 'intermittent', 'passionate' and 'childlike', adjectives some or all of which are also appropriate to such nouns as 'trust', 'loyalty', 'bent', 'aversion', 'hope', 'habit', 'zeal' and 'addiction'. Beliefs, like habits, can be inveterate, slipped into and given up; like partisanships, devotions and hopes they can be blind and obsessing; like aversions and phobias they can be unacknowledged; like fashions and tastes they can be contagious; like loyalties and animosities they can be induced by tricks. A person can be urged or entreated not to believe things, and he may try, with or without success, to cease to do so. Sometimes a person says truly 'I cannot help believing so and so'. But none of these dictions, or their negatives, are applicable to knowing, since to know is to be equipped to get something right and not to tend to act or react in certain manners.

Roughly, 'believe' is of the same family as motive words, where 'know' is of the same family as skill words; so we ask how a person knows this, but only why a person believes that, as we ask how a person ties a clove-hitch, but why he wants to tie a clove-hitch or why he always ties granny-knots. Skills have methods, where habits and inclinations have sources. Similarly, we ask what makes people believe or dread things but not what makes them know or achieve things.

Of course, belief and knowledge (when it is knowledge *that*) operate, to put it crudely, in the same field. The sorts of things that can be described·as known or unknown can also be described as believed or disbelieved, somewhat as the sorts of things that can be manufactured are also the sorts of things that can be exported. A man who believes that the ice is dangerously thin gives warnings, skates warily and replies to pertinent questions in the same ways as the man who knows that it is dangerously thin; and if asked whether he knows it for a fact, he may unhesitatingly claim to do so, until embarrassed by the question how he found it out.

Belief might be said to be like knowledge and unlike trust in persons, zeal for causes, or addiction to smoking, in that it is 'propositional'; but this, though not far wrong, is too narrow. Certainly to believe that the ice is dangerously thin is to be unhesitant in telling oneself and others that it is thin, in acquiescing in other people's assertions to that effect, in objecting to statements to the contrary, in drawing consequences from the original proposition, and so forth. But it is also to be prone to skate warily, to shudder, to dwell in imagination on possible disasters and to warn other skaters. It is a propensity not only to make certain theoretical moves but also to make certain executive and imaginative moves, as well as to have certain feelings. But these things hang together on a common propositional hook. The phrase 'thin ice' would occur in the descriptions alike of the shudders, the warnings, the wary skating, the declarations, the inferences, the acquiescences and the objections.

A person who knows that the ice is thin, and also cares whether it is thin or thick, will, of course, be apt to act and react in these ways too. But to say that he keeps to the edge, because he knows that the ice is thin, is to employ quite a different sense of 'because', or to give quite a different sort of 'explanation', from that conveyed by saying that he keeps to the edge because he believes that the ice is thin.

## (4) *Mental Occurrences.*

There are hosts of ways in which we describe people as now engaged in this, as frequently undergoing that, as having spent several minutes in an activity, or as being quick or slow to achieve a result. An important sub-class of such occurrences are those which exhibit qualities of character and intellect. It must be noticed from the start that it is one thing to say that certain human actions and reactions exhibit qualities of character and intellect; it is, by an unfortunate linguistic fashion, quite another thing to say that there occur mental acts or mental processes. The latter expression traditionally belongs to the two-worlds story, the story that some things exist or occur 'in the physical world', while other things exist and occur not in that world but in another, metaphorical place. Rejection of this story is perfectly compatible with retaining the familiar distinction between, say, babbling and talking sense, or between twitching and signalling; nor does acceptance of the two-worlds story in any degree clarify or consolidate this distinction.

I begin by considering a battery of concepts all of which may be brought under the useful because vague heading of 'minding'. Or they could all alike be described as 'heed concepts'. I refer to the concepts of noticing, taking care, attending, applying one's mind, concentrating, putting one's heart into something, thinking what one is doing, alertness, interest, intentness, studying and trying. 'Absence of mind' is a phrase sometimes used to signify a condition in which people act or react without heeding what they are doing, or without noticing what is going on. We also have in English a more special sense of 'minding', in which to say that a person minds what he eats is to say not only that he notices what he eats, but further that he cares what he eats. Enjoying and disliking entail, but are not entailed by, heeding. 'Enjoy' and 'dislike' belong to the large class of verbs which already connote heeding. We cannot, without absurdity, describe someone as absent-mindedly pondering, searching, testing, debating, planning, listening or relishing. A man may mutter or fidget absent-mindedly, but if he is calculating, or scrutinising, it is redundant to say that he is paying some heed to what he is doing.

Minding, in all its sorts, can vary in degree. A driver can drive a car with great care, reasonable care or slight care, and a student can concentrate hard or not very hard. A person cannot always tell whether he has been applying his whole mind, or only a part of it, to a task, in which he has been engaged. The child who tries to commit a poem to memory may think that he has been attending hard, for he glued his eyes to the page, muttered the words, frowned and stopped up his ears. But if, without there having been any distractions or interruptions, he still cannot recite the poem, say what it was about, or find anything amiss with the erroneous versions recited by his companions, his claim will be rejected by the teacher and even, perhaps, withdrawn by himself.

Some traditional accounts given of consciousness have been, at least in part, attempts to clarify the concepts of heed, usually by claiming to isolate some unique ingredient common to them all. This common ingredient has commonly been described in the idiom of contemplation or inspection, as if part of the difference between having a tickle and noticing it, or between reading a paragraph and studying it, consisted in the fact that the having of the tickle and the reading of the paragraph take place, metaphorically, in a good light and under the eyes of the person concerned. But so far from heeding being a sort of inspecting or monitoring, inspecting and monitoring are themselves special exercises of heed; since whether a person is described literally or metaphorically as a spectator, it is always significant to ask whether he has been a careful or careless spectator, a vigilant or a drowsy one. That someone has been carefully watching a bird on the lawn does not entail that he has also been metaphorically 'watching' his watching; and that he has been applying his mind to the cartoon that he has been drawing does not entail that he has been either watching his fingers at their work or watching anything else at work. Doing something with heed does not consist in coupling an executive performance with a piece of theorising, investigating, scrutinising or 'cognising'; or else doing anything with heed would involve doing an infinite number of things with heed.

The motives for misdescribing heed in the contemplative idiom derive partly from the general intellectualist tradition, according to which theorising is the essential function of minds, and metaphorical contemplation is the essence of theorising. But there is a further and more reputable motive. It is quite true that if a person has been doing or undergoing something and has been paying heed to what he was doing or undergoing, he can then tell what he has been doing or undergoing (provided that he has learned the arts of telling); and he can tell it without rummaging for evidence, without drawing any inferences and without even momentarily wondering what he should say. It is already on the tip of his tongue and he tells it without hesitation or research as he tells anything that is familiar or obvious. And as our standard models of obviousness are taken from the field of familiar things seen from advantageous points of view in good lights, we naturally like to describe all abilities to tell things without work or hesitation as issuing from something like seeing. Hence we like to speak of 'seeing' implications and 'seeing' jokes. But though references to seeing familiar things in favourable circumstances may illustrate, they cannot elucidate the notions of familiarity and obviousness.

Later on we shall have to consider how the readiness to tell what one's actions and reactions have been is involved in having paid some heed to them. Here it is necessary to point out that readiness to answer questions about one's actions and reactions does not exhaust the heed we pay to them. Driving a car with care reduces the risk of accidents as well as enabling the driver to satisfy interrogations about his operations. Applying our minds to things does not qualify us only to give veracious reports about them, and absence of mind is betrayed by other things than merely being nonplussed in the witness-box. The concept of heed is not, save *per accidens*, a cognitive concept. Investigations are not the only occupations in which we apply our minds.

We may now turn to a new feature in the logical behaviour of heed concepts. When a person hums as he walks, he is doing two things at once, either of which he might interrupt without interrupting the other. But when we speak of a person minding what he is saying, or what he is whistling, we are not saying that he is doing two things at once. He could not stop his reading, while continuing his attention to it, or hand over the controls of his car, while continuing to exercise care; though he could, of course, continue to read but cease to attend, or continue to drive but cease to take care. Since the use of such pairs of active verbs as 'read' and 'attend' or 'drive' and 'take care' may suggest that there must be two synchronous and perhaps coupled processes going on whenever both verbs are properly used, it may be helpful to remember that it is quite idiomatic to replace the heed verb by a heed adverb. We commonly speak of reading attentively, driving carefully and conning studiously, and this usage has the merit of suggesting that what is being described is one operation with a special character and not two operations executed in different 'places', with a peculiar cable between them.

What then is this special character? The question is perplexing, since the ways in which heed adverbs qualify the active verbs to which they are attached seem quite unlike the ways in which other adverbs qualify their verbs. A horse may be described as running quickly or slowly, smoothly or jerkily, straight or crookedly, and simple observation or even cinematograph films enable us to decide in which manner the horse was running. But when a man is described as driving carefully, whistling with concentration or eating absent-mindedly, the special character of his activity seems to elude the observer, the camera and the dictaphone. Perhaps knitted brows, taciturnity and fixity of gaze may be evidence of intentness; but these can be simulated, or they can be purely habitual. In any case, in describing him as applying his mind to his task, we do not mean that this is how he looks and sounds while engaged in it; we should not withdraw a statement to the effect that he had been concentrating merely on being told that his expressions and movements had been tranquil. But if this special character is unwitnessable, we seem forced to say either that it is some hidden concomitant of the operation to which it is ascribed, or that it is some merely dispositional property of the agent; either that whistling with concentration is a tandem occurrence, the members of which occur in different 'places', or that the description of the whistling as done with concentration mentions one overt occurrence and makes some open hypothetical statement about its author. To accept the former suggestion would be to relapse into the two-worlds legend. It would also involve us in the special difficulty that since minding would then be a different activity from the overt activity said to be minded, it would be impossible to explain why that minding could not go on by itself as humming can go on without walking. On the other hand, to accept the dispositional account would apparently involve us in saying that though a person may properly be described as whistling now, he cannot be properly described as concentrating or taking care now; and we know quite well that such descriptions are legitimate. But this point must be examined more fully.

If we want to find out whether someone has been noticing what he has been reading, we are generally content to decide the question by cross-questioning him not long afterwards. If he cannot tell us anything about the gist or the wording of the chapter, if he finds no fault with other passages which contradict the original chapter, or if he expresses surprise on being informed of something already mentioned in it, then, unless he has suffered concussion in the interim, or is now excited or sleepy, we are satisfied that he did not notice what he read. To notice what one reads entails being prepared to satisfy some such subsequent tests. In a similar way, certain kinds of accidents or near-accidents would satisfy us that the driver had not been taking care. To take care entails being prepared for certain sorts of emergencies.

But this cannot be the whole story. For one thing, there are plenty of other process verbs which carry analogous dispositional properties with them though they cannot be ranked with heed verbs. 'He is now dying', 'coming to', 'weakening', 'he is now being hypnotised', 'anæsthetised', 'immunised' are all occurrence reports the truth of which requires some testable hypothetical statements about his future to be true. And, on the other side, not only is it allowable to describe someone as now thinking what he is saying, as intermittently noticing the hardness of his chair, or as starting and ceasing to concentrate, but it is proper to order or request someone to apply his mind, as it is not proper to order him to be able or likely to do things. We know, too, that it can be more fatiguing to read attentively than to read inattentively. So while we are certainly saying something dispositional in applying such a heed concept to a person, we are certainly also saying something episodic. We are saying that he did what he did in a specific frame of mind, and while the specification of the frame of mind requires mention of ways in which he was able, ready or likely to act and react, his acting in that frame of mind was itself a clockable occurrence.

To restate the problem, it is possible, if not very common, for two or more overt actions done in quite dissimilar frames of mind to be photographically and gramophonically as similar as you please. A person playing a piece of music on the piano may be doing this for his own pleasure, or to please an audience, or for practice, or for instruction-purposes, or under duress, or as a parody of another pianist, or quite absent-mindedly and by sheer rote. So, since the differences between these performances cannot always be photographically or gramophonically recorded, we are tempted to say that they consist either in the concomitant occurrence of some internal actions and reactions, detectable only by the performer, or else in the satisfaction by the overt performances of different open hypothetical statements. In other words, the description of the player as playing 'Home Sweet Home' as a demonstration of how it should be played has an internal complexity, in respect of one element of which it differs from the description of him as playing 'Home Sweet Home' in parody of another player, though in respect of their witnessed element they are similar. Are these complex descriptions of outwardly similar occurrences to be construed as descriptions of conjunctions of similar overt with dissimilar covert occurrences, or are their differences to be construed in another way? Do they assert dual matters of fact, or singular matters of fact, with different inference-warrants appended?

Neither option seems acceptable, though the second provides an indispensable part of the answer. Like most dichotomies, the logicians' dichotomy 'either categorical or hypothetical' needs to be taken with a pinch of salt. We have here to do with a class or statements the job of which is to straddle just this gulf. Save to those who are spellbound by dichotomies, there is nothing scandalous in the notion that a statement may be in some respects like statements of brute fact and in other respects like inference-licences; or that it may be at once narrative, explanatory and conditionally predictive, without being a conjunctive assemblage of detachable sub-statements. Every statement to the effect that something is so because something else is the case, requires, in order to be true, both that certain matters of fact obtain, and that there is a license to infer one from the other. Nor is such a statement one of which an objector might say that part of it was true, but the other part was false.

The colloquial accusation 'You *would* miss the last train' not only reproaches the culprit for having missed the train, but also declares that he could have been expected to do so. The error that he has in fact committed is just one of the things that could have been predicted. It was just like him to do what he did. The accusation embodies a partially satisfied open hypothetical statement. It is not and could not be wholly satisfied, for it could also have been predicted that if he had gone to a telephone-booth (which perhaps he did not), he would not have had the right change, and if he had meant to post a letter (which perhaps he did not) he would have missed the last collection. I shall call statements like 'You *would* do the thing you did' 'semi-hypothetical' or 'mongrel categorical statements'. Most of the examples ordinarily adduced of categorical statements are mongrel categoricals.

Correspondingly, to say that someone has done something, paying some heed to what he was doing, is not only to say that he was, e.g. ready for any of a variety of associated tasks and tests which might have cropped up but perhaps did not; it is also to say that he was ready for the task with which he actually coped. He was in the mood or frame of mind to do, if required, lots of things which may not have been actually required; and he was, *ipso facto*, in the mood or frame of mind to do at least this one thing which was actually required. Being in that frame of mind, he *would* do the thing he did, as well as, if required, lots of other things none of which is he stated to have done. The description of him as minding what he was doing is just as much an explanatory report of an actual occurrence as a conditional prediction of further occurrences.

Statements of this type are not peculiar to descriptions of the higher level actions and reactions of people. When a sugar-lump is described as dissolving, something more episodic is being said than when it is described as soluble; but something more dispositional is being said than when it is described as moist. When a bird is described as migrating, something more episodic is being said than when it is described as a migrant, but something more dispositional is being said than when it is described as flying in the direction of Africa. The sugar-lump and the bird *would*, in the given situation, do what they actually do as well as lots of other specifiable things, if certain specifiable conditions obtained, which may not obtain.

The description of a bird as migrating has a greater complexity than the description of it as flying in the direction of Africa, but this greater complexity does not consist in its narrating a larger number of incidents. Only one thing need be going on, namely that the bird be at a particular moment flying south. 'It is migrating' tells not more stories, but a more pregnant story than that told by 'It is flying south'. It can be wrong in more ways and it is instructive in more ways.

This point is connected with a very common use of 'because', one which is different from all the uses previously distinguished. The two statements 'the bird is flying south' and 'the bird is migrating' are both episodic reports. The question 'Why is the bird flying south?' could be answered quite properly by saying 'Because it is migrating'. Yet the process of migrating is not a different process from that of flying south; so it is not the cause of the bird's flying south. Nor, since it reports an episode, does the sentence 'because it is migrating' say the same sort of thing as is said in 'because it is a migrant'. We must say that 'it is migrating' describes a flying process in terms which are partly anecdotal, but are also partly predictive and explanatory. It does not state a law, but it describes an event in terms which are law-impregnated. The verb 'migrate' carries a biological message, as the verb 'dissolve' carries a message from chemistry. 'It is migrating' warrants the inference 'it is a migrant', as 'it is dissolving' warrants the inference 'it is soluble'.

So, too, when it is asked why a person is reading a certain book, it is often correct to reply 'because he is interested in what he is reading'. Yet being interested in reading the book is not doing or undergoing two things, such that the interest is the cause of the reading. The interest explains the reading in the same general way, though not the same specific way, as the migrating explains the flying south.

I have pointed out a fact about heed concepts, namely that it is proper to order or request someone to pay heed, exercise caution, take notice, study hard and so on. It is equally proper for a person to tell himself to do so. Now patently one cannot order a person merely to pay heed, or merely to take notice. For the order to be obeyed or disobeyed, it must be understood as specifying just what is to be done with heed. A pupil, a proof-reader and an oculist's patient might all be told, for example, to read carefully a certain paragraph; the pupil will be disobeying his instructions, if he notices the misprints but not the argument; the proof-reader will be disobeying his instructions, if he attends to the arguments but does not detect the misprints; while the oculist's patient is intended to report neither on the argument nor on the misprints, but only on the blurredness or sharpness, the blackness or greyness, the slantingness or the uprightness of the printed letters. Clearly this is true of heeding in general. A person cannot be described merely as taking interest, being absorbed or trying; he must be, for example, reading a leading article with interest, fishing absorbedly or trying to climb this tree. 'Enjoy' and 'dislike' similarly require supplementation by the participle of a specific active verb such as 'swimming', 'listening to Bach' and 'doing nothing'.

When a person is described as applying his mind to some such specifiable action or reaction, it is legitimate to say that he is, in a certain sense of the verb, 'thinking' or 'heeding' what he is doing or experiencing or 'applying his mind' to it. This does not mean that he is necessarily communing with himself about what he is doing or experiencing. He need not, though he may, be murmuring to himself comments, strictures, instructions, encouragements or diagnoses, though if he is doing this, it is again a proper question to ask whether or not he is thinking what he is murmuring. Sometimes an addict of discourse, like Hamlet, is thought not to be applying his mind to a given task just because he is applying his mind to the secondary task of discoursing to himself about his primary task; and sometimes a person who should be trying to converse in French actually distracts himself from his proper business by conversing with himself in English about how he is conducting it. Thinking or heeding what one is doing does not entail constantly or recurrently making intelligent prose moves. On the contrary, making intelligent prose moves is just one example among others of thinking or heeding what one is doing, since it is saying things, thinking what one is saying. It is one species, not the causal condition of heedful performance. But certainly didactic telling, intelligently given and intelligently received, is often an indispensable guide to execution. There are many things which we cannot do, or do well, unless we pay heed to appropriate and timely instructions, even when we ourselves have to be the authors of those instructions. In such cases, trying to do the thing involves both trying to give oneself the right instructions at the right time and trying to follow them.

We should now consider a type of action which, though quite uninventive, involves some degree of heed, as instinctive and purely habitual or reflex actions do not involve heed. A soldier who fixes his bayonet in obedience to an order may go through just the same movements as one who fixes his bayonet for any other purpose. 'Obediently' does not signify a muscularly peculiar manner of operating. Nor does it denote, or connote, any self-communings or self-instructings. For he has not been ordered to do these things, and if he does them they do not explain away his bayonet-fixing, since following self-instructions would simply be another instance of acting obediently. Yet fixing his bayonet obediently is certainly fixing his bayonet with, in some sense, the thought that this is what he was told to do. He would not have done it, had the order been different or been misheard, and if asked why he did it, he would unhesitatingly reply by referring to the order.

Nor is he doing two things, namely both fixing his bayonet and obeying an order, any more than the migrating bird was both flying south and doing or undergoing something else. He obeys the order by fixing his bayonet. The question, 'did he heed the order?' is quite satisfactorily answered by, 'yes, he fixed his bayonet the moment the order was given'. But, of course, he might not have heard the order and merely fixed his bayonet for fun at what happened to be the right moment. In that case it would be false to say that he had fixed his bayonet in obedience to an order.

We might say that his primary object was to obey whatever order was given him by his sergeant. If we ask 'To what was he

applying his mind?' the answer is 'to his orders'. He was only set
to fix his bayonet, if this were to be the thing his sergeant was to
tell him to do. The description of his frame of mind contains a
direct reference to his orders and only an oblique, because
conditional reference to fixing his bayonet. His action of fixing his
bayonet is, so to speak, executed in inverted commas; he does it as
the particular thing actually ordered. He would have done something
else, had the order been different. He is in the frame of mind to do
whatever he is ordered, including fixing his bayonet. His fixing it
is conditionally retro-predictable and a value of the variable condition has been fulfilled.

Similarly a mimic does, perhaps, nothing but utter some words,
or make some gesticulations, but he produces precisely these words
and gesticulations only as representing the precise words and
gesticulations of their original author. Had the original author
spoken or acted in any other way, the mimic would have done so
too. He does not have concomitantly to be telling himself or his
companions that this is how the original author spoke and gesticu-
lated. Showing how he talked and shrugged need not be prefaced
or accompanied by any descriptive commentary; sometimes it
cannot be so prefaced or accompanied, since descriptive skill is
often inferior to histrionic skill. The mimic produces his words and
shrugs as facsimiles of those of the subject mimicked, but he does not
have to be currently asserting that they are facsimiles.

But what is the force of this word 'as', when we say that an
agent does something *as* the action ordered or *as* a facsimile or *as*
practice or *as* a means to an end or *as* a game; or, in general, *as*
the execution of a specific programme? What is the difference
between going merely mechanically through certain movements
and *trying* to satisfy some specific requirement by going through,
perhaps, perfectly similar movements? Or what is the difference
between fixing bayonets in compliance with a command and fixing
bayonets in order to fight?

It is not enough, though it is true, to say that the soldier fixes
his bayonet on purpose, namely on purpose to do what he is told,
or on purpose to defend himself, since our present question amounts
to this: Given that 'the bird is migrating' and 'the soldier is
obediently fixing his bayonet' are both mongrel categorical
statements, what is the difference between them which we signalise

by saying that the soldier is, but the bird is not applying his mind or acting on purpose?

At least a minimal part of the answer is this. To say that a sugar-lump is dissolving, a bird migrating, or a man blinking does not imply that the sugar has learned to go liquid, that the bird has learned to fly south in the autumn, or that the man has learned to blink when startled. But to say that a soldier obediently fixed his bayonet, or fixed it in order to defend himself, does imply that he has learned some lessons and not forgotten them. The new recruit, on hearing the order to fix bayonet, or on seeing an enemy soldier approaching, does not know what to do with his bayonet, how to do it, or when to do it and when not to do it. He may not even know how to construe òr obey orders.

Not all acquired capacities or propensities can be classed as qualities of mind. The habit of going to sleep on one's right side is not a quality of intellect or character; the habit of saying 'Tweedledee', aloud or in one's head, on hearing the word 'Tweedledum', is a trick we have picked up, though we should hardly claim it as a trick that we have learnt. It sticks but we did not try to get it to stick; nor do we ordinarily use or apply it. Picking up things by rote without trying to do so is the vanishing-point of learning. Even learning rhymes by heart, when done with application, though it is a primitive form of learning, does generate not only the trumpery capacity to recite those rhymes, but also the more valuable capacity to learn all sorts of other things by heart, as well as the still more valuable capacity to generate all sorts of capacities by study. It is a primitive lesson in becoming *generally* teachable.

Children, semi-literates, old-fashioned soldiers and some peda-gogues tend to suppose that being taught and trained consist in becoming able merely to echo the exact lessons taught. But this is an error. We should not say that the child had done more than begin to learn his multiplication-tables if all he could do were to go through them correctly from beginning to end. He has not learned them properly unless he can promptly give the right answer to any snap multiplication problem (lower than $12 \times 13$), and unless he can apply his tables by telling us, e.g. how many toes there are in a room in which there are six people. Nor is a man a trained rock-climber who can cope only with the same nursery-climbs over which he was taught, in conditions just like those in which he was taught, and then only by going through the very motions which he had been then made to perform. Learning is becoming capable of doing some correct or suitable thing in *any* situations of certain general sorts. It is becoming prepared for *variable* calls within certain ranges.

To describe someone as now doing something with some degree of some sort of heed is to say not merely that he has had some such preparation, but that he is actually meeting a concrete call and so meeting it that he would have met, or will meet, some of whatever other calls of that range might have cropped up, or may crop up. He is in a 'ready' frame of mind, for he both does what he does with readiness to do just that in just this situation and is ready to do some of whatever else he may be called on to do. To describe a driver as taking care does not entail that it has occurred to him that a donkey may bolt out of that side street. He can be ready for such contingencies without having anticipated them. Indeed, he might have anticipated them without being ready for them.

Earlier in this chapter I undertook to explain why it is that though applying one's mind to a task does not consist in coupling an inspecting or researching operation with the performance of that task, yet we expect a person who applies his mind to anything to be able to tell, without research, what he has been engaged in or occupied with. Heeding is not a secondary occupation of theorising, yet it seems to entail having at the tip of one's tongue the answers to theoretical questions about one's primary occupation. How can I have knowledge of what I have been non-absent-mindedly doing or feeling, unless doing or feeling something with my mind on it at least incorporates some study of what I am doing or feeling? How could I now describe what I had not previously inspected?

Part of the answer seems to be this. Not all talk, and certainly not the most rudimentary talk, consists in imparting items of general knowledge. We do not, for instance, begin by telling the infant the names of things in which he is at the moment not taking an interest. We begin by telling him the names of things in which he is then and there taking an interest. Use of the names of things is thus injected into interest in the things. In a partially similar way we give the child instructions, counsels, demonstrations, rebukes and encouragements for what he is currently essaying; we do not wait until he is unoccupied, before we teach him how things should be done. Nor does the fact that the coaching is concurrent with the performance necessarily render it a distraction from that performance. Trying to comply with the teaching is part of trying to do the thing, and as the child learns to do the thing, he also learns to understand better and apply better the lessons in doing the thing. Hence he learns, too, to double the roles of instructor and pupil; he learns to coach himself and to heed his own coaching, i.e. to suit his deeds to his own words.

The good referee does not blow his whistle at every moment of the game, nor does the trained player cease to apply his mind to the game whenever he attends to the referee's whistle; rather, he shows that he is not applying his mind to the game unless he does attend to the whistle. We are all trained in some degree to be our own referees, and though we are not, all or most of the time, blowing our whistles, we are most of the time ready or half-ready to blow them, if the situation requires it, and to comply with them, when they are blown.

The referee's interventions in the game are normally peremptory rather than descriptive or informative. He is there to help the game to go on rather than to satisfy the journalists about what is going on. He gives rulings and rebukes rather than reports. But to be ready to give an appropriate ruling, when the state of the game requires it, is also to be ready to give a report, if the journalists clamour for it. He knows what fiats to give, so he knows what facts to report. But he does not have to study his fiats in order to glean some facts. Roughly, he needs only to adjust his tone of voice —to tell prosaically what he might otherwise have bellowed peremptorily, or ruled incisively. Telling things in the indicative mood is telling them in the most sophisticated, because most dispassionate manner.

Similarly, we, if duly trained, can, much of the time, deliver to ourselves the injunctions, suggestions and verdicts that are more or less pertinent and contributory to whatever is at that moment occupying us. When we make the transition from telling ourselves the pertinent admonitory or judicial things to telling questioners (who may also be ourselves) the correct descriptive things, we have to do, not research, but re-wording. Knowing what to say pertinently to some requirements is knowing also what to say pertinently to other requirements. Where we cannot talk much to ourselves as coaches or judges, as in inventing jokes, reading characters or composing lyrics, we also cannot tell inquirers much about what we are doing. We then speak of 'inspiration' and 'intuition', and this exempts us from having to answer questions.

(5) *Achievements.*

There is another class of episodic words which, for our purposes, merit special attention, namely the class of episodic words which I have elsewhere labelled 'achievement words', 'success words' or 'got it words', together with their antitheses the 'failure words' or 'missed it words'. These are genuine episodic words, for it is certainly proper to say of someone that he scored a goal at a particular moment, repeatedly solved anagrams, or was quick to see the joke or find the thimble. Some words of this class signify more or less sudden climaxes or dénouements; others signify more or less protracted proceedings. The thimble is found, the opponent checkmated, or the race won, at a specifiable instant; but the secret may be kept, the enemy held at bay, or the lead be retained, throughout a long span of time. The sort of success which consists in descrying the hawk differs in this way from the sort of success which consists in keeping it in view.

The verbs with which we ordinarily express these gettings and keepings are active verbs, such as 'win', 'unearth', 'find', 'cure', 'convince', 'prove', 'cheat', 'unlock', 'safeguard' and 'conceal'; and this grammatical fact has tended to make people, with the exception of Aristotle, oblivious to the differences of logical behaviour between verbs of this class and other verbs of activity or process. The differences, for example, between kicking and scoring, treating and healing, hunting and finding, clutching and holding fast, listening and hearing, looking and seeing, travelling and arriving, have been construed, if they have been noticed at all, as differences between co-ordinate species of activity or process, when in fact the differences are of quite another kind. It has been all the easier to overlook these differences, since we very often borrow achievement verbs to signify the performance of the corresponding task activities, where the hopes of success are good. A runner may be described as winning his race from the start, despite the fact that he may not win it in the end; and a doctor may boast that he is curing his patient's pneumonia, when his treatment does not in fact result in the anticipated recovery. 'Hear' is sometimes used as a synonym of 'listen' and 'mend' as a synonym of 'try to mend'.

One big difference between the logical force of a task verb and that of a corresponding achievement verb is that in applying an achievement verb we are asserting that some state of affairs obtains over and above that which consists in the performance, if any, of the subservient task activity. For a runner to win, not only must he run but also his rivals must be at the tape later than he; for a doctor to effect a cure, his patient must both be treated and be well again; for the searcher to find the thimble, there must be a thimble in the place he indicates at the moment when he indicates it; and for the mathematician to prove a theorem, the theorem must be true and follow from the premisses from which he tries to show that it follows. An autobiographical account of the agent's exertions and feelings does not by itself tell whether he has brought off what he was trying to bring off. He may rashly claim the expected success, but he will withdraw his claim if he discovers that, despite his having done the best he could, something has still gone wrong. I withdraw my claim to have seen a misprint, or convinced the voter, if I find that there was no misprint, or that the voter has cast his vote for my opponent.

It is a consequence of this general point that it is always significant, though not, of course, always true, to ascribe a success partly or wholly to luck. A clock may be repaired by a random jolt and the treasure may be unearthed by the first spade-thrust.

It follows, too, that there can be achievements which are prefaced by no task performances. We sometimes find things without searching, secure appointments without applying and arrive at true conclusions without having weighed the evidence. Things thus got without work are often described as 'given'. An easy catch is 'given', a harder catch is 'offered', a difficult catch is 'made'.

When a person is described as having fought and won, or as having journeyed and arrived, he is not being said to have done two things, but to have done one thing with a certain upshot. Similarly a person who has aimed and missed has not followed up one occupation by another; he has done one thing, which was a failure. So, while we expect a person who has been trying to achieve something to be able to say without research what he has been engaged in, we do not expect him necessarily to be able to say without research whether he has achieved it. Achievements and failures are not occurrences of the right type to be objects of what is often, if misleadingly, called 'immediate awareness'. They are not acts, exertions, operations or performances, but, with reservations for purely lucky achievements, the fact that certain acts, operations, exertions or performances have had certain results.

This is why we can significantly say that someone has aimed in vain or successfully, but not that he has hit the target in vain or successfully; that he has treated his patient assiduously or unassiduously, but not that he has cured him assiduously or unassiduously; that he scanned the hedgerow slowly or rapidly, systematically or haphazardly, but not that he saw the nest slowly or rapidly, systematically or haphazardly. Adverbs proper to task verbs are not generally proper to achievement verbs; in particular, heed adverbs like 'carefully', 'attentively', 'studiously', 'vigilantly', 'conscientiously' and 'pertinaciously' cannot be used to qualify such cognitive verbs as 'discover', 'prove', 'solve', 'detect' or 'see', any more than they can qualify such verbs as 'arrive', 'repair', 'buy' or 'conquer'.

There are many episodic verbs which are used to describe items in the inquisitive life of human beings, and the failure to notice that some of these verbs are achievement verbs while others are task verbs has been the source of some gratuitous puzzles and, accordingly, of some mystery-mongering theories. Special cognitive acts and operations have been postulated to answer to such verbs as 'see', 'hear', 'taste', 'deduce' and 'recall' in the way in which familiar acts and operations do answer to such verbs as 'kick', 'run', 'look', 'listen', 'wrangle' and 'tell'; as if to describe a person as looking and seeing were like describing him as walking and humming instead of being like describing him as angling and catching, or searching and finding. But perception verbs cannot, like search verbs, be qualified by such adverbs as 'successfully', 'in vain', 'methodically', 'inefficiently', 'laboriously', 'lazily', 'rapidly', 'carefully', 'reluctantly', 'zealously', 'obediently', 'deliberately' or 'confidently'. They do not stand for performances, or ways of being occupied; *a fortiori* they do not stand for secret performances, or ways of being privily occupied. To put it crudely, they belong not to the vocabulary of the player, but to the vocabulary of the referee. They are not tryings, but things got by trying or by luck.

Epistemologists have sometimes confessed to finding the supposed cognitive activities of seeing, hearing and inferring oddly elusive. If I descry a hawk, I find the hawk but I do not find my seeing of the hawk. My seeing of the hawk seems to be a queerly transparent sort of process, transparent in that while a hawk is detected, nothing else is detected answering to the verb in 'see a hawk.' But the mystery dissolves when we realise that 'see', 'descry' and 'find' are not process words, experience words or activity words. They do not stand for perplexingly undetectable actions or reactions, any more than 'win' stands for a perplexingly undetectable bit of running, or 'unlock' for an unreported bit of key-turning. The reason why I cannot catch myself seeing or deducing is that these verbs are of the wrong type to complete the phrase 'catch myself. . . .' The questions 'What are you doing?' and 'What was he undergoing?' cannot be answered by 'seeing', 'concluding', or 'checkmating'.

The distinction between task verbs and achievement verbs or 'try' verbs and 'got it' verbs frees us from another theoretical nuisance. It has long been realised that verbs like 'know', 'discover', 'solve', 'prove', 'perceive', 'see' and 'observe' (at least in certain standard uses of 'observe') are in an important way incapable of being qualified by adverbs like 'erroneously' and 'incorrectly'. Automatically construing these and kindred verbs as standing for special kinds of operations or experiences, some epistemologists have felt themselves obliged to postulate that people possess certain special inquiry procedures in following which they are subject to no risk of error. They need not, indeed they cannot, execute them carefully, for they provide no scope for care. The logical impossibility of a discovery being fruitless, or of a proof being invalid, has been misconstrued as a quasi-causal impossibility of going astray. If only the proper road were followed, or if only the proper faculty were given its head, incorrigible observations or self-evident intuitions could not help ensuing. So men are sometimes infallible. Similarly if hitting the bull's eye were construed as a special kind of aiming, or if curing were construed as a special kind of treatment, then, since neither could, in logic, be at fault, it would follow that there existed special fault-proof ways of aiming and doctoring.

There would exist some temporarily infallible marksmen and some occasionally infallible doctors.

Other epistemologists, properly disrelishing the ascription of even temporary infallibility to human beings, have taken up an equally impossible position. Again automatically construing these achievement verbs as standing for special kinds of operations or experiences, they have asserted that the operations or experiences for which they stand are, after all, not fault-proof. We can know what is not the case, prove things fallaciously, solve problems erroneously and see what is not there to be seen, which is like saying that we can hit the bull's eye with an 'outer', cure a patient by aggravating his complaint, or win a race without being first at the tape. There is, of course, no incompatibility between losing a race and lodging a claim to have won it, or between aggravating a complaint and boasting of having cured it. Merely saying 'I see a hawk' does not entail that there is a hawk there, though saying truly 'I see a hawk' does entail this.

This assimilation of certain so-called cognitive verbs to the general class of achievement verbs must not be supposed to elucidate everything. The fact that the logical behaviour of 'deduce' is in some respects like that of 'score', 'checkmate' or 'unlock' does not involve that it is in every respect like that of any of them; nor is arriving at a conclusion in every respect like arriving in Paris. My argument has been intended to have the predominantly negative point of exhibiting both why it is wrong, and why it is tempting, to postulate mysterious actions and reactions to correspond with certain familiar biographical episodic words.

CHAPTER VI

# SELF-KNOWLEDGE

(1) *Foreword.*

A NATURAL counterpart to the theory that minds constitute a world other than 'the physical world' is the theory that there exist ways of discovering the contents of this other world which are counterparts to our ways of discovering the contents of the physical world. In sense perception we ascertain what exists and happens in space; so what exists or happens in the mind must also be ascertained in perception, but perception of a different and refined sort, one not requiring the functioning of gross bodily organs.

More than this, it has been thought necessary to show that minds possess powers of apprehending their own states and operations superior to those they possess of apprehending facts of the external world. If I am to know, believe, guess or even wonder anything about the things and happenings that are outside me, I must, it has been supposed, enjoy constant and mistake-proof apprehension of these selfsame cognitive operations of mine.

It is often held therefore (1) that a mind cannot help being constantly aware of all the supposed occupants of its private stage, and (2) that it can also deliberately scrutinise by a species of non-sensuous perception at least some of its own states and operations. Moreover both this constant awareness (generally called 'consciousness'), and this non-sensuous inner perception (generally called 'introspection') have been supposed to be exempt from error. A mind has a twofold Privileged Access to its own doings, which makes its self-knowledge superior in quality, as well as prior in genesis, to its grasp of other things. I may doubt the evidence of my senses but not the deliverances of consciousness or introspection.

One limitation has always been conceded to the mind's power of finding mental states and operations, namely that while I can

154

have direct knowledge of my own states and operations, I cannot have it of yours. I am conscious of all my own feelings, volitions, emotions and thinkings, and I introspectively scrutinise some of them. But I cannot introspectively observe, or be conscious of, the workings of your mind. I can satisfy myself that you have a mind at all only by complex and frail inferences from what your body does.

This theory of the twofold Privileged Access has won so strong a hold on the thoughts of philosophers, psychologists and many laymen that it is now often thought to be enough to say, on behalf of the dogma of the mind as a second theatre, that its consciousness and introspection discover the scenes enacted in it. On the view for which I am arguing consciousness and introspection cannot be what they are officially described as being, since their supposed objects are myths; but champions of the dogma of the ghost in the machine tend to argue that the imputed objects of consciousness and introspection cannot be myths, since we are conscious of them and can introspectively observe them. The reality of these objects is guaranteed by the venerable credentials of these supposed ways of finding them.

In this chapter, then, I try to show that the official theories of consciousness and introspection are logical muddles. But I am not, of course, trying to establish that we do not or cannot know what there is to know about ourselves. On the contrary, I shall try to show how we attain such knowledge, but only after I have proved that this knowledge is not attained by consciousness or introspection, as these supposed Privileged Accesses are normally described. Lest any reader feels despondency at the thought of being deprived of his twofold Privileged Access to his supposed inner self, I may add the consolatory undertaking that on the account of self-knowledge that I shall give, knowledge of what there is to be known about other people is restored to approximate parity with self-knowledge. The sorts of things that I can find out about myself are the same as the sorts of things that I can find out about other people, and the methods of finding them out are much the same. A residual difference in the supplies of the requisite data makes some differences in degree between what I can know about myself and what I can know about you, but these differences are not all in favour of self-knowledge. In certain quite important respects it is easier for me to find out what I want to know about you than it is for me to find out the same sorts of things about myself. In certain other important respects it is harder. But in principle, as distinct from practice, John Doe's ways of finding out about John Doe are the same as John Doe's ways of finding out about Richard Roe. To drop the hope of Privileged Access is also to drop the fear of epistemological isolationism; we lose the bitters with the sweets of Solipsism.

## (2) *Consciousness.*

Before starting to discuss the philosophers' concept or concepts of consciousness, it is advisable to consider some ways in which the words 'conscious' and 'consciousness' are used, when uncommitted to special theories, in ordinary life.

(a) People often speak in this way; they say, 'I was conscious that the furniture had been rearranged', or, 'I was conscious that he was less friendly than usual'. In such contexts the word 'conscious' is used instead of words like 'found out', 'realised' and 'discovered' to indicate a certain noteworthy nebulousness and consequent inarticulateness of the apprehension. The furniture looked different somehow, but the observer could not say what the differences were; or the man's attitude was unaccommodating in a number of ways, but the speaker could not enumerate or specify them. Though there are philosophically interesting problems about vagueness as well as about the inexpressibility of the very nebulous, this use of 'conscious' does not entail the existence of any special faculties, methods, or channels of apprehension. What we are conscious of, in this sense, may be a physical fact, or a fact about someone else's state of mind.

(b) People often use 'conscious' and 'self-conscious' in describing the embarrassment exhibited by persons, especially youthful persons, who are anxious about the opinions held by others of their qualities of character or intellect. Shyness and affectation are ways in which self-consciousness, in this sense, is commonly exhibited.

(c) 'Self-conscious' is sometimes used in a more general sense to indicate that someone has reached the stage of paying heed to his own qualities of character or intellect, irrespective of whether or not he is embarrassed about other people's estimations of them. When a boy begins to notice that he is fonder of arithmetic, or less homesick, than are most of his acquaintances he is beginning to be self-conscious, in this enlarged sense.

Self-consciousness, in this enlarged sense is, of course, of primary importance for the conduct of life, and the concept of it is therefore of importance for Ethics; but its ingenuous use entails no special doctrines about how a person makes and checks his estimates of his own qualities of character and intellect, or how he compares them with those of his acquaintances.

The Freudian idioms of the 'Unconscious' and the 'Subconscious' are closely connected with this use of 'conscious'; for at least part of what is meant by describing jealousy, phobias or erotic impulses as 'unconscious' is that the victim of them not only does not recognise their strength, or even existence, in himself, but in a certain way *will* not recognise them. He shirks a part of the task of appreciating what sort of a person he is, or else he systematically biases his appreciations. The epistemological question how a person makes his estimates or mis-estimates of his own dispositions is not, or need not be, begged by the Freudian account of the aetiology, diagnosis, prognosis and cure of the tendencies to shirk and bias such estimates.

(*d*) Quite different from the foregoing uses of 'conscious', 'self-conscious' and 'unconscious', is the use in which a numbed or anaesthetised person is said to have lost consciousness from his feet up to his knees. In this use 'conscious' means 'sensitive' or 'sentient' and 'unconscious' means anaesthetised or insensitive. We say that a person has lost consciousness when he had ceased to be sensitive to any slaps, noises, pricks or smells.

(*e*) Different from, though closely connected with this last use, there is the sense in which a person can be said to be unconscious of a sensation, when he pays no heed to it. A walker engaged in a heated dispute may be unconscious, in this sense, of the sensations in his blistered heel, and the reader of these words was, when he began this sentence, probably unconscious of the muscular and skin sensations in the back of his neck, or in his left knee. A person may also be unconscious or unaware that he is frowning, beating time to the music, or muttering.

'Conscious' in this sense means 'heeding'; and it makes sense to say that a sensation is hardly noticed even when the sensation is moderately acute, namely when the victim's attention is fixed very strongly on something else. Conversely, a person may pay sharp heed to very faint sensations; when, for instance, he is scared of appendicitis, he will be acutely conscious, in this sense, of stomachic twinges which are not at all acute. In this sense, too, a person may be keenly conscious, hardly conscious, or quite unconscious, of feelings like twinges of anxiety, or qualms of doubt.

The fact that a person takes heed of his organic sensations and feelings does not entail that he is exempt from error about them. He can make mistakes about their causes and he can make mistakes about their locations. Furthermore, he can make mistakes about whether they are real or fancied, as hypochondriacs do. 'Heeding' does not denote a peculiar conduit of cognitive certainties.

Philosophers, chiefly since Descartes, have in their theories of knowledge and conduct operated with a concept of consciousness which has relatively little affinity with any of the concepts described above. Working with the notion of the mind as a second theatre, the episodes enacted in which enjoy the supposed status of 'the mental' and correspondingly lack the supposed status of 'the physical', thinkers of many sorts have laid it down as the cardinal positive property of these episodes that, when they occur, they occur consciously. The states and operations of a mind are states and operations of which it is necessarily aware, in some sense of 'aware', and this awareness is incapable of being delusive. The things that a mind does or experiences are self-intimating, and this is supposed to be a feature which characterises these acts and feelings not just sometimes but always. It is part of the definition of their being mental that their occurrence entails that they are self-intimating. If I think, hope, remember, will, regret, hear a noise, or feel a pain, I must, *ipso facto*, know that I do so. Even if I dream that I see a dragon, I must be apprised of my dragon-seeing, though, it is often conceded, I may not know that I am dreaming.

It is naturally difficult, if one denies the existence of the second theatre, to elucidate what is meant by describing the episodes which are supposed to take place in it as self-intimating. But some points are clear enough. It is not supposed that when I am wondering, say, what is the answer to a puzzle and am *ipso facto* consciously doing so, that I am synchronously performing two acts of attention, one to the puzzle and the other to my wondering about it. Nor, to generalise this point, is it supposed that my act of wondering and its self-intimation to me are two distinct acts or processes indissolubly welded together. Rather, to relapse perforce into simile, it is supposed that mental processes are phosphorescent, like tropical sea-water, which makes itself visible by the light which it itself emits. Or, to use another simile, mental processes are 'overheard' by the mind whose processes they are, somewhat as a speaker overhears the words he is himself uttering.

When the epistemologists' concept of consciousness first became popular, it seems to have been in part a transformed application of the Protestant notion of conscience. The Protestants had to hold that a man could know the moral state of his soul and the wishes of God without the aid of confessors and scholars; they spoke therefore of the God-given 'light' of private conscience. When Galileo's and Descartes' representations of the mechanical world seemed to require that minds should be salved from mechanism by being represented as constituting a duplicate world, the need was felt to explain how the contents of this ghostly world could be ascertained, again without the help of schooling, but also without the help of sense perception. The metaphor of 'light' seemed peculiarly appropriate, since Galilean science dealt so largely with the optically discovered world. 'Consciousness' was imported to play in the mental world the part played by light in the mechanical world. In this metaphorical sense, the contents of the mental world were thought of as being self-luminous or refulgent.

This model was employed again by Locke when he described the deliberate observational scrutiny which a mind can from time to time turn upon its current states and processes. He called this supposed inner perception 'reflexion' (our 'introspection'), borrowing the word 'reflexion' from the familiar optical phenomenon of the reflections of faces in mirrors. The mind can 'see' or 'look at' its own operations in the 'light' given off by themselves. The myth of consciousness is a piece of para-optics.

These similes of 'over-hearing', 'phosphorescence' or 'self-luminousness' suggest another distinction which needs to be made. It is certainly true that when I do, feel or witness something, I usually could and frequently do pay swift retrospective heed to what I have just done, felt or witnessed. I keep, much of the time, some sort of log or score of what occupies me, in such a way that, if asked what I had just been hearing or picturing or saying, I could usually give a correct answer. Of course, I cannot always be actually harking back to the immediate past; or else, within a few seconds of being called in the morning, I should be recalling that I had just been recalling that I had just been recalling . . . hearing the knock on the door; one event would generate an endless series of recollections of recollections . . . of it, leaving no room for me to pay heed to any subsequent happening. There is, however, a proper sense in which I can be said generally to know what has just been engaging my notice or half-notice, namely that I generally could give a memory report of it, if there was occasion to do so. This does not exclude the possibility that I might sometimes give a misreport, for even short-term reminiscence is not exempt from carelessness or bias.

The point of mentioning this fact that we generally could, if required, report what had just been engaging our notice is that consciousness, as the prevalent view describes it, differs from this log-keeping in one or two important respects. First, according to the theory, mental processes are conscious, not in the sense that we do or could report on them *post mortem*, but in the sense that their intimations of their own occurrences are properties of those occurrences and so are not posterior to them. The supposed deliverances of consciousness, if verbally expressible at all, would be expressed in the present, not in the past tense. Next, it is supposed that in being conscious of my present mental states and acts I know what I am experiencing and doing in a non-dispositional sense of 'know'; that is to say, it is not merely the case that I could, if occasion demanded, tell myself or you what I am experiencing and doing, but that I am actively cognisant of it. Though a double act of attention does not occur, yet when I discover that my watch has stopped, I am synchronously discovering that I am discovering that my watch has stopped; a truth about myself is flashed or shone upon me at the same moment as a truth about my watch is ascertained by me.

I shall argue that consciousness, as so described, is a myth and shall probably therefore be construed as arguing that mental processes are, in some mortifying sense, unconscious, perhaps in the sort of way in which I often cannot tell of my own habitual and reflex movements. To safeguard against this misinterpretation I say quite summarily first, that we do usually know what we are about, but that no phosphorescence-story is required to explain how we are apprised of it; second, that knowing what we are about does not entail an incessant actual monitoring or scrutiny of our doings and feelings, but only the propensity *inter alia* to avow them, when we are in the mood to do so; and, third, that the fact that we generally know what we are about does not entail our coming across any happenings of ghostly status.

The radical objection to the theory that minds must know what they are about, because mental happenings are by definition conscious, or metaphorically self-luminous, is that there are no such happenings; there are no occurrences taking place in a second-status world, since there is no such status and no such world and consequently no need for special modes of acquainting ourselves with the denizens of such a world. But there are also other objections which do not depend for their acceptance upon the rejection of the dogma of the ghost in the machine.

First, and this is not intended to be more than a persuasive argument, no one who is uncommitted to a philosophical theory ever tries to vindicate any of his assertions of fact by saying that he found it out 'from consciousness', or 'as a direct deliverance of consciousness', or 'from immediate awareness'. He will back up some of his assertions of fact by saying that he himself sees, hears, feels, smells or tastes so and so; he will back up other such statements, somewhat more tentatively, by saying that he remembers seeing, hearing, feeling, smelling or tasting it. But if asked whether he really knows, believes, infers, fears, remembers or smells something, he never replies 'Oh yes, certainly I do, for I am conscious and even vividly conscious of doing so'. Yet just such a reply should, according to the doctrine, be his final appeal.

Next, it is supposed that my being conscious of my mental states and operations either is my knowing them, or is the necessary and sufficient ground for my doing so. But to say this is to abuse the logic and even the grammar of the verb 'to know'. It is nonsense to speak of knowing, or not knowing, this clap of thunder or that twinge of pain, this coloured surface or that act of drawing a conclusion or seeing a joke; these are accusatives of the wrong types to follow the verb 'to know'. To know and to be ignorant are to know and not to know that something is the case, for example that that rumble is a clap of thunder or that that coloured surface is a cheese-rind. And this is just the point where the metaphor of light is unhelpful. Good illumination helps us to see cheese-rinds, but we could not say 'the light was too bad for me to know the cheese-rind', since knowing is not the same sort of thing as looking at, and what is known is not the same sort of thing as what is illuminated. True, we can say 'owing to the darkness I could not recognise what I saw for a cheese-rind', but again recognising what I see is not another optical performance. We do not ask for one torch to help us to see and another to help us to recognise what we see. So even if there were some analogy between a thing's being illuminated and a mental process's being conscious, it would not follow that the owner of the process would recognise that process for what it was. It might conceivably explain how mental processes were discernible but it could not possibly explain how we ascertain truths and avoid or correct mistakes about them.

Next, there is no contradiction in asserting that someone might fail to recognise his frame of mind for what it is; indeed, it is notorious that people constantly do so. They mistakenly suppose themselves to know things which are actually false; they deceive themselves about their own motives; they are surprised to notice the clock stopping ticking, without their having, as they think, been aware that it had been ticking; they do not know that they are dreaming, when they are dreaming, and sometimes they are not sure that they are not dreaming, when they are awake; and they deny, in good faith, that they are irritated or excited, when they are flustered in one or other of those ways. If consciousness was what it is described as being, it would be logically impossible for such failures and mistakes in recognition to take place.

Finally, even though the self-intimation supposed to be inherent in any mental state or process is not described as requiring a separate act of attention, or as constituting a separate cognitive operation, still what I am conscious of in a process of inferring, say, is different from what the inferring is an apprehension of. My consciousness is of a process of inferring, but my inferring is, perhaps, of a geometrical conclusion from geometrical premisses. The verbal expression of my inference might be, 'because this is an equilateral triangle, therefore each angle is 60 degrees', but the verbal expression of what I am conscious of might be 'Here I am deducing such and such from so and so'. But, if so, then it would seem to make sense to ask whether, according to the doctrine, I am not also conscious of being conscious of inferring, that is, in a position to say 'Here I am spotting the fact that here I am deducing such and such from so and so'. And then there would be no stopping-place; there would have to be an infinite number of onion-skins of consciousness embedding any mental state or process whatsoever. If this conclusion is rejected, then it will have to be allowed that some elements in mental processes are not themselves things we can be conscious of, namely those elements which constitute the supposed outermost self-intimations of mental processes; and then 'conscious' could no longer be retained as part of the definition of 'mental'.

The argument, then, that mental events are authentic, because the deliverances of consciousness are direct and unimpeachable testimony to their existence, must be rejected. So must the partly parallel argument from the findings of introspection.

(3) *Introspection.*

'Introspection' is a term of art and one for which little use is found in the self-descriptions of untheoretical people. More use is found for the adjective 'introspective', which is ordinarily used in an innocuous sense to signify that someone pays more heed than usual to theoretical and practical problems about his own character, abilities, deficiencies and oddities; there is often the extra suggestion that the person is abnormally anxious about these matters.

The technical term 'introspection' has been used to denote a supposed species of perception. It was supposed that much as a person may at a particular moment be listening to a flute, savouring a wine, or regarding a waterfall, so he may be 'regarding', in a non-optical sense, some current mental state or process of his own. The state or process is being deliberately and attentively scrutinised and so can be listed among the objects of his observation. On the other hand, introspection is described as being unlike sense observation in important respects. Things looked at, or listened to, are public objects, in principle observable by any suitably placed observer, whereas only the owner of a mental state or process is supposed to be able introspectively to scrutinise it. Sense perception, again, involves the functioning of bodily organs, such as the eyes, the ears, or the tongue, whereas introspection involves the functioning of no bodily organ. Lastly, sense perception is never exempt from the possibility of dullness or even of illusion, whereas, anyhow according to the bolder theories, a person's power of observing his mental processes is always perfect; he may not have learned how to exploit his power, or how to arrange or discriminate its findings, but he is immune from any counterparts to deafness, astigmatism, colour-blindness, dazzle or *muscae volitantes*. Inner perception, on these theories, sets a standard of veridical perception, which sense perception can never emulate.

The findings of introspection are reputed to differ in one way at least from the supposed deliverances of consciousness; introspection is an attentive operation and one which is only occasionally performed, whereas consciousness is supposed to be a constant element of all mental processes and one of which the revelations do not require to be receipted in special acts of attention. Moreover we introspect with the intention of finding the answers to particular problems, whereas we are conscious, whether we wish it or not; everyone is constantly conscious, while awake, but only those people introspect who are from time to time interested in what is going on in their minds.

It would be admitted that only people with a special training ever speak of 'introspecting', but in such phrases as 'he caught himself wondering how to do so and so', or 'when I catch myself getting into a panic, I do such and such', the plain man is expressing at least part of what is meant by the word.

Now supposing, (which it is the negative object of this book to deny,) that there did exist events of the postulated ghostly status, there would still be objections to the initially plausible assumption that there also exists a species of perception capable of having any of these events for its proprietary objects. For one thing, the occurrence of such an act of inner perception would require that the observer could attend to two things at the same time. He would, for example, be both resolving to get up early and concomitantly observing his act of resolving; attending to the programme of rising betimes and perceptually attending to his attending to this programme. This objection is not, perhaps, logically fatal, since it might be argued that some people can, anyhow after practice, combine attention to the control of a car with attention to the conversation. The fact that we speak of undivided attention suggests that the division of attention is a possibility, though some people would describe the division of attention as a rapid to-and-fro switch of attention, rather than as a synchronous distribution of it. But many people who begin by being confident that they do introspect, as introspection is officially described, become dubious that they do so, when they are satisfied that they would have to be attending twice at once in order to do it. They are more sure that they do not attend twice at once than that they do introspect.

However, even if it is claimed that in introspecting we are attending twice at once, it will be allowed that there is some limit to the number of possible synchronous acts of attention, and from this it follows that there must be some mental processes which are unintrospectible, namely those introspections which incorporate the maximum possible number of synchronous acts of attention. The question would then arise for the holders of the theory how these acts would be found occurring, since if this knowledge was not introspectively got, it would follow that a person's knowledge of his own mental processes could not always be based on introspection. But if this knowledge does not always rest on introspection, it is open to question whether it ever does. This objection might be countered by appeal to the other form of Privileged Access; we know that we introspect not by introspecting on our introspections, but from the direct deliverances of consciousness. To the guests of Charybdis, Scylla appears the more hospitable resort.

When psychologists were less cautious than they have since become, they used to maintain that introspection was the main source of empirical information about the workings of minds. They were not unnaturally embarrassed to discover that the empirical facts reported by one psychologist sometimes conflicted with those reported by another. They reproached one another, often justly, with having professed to find by introspection just those mental phenomena which their preconceived theories had led them to expect to find. There still occur disputes which should be finally soluble by introspection, if the joint theories of the inner life and inner perception were true. Theorists dispute, for example, whether there are activities of conscience distinct from those of intellect and distinct from habitual deferences to taboos. Why do they not look and see? Or, if they do so, why do their reports not tally? Again, many people who theorise about human conduct declare that there occur certain processes *sui generis* answering to the description of 'volitions'; I have argued that there are no such processes. Why do we argue about the existence of these processes, when the question ought to be as easily decidable as the question whether or not there is a smell of onions in the larder?

There is one last objection to be made against the claims for introspection, that made by Hume. There are some states of mind which cannot be coolly scrutinised, since the fact that we are in those states involves that we are not cool, or the fact that we are cool involves that we are not in those states. No one could introspectively scrutinise the state of panic or fury, since the dispassionateness exercised in scientific observation is, by the definition of 'panic' and 'fury', not the state of mind of the victim of those turbulences. Similarly, since a convulsion of merriment is not the state of mind of the sober experimentalist, the enjoyment of a joke is also not an introspectible happening. States of mind such as these more or less violent agitations can be examined only in retrospect. Yet nothing disastrous follows from this restriction. We are not shorter of information about panic or amusement than about other states of mind. If retrospection can give us the data we need for our knowledge of some states of mind, there is no reason why it should not do so for all. And this is just what seems to be suggested by the popular phrase 'to catch oneself doing so and so'. We catch, as we pursue and overtake, what is already running away from us. I catch myself daydreaming about a mountain walk after, perhaps very shortly after, I have begun the daydream; or I catch myself humming a particular air only when the first few notes have already been hummed. Retrospection, prompt or delayed, is a genuine process and one which is exempt from the troubles ensuing from the assumption of multiply divided attention; it is also exempt from the troubles ensuing from the assumption that violent agitations could be the objects of cool, contemporary scrutiny.

Part, then, of what people have in mind, when they speak familiarly of introspecting, is this authentic process of retrospection. But there is nothing intrinsically ghostly about the objects of retrospection. In the same way that I can catch myself daydreaming, I can catch myself scratching; in the same way that I can catch myself engaged in a piece of silent soliloquy, I can catch myself saying something aloud.

It is true and important that what I recall is always something expressible in the form 'myself doing so and so'. I recall not a clap of thunder but hearing the clap of thunder; or I catch myself swearing, but I do not, in the same sense, catch you swearing. The objects of my retrospections are items in my autobiography. But although personal, they need not be, though they can be, private or silent items of that autobiography. I can recollect seeing things just as much as I can recollect imagining things, my overt acts just as well as my sensations. I can report the calculations that I have been doing in my head, but I can also report the calculations that I have been doing on the blotter.

Retrospection will carry some of the load of which introspection has been nominated for the porter. But it will not carry all of it and in particular it will not carry many of the philosophically precious or fragile parcels. Aside from the fact that even prompt recollection is subject both to evaporations and to dilutions, however accurately I may recollect an action or feeling, I may still fail to recognise its nature. Whether yesterday's twinge which I recall to-day was a pang of genuine compassion or a twinge of guilt, need not be any the more obvious to me for the fact that my memory of it is vivid. Chronicles are not explanatory of what they record.

The fact that retrospection is autobiographical does not imply that it gives us a Privileged Access to facts of a special status. But of course it does give us a mass of data contributory to our appreciations of our own conduct and qualities of mind. A diary is not a chronicle of ghostly episodes, but it is a valuable source of information about the diarist's character, wits and career.

## (4) Self-Knowledge without Privileged Access.

It has been argued from a number of directions that when we speak of a person's mind, we are not speaking of a second theatre of special-status incidents, but of certain ways in which some of the incidents of his one life are ordered. His life is not a double series of events taking place in two different kinds of stuff; it is one concatenation of events, the differences between some and other classes of which largely consist in the applicability or inapplicability to them of logically different types of law-propositions and law-like propositions. Assertions about a person's mind are therefore assertions of special sorts about that person. So questions about the relations between a person and his mind, like those about the relations between a person's body and his mind are improper questions. They are improper in much the same way as is the question, 'What transactions go on between the House of Commons and the British Constitution?'

It follows that it is a logical solecism to speak, as theorists often do, of someone's mind knowing this, or choosing that. The person himself knows this and chooses that, though the fact that he does so can, if desired, be classified as a mental fact about that person. In partly the same way it is improper to speak of my eyes seeing this, or my nose smelling that; we should say, rather, that I see this, or I smell that, and that these assertions carry with them certain facts about my eyes and nose. But the analogy is not exact, for while my eyes and nose are organs of sense, 'my mind' does not stand for another organ. It signifies my ability and proneness to do certain sorts of things and not some piece of personal apparatus without which I could or would not do them. Similarly the British Constitution is not another British political institution functioning alongside of the Civil Service, the Judiciary, the Established Church, the Houses of Parliament and the Royal Family. Nor is it the sum of these institutions, or a liaison-staff between them. We can say that Great Britain has gone to the polls; but we cannot say that the British Constitution has gone to the polls, though the fact that Great Britain has gone to the polls might be described as a constitutional fact about Great Britain.

Actually, though it is not always convenient to avoid the practice, there is a considerable logical hazard in using the nouns 'mind' and 'minds' at all. The idiom makes it too easy to construct logically improper conjunctions, disjunctions and cause-effect propositions such as 'so and so took place not in my body but in my mind', 'my mind made my hand write', 'a person's body and mind interact upon each other' and so on. Where logical candour is required from us, we ought to follow the example set by novelists, biographers and diarists, who speak only of persons doing and undergoing things.

The questions 'What knowledge can a person get of the workings of his own mind?' and 'How does he get it?' by their very wording suggest absurd answers. They suggest that, for a person to know that he is lazy, or has done a sum carefully, he must have taken a peep into a windowless chamber, illuminated by a very peculiar sort of light, and one to which only he has access. And when the question is construed in this sort of way, the parallel questions, 'What knowledge can one person get of the workings of another mind?' and 'How does he get it?' by their very wording seem to preclude any answer at all; for they suggest that one person could only know that another person was lazy, or had done a sum carefully, by peering into another secret chamber to which, *ex hypothesi*, he has no access.

In fact the problem is not one of this sort. It is simply the methodological question, how we establish, and how we apply, certain sorts of law-like propositions about the overt and the silent behaviour of persons. I come to appreciate the skill and tactics of a chess-player by watching him and others playing chess, and I learn that a certain pupil of mine is lazy, ambitious and witty by following his work, noticing his excuses, listening to his conversation and comparing his performances with those of others. Nor does it make any important difference if I happen myself to be that pupil. I can indeed then listen to more of his conversations, as I am the addressee of his unspoken soliloquies; I notice more of his excuses, as I am never absent, when they are made. On the other hand, my comparison of his performances with those of others is more difficult, since the examiner is himself taking the examination, which makes neutrality hard to preserve and precludes the demeanour of the candidate, when under interrogation, from being in good view.

To repeat a point previously made, the question is not the envelope-question 'How do I discover that I or you have a mind?' but the range of specific questions of the pattern, 'How do I discover that I am more unselfish than you; that I can do long division well, but differential equations only badly; that you suffer from certain phobias and tend to shirk facing certain sorts of facts; that I am more easily irritated than most people but less subject to panic, vertigo, or morbid conscientiousness?' Besides such pure dispositional questions there is also the range of particular performance questions and occurrence questions of the patterns, 'How do I find out that I saw the joke and that you did not; that your action took more courage than mine; that the service I rendered to you was rendered from a sense of duty and not from expectation of kudos; that, though I did not fully understand what was said at the time, I did fully understand it, when I went over it in my head afterwards, while you understood it perfectly from the start; that I was feeling homesick yesterday?' Questions of these sorts offer no mysteries; we know quite well how to set to work to find out the answers to them; and though often we cannot finally solve them and may have to stop short at mere conjecture, yet, even so, we have no doubt what sorts of information would satisfy our requirements, if we could get it; and we know what it would be like to get it. For example, after listening to an argument, you aver that you understand it perfectly; but you may be deceiving yourself, or trying to deceive me. If we then part for a day or two, I am no longer in a position to test whether or not you did understand it perfectly. But still I know what tests would have settled the point. If you had put the argument into your own words, or translated it into French; if you had invented appropriate concrete illustrations of the generalisations and abstractions in the argument; if you had stood up to cross-questioning; if you had correctly drawn further consequences from different stages of the argument and indicated points where the theory was inconsistent with other theories; if you had inferred correctly from the nature of the argument to the qualities of intellect and character of its author and predicted accurately the subsequent development of his theory, then I should have required no further evidence that you understood it perfectly. And exactly the same sorts of tests would satisfy me that I had understood it perfectly; the sole differences would be that I should probably not have voiced aloud the expressions of my deductions, illustrations, etc., but told them to myself more perfunctorily in silent soliloquy; and I should probably have been more easily satisfied of the completeness of my understanding than I was of yours.

In short it is part of the *meaning* of 'you understood it' that you could have done so and so and would have done it, if such and such, and the *test* of whether you understood it is a range of performances satisfying the apodoses of these general hypothetical statements. It should be noticed, on the one hand, that there is no single nuclear performance, overt or in your head, which would determine that you had understood the argument. Even if you claimed that you had experienced a flash or click of comprehension and had actually done so, you would still withdraw your other claim to have understood the argument, if you found that you could not paraphrase it, illustrate, expand or recast it; and you would allow someone else to have understood it who could meet all examination-questions about it, but reported no click of comprehension. It should also be noticed, on the other hand, that though there is no way of specifying how many or what sub-tests must be satisfied for a person to qualify as having perfectly understood the argument, this does not imply that no finite set of sub-tests is ever enough. To settle whether a boy can do long division, we do not require him to try out his hand on a million, a thousand, or even a hundred different problems in long division. We should not be quite satisfied after one success, but we should not remain dissatisfied after twenty, provided that they were judiciously variegated and that he had not done them before. A good teacher, who not only recorded the boy's correct and incorrect solutions, but also watched his procedure in reaching them, would be satisfied much sooner, and he would be satisfied sooner still if he got the boy to describe and justify the constituent operations that he performed, though of course many boys can do long division sums who cannot describe or justify the operations performed in doing them.

I discover my or your motives in much, though not quite the same way as I discover my or your abilities. The big practical difference is that I cannot put the subject through his paces in my inquiries into his inclinations as I can in my inquiries into his competences. To discover how conceited or patriotic you are, I must still observe your conduct, remarks, demeanour and tones of voice, but I cannot subject you to examination-tests or experiments which you recognise as such. You would have a special motive for responding to such experiments in a particular way. From mere conceit, perhaps, you would try to behave self-effacingly, or from mere modesty you might try to behave conceitedly. None the less, ordinary day to day observation normally serves swiftly to settle such questions. To be conceited is to tend to boast of one's own excellences, to pity or ridicule the deficiencies of others, to day-dream about imaginary triumphs, to reminisce about actual triumphs, to weary quickly of conversations which reflect un-favourably upon oneself, to lavish one's society upon distinguished persons and to economise in association with the undistinguished. The tests of whether a person is conceited are the actions he takes and the reactions he manifests in such circumstances. Not many anecdotes, sneers or sycophancies are required from the subject for the ordinary observer to make up his mind, unless the candidate and the examiner happen to be identical.

The ascertainment of a person's mental capacities and propensities is an inductive process, an induction to law-like propositions from observed actions and reactions. Having ascertained these long-term qualities, we explain a particular action or reaction by applying the result of such an induction to the new specimen, save where open avowals let us know the explanation without research. These inductions are not, of course, carried out under laboratory conditions, or with any statistical apparatus, any more than is the shepherd's weather-lore, or the general practitioner's understanding of a particular patient's constitution. But they are ordinarily reliable enough. It is a truism to say that the appreciations of character and the explanations of conduct given by critical, unprejudiced and humane observers, who have had a lot of experience and take a lot of interest, tend to be both swift and reliable; those of inferior judges tend to be slower and less reliable. Similarly the marks awarded by practised and keen examiners who know their subject well and are reasonably sympathetic towards the candidates tend to be about right; those of inferior examiners tend to scatter more widely from the proper order. The point of these truisms is to remind us that in real life we are quite familiar with the techniques of assessing persons and accounting for their actions, though according to the standard theory no such techniques could exist.

There is one class of persons whose qualities and frames of mind are specially difficult to appreciate, namely persons who simulate qualities which they lack and dissimulate qualities which they possess. I refer to hypocrites and charlatans, the people who pretend to motives and moods and the people who pretend to abilities; that is, to most of us in some stretches of our lives and to some of us in most stretches of our lives. It is always possible to pretend to motives and abilities other than one's real ones, or to pretend to strengths of motives and levels of ability other than their real strengths and levels. The theatre could not exist, if it was not possible to make such pretences and to make them efficiently. It is, moreover, always possible for a person to take others or himself in by acting a part (as the spectators are not taken in at the theatre, since they have paid to see people act who advertise themselves as actors). At first sight it seems, then, that no one can ever have proper knowledge of his own mind, or of the minds of others, since there is no kind of observable behaviour of which we can say, 'no one could possibly be putting that on'. Certainly we do not ordinarily feel practically embarrassed by this possibility, but some people feel a theoretical embarrassment, since if any particular action or reaction might be a piece of shamming, might not every action or reaction be a piece of shamming? Might not all our appreciations of the conduct of others and of ourselves be uniformly deluded? People sometimes feel an analogous embarrassment about sense perception, for since there is nothing to prevent any particular sensible appearance from being an illusion, there seems to be nothing to prevent all of them from being illusions.

However, the menace of universal shamming is an empty menace. We know what shamming is. It is deliberately behaving in ways in which other people behave who are not shamming. To simulate contrition is to put on gestures, accents, words and deeds like those of people who are contrite. Both the hypocrite and the people whom he deceives must therefore know what it is like for someone to be contrite and not merely to be pretending to be contrite. If we were not usually correct in sizing up contrite people as contrite, we could not be gulled into thinking that the hypocrite was really contrite. Furthermore, we know what it is like to be hypocritical, namely to try to appear actuated by a motive other than one's real motive. We know the sorts of tricks the hypocrite must use. We possess, though we cannot always apply, the criteria by which to judge whether these tricks are being used or not and whether they are being used cleverly or stupidly. So sometimes we can, and sometimes we cannot, detect hypocrisies; but even when we cannot, we know what sorts of extra clues, if we could secure them, would betray the hypocrite. We should, for example, like to see how he would act if told that the cause for which he professed devotion required half his fortune or his life. All that we need, though we often cannot get it, is an *experimentum crucis*, just as the doctor often needs but cannot get an *experimentum crucis* to decide between two diagnoses. To establish hypocrisy and charlatanry is an inductive task which differs from the ordinary inductive tasks of assessing motives and capacities only in being a second order induction. It is trying to discover whether someone is trying to model his actions on what he and we have inductively discovered to be the behaviour of people who are not shamming. When we and the hypocrite have learned how hypocrisy is exposed, we might have to cope with the second order hypocrite, the double-bluffer who has learnt how not to act like a first order hypocrite. There is no mystery about shamming, though it is a tautology to say that skilful shamming is hard to detect and that successful shamming is undetected.

So far we have been considering chiefly those brands of self-knowledge and the knowledge of others which consist in the more or less judicial assessment of long-term propensities and capacities, together with the application of those assessments in explanations of particular episodes. We have been considering how we interpret or understand courses of conduct. But there remains another sense of 'know' in which a person is commonly said to know what he is at this moment doing, thinking, feeling, etc., a sense which is nearer to what the phosphorescence-theory of consciousness tried, but failed, to describe. To bring out the force of this sense of 'know', we should consider first certain kinds of situations in which a person admits that he did not know at the time what he was doing, although what he was doing was not an automatism but an intelligent operation. A person trying to solve a cross-word puzzle is confronted by an anagram; after a short or long pause he gets the answer, but denies that he was aware of taking any specifiable steps, or following any specifiable method, to get it. He may even say that he was thinking, and knew that he was thinking, about some other part of the puzzle. He is in some degree surprised to find that he has got the answer to the anagram, for he had not been aware of going through any shuffling and reshuffling operations, or considering any of the unsuccessful rearrangements of the letters. Yet his solution is correct and he may repeat his success several times in the course of solving the whole puzzle. Our impromptu witticisms often take us by surprise in the same sort of way.

Now usually we are not surprised to catch ourselves having whistled, planned or imagined something and we say, if asked, that we are not surprised, because we knew we were doing these things, while we were doing them. What sort of a rider are we adding when we say 'I did so and so and knew at the time that I was doing it'? The tempting reply is to say 'Well, while I was doing the thing, it must have flashed or dawned upon me that I was doing it; or, if the action was a protracted one, it must have kept on flashing or dawning on me that I was doing the thing'. Yet these metaphors of flashing and dawning leave us uneasy, for we do not ordinarily recall any such occurrences, even when we are quite sure that we knew what we were doing, while we were doing it. Moreover, if there had occurred any such flashings or dawnings, the same question would arise once more. Did you know that you were getting these lightings-up, when they were on, and that you were not getting them, when they were not on? Did it flash on you that it was flashing on you that you were whistling? Or is your knowing that something is going on not always a matter of something flashing on you?

When a person is described as not being surprised when something takes place, he can also be described as having expected it or having been prepared for it. But we use 'expect' in at least two markedly different ways. Sometimes we mean that at a particular moment he considered and accepted the proposition that the event would, or would probably, take place; in this sense, there would be an answer to the question, 'Exactly when did you make this forecast?' But sometimes we mean that whether or not he ever went through the process of making such a forecast, he was continuously prepared or ready for the thing to happen. The gardener who, in this sense, expects rain need not be repeatedly switching his attention from gardening tasks to silent or vocal prognostications of rain; he just leaves the watering-can in the tool-shed, keeps his coat handy, beds out more seedlings, and so on. He anticipates the rain not by delivering occasional or incessant verbal presages, but by gardening appropriately. All the afternoon he is ready and making ready for rain. It may be objected, 'Oh, but he must be constantly considering the proposition that it will rain. That is what makes him keep his coat handy and the watering-pot in the shed.' But the answer to this is easy. 'Tell me at which particular moments he told himself or others that it was going to rain, and then tell me whether he was or was not expecting rain in the intervals between those prognostications.' He prognosticated rain at this, that and the other moment, because he was all the time expecting rain; and he kept his coat handy and the watering-can in the shed for the same reason.

In this sense 'expect' is used to signify not an occurrence but a standing condition or frame of mind. He is all the afternoon in the frame of mind to say certain things in the future tense in certain contingencies, as well as to conduct his gardening-operations in certain ways, to keep his coat handy and so on. To expect, in this sense, is to be prepared; and the giving of warnings, private or public, is only one sort of precautionary measure among others. So when we say that the gardener was not taken by surprise by the rain, or that he was sure that it was going to rain, or that he was ready for rain, we are not referring, save *per accidens*, to any internal flashes of foresight, or to any silent or vocal utterances in the future tense. All his afternoon activities, horticultural and verbal, were performed in a rain-expectant frame of mind.

This lesson can be applied to our problem. There are many tasks in which we are from time to time engaged the execution of which requires continued application; doing the second step requires having done the first step. Sometimes the earlier steps stand to the later as means to ends, as we lay the table in order to have a meal. Sometimes the earlier steps stand in some other relation to the later; we do not eat the first course in order to eat the second, or begin to hum a tune in order to finish humming it. Very often an undertaking, though it requires consecutive application, is only artificially divisible into steps or stages, but it still remains significant to say that it might be broken off short, when only about half or about three-quarters accomplished. Now if the agent is carrying out such a serial operation with any degree of heed, he must at any given stage in it have in mind, in some sense, what is to be done next and what has already been done; he must have kept track of where he has got to and he must be expecting, or even intending, to be getting on to the stages after the present stage. This is sometimes expressed by saying that, in anyhow those serial undertakings that are more or less intelligently performed, the agent must have had from the start a plan or programme of what he is to do and he must continuously consult this plan as he progresses. And this does frequently happen. But it cannot always happen, and even when it does happen, this construction and consultation of programmes is not enough to explain the consecutive and methodical prosecution of the undertaking, since constructing and consulting plans are themselves serial operations intelligently and consecutively prosecuted, and it would be absurd to suggest that an infinite series of serial operations must precede the intelligent performance of any serial operation. Nor can intermittent consultation of a plan explain how we know what to be getting on with between the consultations, how we know which items of the plan to consult at different stages in the task, or how we know that what we are now doing is in accordance with the recently consulted plan.

The prime sense in which a person engaged in a non-sudden task has it in mind what is to be done at later stages is that he is ready to perform step three when the occasion requires, namely when step two is completed; and, what goes with this, that he is ready to tell himself or the world what he would have gone on to do, if he had not been prevented. While engaged in any given step, he is prepared for what should or may follow, and when it does follow, he is not surprised. In this sense he may be alive to what he is doing all the time he is doing it, even though his attention is concentrated on his task and is not divided between the task and any contemplations or chroniclings of his prosecution of it.

In other cases, as when he suddenly makes an unpremeditated witticism, he is surprised to find what he has done and would not describe himself as having known what he was doing, while he did it, or even as having been trying to make a joke. The same thing is true of other sudden acts performed on the spur of the moment. The action may well be the right action to have performed, but the agent does not know how he came to perform it, as he was unprepared for it. His being unprepared for it is not the effect or the cause of his not knowing what he was doing; it is the same thing, differently expressed.

Unlike the man who with surprise catches himself making a good impromptu joke, the man who pursues a new argument is ordinarily alive to what he is doing. He may be surprised by the conclusion at which he arrives, but he is not surprised to find himself arriving at a conclusion. His progressive operation of reasoning was a display of his effort to reach one. So he knew what he was then doing, not in the sense that he had to dilute his consideration of his premises with other acts of considering his consideration of them—he need not have had any such side-issues flash or dawn upon him—but in the sense that he was prepared not only for the steps in reasoning that he was to take, but also for a variety of other eventualities, most of which never occurred, such as being asked what he was doing, what justification he had for taking this rather than that line, and so forth. The phosphorescence-theory of consciousness was in part an attempt to construe concepts of frames of mind like 'prepared', 'ready', 'on the *qui vive*', 'bearing in mind', 'would not be surprised', 'expect', 'realise' and 'alive to' as concepts of special internal happenings.

The same sort of account holds good of not-forgetting. When a person engaged in conversation reaches the middle of a sentence, he has ordinarily not forgotten how his sentence began. In some sense he keeps continuous track of what he has already said. Yet it would be absurd to suggest that he accompanies every word that he utters with an internal repetition of all its predecessors. Apart from the physical impossibility of reciting the previous seventeen words in the moment when the eighteenth word is just giving place to the nineteenth, the process of repetition is itself a serial operation, the execution of the later parts of which would again require that its author had kept track of its earlier parts. Not-to-have-forgotten cannot be described in terms of the performance of actual reminiscences; on the contrary, reminiscences are only one kind of exercise of the condition of not-having-forgotten. Bearing in mind is not recalling; it is what makes recalling, among other things, possible.

Thus the intelligent conduct of serial operations does entail that the agent is throughout the progress of the operation *au fait* both with what he has completed and with what remains to do, but it does not entail that the performance of such operations is backed up by any second order performance or process of monitoring the first order performance. Of course an agent can, from time to time, if he is prompted to do so, announce to himself or the world "Hallo, here I am whistling 'Home Sweet Home'." His ability to do so is part of what is meant by saying that he is in that particular frame of mind that we call 'being alive to what he is doing'. But not only is his actually making such announcements not entailed by the fact that he is concentrating on whistling this tune, but his concentration would be broken each time he produced such a commentary.

I have so far illustrated what I mean by a serial performance by such relatively brief operations as whistling a tune, or uttering a sentence. But in a slightly looser and more elastic sense, an entire conversation may be a serial performance; and so may be the conduct of one's work and recreation during a day or a year. Eating porridge is a non-sudden performance, but so is eating breakfast; giving a lecture is a serial performance, but so is giving a course of lectures.

Now in almost the same way as a person may be, in this sense, alive to what he is doing, he may be alive to what someone else is doing. In the serial operation of listening to a sentence or a lecture delivered by someone else, the listener, like the speaker, does not altogether forget, yet nor does he have constantly to recall the earlier parts of the talk, and he is in some degree prepared for the parts still to come, though he does not have to tell himself how he expects the sentence or lecture to go on. Certainly his frame of mind is considerably different from that of the speaker, since the speaker is, sometimes, creative or inventive, while the listener is passive and receptive; the listener may be frequently surprised to find the speaker saying something, while the speaker is only seldom surprised; the listener may find it hard to keep track of the course taken by the sentences and arguments, while the speaker can do this quite easily. While the speaker intends to say certain fairly specific things, his hearer can anticipate only roughly what sorts of topics are going to be discussed.

But the differences are differences of degree, not of kind. The superiority of the speaker's knowledge of what he is doing over that of the listener does not indicate that he has Privileged Access to facts of a type inevitably inaccessible to the listener, but only that he is in a very good position to know what the listener is often in a very poor position to know. The turns taken by a man's conversation do not startle or perplex his wife as much as they had surprised and puzzled his fiancée, nor do close colleagues have to explain themselves to each other as much as they have to explain themselves to their new pupils.

I have, for expository purposes, treated as separate things the way in which an ordinary person is ordinarily alive to what, at a particular moment, he is occupied with and the ways in which judicially minded persons assess the characters and explain the actions of others and of themselves. There are undoubtedly many big differences. To appraise or examine requires special gifts, interests, training, experience, powers of comparison and generalisation, and impartiality; whereas merely to be alive to what one is whistling or where one is walking, is within the capacities of an ordinary child. None the less, the most naive knowledge of what one is doing shades into the most sophisticated appreciations of particular performances, much as the child's interest in the robins on the bird table shades into ornithology. A boy working out an arithmetical problem is alive in the most primitive way to what he is doing; for while he is thinking about numbers (and not about thinking about numbers), he does not forget the earlier stages of his reckoning, he bears in mind the rules of multiplication and he is not surprised to find himself arriving at the solution. But he differs only in degree of alertness, caution and sophistication from the boy who checks his results, from the boy who tries to find out where he has made a mistake, or from the boy who spots and explains the mistakes in the calculations of someone else; this last boy, again, differs only in degree from the co-operative parent, the professional teacher, or the examiner. The boy who is just capable of working out a simple sum is probably not yet able to state precisely what he is doing, or why he takes the steps that he takes; the examiner can evaluate the actual performances of the candidates in a fairly precise and highly formalised system of marks. But here again the inarticulateness of the beginner's knowledge of what he is doing shades by a series of gradations into the examiner's numerical appraisal code.

A person's knowledge about himself and others may be distributed between many roughly distinguishable grades yielding correspondingly numerous roughly distinguishable senses of 'knowledge.' He may be aware that he is whistling 'Tipperary' and not know that he is whistling it in order to give the appearance of a sang-froid which he does not feel. Or, again, he may be aware that he is shamming sang-froid without knowing that the tremors which he is trying to hide derive from the agitation of a guilty conscience. He may know that he has an uneasy conscience and not know that this issues from some specific repression. But in none of the senses in which we ordinarily consider whether a person does or does not know something about himself, is the postulate of a Privileged Access necessary or helpful for the explanation of how he has achieved, or might have achieved, this knowledge. There are respects in which it is easier for me to get such knowledge about myself than to get it about someone else; there are other respects in which it is harder. But these differences of facility do not derive from, or lead to, a difference in kind between a person's knowledge about himself and his knowledge about other people. No metaphysical Iron Curtain exists compelling us to be for ever absolute strangers to one another, though ordinary circumstances, together with some deliberate management, serve to maintain a reasonable aloofness. Similarly no metaphysical looking-glass exists compelling us to be for ever completely disclosed and explained to ourselves, though from the everyday conduct of our sociable and unsociable lives we learn to be reasonably conversant with ourselves.

(5) *Disclosure by Unstudied Talk.*

Our knowledge of other people and of ourselves depends upon our noticing how they and we behave. But there is one tract of human behaviour on which we pre-eminently rely. When the person examined has learned to talk and when he talks in a language well known to us, we use part of his talk as the primary source of our information about him, that part, namely, which is spontaneous, frank and unprepared. It is, of course, notorious that people are frequently reticent and keep things back, instead of letting them out. It is notorious, too, that people are frequently insincere and talk in manners calculated to give false impressions. But the very fact that utterances can be guarded and studied implies that unguarded, unstudied utterance is possible. To be reticent is deliberately to refrain from being open, and to be hypocritical is deliberately to refrain from saying what comes to one's lips, while pretending to say frankly things one does not mean. In a certain sense of 'natural', the natural thing to do is to speak one's mind, and the sophisticated thing to do is to refrain from doing this, or even to pretend to do this, when one is not really doing so. Furthermore, not only is unstudied talk natural or unsophisticated, it is also the normal way of talking. We have to take special pains to keep things back, only because letting them out is our normal response; and we discover the techniques of insincerity only from familiarity with the modes of unforced conversation that are to be simulated. To say this is not to accord ethical laurels to human nature. Unstudied utterance is not honesty or candour. Honesty is a highly sophisticated disposition, for it is the disposition to abstain from insincerity, just as candour is the disposition to abstain from reticence. A person could not be honest or candid who had never known insincerity or reticence, any more than a person could be insincere or reticent who had never known ingenuous and open utterance.

There are other kinds of studied utterance, some of which will have to be discussed at a later stage, that belong not to normal sociable conversations but only to more serious affairs. The physician, the judge, the preacher, the politician, the astronomer and the geometrician mày give their counsels, verdicts, homilies, theories and formulae by word of mouth, but they are then talking not in the sense of 'chatting' but in the sense of 'pronouncing' or 'propounding'. Perhaps they prepare, but at least they weigh, their words. They do not say the first things that come to their lips, for their discourse is disciplined. What they say would, unlike spontaneous chat, generally tolerate being written down and even printed. It is not impromptu or spontaneous, let fall or blurted out, but delivered. Their authors are considering what to say and how to say it, in order to produce precisely the right effect. This sort of talk is literally prosy.

We need to contrast normal unstudied talk both with studied conversational talk and with studied non-conversational talk, for it is the basis of both of them. We use unstudied, conversational talk not only before we learn to converse guardedly and insincerely and before we learn to discourse weightily; we also continue to occupy a good part of our talking day in saying the first things that come to our lips. Camouflage and gravity are only intermittent necessities.

It is not only in our unembarrassed, uncalculated colloquies with others that we say the first things that come to our lips; we do so also in the easy, unbuttoned colloquies that we hold, commonly in silence, with ourselves.

In unstudied chat we talk about whatever we are at the moment chiefly interested in. It is not a rival interest. We talk about the garden from the motive that prompts us to inspect and potter in the garden, namely interest in the garden. We chat about our dinner not because we are not interested in our dinner, but because we are. We may talk about our dinner because we are hungry, just as we eat it because we are hungry; and we cannot easily help talking about the steepness of the hill, for the same reason that we cannot easily help our steps flagging as we climb it. Spontaneous utterance is not a collateral, competing interest, it is an exercise auxiliary to the taking of any interest in anything whatsoever.

A person who is annoyed with a knotted shoe-lace is, if he has learned to talk, also in the mood to use a verbal expression of annoyance with it. He talks about it in a fretful tone of voice. What he says, together with his way of saying it, discloses cr lets us know his frame of mind, just because his unstudied using of that expression is one of the things that he is in the frame of mind to do. To tug fretfully at the shoe-lace might be another. He is sufficiently aggravated by the knot to talk aggravatedly about it.

Unstudied utterances are not, on the one hand, effects of the frames of mind in which they are used, since frames of mind are not incidents; but nor, on the other hand, are they reports about those frames of mind. If the lorry-driver asks urgently, 'Which is the road to London?' he discloses his anxiety to find out, but he does not make an autobiographical or psychological pronouncement about it. He says what he says not from a desire to inform us or himself about himself, but from a desire to get on to the right road to London. Unstudied utterances are not self-comments, though, as we shall shortly see, they constitute our primary evidence for making self-comments, when we come to be interested in making them.

Now many unstudied utterances embody explicit interest phrases, or what I have elsewhere been calling 'avowals', like 'I want', 'I hope', 'I intend', 'I dislike', 'I am depressed', 'I wonder', 'I guess' and 'I feel hungry'; and their grammar makes it tempting to misconstrue all the sentences in which they occur as self-descriptions. But in its primary employment 'I want . . .' is not used to convey information, but to make a request or demand. It is no more meant as a contribution to general knowledge than 'please'. To respond with 'do you?' or 'how do you know?' would be glaringly inappropriate. Nor, in their primary employment, are 'I hate . . .' and 'I intend . . .' used for the purpose of telling the hearer facts about the speaker; or else we should not be surprised to hear them uttered in the cool, informative tones of voice in which we say 'he hates . . .' and 'they intend. . . .' We expect them, on the contrary, to be spoken in a revolted and a resolute tone of voice respectively. They are the utterances of persons in revolted and resolute frames of mind. They are things said in detestation and resolution and not things said in order to advance biographical knowledge about detestations and resolutions.

A person who notices the unstudied utterances of a speaker, who may or may not be himself, is, if his interest in the speaker has the appropriate direction and if he knows the language in which the utterances are made, especially well situated to pass comments upon the qualities and frames of mind of their author. While careful observation of the subject's other behaviour, such as his other overt actions, his hesitations and his tears and laughter, may tell him much, this behaviour is not *ex officio* made easy to witness, or easy to interpret. But speech is *ex officio* made to be heard and made to be construed. Learning to talk is learning to make oneself understood. No sleuth-like powers are required for me to find out from the words and tones of voice of your unstudied talk, or even of my own unstudied talk, the frame of mind of the talker.

When talk is guarded—and often we do not know whether it is so or not, even in the avowals we make to ourselves—sleuth-like qualities do have to be exercised. We now have to infer from what is said and done to what would have been said, if wariness had not been exercised, as well as to the motives of the wariness. Finding out what is on the pages of an open book is a matter of simple reading; finding out what is on the pages of a sealed book requires hypotheses and evidence. But the fact that concealments have to be penetrated does not imply that non-concealments have to be penetrated.

One of the things often signified by 'self-consciousness' is the notice we take of our own unstudied utterances, including our explicit avowals, whether these are spoken aloud, muttered or said in our heads. We eavesdrop on our own voiced utterances and our own silent monologues. In noticing these we are preparing ourselves to do something new, namely to describe the frames of mind which these utterances disclose. But there is nothing intrinsically proprietary about this activity. I can pay heed to what I overhear you saying as well as to what I overhear myself saying, though I cannot overhear your silent colloquies with yourself.

Nor can I read your diary, if you write it in cipher, or keep it under lock and key. Indeed, not only is this sort of self-study the same in kind as the study of the unguarded and later also the guarded utterances of others, but we learn to make this study of our own talk from first taking part in the public discussion of anyone's talk as well as from reading novelists' illustrative deployment of their characters' talk, together with their explanatory descriptions of it.

Critical readers may ask why I have refrained from using the verb 'to think' instead of such trivial verbs as 'talk', 'chat', 'converse' and 'let out', since clearly the utterances which I have been mentioning are, ordinarily, pertinent utterances, the authors of which mean what they say; I have been mentioning significant and intelligible speech and not things like guffaws, babblings or rigmarole. My reasons are two, and are closely connected. First, the utterances I have been considering belong to sociable interchanges of conversation between speakers and hearers, who may be one and the same persons. Their point is a conversational point. Since many of the utterances that constitute a conversation are not in the indicative mood, but are questions, commands, complaints, quips, scoldings, congratulations, etc., we cannot in their case speak of those epistemological darlings the 'thoughts', 'judgments' or 'propositions' expressed by them. Secondly, we tend to reserve the verb 'to think' for the uses of those studied and severely drilled utterances which constitute theories and policies. Now we learn to chat in the nursery, but we have to go to school to learn even the rudiments of theorising. The techniques of theorising are learned in set lessons, while conversational speech is acquired almost entirely by conversing. So the use of sentences, and particularly of certain sorts of indicative sentences, for the special ends of propounding, i.e. providing premises and delivering conclusions, is a belated and sophisticated use, and necessarily comes later than the conversational uses of sentences and phrases. When a theory or a bit of a theory is voiced aloud, instead of being conveyed in its proper milieu of print, we hesitate to call the voicing by the name of 'talk' and we should flatly refuse to call it 'chat' or 'conversation'. It is meant didactically, not sociably. It is a kind of work, whereas unstudied chat is no kind of work, not even easy or agreeable work.

(6) *The Self.*

Not only theorists but also quite unsophisticated people, including young children, find perplexities in the notion of 'I'. Children sometimes puzzle their heads with such questions as, 'What would it be like if I became you and you became me?' and 'Where was I before I began?' Theologians have been exercised over the question 'What is it in an individual which is saved or damned?', and philosophers have speculated whether 'I' denotes a peculiar and separate substance and in what consists my indivisible and continuing identity. Not all such puzzles arise from the unwitting adoption of the para-mechanical hypothesis, and I propose in this section to try to do justice to one particular family of such enigmas, the expounding and solving of which may be of some general theoretical interest.

The enigmas that I have in mind all turn on what I shall call the 'systematic elusiveness' of the concept of 'I'. When a child, like Kim, having no theoretical commitments or equipment, first asks himself, 'Who or What am I?' he does not ask it from a desire to know his own surname, age, sex, nationality or position in the form. He knows all his ordinary personalia. He feels that there is something else in the background for which his 'I' stands, a something which has still to be described after all his ordinary personalia have been listed. He also feels, very vaguely, that whatever it is that his 'I' stands for, it is something very important and quite unique, unique in the sense that neither it, nor anything like it, belongs to anyone else. There *could* only be one of it. Pronouns like 'you', 'she' and 'we' feel quite unmystifying, while 'I' feels mystifying. And it feels mystifying, anyhow in part, because the more the child tries to put his finger on what 'I' stands for, the less does he succeed in doing so. He can catch only its coat-tails; it itself is always and obdurately a pace ahead of its coat-tails. Like the shadow of one's own head, it will not wait to be jumped on. And yet it is never very far ahead; indeed, sometimes it seems not to be ahead of the pursuer at all. It evades capture by lodging itself inside the very muscles of the pursuer. It is too near even to be within arm's reach.

Theorists have found themselves mocked in a similar way by the concept of 'I'. Even Hume confesses that, when he has tried to sketch all the items of his experience, he has found nothing there to answer to the word 'I', and yet he is not satisfied that there does not remain something more and something important, without which his sketch fails to describe his experience.

Other epistemologists have felt similar qualms. Should I, or should I not, put my knowing self down on my list of the sorts of things that I can have knowledge of? If I say 'no', it seems to reduce my knowing self to a theoretically infertile mystery, yet if I say 'yes', it seems to reduce the fishing-net to one of the fishes which it itself catches. It seems hazardous either to allow or to deny that the judge can be put into the dock.

I shall try before long to explain this systematic elusiveness of the notion of 'I' and with it the apparent non-parallelism between the notion of 'I' and the notions of 'you' and 'he'. But it is expedient first to consider some points which hold good of all personal pronouns alike.

People, including philosophers, tend to raise their questions about what constitutes a self by asking what the words 'I' and 'you' are the names of. They are familiar with the river of which 'Thames' is the name and with the dog called 'Fido'. They are also familiar with the persons of whom their acquaintances' and their own surnames are the surnames. They then feel vaguely that since 'I' and 'you' are not public surnames, they must be names of another and queer sort and must in consequence be the names of some extra individuals hidden away behind or inside the persons who are known abroad by their ordinary surnames and Christian names. As pronouns are not registered at Somerset House, their owners must be different, somehow, from the owners of the Christian and surnames which are registered there. But this way of broaching the question is mistaken from the start. Certainly 'I' and 'you' are not regular proper names like 'Fido' and 'Thames', but they are not irregular proper names either. They are not proper names, or names at all, any more than 'today' is an ephemeral name of the current day. Gratuitous mystification begins from the moment that we start to peer around for the beings named by our pronouns. Sentences containing pronouns do, of course, mention identifiable people, but the way in which the people mentioned are identified by pronouns is quite different from the way in which they are identified by proper names.

This difference can be provisionally indicated in the following manner. There is a class of words (which for ease of reference may be called 'index words') that indicate to the hearer or reader the particular thing, episode, person, place or moment referred to. Thus 'now' is an index word which indicates to the hearer of the sentence 'the train is now going over the bridge' the particular moment of the crossing. The word 'now' can, of course, be used at any moment of any day or night, but it does not mean what is meant by 'at any moment of any day or night'. It indicates that particular moment at which the hearer is intended to hear the word 'now' being uttered. The moment at which the train crosses the bridge is indicated by the utterance at that moment of the word 'now'. The moment at which 'now' is breathed is the moment which it indicates. In a partly similar way the word 'that' is often used to indicate the particular thing at which the speaker's index finger is pointing at the moment when he breathes out the word 'that'. 'Here' indicates, sometimes, that particular place from which the speaker propagates the noise 'here' into the surrounding air; and the page indicated by the phrase 'this page' is the page of which the printed word 'this' occupies a part. Other index words indicate indirectly. 'Yesterday' indicates the day before that on which it is uttered, or printed in a newspaper; 'then', in certain uses, indicates a moment or period standing in a specified relation with that in which it is heard or read.

Now pronouns like 'I' and 'you' are, anyhow sometimes, direct index words, while others, like 'he' and 'they' and, in some uses, 'we' are indirect index words. 'I' can indicate the particular person from whom the noise 'I', or the written mark 'I', issues; 'you' can indicate the one person who hears me say 'you', or it can indicate that person, whoever he is (and there may be several) who reads the 'you' that I write, or have printed. In all cases the physical occurrence of an index word is bodily annexed to what the word indicates. Hence 'you' is not a queer name that I and others sometimes give you; it is an index word which, in its particular conversational setting, indicates to you just who it is to whom I am addressing my remarks. 'I' is not an extra name for an extra being; it indicates, when I say or write it, the same individual who can also be addressed by the proper name 'Gilbert Ryle'. 'I' is not an alias for 'Gilbert Ryle'; it indicates the person whom 'Gilbert Ryle' names, when Gilbert Ryle uses 'I'.

But this is far from being the whole story. We have now to notice that we use our pronouns, as well as our proper names, in a wide variety of different ways. Further mystifications have arisen from the detection, without the comprehension of contrasts between such different uses of 'I' and, to a lesser extent, of 'you' and 'he'.

In the sentence 'I am warming myself before the fire', the word 'myself' could be replaced by 'my body' without spoiling the sense; but the pronoun 'I' could not be replaced by 'my body' without making nonsense. Similarly the sentence 'Cremate me after I am gone' says nothing self-annihilating, since the 'me' and the 'I' are being used in different senses. So sometimes we can, and sometimes we cannot, paraphrase the first personal pronoun by 'my body'. There are even some cases where I can talk about a part of my body, but cannot use 'I' or 'me' for it. If my hair were scorched in a fire, I could say 'I was not scorched; only my hair was', though I could never say 'I was not scorched; only my face and hands were'. A part of the body which is insensitive and cannot be moved at will is mine, but it is not part of me. Conversely, mechanical auxiliaries to the body, such as motor-cars and walking-sticks, can be spoken of with 'I' and 'me; as in 'I collided with the pillar-box', which means the same thing as 'the car which I was driving (or which I owned and was having driven for me in my presence) collided with the pillar-box'.

Let us now consider some contexts in which 'I' and 'me' can certainly not be replaced by 'my body' or 'my leg'. If I say 'I am annoyed that I was cut in the collision', while I might accept the substitution of 'my leg was cut' for 'I was cut', I should not allow 'I am annoyed' to be reconstructed in any such way. It would be similarly absurd to speak of 'my head remembering', 'my brain doing long division', or 'my body battling with fatigue'. Perhaps it is because of the absurdity of such collocations that so many people have felt driven to describe a person as an association between a body and a non-body.

However, we are not yet at the end of our list of elasticities in the uses of 'I' and 'me'; for we find further contrasts breaking out between uses of the first personal pronoun in which none can be paraphrased by mere references to the body. It makes perfect sense to say that I caught myself just beginning to dream, but not that I caught my body beginning to dream, or that my body caught me doing so; and it makes sense to say that a child is telling himself a fairy-story, but nonsense to make his body either narrator or auditor.

Contrasts of these types, perhaps above all the contrasts advertised in descriptions of exercises of self-control, have induced many preachers and some thinkers to speak as if an ordinary person is really some sort of committee or team of persons, all laced together inside one skin; as if the thinking and vetoing 'I' were one person, and the greedy or lazy 'I' were another. But this sort of picture is obviously of no use. Part of what we mean by 'person' is someone who is capable of catching himself beginning to dream, of telling himself stories and of curbing his own greed. So the suggested reduction of a person to a team of persons would merely multiply the number of persons without explaining how it is that one and the same person can be both narrator and auditor, or both vigilant and dreamy, both scorched and amazed at being scorched. The beginning of the required explanation is that in such a statement as 'I caught myself beginning to dream', the two pronouns are not names of different persons, since they are not names at all, but that they are index words being used in different senses in different sorts of context, just as we saw was the case with the statement 'I am warming myself by the fire' (though this is a different difference of sense from the other). In case it seems unplausible to say that inside one sentence the twice used first personal pronoun can both indicate the same person and also have two different senses, it is enough for the moment to point out that the same thing can happen even with ordinary proper names and personal titles. The sentence 'after her wedding Miss Jones will no longer be Miss Jones' does not say that the particular woman will cease to be herself, or cease to be the sort of person she now is, but only that she will have changed her name and status; and the sentence 'after Napoleon returned to France, he was Napoleon no longer' might mean only that his qualities of generalship had altered, and is obviously analogous to the familiar expression 'I am not myself'. The statements 'I was just beginning to dream' and 'I caught myself just beginning to dream' are statements of logically different types, and it follows from their being of different types that the pronoun 'I' is being used with a different logical force in the two sentences.

...ore or less effective. He learns in adolescence
...wn behaviour most of those higher order
...g with the young that are regularly practised
...en said to be growing up.

...t as he had earlier acquired not only the ability,
...nation to direct higher order acts upon the acts
...ow becomes prone, as well as competent, to do the
...wn behaviour; and just as he had earlier learned to
...with the particular performances of others, but also
...positions to conduct such performances, so he now
...me degree both able and ready to take steps, theoretical
... about his own habits, motives and abilities. Nor are
...her order performances, or his dispositions to perform
...way exempted from just the same treatment. For any
...e of any order, it is always possible that there should be
...a variety of higher order actions about it. If I ridicule
...done by you, or by myself, I can, but usually do not
...pass a verbal comment on my amusement, apologise
...let others into the joke; and then I can go on to applaud
...ach myself for doing so, and make a note in my diary that
...alone this.

...ill be seen that what is here under discussion covers much of
...what is ordinarily called 'self-consciousness' and what is
...arily called 'self-control', though it covers much more than
...m. A person can, indeed, and must act sometimes as reporter
upon his own doings and sometimes as prefect regulating his own
conduct, but these higher order self-dealings are only two out of
innumerable brands, just as the corresponding inter-personal dealings
are only two out of innumerable brands.

Nor must it be supposed that the reports which a person makes
to himself upon his own doings, or the régimes which he imposes
upon his own conduct are inevitably free from bias or carelessness.
My reports on myself are subject to the same kinds of defects as
are my reports on you, and the admonitions, corrections and
injunctions which I impose on myself may show me to be as
ineffectual or ill-advised as does my disciplining of others.
Self-consciousness, if the word is to be used at all, must not
be described on the hallowed para-optical model, as a torch
that illuminates itself by beams of its own light reflected from

In considering specifically human behaviour—behaviour, that is,
which is unachieved by animals, infants and idiots—we should for
several reasons notice the fact that some sorts of actions are in
one way or another concerned with, or are operations upon, other
actions. When one person retaliates upon another, scoffs at him,
replies to him or plays hide-and-seek with him, his actions have to
do, in one way or another, with certain actions on the part of the
other; in a sense to be specified later, the performance of the
former involves the thought of the latter. An action on the part
of one agent could not be one of spying or applauding, unless it
had to do with the actions of another agent; nor could I behave as
a customer, unless you or someone else behaved as a seller. One
man must give evidence if another is to cross-examine him; some
people must be on the stage, if others are to be dramatic critics.
It will sometimes be convenient to use the title 'higher order
actions' to denote those the descriptions of which involve the
oblique mention of other actions.

Some, but not all, higher order actions influence the agent dealt
with. If I merely comment on your actions behind your back,
my comment has to do with your actions in the sense that my
performance of my act involves the thought of your performance
of yours; but it does not modify your actions. This is especially
clear where the commentator or critic is operating after the death
of the agent on whose doings he passes his judgments. The historian
cannot change Napoleon's conduct of the battle of Waterloo. On
the other hand, the moment and the methods of my attacking do
affect the timing and the techniques of your defence, and what I
sell has a lot to do with what you buy.

Next, when I speak of the actions of one agent having to do
with those of another, I do not exclude those actions which are
performed under the mistaken impression that the other is doing
something which he is not really doing. The child who applauds
my skill in pretending to be asleep, though I have in fact really
fallen asleep, is doing something which, in the required sense,
presupposes that I am pretending; and Robinson Crusoe really is
having conversationally to do with his parrot, if he believes, or half
believes, that the bird follows what he says, even if this belief is
false.

Finally, there are many kinds of dealings which are concerned with subsequent, or even merely possible, or probable, actions. When I bribe you to vote for me, your voting has not yet taken place and may never take place. A reference to your vote enters into the description of my bribe, but the reference must be of the pattern 'that you shall vote for me', and not of the pattern 'because you did vote', or 'because I thought that you did vote for me'. In the same way my talking to you presupposes only in this way your understanding and agreeing with me, namely that I talk in order that you may understand and agree with me.

So when John Doe counters, detects, reports, parodies, exploits, applauds, mocks, abets, copies or interprets something done by Richard Roe, any description of his action would have to embody an oblique mention of the thing done, or supposed to be done, by Richard Roe; whereas no such description of John Doe's behaviour would have to enter into the description of that of Richard Roe. To talk about John Doe's detection or mockery would involve, but not be involved in, talking about what he had been detecting or mocking, and this is what is meant by saying that John Doe's action is of a higher order than that of Richard Roe. By 'higher' I do not mean 'loftier'. Blackmailing a deserter is of a higher order than his desertion, and advertising is of a higher order than selling. Recollecting the doing of a kindness is not nobler than the doing of it, but it is of a higher order.

It may be hygienic to remember that though the actions of reporting or commenting on the actions of others behind their backs is one species of higher order action, it has no special priority over the other ways of dealing with these actions. Keeping an academic tally of what Richard Roe does is only one way in which John Doe takes steps about Richard Roe's steps. The construction and public or private use of sentences in the indicative is not, as intellectualists love to think, either John Doe's indispensable first move or his Utopian last move. But this point requires us to consider the sense in which performing a higher order action 'involves the thought of' the corresponding lower order action. It does not mean that if, for example, I am to mimic your gestures, I must do two things, namely both verbally describe your gestures to myself and produce gestures complying with the terms employed in that description. Telling myself about your gestures would in itself be a higher order performance, and one which would equally

involve the thought of your g... thought of' does not signify a causal ... of a process of one sort with a ... commenting on your gestures, to b... thinking in a certain way of your gest... be mimicry and not mere replica, mu... certain way of your gestures. But of cour... 'thinking'; it does not denote any sort of ... enunciation of any propositions. It means th... am doing and, since what I am doing is mi... the gestures you made and be using that kn... the mimicking way and not in the reporting o...

Higher order actions are not instinctive. An... be done efficiently or inefficiently, appropriately o... intelligently or stupidly. Children have to learn ... them. They have to learn how to resist, parry and r... forestall, give way and co-operate, how to exchang... reward and punish. They have to learn to make jokes a... and to see some jokes against themselves, to obey ord... them, make requests and grant them, receive marks and a... They have to learn to compose and follow reports, de... and commentaries; to understand and to give criticisms, t... reject, correct and compose verdicts, catechise and be cate... Not least (and also not soonest) they have to learn to keep to th... selves things which they are inclined to divulge. Reticence is ... higher order than unreticence.

My object in drawing attention to these truisms of the playro... and the schoolroom can now be seen. At a certain stage the ... discovers the trick of directing higher order acts upon his ... lower order acts. Having been separately victim and autho... jokes, coercions, catechisms, criticisms and mimicries in... inter-personal dealings between others and himself, he find... how to play both roles at once. He has listened to stories b... and he has told stories before, but now he tells stories to hi... enthralled ear. He has been detected in insincerities and ... detected the insincerities of others, but now he appl... techniques of detection to his own insincerities. He finds ... can give orders to himself with such authority that he so... obeys them, even when reluctant to do so. Self-suasion ...

In considering specifically human behaviour—behaviour, that is, which is unachieved by animals, infants and idiots—we should for several reasons notice the fact that some sorts of actions are in one way or another concerned with, or are operations upon, other actions. When one person retaliates upon another, scoffs at him, replies to him or plays hide-and-seek with him, his actions have to do, in one way or another, with certain actions on the part of the other; in a sense to be specified later, the performance of the former involves the thought of the latter. An action on the part of one agent could not be one of spying or applauding, unless it had to do with the actions of another agent; nor could I behave as a customer, unless you or someone else behaved as a seller. One man must give evidence if another is to cross-examine him; some people must be on the stage, if others are to be dramatic critics. It will sometimes be convenient to use the title 'higher order actions' to denote those the descriptions of which involve the oblique mention of other actions.

Some, but not all, higher order actions influence the agent dealt with. If I merely comment on your actions behind your back, my comment has to do with your actions in the sense that my performance of my act involves the thought of your performance of yours; but it does not modify your actions. This is especially clear where the commentator or critic is operating after the death of the agent on whose doings he passes his judgments. The historian cannot change Napoleon's conduct of the battle of Waterloo. On the other hand, the moment and the methods of my attacking do affect the timing and the techniques of your defence, and what I sell has a lot to do with what you buy.

Next, when I speak of the actions of one agent having to do with those of another, I do not exclude those actions which are performed under the mistaken impression that the other is doing something which he is not really doing. The child who applauds my skill in pretending to be asleep, though I have in fact really fallen asleep, is doing something which, in the required sense, presupposes that I am pretending; and Robinson Crusoe really is having conversationally to do with his parrot, if he believes, or half believes, that the bird follows what he says, even if this belief is false.

Finally, there are many kinds of dealings which are concerned with subsequent, or even merely possible, or probable, actions. When I bribe you to vote for me, your voting has not yet taken place and may never take place. A reference to your vote enters into the description of my bribe, but the reference must be of the pattern 'that you shall vote for me', and not of the pattern 'because you did vote', or 'because I thought that you did vote for me'. In the same way my talking to you presupposes only in this way your understanding and agreeing with me, namely that I talk in order that you may understand and agree with me.

So when John Doe counters, detects, reports, parodies, exploits, applauds, mocks, abets, copies or interprets something done by Richard Roe, any description of his action would have to embody an oblique mention of the thing done, or supposed to be done, by Richard Roe; whereas no such description of John Doe's behaviour would have to enter into the description of that of Richard Roe. To talk about John Doe's detection or mockery would involve, but not be involved in, talking about what he had been detecting or mocking, and this is what is meant by saying that John Doe's action is of a higher order than that of Richard Roe. By 'higher' I do not mean 'loftier'. Blackmailing a deserter is of a higher order than his desertion, and advertising is of a higher order than selling. Recollecting the doing of a kindness is not nobler than the doing of it, but it is of a higher order.

It may be hygienic to remember that though the actions of reporting or commenting on the actions of others behind their backs is one species of higher order action, it has no special priority over the other ways of dealing with these actions. Keeping an academic tally of what Richard Roe does is only one way in which John Doe takes steps about Richard Roe's steps. The construction and public or private use of sentences in the indicative is not, as intellectualists love to think, either John Doe's indispensable first move or his Utopian last move. But this point requires us to consider the sense in which performing a higher order action 'involves the thought of' the corresponding lower order action. It does not mean that if, for example, I am to mimic your gestures, I must do two things, namely both verbally describe your gestures to myself and produce gestures complying with the terms employed in that description. Telling myself about your gestures would in itself be a higher order performance, and one which would equally involve the thought of your gestures. The phrase 'involve the thought of' does not signify a causal transaction, or the concomitance of a process of one sort with a process of another sort. As commenting on your gestures, to be commenting, must itself *be* thinking in a certain way of your gestures, so mimicking them, to be mimicry and not mere replica, must itself *be* thinking in a certain way of your gestures. But of course this is a strained sense of 'thinking'; it does not denote any sort of pondering or entail the enunciation of any propositions. It means that I must know what I am doing and, since what I am doing is mimicking, I must know the gestures you made and be using that knowledge, using it in the mimicking way and not in the reporting or commenting way.

Higher order actions are not instinctive. Any one of them can be done efficiently or inefficiently, appropriately or inappropriately, intelligently or stupidly. Children have to learn how to perform them. They have to learn how to resist, parry and retaliate, how to forestall, give way and co-operate, how to exchange and haggle, reward and punish. They have to learn to make jokes against others and to see some jokes against themselves, to obey orders and give them, make requests and grant them, receive marks and award them. They have to learn to compose and follow reports, descriptions and commentaries; to understand and to give criticisms, to accept, reject, correct and compose verdicts, catechise and be catechised. Not least (and also not soonest) they have to learn to keep to themselves things which they are inclined to divulge. Reticence is of a higher order than unreticence.

My object in drawing attention to these truisms of the playroom and the schoolroom can now be seen. At a certain stage the child discovers the trick of directing higher order acts upon his own lower order acts. Having been separately victim and author of jokes, coercions, catechisms, criticisms and mimicries in the inter-personal dealings between others and himself, he finds out how to play both roles at once. He has listened to stories before, and he has told stories before, but now he tells stories to his own enthralled ear. He has been detected in insincerities and he has detected the insincerities of others, but now he applies the techniques of detection to his own insincerities. He finds that he can give orders to himself with such authority that he sometimes obeys them, even when reluctant to do so. Self-suasion and selfdissuasion become more or less effective. He learns in adolescence to apply to his own behaviour most of those higher order methods of dealing with the young that are regularly practised by adults. He is then said to be growing up.

Moreover, just as he had earlier acquired not only the ability, but also the inclination to direct higher order acts upon the acts of others, so he now becomes prone, as well as competent, to do the same upon his own behaviour; and just as he had earlier learned to cope not only with the particular performances of others, but also with their dispositions to conduct such performances, so he now becomes in some degree both able and ready to take steps, theoretical and practical, about his own habits, motives and abilities. Nor are his own higher order performances, or his dispositions to perform them, in any way exempted from just the same treatment. For any performance of any order, it is always possible that there should be performed a variety of higher order actions about it. If I ridicule something done by you, or by myself, I can, but usually do not go on to pass a verbal comment on my amusement, apologise for it, or let others into the joke; and then I can go on to applaud or reproach myself for doing so, and make a note in my diary that I have done this.

It will be seen that what is here under discussion covers much of both what is ordinarily called 'self-consciousness' and what is ordinarily called 'self-control', though it covers much more than them. A person can, indeed, and must act sometimes as reporter upon his own doings and sometimes as prefect regulating his own conduct, but these higher order self-dealings are only two out of innumerable brands, just as the corresponding inter-personal dealings are only two out of innumerable brands.

Nor must it be supposed that the reports which a person makes to himself upon his own doings, or the régimes which he imposes upon his own conduct are inevitably free from bias or carelessness. My reports on myself are subject to the same kinds of defects as are my reports on you, and the admonitions, corrections and injunctions which I impose on myself may show me to be as ineffectual or ill-advised as does my disciplining of others. Self-consciousness, if the word is to be used at all, must not be described on the hallowed para-optical model, as a torch that illuminates itself by beams of its own light reflected from a mirror in its own insides. On the contrary it is simply a special case of an ordinary more or less efficient handling of a less or more honest and intelligent witness. Similarly, self-control is not to be likened to the management of a partially disciplined subordinate by a superior of perfect wisdom and authority; it is simply a special case of the management of an ordinary person by an ordinary person, namely where John Doe, say, is taking both parts. The truth is not that there occur some higher order acts which are above criticism, but that any higher order act that occurs can itself be criticised; not that something unimprovable does take place, but that nothing takes place which is not improvable; not that any operation is of the highest order, but that for any operation of any order there can be operations of a higher order.

### (7) The Systematic Elusiveness of 'I'.

We are now in a position to account for the systematic elusiveness of the notion of 'I', and the partial non-parallelism between it and the notion of 'you' or 'he'. To concern oneself about oneself in any way, theoretical or practical, is to perform a higher order act, just as it is to concern oneself about anybody else. To try, for example, to describe what one has just done, or is now doing, is to comment upon a step which is not itself, save *per accidens*, one of commenting. But the operation which is the commenting is not, and cannot be, the step on which that commentary is being made. Nor can an act of ridiculing be its own butt. A higher order action cannot be the action upon which it is performed. So my commentary on my performances must always be silent about one performance, namely itself, and this performance can be the target only of another commentary. Self-commentary, self-ridicule and self-admonition are logically condemned to eternal penultimacy. Yet nothing that is left out of any particular commentary or admonition is privileged thereby to escape comment or admonition for ever. On the contrary it may be the target of the very next comment or rebuke.

The point may be illustrated in this way. A singing-master might criticise the accents or notes of a pupil by mimicking with exaggerations each word that the pupil sang; and if the pupil sang slowly enough, the master could parody each word sung by the pupil before the next came to be uttered. But then, in a mood of humility, the singing-master tries to criticise his own singing in the same way, and more than that to mimic with exaggerations each word that he utters, including those that he utters in self-parody. It is at once clear, first, that he can never get beyond the very earliest word of his song and, second, that at any given moment he has uttered one noise which has yet to be mimicked—and it makes no difference how rapidly he chases his notes with mimicries of them. He can, in principle, never catch more than the coat-tails of the object of his pursuit, since a word cannot be a parody of itself. None the less, there is no word that he sings which remains unparodied; he is always a day late for the fair, but every day he reaches the place of yesterday's fair. He never succeeds in jumping on to the shadow of his own head, yet he is never more than one jump behind.

An ordinary reviewer may review a book, while a second order reviewer criticises reviews of the book. But the second order review is not a criticism of itself. It can only be criticised in a further third order review. Given complete editorial patience, any review of any order could be published, though at no stage would all the reviews have received critical notices. Nor can every act of a diarist be the topic of a record in his diary; for the last entry made in his diary still demands that the making of it should in its turn be chronicled.

This, I think, explains the feeling that my last year's self, or my yesterday's self, could in principle be exhaustively described and accounted for, and that your past or present self could be exhaustively described and accounted for by me, but that my today's self perpetually slips out of any hold of it that I try to take. It also explains the apparent non-parallelism between the notion of 'I' and that of 'you', without construing the elusive residuum as any kind of ultimate mystery.

There is another thing which it explains. When people consider the problems of the Freedom of the Will and try to imagine their own careers as analogous to those of clocks or water-courses, they tend to boggle at the idea that their own immediate future is already unalterably fixed and predictable. It seems absurd to suppose that what I am just about to think, feel or do is already preappointed, though people are apt to find no such absurdity in the supposition that the futures of other people are so preappointed. The so-called 'feeling of spontaneity' is closely connected with this inability to imagine that what I am going to think or do can already be anticipated. On the other hand, when I consider what I thought and did yesterday, there seems to be no absurdity in supposing that that could have been forecast, before I did it. It is only while I am actually trying to predict my own next move that the task feels like that of a swimmer trying to overtake the waves that he sends ahead of himself.

The solution is as before. A prediction of a deed or a thought is a higher order operation, the performance of which cannot be among the things considered in making the prediction. Yet as the state of mind in which I am just before I do something may make some difference to what I do, it follows that I must overlook at least one of the data relevant to my prediction. Similarly, I can give you the fullest possible advice what to do, but I must omit one piece of counsel, since I cannot in the same breath advise you how to take that advice. There is therefore no paradox in saying that while normally I am not at all surprised to find myself doing or thinking what I do, yet when I try most carefully to anticipate what I shall do or think, then the outcome is likely to falsify my expectation. My process of pre-envisaging may divert the course of my ensuing behaviour in a direction and degree of which my prognosis cannot take account. One thing that I cannot prepare myself for is the next thought that I am going to think.

The fact that my immediate future is in this way systematically elusive to me has, of course, no tendency to prove that my career is in principle unpredictable to prophets other than myself, or even that it is inexplicable to myself after the heat of the action. I can point to any other thing with my index-finger, and other people can point at this finger. But it cannot be the object at which it itself is pointing. Nor can a missile be its own target, though anything else may be thrown at it.

This general conclusion that any performance can be the concern of a higher order performance, but cannot be the concern of itself, is connected with what was said earlier about the special functioning of index words, such as 'now', 'you' and 'I'. An 'I' sentence indicates whom in particular it is about by being itself uttered or written by someone in particular. 'I' indicates the person who utters it. So, when a person utters an 'I' sentence, his utterance of it may be part of a higher order performance, namely one, perhaps of self-reporting, self-exhortation or self-commiseration, and this

performance itself is not dealt with in the operation which it itself
is. Even if the person is, for special speculative purposes, momentarily concentrating on the Problem of the Self, he has failed and
knows that he has failed to catch more than the flying coat-tails of
that which he was pursuing. His quarry was the hunter.

To conclude, there is nothing mysterious or occult about the
range of higher order acts and attitudes, which are apt to be
inadequately covered by the umbrella-title 'self-consciousness'.
They are the same in kind as the higher order acts and attitudes
exhibited in the dealings of people with one other. Indeed the
former are only a special application of the latter and are learned
first from them. If I perform the third order operation of commenting on a second order act of laughing at myself for a piece of
manual awkwardness, I shall indeed use the first personal pronoun
in two different ways. I say to myself, or to the company, 'I was
laughing at myself for being butter-fingered'. But so far from this
showing that there are two 'Mes' in my skin, not to speak, yet, of
the third one which is still commenting on them, it shows only
that I am applying the public two-pronoun idiom in which we talk
of her laughing at him; and I am applying this linguistic idiom,
because I am applying the method of inter-personal transaction
which the idiom is ordinarily employed to describe.

Before concluding this chapter, it is worth mentioning that
there is one influential difference between the first personal
pronoun and all the rest. 'I', in my use of it, always indicates me
and only indicates me. 'You', 'she' and 'they' indicate different
people at different times. 'I' is like my own shadow; I can never
get away from it, as I can get away from your shadow. There is no
mystery about this constancy, but I mention it because it seems
to endow 'I' with a mystifying uniqueness and adhesiveness.
'Now' has something of the same besetting feeling.

# CHAPTER VII

# SENSATION AND OBSERVATION

(1) *Foreword.*

ONE of the central negative motives of this book is to show that 'mental' does not denote a status, such that one can sensibly ask of a given thing or event whether it is mental or physical, 'in the mind' or 'in the outside world'. To talk of a person's mind is not to talk of a repository which is permitted to house objects that something called 'the physical world' is forbidden to house; it is to talk of the person's abilities, liabilities and inclinations to do and undergo certain sorts of things, and of the doing and undergoing of these things in the ordinary world. Indeed, it makes no sense to speak as if there could be two or eleven worlds. Nothing but confusion is achieved by labelling worlds after particular avocations. Even the solemn phrase 'the physical world' is as philosophically pointless as would be the phrase 'the numismatic world', 'the haberdashery world', or 'the botanical world.'

But it will be urged in defence of the doctrine that 'mental' does denote a status that a special footing must be provided for sensations, feelings and images. The laboratory sciences provide descriptions and correlations of various kinds of things and processes, but our impressions and ideas are unmentioned in these descriptions. They must therefore belong somewhere else. And as it is patent that the occurrence of a sensation, for instance, is a fact about the person who feels the pain or suffers the dazzle, the sensation must be in that person. But this is a special sense of 'in', since the surgeon will not find it under the person's epidermis. So the sensation must be in the person's mind.

Moreover sensations, feelings and images are things the owner of which must be conscious of them. Whatever else may be contained in his stream of consciousness, at least his sensations, feelings and images are parts of that stream. They help to constitute, if they do not completely constitute, the stuff of which minds are composed.

Champions of this argument tend to espouse it with special confidence on behalf of images, such as what 'I see in my mind's eye' and what I have 'running in my head'. They feel certain qualms in suggesting too radical a divorce between sensations and conditions of the body. Stomach-aches, tickles and singings in the ears have physiological attachments which threaten to sully the purity of the brook of mental experiences. But the views which I see, even when my eyes are shut, and the music and the voices that I can hear, even when all is quiet, qualify admirably for membership of the kingdom of the mind. I can, within limits, summon, dismiss and modify them at will and the location, position and condition of my body do not appear to be in any correlation with their occurrences or properties.

This belief in the mental status of images carries with it a palatable corollary. When a person has been thinking to himself, retrospection commonly shows him that at least a part of what has been going on has been a sequence of words heard in his head, as if spoken by himself. So the venerable doctrine that discoursing to oneself under one's breath is the proprietary business of minds reinforces, and is reinforced by, the doctrine that the apparatus of pure thinking does not belong to the gross world of physical noises, but consists instead of the more ethereal stuff of which dreams are made.

However, before we can discuss images, there is a lot that must be said about sensations, and this chapter is concerned entirely with the concepts of sensation and observation. The concept of imaging will be discussed in the next chapter.

For reasons developed in its last section, I am not satisfied with this chapter. I have fallen in with the official story that perceiving involves having sensations. But this is a sophisticated use of 'sensation'. It is not the way in which we ordinarily use the noun 'sensation', or the verb 'to feel'. We ordinarily use these words for a special family of perceptions, namely, tactual and kinaesthetic perceptions and perceptions of temperatures, as well as for localisable pains and discomforts. Seeing, hearing, tasting and smelling do not involve sensations, in this sense of the word, any more than seeing involves hearing, or than feeling a cold draught involves tasting anything. In its sophisticated use, 'sensation' seems to be a semi-physiological, semi-psychological term, the employment of which is allied with certain pseudo-scientific, Cartesian theories. This concept does not occur in what novelists, biographers, diarists or nursemaids say about people, or in what doctors, dentists or oculists say to their patients.

In its familiar, unsophisticated use, 'sensation' does not stand for an ingredient in perceptions, but for a kind of perception. But, neither in its sophisticated use does it signify a notion contained in the notion of perception. People knew how to talk about seeing, hearing and feeling things, before they had mastered any physiological or psychological hypotheses, or heard of any theoretical difficulties about the communications between Minds and their Bodies.

I do not know the right idioms in which to discuss these matters, but I hope that my discussion of them in the official idioms may have at least some internal Fifth Column efficacy.

(2) *Sensations.*

For certain purposes it is convenient to divide sensations into those which enter *ex officio* into sense perception, and those which do not; that is, roughly, into those which are connected with the special organs of sense, namely the eyes, ears, tongue, nose and skin, and those which are connected with the other sensitive but non-sensory organs of the body. But this division is somewhat arbitrary. When the eye is dazzled, and when the nose stings, we incline to rank these sensations with the organic sensations of aches and prickings, and, conversely, when we have certain sensations in the throat or stomach, we are apt to say that we feel the fish-bone or the suet-pudding. A specific muscular sensation might be described indifferently as a sensation of fatigue, or as a feeling of the weight or resistance of the log, and a listener might report to one companion that he heard a very distant train, while he reported to the other that he could barely distinguish the noise from the normal throbbing or singing in his ears.

For obvious reasons we have constantly to refer to the sensations which are connected with the organs of sense, for we are constantly having to mention what we see and do not see, what we hear, smell, taste and feel. But we do not talk about these sensations 'neat'; we ordinarily mention them only in reference to the things or events which we are observing or trying or claiming to observe. People speak of having a glimpse, but only in such contexts as having a glimpse of a robin, or as having a glimpse of something moving. Nor do they break out of this habit, when asked to describe how something looked, or sounded, or tasted; they will normally say that it looked like a haystack, that it sounded like something humming, or that it tasted as if it had pepper in it.

This procedure of describing sensations by referring in a certain way to common objects like haystacks, things that hum, and pepper is of great theoretical importance. A haystack, for example, is something about the description of which everyone could agree. A haystack is something which any observers could observe, and we should expect their accounts of it to tally with one another, or at least to be capable of correction until they did tally. Its position, shape, size, weight, date of construction, composition and function are facts which anyone could establish by ordinary methods of observation and inquiry. But more than this. These methods would also establish how the haystack would look, feel and smell to ordinary observers in ordinary conditions of observation. When I say that something looks like a haystack, (though it may actually be a blanket on a clothes-line), I am describing how it looks in terms of what anyone might expect a haystack to look like, when observed from a suitable angle, in a suitable light and against a suitable background. I am, that is, comparing how the blanket looks to me here and now, not with some other particular glimpse had by me, or had by some other particular person in a particular situation, but with a *type* of glimpse such as any ordinary observers could expect to get in situations of certain sorts, namely in situations where they are in the proximity of haystacks in daylight.

Similarly, to say that something tastes peppery is to say that it tastes to me now as any peppered viands would taste to anybody with a normal palate. It has been suggested that I can never know that pepper-grains do give different people similar sensations, but for the present it is enough to point out that our ordinary ways of imparting information about our own sensations consist in making certain sorts of references to what we think could be established in anyone's observations of common objects. We describe what is personal to ourselves in neutral or impersonal terms.

Indeed, our descriptions would convey nothing unless couched in such terms. These are, after all, the terms which we learned by being taught them by others. We do not and cannot describe haystacks in terms of this or that set of sensations. We describe our sensations by certain sorts of references to observers and things like haystacks.

We follow the same practice in describing organic sensations. When a sufferer describes a pain as a stabbing, a grinding or a burning pain, though he does not necessarily think that his pain is given to him by a stiletto, a drill or an ember, still he says what sort of a pain it is by likening it to the sort of pain that would be given to anyone by such instruments. The same account holds of such descriptions as 'there is a singing in my ears', 'my blood ran cold' and 'I saw stars'. Even to say that one's view is hazy is to liken one's view to the way that common objects look to any observer who is seeing them through an atmospheric haze.

The present point of mentioning these ways of describing our sensations is to show how and why there exists a linguistic difficulty in discussing the logic of concepts of sensation. We do not employ a 'neat' sensation vocabulary. We describe particular sensations by referring to how common objects regularly look, sound and feel to any normal person.

Epistemologists are fond of using words like 'pains', 'itches', 'stabs', 'glows' and 'dazzles' as if they were 'neat' sensation names. But this practice is doubly misleading. Not only do most of these words draw their significance from situations involving common objects like fleas, daggers and radiators, but they also connote that the person who has the sensations likes or dislikes, or might well like or dislike, having them. A pain in my knee is a sensation that I mind having; so 'unnoticed pain' is an absurd expression, where 'unnoticed sensation' has no absurdity.

This point can serve to introduce a conceptual distinction which will shortly turn out to be of cardinal importance, namely, that between having a sensation and observing. When a person is said to be watching, scanning or looking at something, listening to it or savouring it, a part, but only a part, of what is meant is that he is having visual, auditory or gustatory sensations. But to be observing something the observer must also at least be trying to find something out. His scrutiny is accordingly describable as careful or careless, cursory or sustained, methodical or haphazard, accurate or inaccurate, expert or amateurish. Observing is a task which can be one of some arduousness, and we can be more or less successful in it and more or less good at it. But none of these ways of characterising the exercises of one's powers of observation can be applied to the having of visual, auditory or gustatory sensations. One can listen carefully, but not have a singing in one's ears carefully; one can look systematically, but one cannot have a dazzle-sensation systematically; one can try to discriminate flavours, but one cannot try to have sensations of taste. Again we observe, very often, from inquisitiveness or obedience, but we do not have tickles from this or any other motive. We observe on purpose, but we do not have sensations on purpose, though we can induce them on purpose. We can make mistakes of observation, but it is nonsense to speak of either making or avoiding mistakes in sensation; sensations can be neither correct nor incorrect, veridical nor non-veridical. They are neither apprehensions nor misapprehensions. Observing is finding out, or trying to find out, something, but having a sensation is neither finding out, nor trying to find out, nor failing to find out, anything.

This set of contrasts enables us to say that though mention of the degree to which, the ways in which and the objects of which a person is observant or unobservant is a part of the description of his wits and character, mention of his sensory capacities and actual sensations is no part of that description. To use an objectionable phrase, there is nothing 'mental' about sensations. Deafness is not a species of stupidity, nor is a squint any sort of turpitude; the retriever's keenness of scent does not prove him intelligent; and we do not try to train or shame children out of colour-blindness or think of them as mentally defective. It is not for the moralist or the alienist, but for the oculist, to diagnose and prescribe for imperfect vision. Having a sensation is not an exercise of a quality of intellect or character. Hence we are not too proud to concede sensations to reptiles.

Whatever series of sensations an intelligent person may have, it is always conceivable that a merely sentient creature might have had a precisely similar series; and if by 'stream of consciousness' were meant 'series of sensations', then from a mere inventory of the contents of such a stream there would be no possibility of deciding whether the creature that had these sensations was an animal or a human being; an idiot, a lunatic or a sane man; much less whether he was an ambitious and argumentative philologist or a slow-witted but industrious magistrates' clerk.

However, these considerations will not satisfy the theorists who want to make the stream of a person's sensations, feelings and images the stuff of his mind, and thus to back up the dogma that minds are special-status things composed of a special stuff. They will urge, quite correctly, that though the oculist and the dentist can modify the patient's sensations by applying chemical or mechanical treatments to his bodily organs, yet they are debarred from observing the sensations themselves. They may observe what is physiologically amiss with the patient's eyes and gums, but they must rely on the patient's testimony for knowledge of what he sees and feels. Only the wearer knows where the shoe pinches. From this it is argued, plausibly but fallaciously, that there does indeed exist the hallowed antithesis between the public, physical world and the private, mental world, between the things and events which anyone may witness and the things or events which only their possessor may witness. Planets, microbes, nerves and eardrums are publicly observable things in the outside world; sensations, feelings and images are privately observable constituents of our several mental worlds.

I want to show that this antithesis is spurious. It is true that the cobbler cannot witness the tweaks that I feel when the shoe pinches. But it is false that I witness them. The reason why my tweaks cannot be witnessed by him is not that some Iron Curtain prevents them from being witnessed by anyone save myself, but that they are not the sorts of things of which it makes sense to say that they are witnessed or unwitnessed at all, even by me. I feel or have the tweaks, but I do not discover or peer at them; they are not things that I find out about by watching them, listening to them, or savouring them. In the sense in which a person may be said to have had a robin under observation, it would be nonsense to say that he has had a twinge under observation. There may be one or several witnesses of a road-accident; there cannot be several witnesses, or even one witness, of a qualm.

We know what it is like to have and to need observational aids like telescopes, stethoscopes and torches for the observation of planets, heart-beats and moths, but we cannot think what it would be like to apply such instruments to our sensations. Similarly, though we know well what sorts of handicaps impair or prevent our observation of common objects, namely handicaps like fogs, tingling fingers and singings in the ears, we cannot think of analogous impediments getting between us and such sensations as tingles and singings in the ears.

In saying that sensations are not the sorts of things that can be observed, I do not mean that they are unobservable in the way in which infra-microscopic bacteria, flying bullets, or the mountains on the other side of the moon, are unobservable, or that they are unobservable in the way in which the planets are unobservable to the blind. I mean something like this. Every word that can be written down, except words of one letter, has a spelling; some words are more difficult to spell than others and some words have several different spellings. Yet if we are asked how the letters of the alphabet are spelled, we have to answer that they cannot be spelled at all. But this 'cannot' does not mean that the task is one of insuperable difficulty, but only that the question, 'Of what letters arranged in what order does a given letter consist?' is an improper question. As letters are neither easy to spell, nor insuperably hard to spell, so, I argue, sensations are neither observable nor unobservable. Correspondingly, however, just as the fact that we may not even ask how a letter is spelled by no means precludes us from knowing perfectly well how letters are written, so the fact that we may not talk of the observation of sensations by no means precludes us from talking of the notice or heed that people can pay to their sensations, or of the avowals and reports that they can make of the sensations of which they have taken notice. Headaches cannot be witnessed, but they can be noticed, and while it is improper to advise a person not to peep at his tickle, it is quite proper to advise him not to pay any heed to it.

We have seen that observing entails having sensations; a man could not be described as watching a robin who had not got a single glimpse of it, or as smelling a cheese who had not caught a whiff. (I am pretending, what is not true, that words like 'glimpse' and 'whiff' stand for sensations. The fact that a glimpse can be characterised as 'clear' or 'unclear' shows that it is an observation-word and not a 'neat' sensation-word.) An object of observation, like a robin, or a cheese, must therefore be the sort of thing of which it is possible for observers to catch glimpses, or to get whiffs. But many theorists ask us to look away from such common objects as robins and cheeses towards such things as glimpses and whiffs, and we are asked to declare that I, though nobody else, can observe the glimpses and the whiffs that I get, and observe them in the same sense of 'observe' as that in which anyone can observe the robin or the cheese. But to grant this would be to grant that if, when I catch a glimpse of a robin, I can observe that glimpse, then, in doing so, I must get something like a glimpse or a whiff of that glimpse of the robin. If sensations are proper objects of observation, then observing them must carry with it the having of sensations of those sensations analogous to the glimpses of the robin without which I could not be watching the robin. And this is clearly absurd. There is nothing answering to the phrases 'a glimpse of a glimpse' or 'a whiff of a pain' or 'the sound of a tweak' or 'the tingle of a tingle', and if there was anything to correspond, the series would go on for ever.

Again, when a person has been watching a horse-race, it is proper to ask whether he had a good or a bad view of it, whether he watched it carefully or carelessly and whether he tried to see as much of it as he could. So, if it was correct to say that a person observes his sensations, it would be proper to ask whether his inspection of a tickle had been hampered or unhampered, close or casual and whether he could have discerned more of it, if he had tried. No one ever asks such questions, any more than anyone asks how the first letter in 'London' is spelled. There are no such questions to ask. This point is partially obscured by the fact that the word 'observe', though generally used to cover such processes as watching, listening and savouring, or else such achievements as descrying and detecting, is sometimes used as a synonym of 'pay heed to' and 'notice'. Watching and descrying do involve paying heed, but paying heed does not involve watching.

It follows from this that it was wrong from the start to contrast the common objects of anyone's observation, like robins and cheeses, with the supposed peculiar objects of my privileged observation, namely my sensations, since sensations are not objects of observation at all. We do not, consequently, have to rig up one theatre, called 'the outside world', to house the common objects of anyone's observation, and another, called 'the mind', to house the objects of some monopoly observations. The antithesis between 'public' and 'private' was in part a misconstruction of the antithesis between objects which can be looked at, handled and tasted, on the one hand, and sensations which are had but not looked at, handled or tasted, on the other. It is true and even tautologous that the cobbler cannot feel the shoe pinching me, unless the cobbler is myself, but this is not because he is excluded from a peep-show open only to me, but because it would make no sense to say that he was in my pain, and no sense, therefore, to say that he was noticing the tweak that I was having.

Further consequences follow. The properties which we ascertain by observation, or not without observation, to characterise the common objects of anyone's observation cannot be significantly ascribed to, or denied of, sensations. Sensations do not have sizes, shapes, positions, temperatures, colours or smells. In the sense in which there is always an answer to the question, 'Where is?' or 'Where was the robin?', there is no answer to the question, 'Where is?' or 'Where was your glimpse of the robin?' There is indeed a sense in which a tickle is quite properly said to be 'in my foot', or a stinging 'in my nose', but this is a different sense from that in which bones are in my foot, or pepper-grains are in my nose. So in the muddled sense of 'world' in which people say that 'the outside world' or 'the public world' contains robins and cheeses, the locations and connections of which in that world can be found out, there is not another world, or set of worlds, in which the locations and connections of sensations can be found out; nor does the reputed problem exist of finding out what are the connections between the occupants of the public world and those of any such private worlds. Further, while one common object, like a needle, can be inside or outside another, like a haystack, there is no corresponding antithesis of 'inside' to 'outside' applying to sensations. My tweak is not hidden from the cobbler because it is inside me, either as being literally inside my skin, or as being, metaphorically, in a place to which he has no access. On the contrary, it cannot be described, as needles can, as being either internal or external to a common object like myself, nor as being either hidden or unhidden. Nor can letters be classified as either nouns or verbs or adjectives, or described as either obeying or disobeying the rules of English syntax. It is, of course, true and important that I am the only person who can give a first-hand account of the tweaks given me by my ill-fitting shoe, and an oculist who cannot speak my language is without his best source of information about my visual sensations. But the fact that I alone can give first-hand accounts of my sensations does not entail that I have, what others lack, the opportunity of observing those sensations.

Two further connected points must be made. First, there is a philosophically unexciting though important sense of 'private' in which of course my sensations are private or proprietary to me. Namely, just as you cannot, in logic, hold my catches, win my races, eat my meals, frown my frowns, or dream my dreams, so you cannot have my twinges, or my after-images. Nor can Venus have Neptune's satellites, or Poland have Bulgaria's history. This is simply a part of the logical force of those sentences in which the accusative to a transitive verb is a cognate accusative. Such transitive verbs do not signify relations. 'I held my catch' does not assert a relation between me and a catch, such that that catch might conceivably have been in that relation to you instead of to me. It is not like 'I stopped my bicycle'; you might well have anticipated me in stopping my bicycle.

Next, in saying that 'I had a twinge' does not assert a relation, as 'I had a hat' does, I am saying that the phrase 'my twinge' does not stand for any sort of a *thing* or 'term'. It does not even stand for an episode, though 'I had a twinge' asserts that an episode took place. This is part of the reason why it is nonsense to speak of observing, inspecting, witnessing or scrutinising sensations, since the objects proper to such verbs are things and episodes.

Yet when we theorise about sensations, we are forcibly tempted to talk of them as if they were elusive things or episodes. We inadvertently work on such models as that of a solitary man inside his tent who sees spots and patches of light and feels indentations in the inside of the canvas. He then, perhaps, wishes he could see and feel the torches and boots that made those patches of light and indentations in the canvas. But, alas, he can never see those torches, or feel those boots, as the canvas is always in the way. Now illuminated and indented bits of canvas are things; and the momentary illuminations and indentations of the canvas are episodes. So they are the sorts of objects which it is proper to describe as being watched, scrutinised and detected by a man inside his tent; and it is also proper to speak of them being there, but being unwatched and undetected. Moreover a man who can watch or detect illuminated or indented canvas could watch and detect torches and boots, if they were not screened from him. The situation of a man having sensations is, therefore, quite out of analogy with that of the man in the tent. Having sensations is not watching or detecting objects; and watching and detecting things and episodes is not having them in the sense in which one has sensations.

### (3) *The Sense Datum Theory.*

It is apposite at this point to comment on a theory sometimes known as the 'Sense Datum Theory'. This theory is primarily an attempt to elucidate the concepts of sense perception, a part of which task consists in elucidating the notions of sensations of sight, touch, hearing, smelling and tasting.

Our everyday verbs like 'see', 'hear' and 'taste' are not used to designate sensations 'neat', for we speak of seeing horse-races, hearing trains and tasting vintage wines; and horse-races, trains and wines are not sensations. Horse-races do not stop, when I shut my eyes, and vintage wines are not obliterated, when I have catarrh. We therefore seem to need ways of talking about what does stop, when I shut my eyes, and what is obliterated, when I have catarrh, ways which shall not depend on mentions of common events or liquids. An apparently suitable set of nouns is easily found, since it is quite idiomatic to say that my view of the race is interrupted, when I shut my eyes, that the look or appearance of the horses is modified when tears flow, that the flavour of the wine is obliterated by catarrh, and that the noise of the train is dulled, when I stop my ears. We can, it is suggested, talk about sensations 'neat' by talking about 'looks', 'appearances', 'sounds', 'flavours', 'whiffs'' 'tingles', 'glimpses' and so on. It is suggested, too, that it is necessary to adopt some such idioms in order to be able to distinguish the contributions made to our observation of common objects by our sensations from those made to it by tuition, inference, memory, conjecture, habit, imagination and association.

According to the theory, then, having a visual sensation can be described as getting a momentary look, or visual appearance, of something, and having an olfactory sensation as getting a momentary whiff of something. But what is it to get a momentary look, or a momentary whiff? And what sort of an object is the look, or the whiff, which is got? First of all, the look of a horse-race is not a sporting event on a racecourse. In the way in which everyone can witness the horse-race, it is not possible for everyone to witness the momentary look that I get of that race. You cannot get the look that I get, any more than you can suffer the tweak that I suffer. A sense datum, i.e. a momentary look, whiff, tingle or sound, is proprietary to one percipient. Next, the glimpse of a horse-race is described as a momentary patchwork of colour expanses in somebody's field of view. But this has to be qualified by the explanation that it is a patchwork of colour expanses only in a special sense. Ordinarily when people talk of patchworks of colours, they are referring to common objects of anyone's observation such as quilts, tapestries, oil paintings, stage scenery and mildewed plaster, that is, to flattish surfaces of things in front of their noses. But the visual appearances or looks of things, which are described as colour patches momentarily occupying particular fields of view, are not to be thought of as surfaces of flattish common objects; they are simply expanses of colour, not expanses of coloured canvas or plaster. They occupy their owner's private visual space, though he is, of course, subject to the permanent temptation to re-attach them somehow to the surfaces of common objects in ordinary space.

Finally, though holders of the Sense Datum Theory agree that the looks, smells and tingles that I get are inaccessible to anyone else, they are not agreed that it follows from this that they are mental in status or that they exist 'in my mind'. They seem to owe their genesis to the physical and physiological conditions, but not necessarily also to the psychological conditions, of their recipient.

Having, as they think, shown that there exist such momentary and proprietary objects as looks, whiffs, sounds and the rest, holders of the theory next face the question, 'What is it for their recipient to get or have them?' And their answer to this question is simple. In some statements of the theory, he is said to perceive or observe them, in a sense of 'perceive' and 'observe' which makes it proper to say that he sees colour patches, hears sounds, smells whiffs, tastes flavours and feels tickles. Indeed it is often thought not only allowable, but illuminating, to say that people do not really see horse-races, or taste wines; they really only see colour patches and taste flavours; or else, as a concession to ordinary habits of speech, it is admitted that there is indeed a vulgar sense of 'see' and 'taste' in which people may say that they see races and taste wines, but that for theoretical purposes we should use these verbs in a different and more refined sense, saying instead that we see colour patches and taste flavours.

Recently, however, the fashion has grown up of using a new set of verbs. Some holders of the theory now prefer to say that we intuit colour patches, we have direct awareness of smells, we have immediate acquaintanceship with noises, we are in direct cognitive relations with tickles, or, generically, we sense sense data. But what is the cash value of these formidable locutions? Their cash value is this. There are some verbs, like 'guess', 'discover', 'conclude', 'know', 'believe' and 'wonder', which are used only with such complements as '. . . that tomorrow is Sunday', or '. . . whether this is red ink'. There are other verbs, like 'peep at', 'listen to', 'observe', 'espy' and 'come across', the proper complements of which are such expressions as '. . . that robin', '. . . the roll of drums' and '. . . John Doe'. The Sense Datum Theory, according to which looks, whiffs and so on are particular objects or events, has therefore to employ cognition verbs of the second sort in order to construe such verbs as 'get' and 'have' in such expressions as 'get a glimpse' or 'have a tickle'. It has borrowed the ordinary force of verbs like 'observe', 'scan' and 'savour' for its solemnised verbs 'intuit', 'cognise' and 'sense'. The difference is that while laymen speak of observing a robin and scanning a page of *The Times*, this theory speaks instead of intuiting colour patches and having immediate acquaintanceship with smells.

It is not claimed that this account of what it is to have, e.g. a visual sensation—namely that it is to intuit or espy a proprietary patchwork of colours—by itself solves the whole problem of our knowledge of common objects. Disputes continue about the linkages obtaining between horse-races, which we do not 'strictly' or 'directly' see, and the looks of them, which we do 'strictly' or 'directly' see, but which are not on racecourses. But the holders of the theory hope that their elucidation of what sensing is will lead to the elucidation of what watching a horse-race is.

In particular it is claimed that the theory resolves paradoxes in the description of illusions. When the squinter reports that he sees two candles, where there is only one, and when the dipsomaniac says that he sees a snake, where no snake is, their reports can now be reconstrued in the new idiom. The squinter can now be said really to be seeing two 'candle-looks', and the dipsomaniac really does see one 'snake-appearance'. Their only error, if any, lies in their supposing that there also exist two physical candles, or one physical snake. Again, when a person, confronted by a round plate tilted away from him, says that he sees an elliptical object, he is in error if he supposes that the kitchen contains an elliptical piece of crockery, but he is quite correct in saying that he finds something elliptical; for there really is an elliptical patch of white in his field of view, and he really does descry or 'intuit' it there. To argue from what he finds in his field of view to what exists in the kitchen is always hazardous, and in this instance it is wrong. But what he finds in his field of view really is there and really is elliptical.

I shall try to prove that this whole theory rests upon a logical howler, the howler, namely, of assimilating the concept of sensation to the concept of observation; and I shall try to show that this assimilation makes nonsense simultaneously of the concept of sensation and of the concept of observation. The theory says that when a person has a visual sensation, on the occasion, for example, of getting a glimpse of a horse-race, his having this sensation consists in his finding or intuiting a sensum, namely a patchwork of colours. This means that having a glimpse of a horse-race is explained in terms of his having a glimpse of something else, the patchwork of colours. But if having a glimpse of a horse-race entails having at least one sensation, then having a glimpse of colour patches must again involve having at least one appropriate sensation, which in its turn must be analysed into the sensing of yet an earlier sensum, and so on for ever. At each move having a sensation is construed as a sort of espying of a particular something, often gravely called 'a sensible object', and at each move this espying must involve the having of a sensation. The use of awe-inspiring words like 'intuit' in no way exempts us from having to say that for a person to find, watch, listen to, peep at or savour something he must be sensitively affected; and to be sensitively affected is to have at least one sensation. So whether, as we ordinarily think, we see horse-races or whether, as we are instructed to think, we intuit colour patches, the descrying of whatever we descry involves our having sensations. And having sensations is not by itself descrying, any more than bricks are houses, or letters are words.

As has been shown earlier, there is an important logical connection between the concept of sensation and that of observing or perceiving, a connection which by itself entails that they are concepts of different kinds. There is a contradiction in saying that someone is watching or peeping at something, but not getting even one glimpse of it; or in saying that someone is listening to something, though he gets no auditory sensations. Having at least one sensation is part of the force of 'perceiving', 'overhearing', 'savouring' and the rest. It follows that having a sensation cannot itself be a species of perceiving, finding or espying. If all clothes are concatenations of stitches, absurdity results from saying that all stitches are themselves very tiny clothes.

It has already been remarked earlier in this chapter that there are several salient differences between the concepts of sensations and those of observation, scrutinising, detecting and the rest, which are revealed by the uninterchangeability of the epithets by which the different things are described. Thus we can speak of the motives from which a person listens to something, but not of the motives from which he has an auditory sensation; he may show skill, patience and method in peering, but not in having visual sensations. Conversely tickles and tastes may be relatively acute, but his inspections and detections cannot be so described. It makes sense to speak of someone refraining from watching a race or of his suspending his observation of a reptile, but it makes no sense to speak of someone refraining from feeling a pain, or suspending the tingle in his nose. Yet if having a tingle were, as the theory holds, intuiting a special object, it is not clear why this or any discomfort should not be dismissed by suspending the intuition of it.

Sensations then, are not perceivings, observings or findings; they are not detectings, scannings or inspectings; they are not apprehendings, cognisings, intuitings or knowings. To have a sensation is not to be in a cognitive relation to a sensible object. There are no such objects. Nor is there any such relation. Not only is it false, as was argued earlier, that sensations can be objects of observation; it is also false that they are themselves observings of objects.

A champion of the Sense Datum Theory might admit that, for a person to be describable as listening to a train, he must catch at least one sound and so have at least one auditory sensation, and still deny that, by admitting this point, he necessarily set his foot on the suggested Gadarene slope; he need not concede that, for a person to be describable as hearing a sound, he must have yet a prior sensation in his sensing of that sense datum. 'Having a sensation' is merely the vulgar way of reporting the simple intuiting of a special sensible object and to say that a person intuits such an object does not entail his being in any way sensitively affected. He might be an angelic and impassive contemplator of sounds and colour patches, and these might be of any degree of intensity, without anything in him being describable as more or less acute. He may come across tickles without himself being tickled, and the ways in which he becomes acquainted with smells or pains need not involve his being sensitive in any way other than that he is capable of simple detection or inspection of such things.

Such a defence in effect explains the having of sensations as the *not* having any sensations. It avoids the imputed regress by the heroic device of suggesting that sensing is a cognitive process which does not require its owner to be susceptible of stimuli, or to be describable as either highly or slightly sensitive. By construing sensation as the simple observation of special objects, it first does away with the very concept it was professing to elucidate and, in the second stage, makes nonsense of the concept of observation itself, since this concept entails the concept of sensations which are not themselves observings.

Alternatively, the Sense Datum Theory may be defended on a different ground. It may be said that, whatever may be the logical rules governing the concepts of sensation and of observation, it remains an unchallengeable fact that in seeing I am directly presented with patchworks of colours momentarily occupying my field of view, in hearing I am directly presented with noises, in smelling with smells and so forth. That sense data are sensed is beyond question and independent of theory. Two-dimensional colour patches are what I see in the strictest sense of 'see'; and these are not horses and jockeys, but at best the looks, or visual appearances, of horses and jockeys. If there are not two candles, then the squinter does not really see two candles, but he certainly sees two bright somethings, and these can be nothing but two proprietary 'candle-looks' or sense data. The Sense Datum Theory is not inventing factitious entities, it is merely drawing our attention to the immediate objects of sense which, from our ordinary preoccupation with common objects, we are in the habit of cold-shouldering out of conversation. If logical considerations seem to require that having a sensation shall not be on all fours with descrying hawks, or gazing at horse-races, so much the worse for those considerations, since having a visual sensation certainly is a non-inferential discerning of a particular sensible object.

Let us consider, then, the hackneyed instance of a person looking at a round plate tilted away from him, which he may therefore describe as looking elliptical; and let us see what, if anything, requires us to say that he is descrying a something which really is elliptical. It is agreed that the plate is not elliptical but round, and for the argument's sake we may concede that the spectator is veraciously reporting that it looks elliptical, (though round plates, however steeply tilted, do not usually look elliptical). The question is whether the truth of his report that the plate looks elliptical implies that he is really espying, or scanning, an object of sense which is elliptical, something which, not being the plate itself, can claim to be entitled 'a look' or 'a visual appearance of the plate'. We may also grant that if we are bound to say that he has come across an object of sense which is really elliptical and is a visual appearance of the plate, then this elliptical object is a two-dimensional colour patch, momentary in existence and proprietary to one percipient, i.e. that it is a sense datum and therefore that there are sense data.

Now a person without a theory feels no qualms in saying that the round plate might look elliptical. Nor would he feel any qualms in saying that the round plate looks as if it were elliptical. But he would feel qualms in following the recommendation to say that he is seeing an elliptical look of a round plate. Though he talks easily enough in some contexts of the looks of things, and easily enough in other contexts of seeing things, he does not ordinarily talk of seeing or of scanning the looks of things, of gazing at views of races, of catching glimpses of glimpses of hawks, or of descrying the visual appearances of tree-tops. He would feel that, if he mixed his ingredients in these fashions, he would be talking the same sort of nonsense as he would if he moved from talking of eating biscuits and talking of taking nibbles of biscuits to talking of eating nibbles of biscuits. And he would be quite right. He cannot significantly speak of 'eating nibbles', since 'nibble' is already a noun of eating, and he cannot talk of 'seeing looks', since 'look' is already a noun of seeing.

When he says that the tilted plate has an elliptical look, or looks as if it were elliptical, he means that it looks as an elliptical but untilted plate would look. Tilted round things sometimes do look quite or exactly like untilted elliptical things; straight sticks half immersed in water occasionally do look rather like unimmersed bent sticks; solid but distant mountains sometimes do look rather like flat mural decorations quite near to one's nose. In saying that the plate looks elliptical, he is not characterising an extra object, namely 'a look', as being elliptical, he is likening how the tilted round plate does look to how untilted elliptical plates do or would look. He is not saying 'I am seeing a flat elliptical patch of White', but 'I might be seeing an elliptical and untilted piece of white china'. We may say that the nearer aeroplane looks faster than the distant aeroplane, but we could not say that it has 'a faster look'. 'Looks faster' means 'looks as if it is flying faster through the air'. Talking about the apparent speeds of aeroplanes is not talking about the speeds of appearances of aeroplanes.

In other words, the grammatically unsophisticated sentence 'the plate has an elliptical look' does not, as the theory assumes, express one of those basic relational truths which are so much venerated in theory and so seldom used in daily life. It expresses a fairly complex proposition of which one part is both general and hypothetical. It is applying to the actual look of the plate a rule or a recipe about the typical looks of untilted elliptical plates, no matter whether there exist such pieces of china or not. It is what I have elsewhere called a mongrel-categorical statement. It is analogous to saying of someone that he is behaving judicially, or talking like a pedagogue. The squinter, aware of his squint, who reports that it looks just as if there were two candles on the table, or that he might be seeing two candles, is describing how the single candle looks by referring to how pairs of candles regularly look to spectators who are not squinting; and if, not being aware of his squint, he says that there are two candles on the table, he is, in this case, misapplying just the same general recipe. The expressions 'it looks . . .', 'it looks as if . . .', 'it has the appearance of . . .', 'I might be seeing . . .' and plenty of others of the same family contain the force of a certain sort of open hypothetical prescription applied to a case in hand. When we say that someone has a pedantic appearance, we do not mean to suggest that there are two kinds of pedantic beings, namely some men and some appearances of men. We mean that he looks rather like some pedantic people look. Similarly there are not two kinds of elliptical objects, namely some platters and some looks; there are only some platters which are elliptical and others which look as if they were elliptical.

In ordinary life there are certain ways in which we are quite ready to speak of patches and splashes of colour. A housewife might say that her sitting-room needed a splash of crimson, without specifying crimson paper, crimson flowers, crimson rugs, or crimson curtains. She might ask her husband to go out and buy 'an expanse of crimson . . .', leaving it to him to fill in the lacuna with 'geraniums', 'distemper', 'cretonne', or whatever else would meet her requirements. In a similar way an observer peering through a gap in a hedge might say that he saw an area of yellow . . . , but be unable to specify whether what he had seen were yellow daffodils, yellow charlock, yellow canvas or any other specific kind of common object or material. To complete his sentence he could say only 'I saw something yellow'.

In contrast with this ordinary use of lacuna-expressions like 'a patch of yellow . . .' and 'a splash of crimson something or other', the Sense Datum Theory recommends another idiom in which we are to say 'I see a patch of White' (and not 'I see a patch of white . . .') or 'he espied a two-dimensional, elliptical expanse of Blue' (and not 'a flat-looking, elliptical-looking blue something or other').

Now I am denying that having a visual sensation is a sort of observation describable as the sensing or intuiting of colour patches. But I am not denying that a woman can properly ask her husband to buy a splash of crimson . . . , or that a pedestrian can properly be said to espy an expanse of yellow something or other through a hole in the hedge. What the Sense Datum Theory has done is to try to skim an ethereal cream off such ordinary lacuna-descriptions of common objects; to talk as if it had found a new class of objects, where it has only misconstrued a familiar range of statements mentioning how otherwise unparticularised common objects are found to look.

Talking about looks, sounds and smells, about expanses, shapes and colours, just as much as talking about perspectives, hazes, focuses and twilights, is already talking about common objects, since it is applying learned perception recipes for the typical appearances of common objects to whatever one is trying to make out at the moment. To say that someone caught a glimpse, or heard a sound, is already to say more than would be involved in barely describing his visual and auditory sensations, for it is already to range what he is attending to under fairly general perception recipes.

This point may be illustrated by reference to the historic doctrine of Secondary Qualities. It was half-correctly observed that when a common object is described as green, bitter, chilly, pungent or shrill, it is being characterised as looking, tasting, feeling, smelling or sounding so and so to a sentient observer; it was correctly noticed, too, that conditions which affect his sensitivity make a difference in how the things look, taste, feel, smell or sound to him. How loud a train sounds depends in part upon the distance of the observer from the train, upon his degree of hardness of hearing, upon the direction in which his head is turned, upon whether his ears are covered and so forth. Whether water of a certain thermometer-temperature feels chilly or cosy depends on the prior thermometer-temperature of his hands. From such facts the theoretical jump was made to the doctrine that to say that an object is green is to say something about the visual sensations of the particular observer who reports that it is green. It was supposed that 'green', 'bitter', 'chilly' and the rest are adjectives which properly apply to sensations and are only improperly applied to common objects. And then, as it is obviously absurd to say that a sensation is a green thing, or an elliptical thing, or a chilly thing, it seemed necessary to allot to sensations their own peculiar objects, so that 'green' might be suitably applied not to the having of a sensation but to a peculiar object internally nursed by that sensation. The ban on characterising common objects of anyone's observation by Secondary Quality adjectives led to the invention of some counterpart, privy objects to carry those adjectives. Because Secondary Quality adjectives would not behave except as predicates in observation reports, sensations had to be construed as being themselves observations of special objects.

But when I describe a common object as green or bitter, I am not reporting a fact about my present sensation, though I am saying something about how it looks or tastes. I am saying that it would look or taste so and so to anyone who was in a condition and position to see or taste properly. Hence I do not contradict myself if I say that the field is green, though at the moment it looks greyish-blue to me; or that the fruit is really bitter, though it appears to me quite tasteless. And even when I say that the grass, though really green, looks greyish-blue to me, I am still describing my momentary sensation only by assimilating it to how common objects that are really greyish-blue normally look to anyone who can see properly. Secondary Quality adjectives are used and are used only for the reporting of publicly ascertainable facts about common objects; for it is a publicly ascertainable fact about a field that it is green, i.e. that it would look so and so to anyone in a position to see it properly. What else could the people who teach other people to talk, teach them about the use of these adjectives? It must be noticed that the formula 'it would look so and so to anyone' cannot be paraphrased by 'it would look *green* to anyone', for to say that something looks green is to say that it looks as it would if it were green and conditions were normal. We cannot *say* how something looks, or would look, except by mentioning the ascertainable properties of common objects, and then saying that this looks now as that can be expected to look.

So while it is true that to say 'the field is green' entails propositions about observers with certain optical equipments and opportunities, it is not true that it tells an anecdote about its author. It is analogous to the proposition 'this bicycle costs £12', which entails hypothetical propositions about any actual or possible purchaser, but does not state or entail any categorical proposition about its author. That an article has a price is a fact about the article and about customers, but it is not a fact about an article and about a given customer; still less is it a fact merely about a given customer.

A person who says 'the searchlight is dazzling' need not himself have any dazzle-discomforts; but still he is talking about dazzle-discomforts in another way, though it is a way which involves also talking about the searchlight. It is fallacious to argue that a searchlight cannot be said to be dazzling, unless the speaker is being dazzled, and that therefore dazzlingness is not a quality of the searchlight, but is a quality of that individual's sense data. To say that the searchlight is dazzling does not imply that it is now dazzling someone; it says only that it would dazzle anyone of normal eyesight who was looking at it from a certain distance without any protection. My statement 'the searchlight is dazzling' no more reports a sensation that I am having than 'the bicycle costs £12' reports money that I am handling. In the sense of 'subjective' usually intended, Secondary Qualities are not subjective, though it remains true that in the country of the blind adjectives of colour would have no use, while adjectives of shape, size, distance, direction of motion and so on would have the uses that they have in England.

Arguments for the subjectivity of Secondary Qualities are apt to hinge in fact upon an interesting verbal trick. Adjectives like 'green', 'sweet' and 'cold' are assimilated to adjectives of discomfort and their opposites, like 'dazzling', 'palatable', 'scalding' and 'chilly'. Even so, as we have seen, the conclusion drawn does not follow. To call the water 'painfully hot' is not to say that the author of the statement or anyone else is in pain. However, it does refer in a more indirect way to people being in pain, and as being in pain is a state of mind, namely one of distress, we can say that 'painfully hot' alludes indirectly and *inter alia* to a state of mind. But it certainly does not follow that 'the water is lukewarm' and 'the sky is blue' allude even in this indirect way to states of mind. 'Lukewarm' and 'blue' are not adjectives of discomfort or gratification. One road may be described as more boring than a second road and as longer than a third road; but in the way in which the first description does allude to wayfarers feeling bored, the second does not allude to wayfarers' moods at all.

A linguistic consequence of all this argument is that we have no employment for such expressions as 'object of sense', 'sensible object', 'sensum', 'sense datum', 'sense-content', 'sense field' and 'sensibilia'; the epistemologist's transitive verb 'to sense' and his intimidating 'direct awareness' and 'acquaintance' can be returned to store. They commemorate nothing more than the attempt to give to concepts of sensation the jobs of concepts of observation, an attempt which inexorably ended in the postulation of sense data as counterparts to the common objects of observation.

It also follows that we need erect no private theatres to provide stages for these postulated extra objects, nor puzzle our heads to describe the indescribable relations between these postulated objects and everyday things.

## (4) *Sensation and Observation.*

It is no part of the object of this book to swell the ranks of theories of knowledge in general, or of theories of perception in particular. It is, rather, one of its motives to show that a lot of the theories that go by those names are, or embody, unwanted para-mechanical hypotheses. When theorists pose such 'wires and pulleys' questions as, 'How are past experiences stored in the mind?', 'How does a mind reach out past its screen of sensations to grasp the physical realities outside?', 'How do we subsume the data of sense under concepts and categories?', they are apt to pose these problems as if they were problems about the existence and interconnections of hidden bits of ghostly apparatus. They talk as if they were doing something like speculative anatomy or even counter-espionage.

Since, however, we do not regard the fact that a person has a sensation as a fact about his mind, whereas the fact that he observes something and the fact that he tends not to observe things of certain sorts do belong to the description of his mental operations and powers, it is proper to say more about this difference.

We use the verb 'to observe' in two ways. In one use, to say that someone is observing something is to say that he is trying, with or without success, to find out something about it by doing at least some looking, listening, savouring, smelling or feeling. In another use, a person is said to have observed something, when his exploration has been successful, i.e. that he has found something out by some such methods. Verbs of perception such as 'see', 'hear', 'detect', 'discriminate' and many others are generally used to record observational successes, while verbs like 'watch', 'listen', 'probe', 'scan' and 'savour' are used to record observational undertakings, the success of which may be still in question. Hence it is proper to speak of someone watching carefully and successfully, but not of his seeing carefully or successfully, of his probing systematically, but not of his discovering systematically, and so on. The simple-seeming assertion 'I see a linnet' claims a success, where 'I am trying to make out what is moving' reports only an investigation.

In our present inquiry it will sometimes be convenient to use the ambiguous word 'observe' just because it can be used as well to signify discovery as to signify search. The words 'perception' and 'perceive' which are often used as cardinal in these inquiries, are too narrow since they cover only achievements, as do the specific verbs of perception 'see', 'hear', 'taste', 'smell' and, in one sense, 'feel'.

It has already been remarked that observing entails having at least one sensation, though having sensations does not entail observing. We might now ask, 'What more is there in observing than having at least one sensation?' But this formulation of the question is misleading, since it suggests that visually observing a robin consists in both having at least one visual sensation and doing or having something else as well, i.e. in two states or processes coupled together, as humming and walking can be coupled together; and this need not be the case. As was argued in Chapter V (Section 4) there is a crucial difference between doing something with heed and doing it, e.g. in absence of mind, but this difference does not consist in heeding being a concomitant act, occurring in another 'place'. So we should ask, not, 'What is an observer doing besides having sensations?', but, 'What does the description of an observer embody over and above the description of him as having those sensations?' This point will be important before long.

We should begin by dismissing a model which in one form or another dominates many speculations about perception. The beloved but spurious question, 'How can a person get beyond his sensations to apprehension of external realities?' is often posed as if the situation were like this. There is immured in a windowless cell a prisoner, who has lived there in solitary confinement since birth. All that comes to him from the outside world is flickers of light thrown upon his cell-walls and tappings heard through the stones; yet from these observed flashes and tappings he becomes, or seems to become, apprised of unobserved football-matches, flower-gardens and eclipses of the sun. How then does he learn the ciphers in which his signals are arranged, or even find out that there are such things as ciphers? How can he interpret the messages

which he somehow deciphers, given that the vocabularies of those
messages are the vocabularies of football and astronomy and not
those of flickers and tappings?

This model is of course the familiar picture of the mind as a
ghost in a machine, about the general defects of which nothing
more need be said. But certain particular defects do need to be
noticed. The use of this sort of model involves the explicit or
implicit assumption that, much as the prisoner can see flickers and
hear tappings, but cannot, unfortunately, see or hear football
matches, so we can observe our visual and other sensations, but
cannot, unfortunately, observe robins. But this is doubly to abuse
the notion of observation. As has been shown, on the one hand,
it is nonsense to speak of a person witnessing a sensation, and, on
the other, the ordinary use of verbs like 'observe', 'espy', 'peer at'
and so on is in just such contexts as 'observe a robin', 'espy a lady-
bird' and 'peer at a book'. Football matches are just the sorts of
things of which we do catch glimpses; and sensations are the sorts
of things of which it would be absurd to say that anyone caught
glimpses. In other words, the prison model suggests that, in finding
out about robins and football matches, we have to do something
like inferring from sensations, which we do observe, to birds and
games, which we never could observe; whereas in fact it is robins
and games that we observe, and it is sensations that we never could
observe. The question, 'How do we jump from descrying or
inspecting sensations to becoming apprised of robins and football
matches?' is a spurious how-question.

Now there is no unique and central problem of perception.
There is a range of partially overlapping questions, most of which
will cease to be intriguing, the moment that a few of them have
been cleared up. We can illustrate certain of the problems which
belong to this range in this way. To describe someone as finding a
thimble is to say something about his having visual, tactual or
auditory sensations, but it is to say more than that. Similarly to
describe someone as trying to make out whether what he sees is a
chaffinch or a robin, a stick or a shadow, a fly on the window or a
mote in his eye, is to say something about his visual sensations,
but it is to say more than that. Finally, to describe someone as
'seeing' a snake that is not there, or as 'hearing' voices, where all is
silent, seems to be saying something about his images, if not about his

sensations, but it is to say more than that. What more is being said? Or, what is the specific force of such descriptions in respect of which they differ both from one another and from 'neat' descriptions of sensations, supposing that we could produce such descriptions? The questions, that is, are not questions of the para-mechanical form 'How do we see robins?', but questions of the form, 'How do we use such descriptions as "he saw a robin"?'

When we describe someone as having detected a mosquito in the room, what more are we saying than that there was a certain sort of singing in his ears? We begin by answering that he not only had a singing in his ears but also recognised or identified what he heard as the noise of a fairly adjacent mosquito; and we are inclined to go on to say in more generic terms that he was not only having a singing in his ears, but was also thinking certain thoughts; perhaps that he was subsuming the singing under a concept, or that he was coupling an intellectual process with his sensitive state. But in saying this sort of thing, though we have one foot on the right track, we also have one foot on the wrong track. We are beginning to go on the wrong track, when we say that there must have taken place such and such conceptual or discursive processes; since this is in effect, if not in intention, to say that detecting a mosquito could not happen, unless some special but unobserved ghostly wheels had gone round, wheels whose existence and functions only epistemologists are clever enough to diagnose. On the other hand, in saying this sort of thing we are also on the right track. It is certainly true that a man could not detect a mosquito if he did not know what mosquitoes were and what they sounded like; or if, through absent-mindedness, panic or stupidity, he failed to apply this knowledge to the present situation; for this is part of what 'detecting' means.

We do not, that is, want tidings or hypotheses about any other things which the listener may have privily done or undergone. Even if there had taken place three, or seventeen, such *entr'actes*, news about them would not explain how detecting a mosquito differs from having a shrill singing in the ears. What we want to know is how the logical behaviour of 'he detected a mosquito' differs from that of 'there was a singing in his ears', from that of 'he tried in vain to make out what was making the noise', and from that of 'he mistook it for the noise of the wind in the telephone wires'.

Let us consider a slightly different situation in which a person would be described as not merely hearing something, and not merely listening to something, and not merely trying to make out what he was hearing, but as identifying or recognising what he heard, namely the case of a person who recognises a tune. For this situation to obtain, there must be notes played in his hearing, so he must not be deaf, or anaesthetised, or fast asleep. Recognising what he hears entails hearing. It also entails heeding; the absent-minded or distracted man is not following the tune. But more than this, he must have met this tune before; and he must not only have met it, but also have learned it and not forgotten it. If he did not in this sense already know the tune, he could not be said to recognise it on listening to it now.

What then is it for a person to know a tune, that is to have learned and not forgotten it? It certainly does not entail his being able to tell its name, for it may have no name; and even if he gave it the wrong name, he might still be said to know the tune. Nor does it entail his being able to describe the tune in words, or write it out in musical notation, for few of us could do that, though most of us can recognise tunes. He need not even be able to hum or whistle the tune, though if he can do so, he certainly knows the tune; and if he can hum or whistle plenty of other tunes, but cannot produce this one, even when prompted, we suspect that he does not know this tune. To describe him as knowing the tune is at the least to say that he is capable of recognising it, when he hears it; and he will be said to recognise it, when he hears it, if he does any, some or all of the following things: if, after hearing a bar or two, he expects those bars to follow which do follow; if he does not erroneously expect the previous bars to be repeated; if he detects omissions or errors in the performance; if, after the music has been switched off for a few moments, he expects it to resume about where it does resume; if, when several people are whistling different tunes, he can pick out who is whistling this tune; if he can beat time correctly; if he can accompany it by whistling or humming it in time and tune, and so on indefinitely. And when we speak of him expecting the notes which are due to follow and not expecting notes or bars which are not due to follow, we do not require that he be actually thinking ahead. Given that he is surprised, scornful or amused, if the due notes and bars do not come at their due times, then it is true to say that he was expecting them, even though it is false to say that he went through any processes of anticipating them.

In short, he is now recognising or following the tune, if, knowing how it goes, he is now using that knowledge; and he uses that knowledge not just by hearing the tune, but by hearing it in a special frame of mind, the frame of mind of being ready to hear both what he is now hearing and what he will hear, or would be about to hear, if the pianist continues playing it and is playing it correctly. He knows how it goes and he now hears the notes as the progress of that tune. He hears them according to the recipe of the tune, in the sense that what he hears is what he is listening for. Yet the complexity of this description of him as both hearing the notes, as they come, and listening for, or being ready for, the notes that do, and the notes that should, come does not imply that he is going through a complex of operations. He need not, for example, be coupling with his hearing of the notes any silent or murmured prose-moves, or 'subsuming' what he hears 'under the concept of the tune'. Indeed, if he were told to think the thought of 'Lillibullero', without producing, imagining or actually listening to the tune itself, he would say that there was nothing left for him to think; and if he were told that the fact that he could recognise the tune, even though played in various ways in various situations, meant that he had a Concept, or Abstract Idea, of the tune, he would properly object that he could not think what it would be like to be considering or applying the Abstract Idea of 'Lillibullero', unless this meant merely that he could recognise the tune, when he heard it, detect mistakes and omissions in it, hum snatches from it and so on.

This enables us to reconsider what was said earlier, namely, that a person who recognises what he hears is not only having auditory sensations, but is also thinking. It is not true that a person following a familiar tune need be thinking thoughts such that there must be an answer to the question, 'What thoughts has he been thinking?' or even 'What general concepts has he been applying?' It is not true that he must have been pondering or declaring propositions to himself, or to the company, in English or French; and it is not true that he must have been marshalling any visual or auditory images. What is true is that he must have been in some degree vigilant, and the notes that he heard must have fallen as he expected them to fall, or shocked him by not doing so. He was neither merely listening, as one might listen to an unfamiliar air, nor yet was he necessarily coupling his listening with some other process; he was just listening according to the recipe.

To clarify further the senses in which following a known tune is and is not 'thinking', let us consider the case of a person hearing a waltz for the first time. He does not know how this tune goes, but since he knows how some other waltz tunes go, he knows what sorts of rhythms to expect. He is partially but not fully prepared for the succeeding bars, and he can partially but not completely place the notes already heard and now being heard. He is wondering just how the tune goes, and in wondering he is trying to piece out the arrangement of the notes. At no moment is he quite ready for the note that is due next. That is, he is thinking in the special sense of trying to puzzle something out.

But, in contrast with him, the person who already knows the tune follows the tune without any business of puzzling or trying to make out how the tune goes. It is completely obvious to him all the time. There need be no activity, not even a very swift and very easy activity, of trying to resolve uncertainties, for there are no uncertainties. He is not listening in a worrying-out way; he is just listening. Yet he is not merely hearing notes, for he is hearing 'Lillibullero'. Not only are the notes clearly audible to him (perhaps they are not), but the tune is quite obvious to him; and the obviousness of the tune is not a fact about his auditory sensitiveness, it is a fact about what he has learned and not forgotten and his present application of those lessons.

Finally, though following a familiar tune entails having become familiarised with it, it does not require going through any operations of reminiscence. Memories of past hearings of the tune need not well up, or be called up. The sense of 'thinking' in which a person following a familiar tune can be said to be thinking what he is hearing, is not that thoughts of past auditions are occurring to him. He has not forgotten how it goes, but he is not recalling how it formerly went.

Roughly, to know how a tune goes is to have acquired a set of auditory expectation propensities, and to recognise or follow a tune is to be hearing expected note after expected note. And this does not entail the occurrence of any other exercises of expectation than listening for what is being heard and what is due to be heard. The description of a person hearing expected notes is indeed different from that of a person hearing unexpected notes and from that of a person who hears notes without any expectations at all, (like a person who is hearing but not listening); but this does not mean that there is something extra going on in the first person which is not going on in the second or the third. It means that the hearing is going on in a different way, the description of which difference involves, not a report of extra occurrences, but only the characterisation of his hearing as specially schooled hearing. That a person is following a tune is, if you like, a fact both about his ears and about his mind; but it is not a conjunction of one fact about his ears and another fact about his mind, or a conjoint report of one incident in his sensitive life and another incident in his intellectual life. It is what I have called a 'semi-hypothetical', or 'mongrel-categorical', statement.

We can now turn to consider some of the kinds of perceptual episodes which are ordinarily taken as the standard models of perceptual recognition. We shall see that they are in many important respects of a piece with the recognition of a tune. I chose to start with the example of someone following a familiar tune, because this is a protracted occupation. We can see a gate-post in a flash, but we cannot hear 'Lillibullero' in a flash. There is here, consequently, no temptation to postulate the occurrence of lightning intellectual processes, processes too rapid to be noticed, but intellectual enough to execute all the Herculean labours demanded by epistemologists.

When a person is described as having seen the thimble, part of what is said is that he has had at least one visual sensation, but a good deal more is said as well. Theorists commonly construe this as meaning that a description of a person as having seen the thimble both says that he had at least one visual sensation and says that he did or underwent something else as well; and they ask accordingly, 'What else did the finder of the thimble do or undergo, such that he would not have found the thimble if he had not done or undergone these extra things?' Their queries are then answered by stories about some very swift and unnoticed inferences, or some sudden and unrememberable intellectual leaps, or some fetching up of concepts and clapping them upon the heads of the visual data. They assume, that is, that because the proposition 'he espied the thimble' has a considerable logical complexity, it therefore reports a considerable complication of processes. And as these processes are not witnessed going on, it is postulated that they must be going on in a place where they cannot be witnessed, namely, in the finder's stream of consciousness.

Our analysis of what we have in mind, when we say that someone recognises a tune, can be applied to the new case. Certainly a person who espies the thimble is recognising what he sees, and this certainly entails not only that he has a visual sensation, but also that he has already learned and not forgotten what thimbles look like. He has learned enough of the recipe for the looks of thimbles to recognise thimbles, when he sees them in ordinary lights and positions at ordinary distances and from ordinary angles. When he espies the thimble on this occasion, he is applying his lesson; he is actually doing what he has learned to do. Knowing how thimbles look, he is ready to anticipate, though he need not actually anticipate, how it will look, if he approaches it, or moves away from it; and when, without having executed any such anticipations, he does approach it, or move away from it, it looks as he was prepared for it to look. When the actual glimpses of it that he gets are got according to the thimble recipe, they satisfy his acquired expectation-propensities; and this is his espying the thimble.

As with the tune, so with the thimble; if the recognition is impeded by no difficulties, if, that is, the thimble is obvious to the observer from the first glance, then no extra thinking or pondering, no puzzlings or reminiscences need be performed. He need not say anything in English or in French, to himself or to the world; he need not marshal memory images or fancy images; he need not wonder, make conjectures, or take precautions; he need not recall past episodes; he need do nothing that would be described as the thinking of thoughts, though, if linguistically equipped, he can be expected to be ready to do some of these things, if there arises any call to do so. The sense in which he is thinking and not merely having a visual sensation, is that he is having a visual sensation in a thimble-seeing frame of mind. Just as a person who recognises a tune from the first few bars is prepared both retrospectively for those already heard and those now being heard and prospectively for the bars that are to follow, though he goes through no additional operations of preparing for them, so a person who recognises a cow at sight is prepared for a multifarious variety of sights, sounds and smells, of none of which need the thought actually occur to him.

The difficulty will probably be felt that even if this sort of account of the visual obviousness of thimbles and the auditory obviousness of tunes is true, the real question remains unanswered. How do we learn that there are thimbles in the first place? How can a person who starts with mere sensations reach the stage of finding out that there are physical objects? But this is a queer sort of how-question, since, construing it in one way, we all know the answer perfectly well. We know how infants come to learn that some noises do, and others do not, belong to tunes; that some tuneless sequences of noises, like nursery rhymes, have recognisable rhythms; others, like clock-noises, have recognisable monotonies; while yet others, like rattle-noises, are random and disorderly. We know, too, the sorts of games and exercises by which mothers and nurses teach their infants lessons of these sorts. There is no more of an epistemological puzzle involved in describing how infants learn perception recipes than there is in describing how boys learn to bicycle. They learn by practice, and we can specify the sorts of practice that expedite this learning.

Now clearly stories about learning by practice will not be felt to give the solution of the how-question asked above. This question was not intended as a question about the stages through which capacities and interests develop, or about the aids and impediments to their development. What then was intended? Perhaps its poser might say something like this. 'There is, perhaps, no philosophical puzzle about how children learn tunes, or recognise them, when they have once learned them. Nor perhaps is there a puzzle about analogous learning of recipes in respect of sights, tastes and smells. But there is a big difference between learning a tune and finding out that there are such things as violins, thimbles, cows and gate-posts. Finding out that there are material objects requires, as learning tunes does not, getting beyond noises, sights, tastes and smells to public existents other than, and independent of, our personal sensations. And by the metaphorical expression 'getting beyond' is meant getting to know that such objects exist on the basis of originally knowing only that these sensations exist. Our puzzle is, therefore, in accordance with what principles, and from what premisses, can a person validly conclude that cows and gate-posts exist? Or, if by some lucky instinct he correctly believes such things without inferences, by what inferences can he justify these instinctive beliefs?' That is, the how-question is to be construed as a Sherlock Holmes question of the type 'what evidence had the detective ascertained which enabled him to confirm his suspicion that the gamekeeper was the murderer?' And construing the question in this way, we can swiftly see that it is an improper question. When we speak of the evidence ascertained by the detective, we are thinking of things which he or his informants had observed or witnessed, such as fingerprints found on glasses and conversations overheard by eavesdroppers. But a sensation is not something which its owner observes or witnesses. It is not a clue. Listening to a conversation entails having auditory sensations, for listening is heedful hearing, and hearing entails getting auditory sensations. But having sensations is not discovering clues. We discover clues by listening to conversations and looking at fingerprints. If we could not observe some things, we should not have clues for other things, and conversations are just the sorts of things to which we do listen, as fingerprints and gate-posts are just the sorts of things at which we do look.

This improper how-question is tempting, partly because there is a tendency mistakenly to suppose that all learning is discovery by inference from previously ascertained evidence; and then a process of sensing sense data is cast for the role of ascertaining the initial evidence. In fact, of course, we learn how to make inferences from previously ascertained facts just as we learn how to play chess, ride bicycles, or recognise gate-posts, namely by practice, reinforced, maybe, by some schooling. The application of rules of inference is not a condition of learning by practice; it is just one of the countless things learned by practice.

As has been shown, listening and looking are not merely having sensations; nor, however, are they joint processes of observing sensations and inferring to common objects. A person listening or looking is doing something which he would not do, if he were deaf or blind; or, what is quite different, if he were absent-minded, distracted or quite uninterested; or, what is quite different again, if he had not learned to use his ears and eyes. Observing is using one's ears and eyes. But using one's ears and eyes does not entail using, in a different sense, one's visual and auditory sensations as clues. It makes no sense to speak of 'using' sensations. It will not even do to say that in watching a cow, I am finding out about the cow 'by means of' visual sensations, since this too would suggest that sensations are tools, objects which can be handled in the same sorts of ways as the things seen and heard can be handled. And this would be even more misleading than it would be to say that manipulating a hammer involves first manipulating my fingers, or that I control the hammer by dint of controlling my fingers.

There is another favourite model for the description of sensations. As flour, sugar, milk, eggs and currants are among the raw materials out of which the confectioner concocts cakes, or as bricks and timber are among the raw materials of the builder, so sensations are often spoken of as the raw materials out of which we construct the world we know. As a counterblast to even more misleading stories this story had some important merits. But the notions of collecting, storing, sorting, unpacking, treating, assembling and arranging, which apply to the ingredients of cakes and the materials of houses do not apply to sensations. We can ask what a cake is made of, but not what knowledge is made of; we can ask what those ingredients are to be made into, but not what is going to be concocted or constructed out of the visual and auditory sensations which the child has recently been having.

We can conclude, then, that there is no difference of principle, though there are plenty of differences in detail, between recognising tunes and recognising gate-posts. One such difference may be mentioned, before we leave the subject. At a fairly early stage of infancy, the child learns to co-ordinate, for example, the sight recipes, the sound recipes and the feel recipes of things like rattles and kittens; and having begun to learn how things of particular sorts can be expected to look, sound and feel, he then begins to learn how they behave; when, for example, the rattle or the kitten makes a noise and when it makes none. He now observes things in an experimental way. But the relatively contemplative business of learning tunes does not, by itself, involve much co-ordination of looks with sounds, or give much room for experimentation. But this is a difference of degree, not one of kind.

One or two residual points should receive brief notice. First, in talking of a person learning a perception recipe, I am not talking of his discovering any causal laws, such as those of physiology, optics or mechanics. The observation of common objects is prior to the discovery of general correlations between special kinds of common objects. Next, in talking of a person knowing a perception recipe, e.g. knowing how common objects are due to look, sound and feel, I am not crediting him with the ability to formulate or impart this recipe. Somewhat as most people know how to tie a few different sorts of knots, but are quite incapable of describing those knots, or following spoken or printed descriptions of them, so we all know how to identify a cow at sight a very long time before we can tell the world anything about the visible marks by which we recognise it, and quite an appreciable time before we can draw, paint or even recognise pictures of cows. Indeed, if we did not learn to recognise things on sight or hearing, before we had learnt to talk about them, we could never start at all. Talking and understanding talk themselves involve recognising words on saying and hearing them.

Though I have drawn most of my instances of seeing according to perception recipes from cases of non-mistaken observation, such as espying a gate-post, where there is a gate-post, the same general account holds for mistaken observations such as 'espying' a huntsman, where there is really a pillar box, 'discerning' a stick, where there is really a shadow, or 'seeing' a snake on the eiderdown, when there is really nothing on the eiderdown. Getting a thing wrong entails what getting it right entails, namely, the use of a technique. A person is not careless, if he has not learned a method, but only if he has learned it and does not apply it properly. Only a person who can balance can lose his balance; only a person who can reason can commit fallacies; only a person who can discriminate huntsmen from pillar boxes can mistake a pillar box for a huntsman; and only a person who knows what snakes look like can fancy he sees a snake without realising that he is only fancying.

(5) *Phenomenalism.*

It is of topical interest to say a few words about a theory known as 'Phenomenalism'. This theory maintains that somewhat as talking about a cricket team is talking in certain ways about the eleven individuals who compose it, so talking about a common object like a gate-post is talking in certain ways about the sense data which observers do or might get in seeing, hearing and feeling it. Just as there is nothing to report in the history of a cricket team, save a certain selection of the actions and experiences of its members, when playing, travelling, dining and conversing as a team, so it is argued, there is nothing more to be said about the gate-post than how it does or would look, sound, feel, etc. Indeed, even to talk about how *it* looks, etc., is misleading; for 'it' is simply a succinct way of collecting mentions of these looks, sounds, etc., which it is proper to team together. It is conceded that this programme cannot in fact be carried out. Whereas we could, at the cost of long-windedness, relate the fortunes of a team by compiling accounts of the team-activities, habits and sentiments of its several members, we could not actually say all we know about the gate-post by describing the pertinent sensations which observers have, or could have. We have no 'neat' sensation vocabulary. We can in fact specify our sensations only by mention of common objects, including persons. But it is suggested that this is an accidental defect of language which would be obviated in a language designed to meet the needs of complete logical candour.

One of the commendable motives of this theory was the desire to dispense with occult agencies and principles. Its holders found that current theories of perception postulated unobservable entities or factors to endow things like gate-posts with properties which sensations were debarred from revealing. A gate-post is lasting, while sensations are fleeting; it is accessible to anyone, while sensations are proprietary; it observes causal regularities, while sensations are disorderly; it is unitary, while sensations are plural. So there had been a tendency to say that behind what is revealed to the senses there lie some ulterior and very important properties of the gate-post, namely that it is an Enduring Substance, a Thing-in-Itself, a Centre of Causation, an Objective Unity and a variety of other theorists' solemnities. Phenomenalism, accordingly, attempts to dispense with these unavailing theorists' nostrums, though, as I hope to show, it tries to dispense with the nostrums without diagnosing or curing the maladies which they were vainly adduced to remedy.

Phenomenalism also derives from another motive, this time not a commendable motive; and it is a motive from which derived also the theories against which Phenomenalism was a revolt. Namely it supposed that having a sensation is itself a finding of something, or that something is 'revealed' in sensation. It assumed the principle of the Sense Datum Theory, that having a sensation is itself a piece of observing, and indeed the only sort of observing which, being proof against mistakes, merited the name 'observation'. We can only really find out by observation facts about those objects which are directly given in sensations, i.e. such things as colour patches, noises, prickings and whiffs. Only propositions about such objects were observationally verifiable. It seemed to follow that we cannot really observe gate-posts and cannot therefore find out by observation the things that we all know quite well about gate-posts.

We can now see that both Phenomenalism and the theory that Phenomenalism was opposing were in error from the start. The latter said that since we can observe only sensible objects, gate-posts must be partly constituted of elements which cannot be found out by observation. Phenomenalism said that since we can observe only sensible objects, propositions about gate-posts must be translatable into propositions about sensible objects. The truth is that 'sensible object' is a nonsensical phrase, so 'propositions about sensible objects' is a nonsensical phrase; and so far from it being true that we cannot observe gate-posts, 'gate-posts' is a specimen of the sorts of complements which alone can be significantly given to such expressions as 'John Doe is looking at a so and so'. Such facts as that gate-posts last a very long time, especially if well creosoted, that, unlike wisps of smoke, they are hard and tough, that, unlike shadows, anybody can find them, whether by night or day, that they support the weight of gates, but can be consumed by fire, can be and are found out by observation and experiment. It can also be found out in the same way that gate-posts can look very much like trees or men; and that in certain conditions it is very easy to make mistakes about their sizes and distances. Certainly such facts about gate-posts are not directly given to sense, or immediately revealed in sensation; but nothing is so given or revealed, since having a sensation is not a finding.

This shows, too, why language does not enable us to formulate the propositions into which, according to Phenomenalism, propositions about gate-posts should be translatable. It is not because our vocabularies are incomplete, but because there are no such objects

as those for which the extra dictions are desiderated. It is not that
we have a vocabulary for common objects and lack a vocabulary
for sensible objects, but that the notion of sensible objects is absurd.
Not only is it false, then, that ideally we should talk, not in the
vocabulary of gate-posts, but only in the vocabulary of sensations,
but we cannot describe sensations themselves without employing
the vocabulary of common objects.

The objection may be made that it is improper to give the
honorific title of 'observation' to the operations by which we and
astronomers ordinarily satisfy ourselves about robins and spiral
nebulae. Not only do we often mistake things for other things,
but we never have a certificate guaranteeing that we are not making
such a mistake. 'Observation' ought to be reserved for a mistake-
proof process.

But why? If it makes sense to call one man a careful and another
a careless observer, why should we then retract and say that neither
is genuinely observing, since no degree of cautiousness is ever
absolute? We do not say that no one ever reasons, just because no
one ever has a certificate guaranteeing that he has not committed
a fallacy, so why should it be supposed that there is a kind of
mistake-proof operation to which alone the verb 'to observe' is
consecrated? Indeed 'observing', in its task-sense, is just one of the
verbs to which adverbs like 'carefully', 'carelessly', 'successfully',
'unavailingly' are appropriate, which shows that there could not
be a sort of observing, in this sense, where there was neither need
nor room for precautions against mistakes.

One motive for demanding a guaranteed mistake-proof brand of
observation seems to be this. It would be absurd to say that there
are, or might be, matters of empirical fact which could not, in
principle, be found out by observation; so, since any ordinary
observation actually made might be mistaken, there must be a special
sort of mistake-proof observation, in order that 'empirical' may be
defined in terms of it. And then sensing is invented to play this role,
for it is certainly improper to speak of a mistaken sensation. But the
reason why sensation cannot be mistaken is not because it is a
mistake-proof observing, but because it is not an observing at all.
It is as absurd to call a sensation 'veridical' as to call it 'mistaken'.
The senses are neither honest nor deceitful. Nor does the argument
justify us in postulating any other kind of automatically veridical

observation. All it requires is what familiar facts provide, namely that observational mistakes, like any others, are detectable and corrigible; so no empirical fact which has in fact been missed by a lapse, need be missed by an endless series of lapses. What is wanted is not any peculiar certificated process, but the ordinary careful processes; not any incorrigible observations, but ordinary corrigible observations; not inoculation against mistakes, but ordinary precautions against them, ordinary tests for them and ordinary corrections of them. Ascertaining is not a process which bases upon a fund of certainties a superstructure of guesses; it is a process of making sure. Certainties are what we succeed in ascertaining, not things which we pick up by accident or benefaction. They are the wages of work, not the gifts of revelation. When the sabbatical notion of 'the Given' has given place to the week-day notion of 'the ascertained', we shall have bade farewell to both Phenomenalism and the Sense Datum Theory.

There was another motive for desiderating a mistake-proof brand of observation, namely that it was half-realised that some observation words, such as 'perceive', 'see', 'detect', 'hear' and 'observe' (in its 'find' sense) are what I have called 'achievement verbs'. Just as a person cannot win a race unsuccessfully, or solve an anagram incorrectly, since 'win' means 'race victoriously' and 'solve' means 'rearrange correctly', so a person cannot detect mistakenly, or see incorrectly. To say that he has detected something means that he is not mistaken, and to say that he sees, in its dominant sense, means that he is not at fault. It is not that the perceiver has used a procedure which prevented him from going wrong or set a Faculty to work which is fettered to infallibility, but that the perception verb employed itself connotes that he did not go wrong. But when we employ the task verbs 'scan', 'listen', 'search' and the rest, it always makes sense to say that the operations denoted by them might go wrong, or be fruitless. There is nothing to prevent a scrutiny from being bungled or unavailing. Simple logic 'prevents' curing, finding, solving and hitting the bull's eye from being bungled or unavailing. The fact that doctors cannot cure unsuccessfully does not mean that they are infallible doctors; it only means that there is a contradiction in saying that a treatment which has succeeded has not succeeded.

This is why a person who claims to have seen a linnet, or heard a nightingale, and is then persuaded that there was no linnet or nightingale, at once withdraws his claim to have seen the linnet, or heard the nightingale. He does not say that he saw a linnet which was not there, or that he heard an unreal nightingale. Similarly, a person who claims to have solved an anagram and is then persuaded that that is not the solution, withdraws his claim to have solved it. He does not say that in a 'strict' or 'refined' sense of the verb he solved a 'solution-object', which happened not to coincide with the word camouflaged in the anagram.

Underlying most, if not all of the views criticised in this chapter there seems to be one general assumption; the assumption that whatever is known is learned either by inference from premisses, or, in the case of the ultimate premisses, by some sort of non-inferential confrontation. This confrontation has been traditionally labelled 'consciousness', 'immediate awareness', 'acquaintance', 'direct inspection', 'intuition', etc., words which no one without an epistemological theory to support ever uses for chronicling special episodes in his daily life.

This pet dichotomy 'either by inference or by intuition' seems to have its historical origin in the deference of epistemologists to Euclidean geometry. The truths of geometry are either theorems or axioms, and since geometry was, for a time, the exemplar of scientific knowledge, all other procedures for finding out truths, or establishing them, were piously mis-assimilated to this one special procedure.

But the assumption of similarity is false. There are lots of different ways of ascertaining things which are neither blank acquiescent gazings, nor yet inferrings. Consider the replies we should expect to get to the following 'How-do-you-know?' questions. 'How do you know that there are twelve chairs in the room?' 'By counting them'. 'How do you know that $9 \times 17$ makes 153?' 'By multiplying them and then checking the answer by subtracting 17 from $10 \times 17$'. 'How do you know the spelling of "fuchsia"?' 'By consulting the dictionary'. 'How do you know the dates of the Kings of England?' 'By learning them by heart for a strict schoolmaster'. 'How do you know that the pain is in your leg and not in your shoulder?' 'They are my leg and shoulder, aren't they?' 'How do you know that the fire is out?' 'I looked twice and felt with my hand'.

In none of these situations should we press to be told the steps of any inferences, or the counterparts of any axioms; nor should we grumble at the adoption of these different techniques of discovery, but only, in cases of doubt, at the carelessness of their execution. Nor do we require that tennis should be played as if it were, at bottom, a variety of Halma.


## (6)  *Afterthoughts.*

As I said in the Foreword, there is something seriously amiss with the discussions occupying this chapter. I have talked as if we know how to use the concept or concepts of sensation; I have spoken with almost perfunctory regret of our lack of 'neat' sensation words; and I have glibly spoken of auditory and visual sensations. But I am sure that none of this will do.

Sometimes we use the word 'sensation' in a sophisticated tone of voice to show that we are conversant with modern physiological, neurological and psychological hypotheses. We use it in the same breath with scientific words like 'stimulus', 'nerve-endings' and 'rods and cones'; and when we say that a flash of light causes a visual sensation, we think that experimentalists are now able, or will one day be able, to tell us what sort of a thing such a visual sensation is. But quite different from this is an unsophisticated use of 'sensation' and 'feeling'; the sense in which I say, without thinking about theories, that the electric shock gave me a tingling feeling up my arm, or that sensation is now returning to my numbed leg. In this use, we are quite ready to say that a piece of grit, or a dazzling light, gives us disagreeable sensations in our eyes; but in this use we should never say that the things we ordinarily look at give us any sensations in our eyes at all. When the grit is removed, we can reply to the question, 'How does your eye feel now?'. But when we switch our gaze from the field to the sky, we can give no answer to the question, 'How has that switch modified the feelings in your eyes?'. We can say from our own knowledge how the view has changed; and we can say, on hearsay knowledge of special theories, that presumably there have been a change of stimuli and a change in the reactions of our rods and cones. But there was nothing which we should ordinarily call 'a feeling' in our eyes at either stage.

Similarly, a few pungent or acrid smells give us special and describable feelings inside our noses and throats; but most smells give us no such sensations inside our noses. I can distinguish the smell of roses from the smell of bread, but I do not naively describe this difference by saying that roses give me one, and bread another, sort of sensation or feeling, as electric shocks and hot water do give me different sorts of sensations in my hand.

In our ordinary use of them, the words 'sensation', 'feel' and 'feeling' originally signify perceptions. A sensation is a sensation of something and we feel the ship vibrating, or rolling, as we see its flag flying, or hear its siren hooting. We can, in this sense, feel things distinctly or indistinctly, as we can smell them distinctly or indistinctly. As we see with our eyes and hear with our ears, so we feel things with our hands, lips, tongues or knees. To find out whether or not a common object is sticky, warm, lissom, hard or gritty, we have not to look, listen, sniff or savour, but to feel the thing. Reporting a sensation is, in this ordinary, unsophisticated use, reporting something found out by tactual or kinaesthetic observation.

True, we often use 'feel' and 'sensation' in a different, though derivative way. When a person with sore eyes says that there is a gritty feeling under his eyelids, or when a feverish person says that his head feels hot and his feet feel cold, they would not withdraw their statements on being assured that there was no grit under the eyelids, or that the head and feet were of the same temperature. For here their 'feel' means 'feels as if', just as 'looks' often means 'looks as if' and 'sounds' means 'sounds as if'. But what is needed to complete the 'as if' clause is a reference to some state of affairs, which, if it really obtained, would be found out by feeling in the primary sense of this word—the sense in which 'I feel a piece of grit under my eyelid' would be withdrawn, when the speaker was satisfied that there was no grit there. We might call this a 'post-perceptual' use of the verbs 'feel', 'look', 'sound' and the rest.

There is, however, an important disparity between 'feel' on the one hand and 'see', 'hear', 'taste' and 'smell' on the other. A person whose foot is numbed may say not only that he cannot feel things with his foot, but also that he cannot feel his foot, whereas a momentarily blinded or deafened person would say that he could not see or hear things with his right eye or right ear, but not that he could not see his eye or hear his ear. When sensation returns to the numbed foot its owner resumes his ability to report things both about the pavement and about the foot.

It is obvious that this primary concept of sensation is not a component of the generic concept of perception, since it is just a species of that genus. I can see something without feeling anything, just as I can feel something without seeing anything.

What then of the other, sophisticated sense of 'sensation', the sense in which it is said that seeing involves having visual sensations or impressions? Sensations or impressions in this sense are not things that people mention, until they have at least a hearsay knowledge of physiological, psychological or epistemological theories. Yet long before they reach this level of edification, they know how to use verbs of perception, like 'see', 'hear', 'taste', 'smell' and 'feel', and they use them then just as they continue to use them after edification. So the sophisticated concept of sensations or impressions is not a component of their concepts of perception. We could, and should do well to discuss with Plato the notion of perception; if we did so, we should never have occasion to complain that he had not yet graduated to the use of the concepts of seeing, hearing and feeling, since he had not yet been told latter-day theories about sensory stimuli.

Physiologists and psychologists sometimes lament, or boast, that they cannot find a bridge across the gulf separating impressions and the nervous excitations which cause them. They take for granted the existence of these impressions; it is only the mechanism of their causation which, not unnaturally, perplexes them. How could one question the existence of sense impressions? Has it not been notorious, at least since the time of Descartes, that these are the original, the elementary and the constant contents of consciousness?

Now when we say that a person is conscious of something, part of what we normally mean is that he is ready to avow or report it without research or special tuition. Yet just this is what no one ever does with his alleged impressions. People are ordinarily ready to tell what they see, hear, taste, smell or feel; they are ready, too, to tell that it looks as if so and so, or that it sounds or feels as if such and such. But they are not ready, indeed they are not even linguistically equipped, to tell what impressions they are or have been having. So the notion that such episodes occur does not derive from study of what ordinary sensible people are found telling. They are not mentioned in the deliverances of untutored 'consciousness'. Rather, the notion derives from a special causal hypothesis—the hypothesis that my mind can get in touch with a gate-post, only if the gate-post causes something to go on in my body, which in its turn causes something else to go on in my mind. Impressions are ghostly impulses, postulated for the ends of a para-mechanical theory. The very word 'impression', borrowed as it was from the description of dents made in wax, betrays the motives of the theory. It is a philosophical misfortune that the theory was able to trade on, and pervert, the vocabulary in which we tell the things that we find out by feeling. It is not a specialists' theory, but a piece of common knowledge, that we find out by sensation that things are warm, sticky, vibrating and tough. It was, accordingly, made to seem just a more general piece of common knowledge that we have sensations when we see, hear and smell. The sophisticated notion of sense impressions has been smuggled in under the umbrella of the ordinary idea of perception by touch.

I must not omit to mention another unsophisticated use of words like 'sensation' and 'feel'. Sometimes a person will say, not that he feels a piece of grit under his eyelid, and not that he feels a gritty feeling under his eyelids, but that he feels a pain in his eye, or has a painful sensation in his eye. Nouns of discomfort, like 'pain', 'itch' and 'qualm' come then to be treated by some theorists as names of specific sensations, where 'sensation' is used in its sophisticated sense as a synonym of the other sophisticated word 'impression'. But if a sufferer is asked just what he feels, he does not satisfy the questioner by replying 'a pain' or 'a discomfort', but only by replying 'a stabbing feeling', 'a gritty feeling', or 'a burning feeling'. He has to use a post-perceptual expression to the effect that it feels as if something sharp were stabbing him, something gritty were scratching him, or something red-hot were scorching him. That he is in slight, great or intense distress is information of a different sort, given in answer to a different sort of question. So the suggestion is mistaken that in nouns like 'pain', 'itch' and 'qualm' we do, after all, possess the beginnings of a vocabulary in which to report or describe impressions. There remains, however, an interesting and perhaps important difference between the sense in which a piece of grit hurts me and the sense in which a heard discord, or a seen clash of colours, hurts me. The grit literally hurts my eye, where the discord only metaphorically hurts my ears. I should not ask the chemist for an optical anodyne to stop the distress given to me by a clash of colours, and if asked whether the clash hurt my right eye more than it hurt my left eye, I should refuse to answer, unless by saying that it did not literally hurt my eyes at all, as grit and dazzling lights do literally hurt my eyes.

Words like 'distress', 'distaste', 'grief' and 'annoyance' are names of moods. But 'hurt', 'itch' and 'qualm', when used literally, are not the names of moods. We locate hurts and itches where we locate the grit, or the straw, that we feel, or fancy we feel. Yet 'hurt' and 'itch' are not nouns of perception either. Hurts and itches cannot, for instance, be distinct or indistinct, clear or unclear. Whereas finding something out by sight or touch is an achievement, 'I itch terribly' does not report an achievement, or describe anything ascertained. I do not know what more is to be said about the logical grammar of such words, save that there is much more to be said.

CHAPTER VIII

# IMAGINATION

(1) *Foreword.*

I HAVE mentioned the terminological fact that 'mental' is occasionally used as a synonym of 'imaginary'. A hypochondriac's symptoms are sometimes discounted as 'purely mental'. But much more important than this linguistic oddity is the fact that there exists a quite general tendency among theorists and laymen alike to ascribe some sort of an other-worldly reality to the imaginary and then to treat minds as the clandestine habitats of such fleshless beings. Operations of imagining are, of course, exercises of mental powers. But I attempt in this chapter to show that to try to answer the question, 'Where do the things and happenings exist which people imagine existing?' is to try to answer a spurious question. They do not exist anywhere, though they are imagined as existing, say, in this room, or in Juan Fernandez.

The crucial problem is that of describing what is 'seen in the mind's eye' and what is 'heard in one's head'. What are spoken of as 'visual images', 'mental pictures', 'auditory images' and, in one use, 'ideas' are commonly taken to be entities which are genuinely found existing and found existing elsewhere than in the external world. So minds are nominated for their theatres. But, as I shall try to show, the familiar truth that people are constantly seeing things in their minds' eyes and hearing things in their heads is no proof that there exist things which they see and hear, or that the people are seeing or hearing. Much as stage-murders do not have victims and are not murders, so seeing things in one's mind's eye does not involve either the existence of things seen or the occurrence of acts of seeing them. So no asylum is required for them to exist or occur in.

The afterthoughts expressed at the end of the last chapter cover also some of the things said about sensations in this chapter.

## (2) *Picturing and Seeing*.

To see is one thing; to picture or visualise is another. A person can see things, only when his eyes are open, and when his surroundings are illuminated; but he can have pictures in his mind's eye, when his eyes are shut and when the world is dark. Similarly, he can hear music only in situations in which other people could also hear it; but a tune can run in his head, when his neighbour can hear no music at all. Moreover, he can see only what is there to be seen and hear only what is there to be heard, and often he cannot help seeing and hearing what is there to be seen and heard; but on some occasions he can choose what pictures shall be before his mind's eye and what verses or tunes he shall go over in his head.

One way in which people tend to express this difference is by writing that, whereas they see trees and hear music, they only 'see', in inverted commas, and 'hear' the objects of recollection and imagination. The victim of *delirium tremens* is described by others, not as seeing snakes, but as 'seeing' snakes. This difference of idiom is reinforced by another. A person who says that he 'sees' the home of his childhood is often prepared to describe his vision as 'vivid', 'faithful' or 'lifelike', adjectives which he would never apply to his sight of what is in front of his nose. For while a doll can be called 'lifelike', a child cannot; or while a portrait of a face may be faithful, the face cannot be any such thing. In other words, when a person says that he 'sees' something which he is not seeing, he knows that what he is doing is something which is totally different in kind from seeing, just because the verb is inside inverted commas and the vision can be described as more or less faithful, or vivid. He may say 'I might be there now', but the word 'might' is suitable just because it declares that he is not there now. The fact that in certain conditions he fails to realise that he is not seeing, but only 'seeing', as in dreams, delirium, extreme thirst, hypnosis and conjuring-shows, does not in any degree tend to obliterate the distinction between the concept of seeing and that of 'seeing', any more than the fact that it is often difficult to tell an authentic from a forged signature tends to obliterate the distinction between the concept of a person signing his own name and that of someone else forging it. The forgery can be described as a good or bad imitation of the real thing; an authentic signature could not be characterised as an imitation at all, since it is the real thing without which the forger would have nothing to imitate.

As visual observation has pre-eminence over observation by the other senses, so with most people visual imagination is stronger than auditory, tactual, kinaesthetic, olfactory and gustatory imagination, and consequently the language in which we discuss these matters is largely drawn from the language of seeing. People speak, for example, of 'picturing' or 'visualising' things, but they have no corresponding generic verbs for imagery of the other sorts.

An unfortunate result ensues. Among the common objects of visual observation there exist both visible things and visible simulacra of them, both faces and portraits, both signatures and forged signatures, both mountains and snapshots of mountains, both babies and dolls; and this makes it natural to construe the language in which we describe imaginations in an analogous way.

If a person says that he is picturing his nursery, we are tempted to construe his remark to mean that he is somehow contemplating, not his nursery, but another visible object, namely a picture of his nursery, only not a photograph or an oil-painting, but some counterpart to a photograph, one made of a different sort of stuff. Moreover, this paperless picture, which we suppose him to be contemplating, is not one of which we too can have a view, for it is not in a frame on the wall in front of all of our noses, but somewhere else, in a gallery which only he can visit. And then we are inclined to say that the picture of his nursery which he contemplates must be in his mind; and that the 'eyes' with which he contemplates it are not his bodily eyes, which perhaps we see to be shut, but his mind's eyes. So we inadvertently subscribe to the theory that 'seeing' is seeing after all, and what is 'seen' by him is as genuine a likeness and as genuinely seen as is the oil-painting which is seen by everyone. True, it is a short-lived picture, but so are cinematograph-pictures. True, too, it is reserved for the one spectator to whom it and its gallery belong; but monopolies are not uncommon.

I want to show that the concept of picturing, visualising or 'seeing' is a proper and useful concept, but that its use does not entail the existence of pictures which we contemplate or the existence of a gallery in which such pictures are ephemerally suspended. Roughly, imaging occurs, but images are not seen. I do have tunes running in my head, but no tunes are being heard, when I have them running there. True, a person picturing his nursery is, in a certain way, like that person seeing his nursery, but the similarity does not consist in his really looking at a real likeness of his nursery, but in his really seeming to see his nursery itself, when he is not really seeing it. He is not being a spectator of a resemblance of his nursery, but he is resembling a spectator of his nursery.

(3) *The Theory of Special Status Pictures.*

Let us first consider some implications of the other doctrine, that in visualising I am, in a nearly ordinary sense of the verb, seeing a picture with a special status. It is part of this doctrine that the picture that I see is not, as snapshots are, in front of my face; on the contrary, it has to be not in physical space, but in a space of another kind. The child, then, who imagines her wax-doll smiling is seeing a picture of a smile. But the picture of the smile is not where the doll's lips are, since they are in front of the child's face. So the imagined smile is not on the doll's lips at all. Yet this is absurd. No one can imagine an unattached smile, and no doll-owner would be satisfied with an unsmiling doll plus a separate and impossible simulacrum of a smile suspended somewhere else. In fact she does not really see a Cheshire smile elsewhere than on the doll's lips; she fancies she sees a smile on the doll's lips in front of her face, though she does not see one there and would be greatly frightened if she did. Similarly the conjuror makes us 'see' (not see) rabbits coming out of the hat in his hand on the stage in front of our noses; he does not induce us to see (not 'see') shadow-rabbits coming out of a second spectral hat, which is not in his hand, but in a space of another kind.

The pictured smile is not, then, a physical phenomenon, i.e. a real contortion of the doll's face; nor yet is it a non-physical phenomenon observed by the child taking place in a field quite detached from her perambulator and her nursery. There is not a smile at all, and there is not an effigy of a smile either. There is only a child fancying that she sees her doll smiling. So, though she is really picturing her doll smiling, she is not looking at a picture of a simile; and though I am fancying that I see rabbits coming out of the hat, I am not seeing real phantasms of rabbits coming out of real phantasms of hats. There is not a real life outside, shadowily mimicked by some bloodless likenesses inside; there are just things and events, people witnessing some of these things and events, and people fancying themselves witnessing things and events that they are not witnessing.

Take another case. I start to write down a long and unfamiliar word and after a syllable or two, I find that I am not sure how the word should go on. I then, perhaps, imagine myself consulting a dictionary and in some cases I can then 'see' how the last three syllables are printed. In this sort of case it is tempting to say that I am really seeing a picture of a printed word, only the picture is 'in my head', or 'in my mind', since reading off the letters of the word that I 'see' feels rather like reading off the letters from a dictionary-item, or a photograph of such an item, which I really do see. But in another case, I start writing the word and I 'see' the next syllable or two on the page on which I am writing and in the place where I am to write them. I feel rather as if I were merely inking in a word-shadow lying across the page. Yet here it is impossible to say that I am having a peep at a picture or ghost of a word in a queer space other than physical space, for what I 'see' is on my page just to the right of my nib. Again we must say that though I picture the word in a certain place, printed in a certain type, or written in a certain handwriting, and though I can read off the spelling of the word from the way I picture it as printed or written, yet there exists no picture, shadow or ghost of the word and I see no picture, shadow or ghost of it. I seem to see the word on the page itself, and the more vividly and sustainedly I seem to see it, the more easily can I transcribe what I seem to see on to my paper with my pen.

Hume notoriously thought that there exist both 'impressions' and 'ideas', that is, both sensations and images; and he looked in vain for a clear boundary between the two sorts of 'perceptions'. Ideas, he thought, tend to be fainter than impressions, and in their genesis they are later than impressions, since they are traces, copies or reproductions of impressions. Yet he recognised that impressions can be of any degree of faintness, and that though every idea is a copy, it does not arrive marked 'copy' or 'likeness', any more than impressions arrive marked 'original' or 'sitter'. So, on Hume's showing, simple inspection cannot decide whether a perception is an impression or an idea. Yet the crucial difference remains between what is heard in conversation and what is 'heard' in day-dreams, between the snakes in the Zoo and the snakes 'seen' by the dipsomaniac, between the study that I am in and the nursery in which 'I might be now'. His mistake was to suppose that 'seeing' is a species of seeing, or that 'perception' is the name of a genus of which there are two species, namely impressions and ghosts or echoes of impressions. There are no such ghosts, and if there were, they would merely be extra impressions; and they would belong to seeing, not to 'seeing'.

Hume's attempt to distinguish between ideas and impressions by saying that the latter tend to be more lively than the former was one of two bad mistakes. Suppose, first, that 'lively' means 'vivid'. A person may picture vividly, but he cannot see vividly. One 'idea' may be more vivid than another 'idea', but impressions cannot be described as vivid at all, just as one doll can be more lifelike than another, but a baby cannot be lifelike or unlifelike. To say that the difference between babies and dolls is that babies are more lifelike than dolls is an obvious absurdity. One actor may be more convincing than another actor; but a person who is not acting is neither convincing nor unconvincing, and cannot therefore be described as more convincing than an actor. Alternatively, if Hume was using 'vivid' to mean not 'lifelike' but 'intense', 'acute' or 'strong', then he was mistaken in the other direction; since, while sensations can be compared with other sensations as relatively intense, acute or strong, they cannot be so compared with images. When I fancy I am hearing a very loud noise, I am not really hearing either a loud or a faint noise; I am not having a mild auditory sensation, as I am not having an auditory sensation at all, though I am fancying that I am having an intense one. An imagined shriek is not ear-splitting, nor yet is it a soothing murmur, and an imagined shriek is neither louder nor fainter than a heard murmur. It neither drowns it nor is drowned by it.

Similarly, there are not two species of murderers, those who murder people, and those who act the parts of murderers on the stage; for these last are not murderers at all. They do not commit murders which have the elusive attribute of being shams; they pretend to commit ordinary murders, and pretending to murder entails, not murdering, but seeming to murder. As mock-murders are not murders, so imagined sights and sounds are not sights or

sounds. They are not, therefore, dim sights, or faint sounds. And
they are not private sights or sounds either. There is no answer to
the spurious question, 'Where have you deposited the victim of
your mock-murder?' since there was no victim. There is no answer
to the spurious question, 'Where do the objects reside that we fancy
we see?' since there are no such objects.

It will be asked, 'How can a person seem to hear a tune running
in his head, unless there is a tune to hear?' Part of the answer is
easy, namely that he would not be seeming to hear, or fancying that
he heard, a tune, if he were really hearing one, any more than the
actor would be simulating murder, if he were really murdering
someone. But there is more to be said than this. The question,
'How can a person seem to hear a tune, when there is no tune to be
heard?' has the form of a 'wires and pulleys' question. It suggests
that there exists a mechanical or para-mechanical problem, (like
those that are properly asked about conjuring-tricks and automatic
telephones), and that we need to have described to us the hidden
workings that constitute what a person does, when he fancies himself
listening to a tune. But to understand what is meant by saying that
someone is fancying that he hears a tune does not require information about any ulterior processes which may be going on when he
does so. We already know, and have known since childhood, in
what situations to describe people as imagining that they see or
hear or do things. The problem, so far as it is one, is to construe
these descriptions without falling back into the idioms in which we
talk of seeing horse-races, hearing concerts and committing murders.
It is into these idioms that we fall back the moment we say that
to fancy one sees a dragon is to see a real dragon-phantasm, or that
to pretend to commit a murder is to commit a real mock-
murder, or that to seem to hear a tune is to hear a real mental tune.
To adopt such linguistic practices is to try to convert into species-
concepts concepts which are designed, anyhow partly, to act
as factual disclaimers. To say that an action is a mock-murder
is to say, not that a certain sort of mild or faint murder has been
committed, but that no sort of murder has been committed; and to
say that someone pictures a dragon is to say, not that he dimly sees
a dragon of a peculiar kind, or something else very like a dragon,
but that he does not see a dragon, or anything dragon-like at all.
Similarly a person who 'sees Helvellyn in his mind's eye' is not

seeing either the mountain, or a likeness of the mountain; there is neither a mountain in front of the eyes in his face, nor a mock-mountain in front of any other non-facial eyes. But it is still true that he 'might be seeing Helvellyn now' and even that he may fail to realise that he is not doing so.

Let us consider another sort of imaging. Sometimes, when someone mentions a blacksmith's forge, I find myself instantaneously back in my childhood, visiting a local smithy. I can vividly 'see' the glowing red horseshoe on the anvil, fairly vividly 'hear' the hammer ringing on the shoe and less vividly 'smell' the singed hoof. How should we describe this 'smelling in the mind's nose'? Ordinary language provides us with no means of saying that I am smelling a 'likeness' of a singed hoof. As has been said already, in the ordinary daylit world there are visible faces and mountains, as well as other visible objects, which are pictures of faces and mountains; there are visible people and visible effigies of people. Both trees and reflections of trees can be photographed or reflected in mirrors. The visual comparison of seen things with the seen likenesses of those things is familiar and easy. With sounds we are not quite so well placed, but there are heard noises and heard echoes of noises, songs sung and recordings of songs played, voices and mimicries of them. So it is easy and tempting to describe visual imaging as if it were a case of looking at a likeness instead of looking at its original, and it may pass muster to describe auditory imaging as if it were a case of hearing a sort of echo or recording, instead of hearing the voice itself. But we have no such analogies for smelling, tasting or feeling. So when I say that I 'smell' the singed hoof, I have no way of paraphrasing my statement into a form of words which says instead 'I smell a copy of a singed hoof'. The language of originals and copies does not apply to smells.

None the less, I may certainly say that I vividly 'smell' the singed hoof, or that its smell comes back to me vividly, and the use of this adverb shows by itself that I know that I am not smelling, but only 'smelling'. Smells are not vivid, faithful or lifelike; they are only more or less strong. Only 'smells' can be vivid, and correspondingly they cannot be more or less strong, though I can seem to be getting a more or less strong smell. However vividly I may be 'smelling' the smithy, the smell of lavender in my room, however faint, is in no degree drowned. There is no competition between a smell and a 'smell', as there can be a competition between the smell of onions and the smell of lavender.

If a person who has recently been in a burning house reports that he can still 'smell' the smoke, he does not think that the house in which he reports it is itself on fire. However vividly he 'smells' the smoke, he knows that he smells none; at least, he realises this, if he is in his right mind, and if he does not realise it, he will say not that the 'smell' is vivid, but, erroneously, that the smell is strong. But if the theory were true that to 'smell' smoke were really to smell a likeness of smoke, he could have no way of distinguishing between 'smelling' and smelling, corresponding to the familiar ways in which we distinguish between looking at faces and looking at likenesses of them, or between hearing voices and hearing recordings of voices.

There are usually ocular ways of distinguishing between things and snapshots or effigies of them; a picture is flat, has edges and perhaps a frame; it can be turned round and turned upside down, crumpled and torn. Even an echo, or a recording, of a voice can be distinguished, if not audibly, at least by certain mechanical criteria from the voice itself. But no such discriminations can be made between a smell and a copy of a smell, a taste and a likeness of a taste, a tickle and a dummy-tickle; indeed, it makes no sense to apply words like 'copy', 'likeness' and 'dummy' to smells, tastes and feelings. Consequently we have no temptation to say that a person who 'smells' the smithy is really smelling a facsimile or likeness of anything. He seems to smell, or he fancies he smells, something, but there is no way of talking as if there existed an internal smell replica, or smell facsimile, or smell echo. In this case, therefore, it is clear that to 'smell' entails not smelling and therefore that imaging is not perceiving a likeness, since it is not perceiving at all.

Why, then, is it tempting and natural to misdescribe 'seeing things' as the seeing of pictures of things? It is not because 'pictures' denotes a genus of which snapshots are one species and mental pictures are another, since 'mental pictures' no more denotes pictures than 'mock-murders' denotes murders. On the contrary, we speak of 'seeing' as if it were a seeing of pictures, because the familiar experience of seeing snapshots of things and persons so often induces the 'seeing' of those things and persons. This is what snapshots are for. When a visible likeness of a person is in front of my nose, I often seem to be seeing the person himself in front of my nose, though he is not there and may be long since dead. I should not keep the portrait if it did not perform this function. Or when I hear a recording of a friend's voice, I fancy I hear him singing or speaking in the room, though he is miles away. The genus is seeming to perceive, and of this genus one very familiar species is that of seeming to see something, when looking at an ordinary snapshot of it. Seeming to see, when no physical likeness is before the nose, is another species. Imaging is not having shadowy pictures before some shadow-organ called 'the mind's eye'; but having paper pictures before the eyes in one's face is a familiar stimulus to imaging.

An oil painting of a friend is described as lifelike, if it makes me seem to see the friend in great clarity and detail, when I am not actually seeing him. A mere cartoon may be lifelike without being at all similar to a lifelike oil painting of the same person. For a picture to be lifelike it is not necessary or sufficient that it should be an accurate replica of the contours or colouring of the subject's face. So when I vividly 'see' a face, this does not entail my seeing an accurate replica, since I might see an accurate replica without being helped to 'see' the face vividly and *vice versa*. But finding a picture of a person lifelike or 'speaking' entails being helped to seem to see the person, since that is what 'lifelike' and 'speaking' mean.

People have tended to describe 'seeing' as a seeing of genuine but ghostly likenesses, because they wanted to explain vividness or lifelikeness in terms of similarity, as if, for me vividly to 'see' Helvellyn, I must be actually seeing something else very similar to Helvellyn. But this is erroneous. Seeing replicas, however accurate, need not result in 'seeing' vividly, and the speakingness of a physical likeness has to be described, not in terms of similarity, but in terms of the vividness of the 'seeing' which it induces.

In short, there are no such objects as mental pictures, and if there were such objects, seeing them would still not be the same thing as seeming to see faces or mountains. We do picture or visualise faces and mountains, just as we do, more rarely, 'smell' singed hoofs, but picturing a face or a mountain is not having before us a picture of the face or mountain, it is something that having a physical likeness in front of one's nose commonly helps us to do, though we can and often do do it without any such promptings. Dreaming, again, is not being present at a private cinematograph show; on the contrary, witnessing a public cinematograph show is one way of inducing a certain sort of dreaming. The spectator there is seeing a variously illuminated sheet of linen, but he is 'seeing' rolling prairies. So it would invert the true state of affairs to say that the dreamer is regarding a variously illuminated sheet of 'mental' linen; for there is no mental linen, and if there were, seeing it variously illuminated would not be dreaming that one was galloping over the prairies.

The tendency to describe visualising as seeing genuine, but internal, likenesses, reinforces and is reinforced by the Sense Datum Theory. Many holders of this theory, supposing, erroneously, that in 'seeing' I am seeing a peculiar paper-less snapshot, though one which, oddly, cannot be turned upside down, think that *a fortiori* in seeing proper I am seeing a peculiar non-physical colour expanse. And supposing, erroneously, that having a visual sensation is descrying a flat patchwork of colours spread out in 'a private space', they find it all the easier to say that in imaging we are scanning a more ghostly patchwork of colours hung up in the same gallery with that original patchwork of colours. As in my study there may be both a person and a shadow or a portrait of that person, so in my private sight-gallery there might be both sense data and reproductions of sense data. My objections to the interpretation of picturing as picture-seeing do not in themselves demolish the Sense Datum Theory of sensations; but they do demolish, I hope, the ancillary theory that picturing is looking at reproductions of sense data. And if I am right in saying that having a visual sensation is wrongly described as some sort of observing of a patchwork of colours, since the concept of sensation is different from the concept of observing, it will follow, as can be established on other grounds, that imaging is not only not any sort of observing of anything; it is also not having a sensation of a special sort. Seeming to hear a very loud noise is not being in any degree deafened, nor is seeming to see a very bright light being in any degree dazzled. So far are ideas from being impressions of a special sort, that to describe something as an idea, in this sense, is to deny that an impression is being had.

(4) *Imagining.*

It will probably be asked, 'What then is it for a person to fancy that he sees or smells something? How can he seem to hear a tune that he does not really hear? And, in particular, how can a person fail to be aware that he is only seeming to hear or see, as the dipsomaniac certainly fails? In what precise respects is 'seeing' so like seeing that the victim often cannot, with the best will and the best wits, tell which he is doing?' Now if we divest these questions of associations with any 'wires and pulleys' questions, we can see that they are simply questions about the concept of imagining or make-believe, a concept of which I have so far said nothing positive. I have said nothing about it so far, because it seemed necessary to begin by vaccinating ourselves against the theory, often tacitly assumed, that imagining is to be described as the seeing of pictures with a special status.

But I hope I have now shown that what people commonly describe as 'having a mental picture of Helvellyn' or 'having Helvellyn before the mind's eye' is actually a special case of imagining, namely imagining that we see Helvellyn in front of our noses, and that having a tune running in one's head is imagining that one has the tune being played in one's hearing, maybe in a concert-hall. If successful, then I have also shown that the notion that a mind is a 'place', where mental pictures are seen and reproductions of voices and tunes are heard, is also wrong.

There are hosts of widely divergent sorts of behaviour in the conduct of which we should ordinarily and correctly be described as imaginative. The mendacious witness in the witness-box, the inventor thinking out a new machine, the constructor of a romance, the child playing bears, and Henry Irving are all exercising their imaginations; but so, too, are the judge listening to the lies of the witness, the colleague giving his opinion on the new invention, the novel reader, the nurse who refrains from admonishing the 'bears' for their subhuman noises, the dramatic critic and the theatre-goers. Nor do we say that they are all exercising their imaginations because we think that, embedded in a variety of often widely different operations, there is one common nuclear operation which all alike are performing, any more than we think that what makes two men both farmers is some nuclear operation which both do in exactly the same way. Just as ploughing is one farming job and tree-spraying is another farming job, so inventing a new machine is one way of being imaginative and playing bears is another. No one thinks that there exists a nuclear farming operation by the execution of which alone a man is entitled to be called 'a farmer'; but the concepts wielded in theories of knowledge are apt to be less generously treated. It is often assumed that there does exist one nuclear operation in which imagination proper consists; it is assumed, that is, that the judge following the witness's mendacities, and the child playing bears, are both exercising their imaginations only if they are both executing some specifically identical ingredient operation. This supposed nuclear operation is often supposed to be that of seeing things in the mind's eye, hearing things in one's head and so on, i.e. some piece of fancied perceiving. Of course, it is not denied that the child is doing lots of other things as well; he roars, he pads around the floor, he gnashes his teeth and he pretends to sleep in what he pretends is a cave. But, according to this view, only if he sees pictures in his mind's eye of his furry paws, his snowbound den and so on, is he imagining anything. His noises and antics may be a help to his picturing, or they may be special effects of it, but it is not in making these noises, or performing these antics, that he is exercising his imagination, but only in his 'seeing', 'hearing', 'smelling', 'tasting' and 'feeling' things which are not there to be perceived. And the corresponding things will be true of the attentive, if sceptical, judge.

Put as bluntly as this, the doctrine is patently absurd. Most of the things for which we ordinarily describe children as imaginative are ruled out in favour of a limited number of operations the occurrence and qualities of which it is difficult to ascertain, especially from relatively inarticulate children. We see and hear them play, but we do not see or hear them 'seeing' or 'hearing' things. We read what Conan Doyle wrote, but we do not get a view of what he saw in his mind's eye. So, on this theory, we cannot easily tell whether children, actors or novelists are imaginative or not, though the word 'imagination' came to be wielded in theories of knowledge just because we all know how to wield it in our everyday descriptions of children, actors and novelists.

There is no special Faculty of Imagination, occupying itself single-mindedly in fancied viewings and hearings. On the contrary, 'seeing' things is one exercise of imagination, growling somewhat like a bear is another; smelling things in the mind's nose is an uncommon act of fancy, malingering is a very common one, and so forth. Perhaps the chief motive from which many theorists have limited the exercises of imagination to the special class of fancied perceptions is that they have supposed that, since the mind is officially tri-partitioned into the Three Estates of Cognition, Volition and Emotion, and since imagination was born into the first, it must therefore be excluded from the others. Cognitive malpractices are notoriously due to the pranks of undisciplined Imagination, and some cognitive successes are in debt to its primmer activities. So, being an (erratic) Squire of Reason, it cannot serve the other masters. But we need not pause to discuss this feudal allegory. Indeed, if we are asked whether imagining is a cognitive or a non-cognitive activity, our proper policy is to ignore the question. 'Cognitive' belongs to the vocabulary of examination papers.

## (5) *Pretending.*

Let us begin by considering the notion of pretending, a notion which is partly constitutive of such notions as those of cheating, acting a part, playing bears, shamming sick and hypochondria. It will be noticed that in some varieties of make-believe, the pretender is deliberately simulating or dissimulating, in some varieties he may not be quite sure to what extent, if any, he is simulating or dissimulating, and in other varieties he is completely taken in by his own acting. On a small scale this can be illustrated by the child playing bears, who knows, while in the well-lit drawing-room, that he is only playing an amusing game, but feels faint anxieties when out on the solitary landing, and cannot be persuaded of his safety when in the darkness of a passage. Make-believe is compatible with all degrees of scepticism and credulity, a fact which is relevant to the supposed problem, 'How can a person fancy that he sees something, without realising that he is not seeing it?' But if we pose the parallel questions, 'How can a child play bears, without being all the time quite sure that it is only a game? How can the malingerer fancy that he has symptoms, without being perfectly confident that they are only his fancies?' we see that these questions, and many others like them, are not genuine how-questions at all. The fact that people can fancy that they see things, are pursued by bears, or have a grumbling appendix, without realising that it is nothing but fancy, is simply a part of the unsurprising general fact that not all people are, all the time, at all ages and in all conditions, as judicious or critical as could be wished.

To describe someone as pretending is to say that he is playing a part, and to play a part is to play the part, normally, of someone who is not playing a part, but doing or being something ingenuously or naturally. A corpse is motionless, and so is a person pretending to be a corpse. But a person pretending to be a corpse is, unlike the corpse, trying to be motionless, and, again unlike the corpse, he is motionless from the wish to resemble a corpse. He is, perhaps, deliberately, skilfully and convincingly motionless, whereas the corpse is just motionless. Corpses have to be dead, but mock-corpses have to be alive. Indeed, they have to be not only alive, but also awake, non-absent-minded and applying their minds to the part they are playing.

Talking about a person pretending to be a bear or a corpse involves talking obliquely about how bears and corpses behave, or are supposed to behave. He plays these parts by growling as bears growl and lying still as corpses lie still. One cannot know how to play a part without knowing what it is like to be or do ingenuously that which one is staging; nor can one find a mock-performance convincing or unconvincing, or dub it skilful or inefficient, without knowing how the ingenuous performance itself is conducted. Pretending to growl like a bear, or lie still like a corpse, is a sophisticated performance, where the bear's growling and the corpse's immobility are naive.

The difference is parallel to that between quoting an assertion and making it. If I quote what you asserted, then what I say is just what you said; I may even say it in just your tone of voice. Yet the full description of my action is not at all like that of yours. Yours was, perhaps, an exercise of the skill of a preacher; mine is that of a reporter or mimic; you were being original; I am being an echo: you said what you believed; I say what I do not believe. In short, the words I utter are uttered, so to speak, as they would be written, inside inverted commas. The words you uttered were not. You spoke in *oratio recta*; I may intend what I say to be taken as if in *oratio obliqua*. In the same sort of way, while the bear just growls, the child's growling is, so to speak, inside inverted commas. His direct action is, unlike the bear's, one of representation, and this obliquely embodies growling. Yet the child is not doing two things at once, any more than I, in quoting you, am saying two things at once. A mock-performance differs from the ingenuous performance which it represents, not in being a complex of performances, but in being a performance with a certain sort of complex description. A mention of the ingenuous performance is an ingredient in the description of the mock-performance. The noises issuing from the child may be as similar as you please to those issuing from the bear, just as the noises issuing from my lips may be as similar as you please to the noises you made in your homily, but the concept of such mock-performances is logically very different from that of the ingenuous performances. In describing their authors, we use quite different batteries of predicates.

Is a forged signature the same sort of thing as a genuine signature, or is it a different sort of thing? If the forgery is perfect, then the one cheque really is indistinguishable from the other and so, in this sense, they are exactly the same sort of thing. But forging a signature is quite unlike signing; the one requires what the other does not, the wish and the ability to produce marks indistinguishable from a signature. In this sense they are completely different sorts of things. The whole ingenuity of the forger is exerted in trying to make his cheque a perfect facsimile of the authentic cheque, the signing of which had taken no ingenuity. What he is after has to be described in terms of the similarity between writings, just as what the child was after has to be described in terms of the similarity between his noises and the bear's noises. Deliberate verisimilitude is a part of the concept of copying. The very likenesses between copies and their originals are what make activities of copying different in type from the activities copied.

There are lots of different sorts of pretending, different motives from which people pretend and different criteria by which pretences are assessed as skilful or unskilful. The child pretends for fun, the hypocrite for profit, the hypochondriac from morbid egotism, the spy, sometimes, from patriotism, the actor, sometimes, for art's sake, and the cooking instructress for demonstration purposes. Let us consider the case of the boxer sparring with his instructor. They go through the motions of serious fighting, though they are not fighting seriously; they pretend to attack, retreat, punish and retaliate, though no victory is aimed at, or defeat feared. The pupil is learning manoeuvres by playing at them, the instructor is teaching them by playing at them. Yet though they are only mock-fighting, they need not be carrying on two collateral activities. They need not be both punching and also pulling their punches; both laying traps and also betraying the traps they lay; or both plying their fists and also plying propositions. They may be going through only one set of movements, yet they are making these movements in a hypothetical and not in a categorical manner. The notion of hurt enters only obliquely into the description of what they are trying to do. They are not trying either to hurt or to avoid hurt, but only to practise ways in which they would hurt and would avoid hurt, if engaged in serious fights. The cardinal thing in sparring is abstaining from giving punishing blows, when one could, i.e. in situations in which one would give such blows if the fight were serious. Sham-fighting is, to put it crudely, a series of calculated omissions to fight.

The central point illustrated by these cases is that a mock-performance may be unitary as an action though there is an intrinsic duality in its description. Only one thing is done, yet to say what is done requires a sentence containing, at the least, both a main clause and a subordinate clause. To recognise this is to see why there is no more than a verbal appearance of a contradiction in saying of an actor, playing the part of an idiot, that he is grimacing in an idiotic manner in a highly intelligent manner; or of a clown that he is deftly clumsy and brilliantly inane. The scathing adjective attaches to the conduct mentioned in the subordinate clause of the description and the flattering adjective or adverb to the activity mentioned in the main clause, yet only one set of motions is executed. Similarly, if I quote a statement, you might correctly characterise what I say both as 'accurate' and as 'inaccurate', for it might be a highly inaccurate statement of the size of the National Debt quite accurately quoted, or *vice versa*. Yet I have uttered only one statement.

Acts of pretending are not the only ones the descriptions of which incorporate this dualism between the direct and the oblique. If I obey an order, I do the thing I am told to do and I comply with the command; but as I comply with the command by doing the thing, I execute only one action. Yet the description of what I do is complex in such a way that it would often be correct to characterise my conduct by two seemingly conflicting predicates. I do what I am told from force of habit, though what I am ordered to do is something which I am not in the habit of doing; or I obey like a good soldier, though what I am ordered to do is something which it is a mark of a bad soldier to do. Similarly, I may do wisely in following advice to do something unwise, and I may with difficulty carry out a resolve to do something easy. In Chapter VI, Section (6) we found it convenient to distinguish verbally between higher order tasks and lower order tasks, and between higher order performances and lower order performances, meaning by a 'higher order task', one the description of which incorporates the mention of another task of a less complex description. It will be realised that the fact that the movements made in the execution of one task are entirely similar to those made in the execution of another is compatible with the descriptions of the tasks being not only different but different in type in the way indicated.

To return to pretending. The frame of mind of a person pretending to be cross is different from that of a person who is cross, and different from it not just in the fact that the former is not cross. He is not cross, though he acts as if he were; and this simulation involves, in some way, the thought of crossness. He must not only possess, but in some way be using, the knowledge of what it is for someone to be cross. He intentionally models his actions upon those of a cross man. But when we say that putting on the behaviour of a cross man involves having the thought of crossness, we run a certain risk, namely the risk of suggesting that pretending to be cross is a tandem process consisting of one operation of meditating about crossness, shepherding a second operation of performing the quasi-cross actions. Such a suggestion would be wrong. Whether or not pieces of make-believe happen to be preceded by, or interlarded with, pieces of describing or planning, it is not in this way that make-believe involves the thought of what is simulated. The business of trying to behave in ways in which a cross man would behave is itself, in part, the thought of how he would behave; the more or less faithful muscular representation of his poutings and stampings is the active utilisation of the knowledge of how he would comport himself. We concede that a person knows what the publican's temper is like if, though he is unable to give to himself, or to us, even a lame verbal description of it, he can yet play the part to the life; and if he does so, he cannot then say that he is unable to think how the publican behaves when annoyed. Mimicking him *is* thinking how he behaves. If we ask the person how he thinks the publican acted, we shall not reject a response given by impersonation and demand instead a response given in prose. Indeed, so far from the concept of pretending to be cross requiring for its elucidation a causal story about operations of planning shepherding operations of acting quasi-crossly, the converse is the case. To explain the sense in which planning a line of conduct leads to the pursuance of that line of conduct, it is necessary to show that executing a planned task, is doing, not two things, but one thing. But the thing done is an act of a higher order, since its description has a logical complexity, like that which characterises the descriptions of pretending and obeying. To do what one has planned to do and to growl like a bear are both relatively sophisticated occupations. To describe them, we have obliquely to mention doings, whose description embodies no corresponding oblique mentions. Of the same type are acts of repenting of what one has done, keeping a resolution, jeering at another's performance and complying with the rules. In all these cases, as well as in many others, the doing of the higher order acts involves the thought of the lower order acts; yet the phrase 'involves the thought of' does not connote the collateral occurrence of another, cogitative act.

One variety of pretending is worthy of mention at this point. A person engaged in a planning or theorising task may find it useful or amusing to go through the motions of thinking thoughts which are not, or are not yet, what he is disposed ingenuously to think. Assuming, supposing, entertaining, toying with ideas and considering suggestions are all ways of pretending to adopt schemes or theories. The sentences in which the propositions entertained are expressed are not being ingenuously used; they are being mock-used. There are, metaphorically speaking, inverted commas round them. Their employer is wielding them with his intellectual tongue in his cheek; he utters them in a hypothetical, not in a categorical frame of mind. Very likely he advertises the fact that he is wielding his sentences in a sophisticated and not in a naive way by using such special signals as the words 'if', 'suppose', 'granting', 'say' and so on. Or, he may talk aloud, or to himself, in a sparring, instead of a fighting tone of voice. But he may still be misunderstood and accused of seriously meaning what he says, and then he has to explain that he had not been committing himself to what he had been asserting, but only considering just what he would have been committing himself to, had he done so. He had been trying out the thought, perhaps to give himself practice in it. That is to say, supposing is a more sophisticated operation than ingenuous thinking. We have to learn to give verdicts before we can learn to operate with suspended judgments.

This point is worth making, partly for its intimate connection with the concept of imagining and partly because logicians and epistemologists sometimes assume, what I for a long time assumed, that entertaining a proposition is a more elementary or naive performance than affirming that something is the case, and, what follows, that learning, for example, how to use 'therefore' requires first having learned to use 'if'. This is a mistake. The concept of make-believe is of a higher order than that of belief.

(6) *Pretending, Fancying and Imaging.*

There is not much difference between a child playing at being a pirate, and one fancying that he is a pirate. So far as there is a difference, it seems to come to this, that we use words like 'play', 'pretend' and 'act the part', when we think of spectators finding the performance more or less convincing, whereas we use words like 'fancy' and 'imagine' when we are thinking of the actor himself being half-convinced; and we use words like 'play' and 'pretend' for deliberate, concerted and rehearsed performances, whereas we are more ready to use words like 'fancy' and 'imagine' for those activities of make-believe into which people casually and even involuntarily drift. Underlying these two differences there is, perhaps, this more radical difference, that we apply the words 'pretend' and 'act the part', where an overt and muscular representation is given of whatever deed or condition is being put on, while we tend, with plenty of exceptions, to reserve 'imagine' and 'fancy' for some things that people do inaudibly and invisibly because 'in their heads', i.e. for their fancied perceptions and not for their mock-actions.

It is with this special brand of make-believe that we are here chiefly concerned, namely what we call 'imaging', 'visualising', 'seeing in the mind's eye' and 'going through in one's head'.

Even people who might allow that sparring consists in going through some of the motions of fighting in a hypothetical manner will not readily allow that the same sort of account holds good of seeing Helvellyn in one's mind's eye. What motions are there here to go through in a hypothetical manner? Even though in describing how the dipsomaniac 'sees' snakes we use inverted commas, as we do in describing how the child 'scalps' his nurse, or how the boxer 'punishes' his sparring partner, it will be urged that the force of these commas is not the same in the two sorts of cases. Picturing is not sham-seeing in the way that sparring is sham-fighting.

We have, I hope, got rid of the idea that picturing Helvellyn is seeing a picture of Helvellyn, or that having 'Lillibullero' running in one's head is listening to a private reproduction, or internal echo, of that tune. It is necessary now to get rid of a more subtle superstition. Epistemologists have long encouraged us to suppose that a mental picture, or a visual image, stands to a visual sensation in something like the relation of an echo to a noise, a bruise to a blow or a reflection in a mirror to the face reflected. To make this point more specific, it has been supposed that what is taking place, when I 'see', or 'hear', or 'smell', corresponds to that element in perceiving which is purely sensuous; and not to that element which constitutes recognising or making out; i.e. that imaging is a piece of near-sentience and not of a function of intelligence, since it consists in having, not indeed a proper sensation, but a shadow-sensation.

But this opinion is completely false. Whereas an unknown tune may be played in a person's hearing, so that he hears the tune without knowing how it goes, we cannot say of a person in whose head a tune is running that he does not know how it goes. Having a tune running in one's head is one familiar way in which knowledge of how that tune goes is utilised. So having a tune running in one's head is not to be likened to the mere having of auditory sensations; it is to be likened rather to the process of following a familiar tune, and following a heard tune is not a function of sentience.

Similarly, if I peer through a hole in a hedge on a misty day, I may not be able to identify what I see as a watercourse flowing in spate down a mountainside. But it would be absurd for someone to say 'I vividly see something in my mind's eye, but I cannot make out even what sort of a thing it is'. True, I can see a face in my mind's eye and fail to put a name to its owner, just as I can have a tune in my head, the name of which I have forgotten. But I know how the tune goes and I know what sort of a face I am picturing. Seeing the face in my mind's eye is one of the things which my knowledge of the face enables me to do; describing it in words is another and a rarer ability; recognising it at sight in the flesh is the commonest of all.

We saw in the previous chapter that perceiving entails both having sensations and something else which can be called, in a strained sense, 'thinking'. We can now say that to picture, image or fancy one sees or hears also entails thinking, in this strained sense. Indeed, this should be obvious, if we consider that our picturing of something must be characterisable as more or less vivid, clear, faithful and accurate, adjectives which connote not merely the possession but the use of the knowledge of how the object pictured does or would really look. It would be absurd for me to say that the smell of burning peat comes vividly back to me, but that I should not recognise the smell, if the peat were smoking in my presence. Imaging, therefore, is not a function of pure sentience; and a creature which had sensations, but could not learn, could not 'see', or picture, things any more than it could spell.

A person with a tune running in his head is using his knowledge of how the tune goes; he is in a certain way realising what he would be hearing, if he were listening to the tune being played. Somewhat as the boxer, when sparring, is hitting and parrying in a hypothetical manner, so the person with a tune running in his head may be described as following the tune in a hypothetical manner. Further, just as the actor is not really murdering anyone, so the person picturing Helvellyn is not really seeing Helvellyn. Indeed, as we know, he may have his eyes shut, while he pictures the mountain. Picturing Helvellyn, so far from having, or being akin to having, visual sensations, is compatible with having no such sensations and nothing akin to them. There is nothing akin to sensations. Realising, in this way, how Helvellyn would look is doing something which stands in the same relation to seeing Helvellyn as sophisticated performances stand to those more naive performances, whose mention is obliquely contained in the description of the higher order performances.

But there remains, or appears to remain, a crucial difference, which may be brought out thus. A sailor, asked to demonstrate how a certain knot is tied, finds that he has no cord with which to demonstrate. However, he does nearly as well by merely going through the motions of knotting a cord empty-handed. His spectators see how he would tie the knot by seeing how he manoeuvres his hands and fingers without any cord in them. Now although he is, so to speak, hypothetically knotting cord, still he is really moving his hands and fingers. But a person picturing Helvellyn with his eyes shut, while he is certainly enjoying, so to speak, only a hypothetical view of the mountain, does not seem to be really doing anything. Perhaps his non-existent visual sensations correspond to the sailor's non-existent piece of string, but what corresponds to the movements of his hands and fingers? The sailor does show the spectators how the knot would be tied; but the person visualising Helvellyn does not thereby show to his companion its contours or its colouring. Does he even show them to himself?

This difference between the two varieties of make-believe is, however, nothing but a consequence of the difference between perceiving something and bringing something about. This difference is not a difference between bringing something about privily and bringing something about overtly, for perceiving is not bringing anything about. It is getting something or, sometimes, keeping something; but it is not effecting anything. Seeing and hearing are neither witnessed nor unwitnessed doings, for they are not doings. It makes no sense to say 'I saw you seeing the sunset', or 'I failed to watch myself hearing the music'. And if it makes no sense to speak of my witnessing, or failing to witness, a piece of hearing or seeing, *a fortiori* it makes no sense to speak of my witnessing, or failing to witness, a piece of fancied hearing or fancied seeing. No hearing or seeing is taking place.

In the concert-hall a man's neighbour can, perhaps, see him beating time to the music and even overhear him half-whistling or half-humming to himself the tune the band is playing. But not only do we not say that his neighbour sees, or overhears, him hearing the music, as he sees or overhears him accompanying it, but we do not say, either, that his neighbour fails to witness him hearing the music. 'Secretly' and 'openly' do not attach to 'hearing', as they can attach to 'cursing' and 'plotting'. *A fortiori*, while his neighbour in the train may detect him beating time to a tune that is running in his head, he does not claim either to detect, or to fail to detect, his 'hearing' of the imagined tune.

Next, as we saw in the last chapter, following a known tune involves not only hearing the notes, but also much more than that. It involves, so to speak, having the proper niche ready for each note as it comes. Each note comes as and when it was expected to come; what is heard is what was listened for. This listening for the due notes entails having learned and not forgotten the tune and is therefore a product of training and is not a mere function of aural sensitiveness. A deafish man may follow a tune better than one who hears it better.

A person listening to a moderately familiar tune may on some occasions describe himself as having got the tune wrong, meaning by this that, though he was not himself playing or humming the tune, but only listening to it, yet here and there he listened for notes other than those which were really due to come; and he was taken by surprise to hear a particular movement beginning when it did, though he also recognised that it was his mistake to be surprised. It must be noticed that his error about the course of the tune need not have been, and ordinarily would not have been, formulated in a false sentence, private or public; all he 'did' was to be listening for what was not due to come, in place of what was due to come, and this listening for notes is not a deed done, or a series of deeds done.

This very point brings us to the case of a person following an imagined tune. To expect a tune to take one course, when it is actually taking another, is already to suppose, fancy or imagine. When what is heard is not what was listened for, what was listened for can be described only as notes which might have been heard, and the frame of mind in which they were listened for was therefore one of erroneous expectancy. The listener is disappointed, or abashed, by what he actually hears. A person going through a tune entirely in his head is in a partially similar case. He, too, listens for something which he does not get, though he is well aware all the time that he is not going to get it. He too can get the tune wrong, and either realise, or fail to realise, that he does so, a fact which by itself shows that imaging is not merely the having of sensations or sensation-echoes, since this could not be characterised as the acceptance of either a wrong or a correct version of a tune.

Going through a tune in one's head is like following a heard tune and is, indeed, a sort of rehearsal of it. But what makes the imaginative operation similar to the other is not, as is often supposed, that it incorporates the hearing of ghosts of notes similar in all but loudness to the heard notes of the real tune, but the fact that both are utilisations of knowledge of how the tune goes. This knowledge is exercised in recognising and following the tune, when actually heard; it is exercised in humming or playing it; in noticing the errors in its misperformance; it is also exercised in fancying oneself humming or playing it and in fancying oneself merely listening to it. Knowing a tune just is being able to do some such things as recognise and follow it, produce it, detect errors in the playing of it and go through it in one's head. We should not allow that a person had been unable to think how the tune went, who had whistled it correctly or gone through it in his head. Doing such things *is* thinking how the tune goes.

But the purely imaginative exercise is more sophisticated than that of following the tune, when heard, or than that of humming it; since it involves the thought of following or producing the tune, in the way in which sparring involves the thought of fighting in earnest, or in the way in which uttering something at second hand involves the thought of its first hand utterance. Fancying one is listening to a known tune involves 'listening for' the notes which would be due to be heard, were the tune being really performed. It is to listen for those notes in a hypothetical manner. Similarly, fancying one is humming a known tune involves 'making ready' for the notes which would be due to be hummed, were the tune actually being hummed. It is to make ready for those notes in a hypothetical manner. It is not humming very, very quietly, but rather it is deliberately not doing those pieces of humming which would be due, if one were not trying to keep the peace. We might say that imagining oneself talking or humming is a series of abstentions from producing the noises which would be the due words or notes to produce, if one were talking or humming aloud. That is why such operations are impenetrably secret; not that the words or notes are being produced in a hermetic cell, but that the operations consist of abstentions from producing them. That, too, is why learning to fancy one is talking or humming comes later than learning to talk or hum. Silent soliloquy is a flow of pregnant non-sayings. Refraining from saying things, of course, entails knowing both what one would have said and how one would have said it.

Doubtless some people on some occasions of imagining tunes fancy themselves not merely passively hearkening but also actively producing the notes, just as most imagined discourse contains not only imagined hearing but also imagined speaking. Very likely, too, people who imagine themselves producing noises tend to activate slightly those muscles which they would be activating fully, if they were singing or talking aloud, since complete abstention is harder than partial abstention. But these are questions of fact with which we are not concerned. Our concern is to find out what it means to say, e.g. that someone 'hears' something that he is not hearing.

The application of this account to visual and other imagery is not difficult. Seeing Helvellyn in one's mind's eye does not entail, what seeing Helvellyn and seeing snapshots of Helvellyn entail, the having of visual sensations. It does involve the thought of having a view of Helvellyn and it is therefore a more sophisticated operation than that of having a view of Helvellyn. It is one utilisation among others of the knowledge of how Helvellyn should look, or, in one sense of the verb, it is thinking how it should look. The expectations which are fulfilled in the recognition at sight of Helvellyn are not indeed fulfilled in picturing it, but the picturing of it is something like a rehearsal of getting them fulfilled. So far from picturing involving the having of faint sensations, or wraiths of sensations, it involves missing just what one would be due to get, if one were seeing the mountain.

Certainly not all imaging is the picturing of real faces and mountains, or the 'hearing' of familiar tunes and known voices. We can fancy ourselves looking at fabulous mountains. Composers, presumably, can fancy themselves listening to tunes that have never yet been played. It may be supposed, accordingly, that in such cases there is no question of the imaginary scene being pictured right, or of the tune still under composition being 'heard' to go otherwise than as it really goes; any more than Hans Andersen could be either accused of misreporting the careers of his characters, or praised for the factual fidelity of his narratives.

Consider the parallels of pretending and quoting. An actor on one day plays the part of a Frenchman; on the next day he has to

play the part of a visitor from Mars. We know how the former
representation might be convincing or unconvincing; but how could
the latter? Or I might start by quoting what you have said and go
on by giving utterance to what you would or could have said. We
know what it is for a quotation to be accurate, but a pretence
quotation cannot be either accurate or inaccurate; it can only be,
in some remoter sense, in character or out of character, by being,
or failing to be, the sort of thing that you would or could have said.
None the less, the actor is pretending to give a convincing representation of the man from Mars, and I am pretending that I am
quoting your very words. It is just a piece of double representation. A
boy mimicking a boxer sparring is in a similar case, for he is not
fighting and he is not rehearsing fighting; he is staging some of
the moves of a person rehearsing fighting. He is mock-mock-
fighting. As the predicates by which we comment on fighting do
not attach to sparring, so the predicates by which we comment on
sparring do not attach to mimicries of sparring. Correspondingly,
not only do the predicates by which we comment on our view of
Helvellyn not attach to the manner in which we picture Helvellyn,
but also the predicates by which we comment on our visualisations
of Helvellyn do not attach to our visualisations of Atlantis or Jack's
Beanstalk. None the less, we pretend that this is how Atlantis and
the Beanstalk would have looked. We are doing a piece of double
imagining.

     We are now in a position to locate and correct an error made by
Hume. Supposing, wrongly, that to 'see' or 'hear' is to have a
shadow-sensation, (which involves the further error of supposing
that there could be shadow-sensations), he put forward the causal
theory that one could not have a particular 'idea' without having
previously had a corresponding sensation, somewhat as having an
angular bruise involves having been previously struck by an angular
object. The colours that I see in my mind's eye are, he seems to
have thought, traces somehow left by the colours previously seen
by me with my eyes open. The only thing that is true in this account
is that what I see in my mind's eye and what I hear 'in my
head' is tied in certain ways to what I have previously seen and
heard. But the nature of this tie is not at all what Hume supposed.

     We saw that mock-actions presuppose ingenuous actions, in the
sense that performing the former involves, in a special sense, the

thought of the latter. A person who had not learned how bears growl, or how murderers commit murders, could not play bears, or act murders. Nor could he criticise the acting. In the same way, a person who had not learned how blue things look, or how the postman's knock sounds, could not see blue things in his mind's eye, or 'hear' the postman's knock; nor could he recognise blue things, or postman's knocks. Now we learn how things look and sound chiefly and originally by seeing and hearing them. Imaging, being one among many ways of utilising knowledge, requires that the relevant knowledge has been got and not lost. We no more need a para-mechanical theory of traces to account for our limited ability to see things in our mind's eyes than we need it to account for our limited ability to translate French into English. All that is required is to see that learning perceptual lessons entails some perceiving, that applying those lessons entails having learned them, and that imaging is one way of applying those lessons. Addicts of the trace theory should try to fit their theory to the case of a tune running in someone's head. Is this a revived trace of an auditory sensation; or a series of revived traces of a series of auditory sensations?

(7) *Memory.*

It is convenient to append to this discussion of imagination a brief excursus on remembering. We must begin by noticing two widely different ways in which the verb 'to remember' is commonly used.

(a) By far the most important and the least discussed use of the verb is that use in which remembering something means having learned something and not forgotten it. This is the sense in which we speak of remembering the Greek alphabet, or the way from the gravel-pit to the bathing-place, or the proof of a theorem, or how to bicycle, or that the next meeting of the Board will be in the last week of July. To say that a person has not forgotten something is not to say that he is now doing or undergoing anything, or even that he regularly or occasionally does or undergoes anything. It is to say that he *can* do certain things, such as go through the Greek alphabet, direct a stranger back from the bathing-place to the gravel-pit and correct someone who says that the next meeting of the Board is in the second week in July.

What, in this use, is said to be remembered is any learned lesson, and what is learned and not forgotten need have nothing to do with the past, though the learning of it of course precedes the condition of not having forgotten it. 'Remember' in this use is often, though not always, an allowable paraphrase of the verb 'to know'.

(b) Quite different from this is the use of the verb 'to remember' in which a person is said to have remembered, or been recollecting, something at a particular moment, or is said to be now recalling, reviewing or dwelling on some episode of his own past. In this use, remembering is an occurrence; it is something which a person may try successfully, or in vain, to do; it occupies his attention for a time and he may do it with pleasure or distress and with ease or effort. The barrister presses the witness to recall things, where the teacher trains his pupils not to forget things.

Recalling has certain features in common with imagining. I recall only what I myself have seen, heard, done and felt, just as what I imagine is myself seeing, hearing, doing and noticing things; and I recall as I imagine, relatively vividly, relatively easily and relatively connectedly. Moreover, much as I imagine things sometimes deliberately and sometimes involuntarily, so I recall things sometimes deliberately and sometimes involuntarily.

There is an important connection between the notion of not-forgetting and the notion of recollecting. To say that a person either actually is recalling something, or can recall, or be reminded of it, implies that he has not forgotten it; whereas to say that he has not forgotten something does not entail that he ever does or could recall it. There would be a contradiction in saying that I can or do recollect the incidents that I witnessed taking place at a picnic, though I no longer know what occurred there. There is no contradiction in saying that I know when I was born, or that I had my appendix removed, though I cannot recall the episodes. There would be an absurdity in saying that I do or can recall Napoleon losing the Battle of Waterloo, or how to translate English into Greek, though I have not forgotten these things; since these are not the sorts of things that can be recalled, in the sense of the verb in which what I recall must be things that I have myself witnessed, done or experienced.

Theorists speak sometimes of memory-knowledge, memory-belief and the evidence of memory, and, when discussing the 'sources' of knowledge and the ways by which we come to know things, they sometimes talk as if memory were one such 'source' and as if remembering were one such way of coming to know things. Memory is, accordingly, sometimes ranged alongside of perception and inference as a cognitive faculty or power; or remembering is ranged alongside of perceiving and inferring as a cognitive act or process.

This is a mistake. If a witness is asked how he knows that something took place, he may reply that he witnessed it, or that he was told of it, or that he inferred to it from what he witnessed or was told. He could not reply that he found out what took place either by not forgetting what he had found out, or by recalling finding it out. Reminiscence and not-forgetting are neither 'sources' of knowledge, nor, if this is anything different, ways of getting to know. The former entails having learned and not forgotten; the latter is having learned and not forgotten. Neither of them is a sort of learning, discovering or establishing. Still less is recalling what took place using a piece of evidence from which certain or probable inferences are made to what took place, save in the sense that the jury may infer from what the witness narrates. The witness himself does not argue 'I recall the collision occurring just after the thunder-clap, so probably the collision occurred just after the thunder-clap'. There is no such inference; and even if there were, the good witness is one who is good at recollecting, not one who is good at inferring.

Certainly the witness may be forced to admit, even to his surprise, that he must have been drawing on his imagination, since, for one reason or another, he could not have been recalling what he professed to be recalling; in other circumstances he may volunteer that he himself has doubts whether he is recalling, or making things up. But it does not follow from the fact that alleged reminiscences may be fabrications that veracious reminiscences are discoveries or successful investigations. A person who is asked to tell what is known of the Milky Way, or to draw a map of the rivers and railways of Berkshire, may say and draw things which he does not know to represent the facts, and he may be surprised to find that he has been doing this, or be uncertain whether he is doing it. But no one thinks that telling and drawing are 'sources' of knowledge, ways of finding things out, or bits of evidence from which discoveries can be made by inference. Telling and drawing things are, at best, ways of conveying lessons already learned. So is recalling a conning of something already learned. It is going over something, not getting to something ; it is like recounting, not like researching. A person may recall a particular episode twenty times in a day. No one would say that he twenty times discovered what happened. If the last nineteen reviewings were not discoveries, nor was the first.

The stock accounts given of reminiscence give the impression that when a person recalls an episode belonging to his own past history, the details of the episode must come back to him in imagery. He must 'see' the details 'in his mind's eye', or 'hear' them 'in his head'. But there is no 'must' about it. If a concert-goer wishes to recollect just how the violinist misplayed a certain piece, he may whistle the bungled tune, or play it on his own fiddle just as the artist had done it; and, if he repeats the mistake faithfully, he is certainly recollecting the artist's error. This might be his only way of recalling how the artist had gone wrong, since he may be poor at going over tunes in his head. Similarly a good mimic might recapture the preacher's gestures and grimaces only by reproducing them with his own hands and on his own face, since he may be poor at seeing things in his mind's eye. Or a good draughts-man may fail to recollect the lines and the rigging of a yacht, until he is given a pencil with which to delineate them on paper. If their mimicries and delineations are good and if, when they go wrong, their authors duly correct them without being prompted, their companions will be satisfied that they have recollected what they had seen, without desiring any additional information about the vividness, copiousness or connectedness of their visual imagery or even about its existence.

No one would say that the concert-goer, the mimic or the draughtsman had got to know anything by reproducing the misplayed tune, the preacher's gestures, or the lines of the yacht, but only that they had shown how the tune had been heard to be misplayed, how the preacher had been seen to gesticulate and how the yacht had been seen to be shaped and rigged. Reminiscence in imagery does not differ in principle, though it tends to be superior in speed, if otherwise greatly inferior in efficiency; and it is, of course, of no direct public utility.

People are apt grossly to exaggerate the photographic fidelity of their visual imagery. The main reason for this exaggeration seems to be that they find that very often, particularly when suitably prompted and questioned, they can give very comprehensive, detailed and well-ordered verbal descriptions of episodes at which they have been present. They are then tempted to suppose that, since they can describe such bygone episodes nearly as well now as they could have done during their occurrence, they must be checking their narratives against some present replicas or souvenirs of the vanished scene. If a description of a face is about as good in the absence as in the presence of the face, this must be due to the presence of something like a photograph of the face. But this is a gratuitous causal hypothesis. The question, 'How can I faithfully describe what I once witnessed?' is no more of a puzzle than the question, 'How can I faithfully visualise what I once witnessed?' Ability to describe things learned by personal experience is one of the knacks we expect of linguistically competent people; ability to visualise parts of it is another thing that we expect in some degree of most people and in high degree of children, dress-designers, policemen and cartoonists.

Reminiscing, then, can take the form of faithful verbal narration. When it does so, it differs from reminiscence by mimicry and reminiscence by sketching inasmuch as what took place is told and not portrayed (though the telling often embodies some dramatic portrayal as well). Clearly, here, too, no one would wish to speak as if narration were either a 'source' of knowledge, or a way of acquiring knowledge. It belongs not to the stages of manufacture and assembly, but to the stage of export. It is akin not to learning lessons, but to reciting them.

People are, however, strongly tempted to think that vivid visual recall must be a sort of seeing and therefore a sort of finding. One motive of this mistake may be brought out as follows. If a person learns that a naval engagement has taken place, without himself having been a witness of it, he may deliberately or involuntarily picture the scene in visual imagery. Very likely he soon settles down to picturing it in a fairly uniform way whenever he thinks of the battle, much as he is likely to settle down to describing the episode in a fairly uniformly worded narrative, whenever he is called on to tell the story. But though he cannot, perhaps, easily help picturing the scene in his now routine manner, still he recognises a difference between his habitual way of picturing scenes of which he was not a witness and the way in which unforgotten episodes of which he was a witness 'come back' to him in visual imagery. These, too, he cannot help picturing in a uniform way, but their uniformity seems to him compulsory and not merely settled by repetition. He cannot now 'see' the episode as he pleases, any more than he could originally have seen it as he pleased. He could not originally have seen the thimble elsewhere than on the corner of the mantelpiece, since that is where it was. Nor, however hard he tries, can he now recall seeing it elsewhere, for all that he can, if he likes, imagine seeing it lying in the scuttle. Indeed he may well imagine seeing it in the scuttle, while repudiating someone else's allegation that that is where it was.

The reader of a report of a race can, subject to certain restrictions imposed by the text of the report, first picture the race in one way and then deliberately or involuntarily picture it in a different and perhaps conflicting way; but a witness of the race feels that, while he can call back further views of the race, yet alternative views are rigidly ruled out. This is what makes it tempting to say that reminiscence by imaging has in it something analogous to scanning a photograph, or to listening to a gramophone record. The 'cannot' in 'I cannot "see" the episode save in one way' is tacitly assimilated to the mechanical 'cannot' in 'the camera cannot lie', or in 'the record cannot vary the tune'. But in fact the 'cannot', in 'I cannot "see" the episode save in one way' is like that in 'I cannot spell "Edinburgh" as I like'. I cannot write down the correct letters in the correct order and at the same time be writing down any other arrangement of letters; I cannot be spelling out 'Edinburgh' as I know it should be spelled out and also be spelling it out in any other way. Nothing forces my hand to spell it in one way rather than another; but simple logic excludes the possibility of my both producing what I know to be the required spelling and producing an arbitrary spelling in one and the same operation. Similarly, nothing forces me to do any picturing at all, or to do my picturing in this way rather than that; but if I am recalling how the scene looked when I witnessed it, then my picturing is not arbitrary. Nor in making my way from the gravel-pit to the bathing-place am I forced to take this rather than any other footpath. But if I know that this is the right path, then I cannot, in logic, both take the path known to be the correct one and also take any other path.

Consider again the case of the concert-goer who reproduces the violinist's mistake by whistling the bars as the violinist had misplayed them. The only sense in which he 'has' to whistle as he does, is that he will not be reproducing the violinist's mistake if he whistles anything else. He whistles what he whistles because he has not forgotten what he heard the violinist do. But this is not a cause-effect 'because'. His whistling is not causally controlled or governed either by the violinist's misperformance, or by his own original hearing of it. Rather, to say that he has not forgotten what he heard is to say that he can do some such things as faithfully reproduce the mistake by whistling it. As long as he continues to bear in mind the violinist's mistake, he continues to be able and ready to do some such things as to show what the mistake was by faithfully re-performing it. This is what is meant by 'bear in mind'.

If a child is set to recite a poem, but gets it wrong, or partly wrong, we do not say that he has recited the poem. Nor is a mis-quotation a sort of quotation. If we are told that someone has spelled or construed something, we do not ask, 'But did he get it right?', since it would not be spelling or construing if it were misspelling or misconstruing. But of course there do exist uses of these verbs in which they have the same force as the phrases 'try to spell', or 'try to construe'. In these uses they can be significantly qualified by 'unsuccessfully'.

'Recall', save when it means 'try to recall', is in the same way a 'got it' verb. 'Recall unsuccessfully' and 'recall incorrectly' are illegitimate phrases. But this does not mean that we have a privileged faculty which, given its head, carries us to our destination without our having to be careful. It means only that if, for example, we picture incidents otherwise than as we know they looked, then we are not recalling, any more than we are quoting, if we ascribe other words to a speaker than those which we know he uttered. Recalling is something which we sometimes have to try hard and which we often fail to bring off; and very often we do not know whether we have brought it off or not. So we may claim to have recalled something and later be persuaded to withdraw the claim. But though 'recall' is a 'got it' verb, it is not a verb of finding, solving or proving. Rather, like 'reciting', 'quoting', 'depicting' and 'mimicking', it is a verb of showing, or is at least affiliated to such verbs. Being good at recalling is not being good at investigating, but being good at presenting. It is a narrative skill, if 'narrative' be allowed to cover non-prosaic as well as prosaic representations. That is why we describe recollections as relatively faithful, vivid and accurate and not as original, brilliant or acute. Nor do we call people 'clever' or 'observant' merely because things come back to them well. An anecdotalist is not a sort of detective.

# CHAPTER IX

# THE INTELLECT

## (1) *Foreword.*

So far I have said little positive about Reason, the Intellect or the Understanding, about thought, judgment, inference or conception. Indeed, what little I have said has largely been of a deflationary tendency, since I have repeatedly argued against the common assumption that the use of such epithets as 'purposive', 'skilful', 'careful', 'ambitious' and 'voluntary' entails, as a causal pre-requisite, the occurrence of cogitative or theorising operations. I have probably left the impression that since planning and theorising operations can themselves be characterised as purposive, skilful, careful, ambitious, voluntary and the rest, I regard these operations merely as special occupations on all fours with such occupations as tying knots, following tunes or playing hide-and-seek.

Such a democratisation of the offices of the old élite will have seemed all the more shocking, since there exists a widespread habit of using 'mind' and 'mental' as synonyms of 'the intellect' and 'intellectual'. It is quite idiomatic to ask an examiner what sort of a mind a candidate has, when all that is wanted is to be told how well he can tackle certain sorts of academic tasks. The questioner would be surprised to be answered that the candidate was fond of animals, bashful, musical and witty.

It is now time to discuss certain features of the concepts of specifically intellectual powers, propensities and performances. It will be found that these have indeed a primacy of a certain sort, though not that causal anteriority which is commonly postulated for them.

## (2) *The Demarcation of the Intellect.*

The place of the intellect in human life is apt to be described, with or without consciousness of metaphor, after certain models.

Sometimes the Intellect is talked of as a special organ, and strong or weak intellects are assimilated to strong or weak eyes and biceps. Sometimes the Understanding is talked of as a sort of publishing firm or mint which issues its products *via* the retail traders and banks to the customers. And sometimes Reason is talked of as a sapient lecturer or magistrate, who tells his audience from his place in its midst what he knows, commands and recommends. We need not trouble, now, to argue that these and kindred models are unsuited to provide the terms on which our discussions are to be hinged. But there is one underlying promise made by all these models of which we need to be suspicious from the start. We can tell pretty exactly what are the things which strength or weakness of eyes and biceps enables us to do, or prevents us from doing; we can tell just which products are issued, and which are not issued, by this publishing firm and that mint; and we can tell just what was, and what was not, imparted by a particular lecturer in a particular lecture. But if asked just which human actions and reactions should be classed as intellectual, we have no similar criteria. Mathematical calculation should certainly be so classed, but what if it is full of mistakes and lucky guesses, or is done by sheer rote? Forensic argumentation, but what if its motive is the desire to make the worse seem the better cause? Philosophising, but what if the thinking is wishful? The collection and colligation of facts, but what if their collection is jackdaw-like and their colligation fanciful?

On some accounts it is a defining property of intellectual operations that they are governed by the purpose of discovering truth. But bridge and chess are intellectual games in which the purpose of performing the required intellectual operations is victory and not discovery. The engineer and the general plan with their heads, but they do not aim at adding to knowledge. The legislator has to think in abstract terms and in a systematic way, but his labours issue not in theorems but in Bills. Conversely, the reminiscences of the aged may pile up into formidable bodies of truths, but we hesitate to class these recollections as exercises of more than minimal intellectual powers. The aged do not think out what once happened; it just comes back to them. Nor do we ordinarily regard the observant child's incessant discoveries of things by eye, ear, nose, tongue and fingers as exercises of intellectual powers. He does not win scholarships by them.

Nor are the boundaries between what is and what is not intellectual made much clearer by referring to the notion of thinking,
since 'thinking' is not only just as vague as 'intellectual', but also
has extra ambiguities of its own. In one sense, the English verb
'think' is a synonym of 'believe' and 'suppose'; so it is possible for
a person, in this sense, to think a great number of silly things, but,
in another sense, to think very little. Such a person is both credulous
and intellectually idle. There is yet another sense in which a person
may be said to be 'thinking hard what he is doing', when he is
paying close heed to, say, playing the piano; but he is not pondering or being in any way pensive. If asked what premisses he had
considered, what conclusions he had drawn or, in a word, what
thoughts he had had, his proper answer might well be, 'None. I had
neither the time nor the interest to construct or manipulate any
propositions at all. I was applying my mind to playing, not to
speculating on problems, or even to lecturing to myself on how to
play.'

It is sometimes said that by an 'intellectual process' or by
'thinking', in the special sense required, is meant an operation with
symbols such as, *par excellence*, words and sentences. 'In thinking
the soul is talking to itself'. But this is both too wide and too narrow.
A child reciting by pure rote a nursery rhyme, or the multiplica-
tion-table, is going through a sort of expression-wielding process,
but he is not attending to what his words and sentences mean;
he is not using his expressions, but parroting them, as he might
parrot a tune. Nor yet will it do to say that a thinker is a person
who operates purposefully and attentively with expressions; for if
a jigsaw puzzle was constructed out of fragments of a once-learned
foreign nursery rhyme, a child might work hard and efficiently
at rearranging them in their proper order, though he had
no idea what the sentences of the rhyme meant. It will not
do even to say that thinking consists in constructing complexes
of expressions as vehicles of specific meanings, for we allow
that a person is thinking who is merely following expressions delivered by someone else. He is not putting his
own ideas into words but getting ideas from someone else's
words.

On the other hand, we have to allow that a person is doing
genuine intellectual work in some situations where no expressions

at all are being used, whether words, code-symbols, diagrams or pictures. Tracing out the intricacies of a tangled skein of wool, studying the position of the game on the chessboard, and trying to place a piece of a jig-saw puzzle, would usually be allowed to be cogitation, even though unaccompanied by any self-colloquy.

Lastly, to apply a point made earlier, the distinction between unstudied and studied utterance becomes of importance here. In the greater part of our ordinary sociable chat we say the first things that come to our lips without deliberating what to say, or how to say it; we are confronted by no challenge to vindicate our statements, to elucidate the connections between our utterances, or to make plain the purport of our questions, or the real point of our coaxings. Our talk is artless, spontaneous and unweighed. It is not work and it is not meant to edify, to be remembered, or to be recorded. None the less our remarks have their points and the listener understands them and responds appropriately.

Yet this is not the sort of talk we have in mind when we speak of someone judging, pondering, reasoning or thinking something out. We do not judge a person's intellectual powers by most of the ways in which he chats. We judge them rather by the ways in which he talks when his talk is guarded, disciplined, and serious, uttered in his on-duty tone of voice and not in any of his off-duty tones of voice. We do, however, judge a person's intellectual potentialities partly by the jokes he makes and appreciates even though these belong to his out-of-school conversations. Theorists are inclined to assume that the differences between unstudied chat and weighed discourse is one only of degree, so that the things that come straight to our lips reflect the same sorts of intellectual processes as those reflected by seriously delivered pronouncements. But in practice we consider only the latter when assessing a person's judiciousness, acumen and grasp. So in practice we do not regard all intelligent expression-using as thinking but only or chiefly that which is done as work. We do not regard unstudied chat as low-level theorising or planning, and we are quite right not to do so. It is not the object of ordinary chat to advance anyone's theories or plans. Nor do we regard strolling and humming as gentle toil. But, after all, does it matter if all attempts at giving a hard-edged definition of 'intellectual' and 'thought' break down somewhere or other? We know well enough how to distinguish urban from rustic areas, games from work, and spring from summer, and are unembarrassed by the discovery of undecidable marginal cases. We know that solving a mathematical problem is an intellectual task, hunting the thimble is a non-intellectual task, while looking for an apposite rhyme is a halfway house. Bridge is an intellectual game, Snap an unintellectual game and Beggar-my-neighbour is betwixt and between. Our daily use of the concepts of the intellect and of thought is unembarrassed by the discovery of a moderate number of borderline cases.

Certainly for some purposes this does not matter. But it does matter a lot to us. It means that the same thing is wrong both with the older theories which spoke of Reason, the Intellect or the Understanding as a specific Faculty or occult organ, and with the newer theories which speak of the specific intellectual processes of judging, conceiving, supposing, reasoning and the rest. They are pretending to have identification-marks for things which they cannot in fact always identify. We do not always know when to apply, and when not to apply, the trade-names of epistemology.

Let us start again. There is one idea not far from the forefront of most people's minds when they contrast intellectual powers and performances with other powers and performances, namely that of schooling. The intellectual powers are those which are developed by set lessons and tested by set examinations. Intellectual tasks are those or some of those which only the schooled can perform. Intellectuals are persons who have profited from the highest available education, and intellectual talk is edified and edifying talk. Native or untutored knacks are not classed with intellectual proficiencies, and even arts learned mainly by sheer imitation, like skipping, playing Snap and chatting, are not spoken of as intellectual accomplishments. This certificate is reserved for exploitations of lessons learned at least in part from books and lectures, or, in general, from didactic discourse.

It is clear (1) that no one could follow or use didactic discourse who had not already learned to follow and use conversational talk, and (2) that didactic discourse is itself a species of studied discourse. It is discourse in which schooling is given, and it is discourse which is itself in some degree the product of schooling. It has its own drills and it is spoken or written not in the sociable, conversational, but in the non-sociable, drill style. It is delivered magisterially. Even if a bright conversational style is affected, a merely conversational reception of it is known to be inappropriate, so the conversational style is recognised to be fraudulent. The teacher is only pretending that she and the pupils are not really working. We shall see later that behind this seemingly trivial way of demarcating what is intellectual from what is not, in terms of the academic machinery by which certain things come to be learnt, there lies something very important.

It is now necessary to discuss some of the concepts of thought and thinking. We must distinguish clearly between the sense in which we say that someone is engaged in thinking something out from the sense in which we say that so and so is what he thinks, i.e. between the sense of 'thought' in which thought can be hard, protracted, interrupted, careless, successful or unavailing from the sense in which a person's thoughts are true, false, valid, fallacious, abstract, rejected, shared, published or unpublished. In the former sense we are talking about work in which a person is at times and for periods engaged. In the latter sense we are talking about the results of such work. The importance of drawing this distinction is that the prevalent fashion is to describe the work of thinking things out in terms borrowed from descriptions of the results reached. We hear stories of people doing such things as judging, abstracting, subsuming, deducing, inducing, predicating and so forth, as if these were recordable operations actually executed by particular people at particular stages of their ponderings. And, since we do not witness other people in the act of doing these things, or even catch ourselves in the act of doing them, we feel driven to allow that these acts are very subterranean happenings, the occurrences of which are found out only by the inferences and divinations of expert epistemologists. These experts seem to tell us that we do these things somewhat as anatomists tell us of the digestive and cerebral processes that go on inside us without our knowledge. So our intellects must be fleshless organs, since these para-anatomists find out so much about their clandestine functionings.

I hope to show that the words 'judgment', 'deduction', 'abstraction' and the rest belong properly to the classification of the products of pondering and are mis-rendered when taken as denoting acts of which pondering consists. They belong not to the vocabulary of biography but to the vocabulary of reviews of books, lectures, discussions and reports. They are referees' nouns, not biographers' nouns.

(3) *The Construction, Possession and Utilisation of Theories.*

Although there are plenty of avocations, both games and work, which we describe as intellectual without implying that their purpose is to discover truths, there are good reasons for giving early consideration to that special family of avocations in which we are concerned to discover truths. I say 'family of avocations', since nothing is to be gained by pretending that Euclid, Thucydides, Columbus, Adam Smith, Newton, Linnaeus, Porson and Bishop Butler were all in partnership.

The work for which each of these men got his reputation can be called the work of 'theory building', though the word 'theory' has widely different senses. Sherlock Holmes' theories were not built by the same methods as those of Marx, nor were the uses or applications of them similar to those of Marx. But both were alike in delivering their theories in didactic prose.

Before we say anything more specific about the operations or processes of building theories we should consider what it means to say that someone *has* a theory. Building a theory is trying to get a theory, and to have a theory is to have got and not forgotten it. Building a theory is travelling; having a theory is being at one's destination.

To have a theory or a plan is not itself to be doing or saying anything, any more than to have a pen is to be writing with it. To have a pen is to be in a position to write with it, if occasion arises to do so; and to have a theory or plan is to be prepared either to tell it or to apply it, if occasion arises to do so. The work of building a theory or plan is the work of getting oneself so prepared.

I say that the possessor of a theory is prepared to state it or otherwise apply it. What is this distinction? To be in a position to tell a theory is to be able to give a good answer to someone, the theorist himself maybe, who wants or needs to learn, or learn better, what the theory is, i.e. to deliver, by word of mouth or in writing, an intelligible statement of the conclusions of the theory, the problems which they solve and perhaps also the reasons for accepting these and rejecting rival answers. Having a theory involves being able to deliver lessons or refresher-lessons in it. The intelligent recipient of such lessons comes himself to have the theory or else, if he is sophisticated enough, to grasp without adopting it. But we do not build theories, any more than we build plans, merely or primarily in order to be equipped to tell them. The chief point of giving didactic exercises to oneself, or to other pupils, is to prepare them to use these lessons for other than further didactic ends. Columbus did not explore only to add to what was recited in geography lessons. Having a theory or plan is not merely being able to tell what one's theory or plan is. Being able to tell a theory is, in fact, being able to make just one, namely the didactic exploitation of it. Mastery of Euclid's theorems is not merely ability to cite them; it is also ability to solve riders to them, meet objections to them and find out the dimensions of fields with their aid.

There is no single-track answer to the question, 'How is a theory turned to accounts other than didactic accounts?' Sherlock Holmes' theories were primarily intended to be applied in the apprehension and conviction of criminals, the thwarting of planned crimes and the exculpation of innocent suspects. They might also have been intended to be used as instructive examples of effective detection-techniques. His theories were applied, if further deductions were actually made from them, and if criminals were arrested and suspects released in accordance with them. Newton's theories were used when correct predictions and retrodictions were made on the basis of them, when machines were designed in accordance with them, when the hope of building perpetual-motion machines was given up, when some other theories were abandoned, or else were codified with his, when books were produced and lectures delivered enabling students to grasp the whole or parts of his theories and, lastly, when some or all of his theory-building techniques were learned from his example and successfully applied in new investigations. To be a Newtonian was not just to say what Newton had said, but also to say and do what Newton would have said and done. Having a theory is being prepared to make a variety of moves, only some of which are teachings; and to teach something to someone, oneself or another, is, in its turn, to prepare him for a variety of tasks, only some of which will be further teachings.

We might say, therefore, that in theorising the soul is, *inter alia*, preparing itself to talk or write didactically; and that the intended benefits to the recipient consist of acquired preparednesses to act and react in various new ways, only some of which will themselves be further didactic pronouncements. This shows part of what is wrong with the notion of Reason as the power merely to give and receive didactic talks. But some of the operations learned certainly will be further didactic talkings, since at least one thing that is learned in listening attentively to didactic talking is how to say just those same things, or things to the same effect, or at least how to talk in that manner. At the very least the recruit learns the words of command and how N.C.O.s deliver them. A lesson in anything is also a lesson in giving and receiving lessons of that sort. Galileo, in teaching about the behaviour of stars, pendulums and telescopes, also taught by his example how to talk scientifically about any other subject.

To come now to the work of building theories. First, I am not restricting this phrase to those operations which, like mathematics, jurisprudence, philology and philosophy, can be done in an arm-chair or at the desk. Columbus could not have given his account of the west side of the Atlantic without voyaging thither, nor could Kepler have given his account of the solar system, unless he and Tycho Brahe had spent weary hours visually studying the heavens. None the less we distinguish the theories, which they finally built and then taught to the educated world by word of mouth or in print, from the exertions and observations without which they would not have built those theories. The formulations of their theories embody reports of, or references to, the courses set and the observations made, but they do not embody the courses set, or the observations themselves. The results of research can be delivered in prose, but researching does not generally consist only in operating with pens, but also in operating with microscopes and telescopes, balances and galvanometers, log-lines and litmus-papers.

Next, in talking of building theories I am not referring only to the classical examples of famous discoveries but to a class of tasks in which all people who have had any education participate in some degree on some occasions. The housewife trying to find out whether a carpet will fit a floor is engaged in an unambitious task of theorising. She is investigating something and the results of her investigations will be statable. Both what she reports to her husband and what she does with the carpet will show what theory she has reached, since her morning's work with tape-measure, pencil and paper was preparing her both to lay the carpet this way round and not that, and to tell her husband that the carpet will go there that way round, since the shape and size of the floor and of the carpet are so and so. I am also using the word 'theory' to cover the results of any kind of systematic inquiry, whether or not these results make up a deductive system. An historian's account of the course of a battle is his theory.

If a farmer has made a path, he is able to saunter easily up and down it. That is what the path was made for. But the work of making the path was not a process of sauntering easily, but one of marking the ground, digging, fetching loads of gravel, rolling and draining. He dug and rolled where there was yet no path, so that he might in the end have a path on which he could saunter without any more digging or rolling. Similarly a person who has a theory can, among other things, expound to himself, or the world, the whole theory or any part of it; he can, so to speak, saunter in prose from any part to any other part of it. But the work of building the theory was a job of making paths where as yet there were none. The point of the analogy is this. Epistemologists very frequently describe the labours of building theories in terms appropriate only to the business of going over or teaching a theory that one already has; as if, for example, the chains of propositions which constitute Euclid's 'Elements' mirrored a parallel succession of theorising moves made by Euclid in his original labours of making his geometrical discoveries; as if, that is, what Euclid was equipped to do when he had his theory, he was already equipped to do when constructing it. But this is absurd. On the other hand, epistemologists sometimes tell the opposite story, describing what Euclid did in delivering his theories when he had them, as if it was some recrudescence of the original theorising work. This, too, is absurd. These epistemologists describe using a path, as if it were a piece of path-making; the others describe the path-making, as if it were a piece of path-using.

Now just as the farmer, in toiling at making paths, is preparing the ground for effortless sauntering, so a person in toiling at building a theory is preparing himself for, among other things, the effortless exposition of the theories which he gets by building them. His theorising labours are self-preparations for, among other things, didactic tasks which are not further self-preparations, but preparations of other students. Naturally there are halfway houses. There is a stage at which a thinker has his theory, but has not yet got it perfectly. He is not yet completely at home in it. There are places where he sometimes slips, stumbles and hesitates. At this stage he will go over his theory, or parts of it, in his head, or on paper, not yet with the ease begotten by much practice, nor with the trouble that it had cost him to do the original building. He is like the farmer, whose path is still sufficiently rough to require him to tread up and down it somewhat heavy-footedly, in order to smooth out some remaining inequalities of the surface. As the farmer is both half-sauntering and still preparing the ground for more effortless sauntering, so the thinker is both using his near-mastery of his theory and still schooling himself to master it perfectly. Telling himself his theory is still somewhat toilsome and one of the objects of this toil is to prepare himself for telling it without toil.

Now when we are told that a proper use of an indicative sentence reflects an act of 'judging', or 'making a judgment', and that a proper use of an indicative sentence embodying conjunctions like 'if', 'so' and 'because' reflects an act of 'reasoning', 'inferring' or 'drawing a conclusion from premisses', we ought to ask whether these proper uses of such indicative sentences are supposed to occur, when their user is building his theory, or whether they are supposed to occur, when he already has his theory and is delivering it in didactic prose, spoken or written, with the facility borne of adequate practice. Are conceptions, judgments and inferences or, compendiously, thoughts, path-making moves, or are they a certain class of path-using moves, namely path-showing or path-teaching moves? Are they steps and stages in learning something, or are they bits of the lesson that we teach, on demand, when we have learned it? It is a truism to say that the expert who is thoroughly at home with his theory expounds the several elements of it with complete facility; he is not now having to study what to say, or else he could not be described as being thoroughly at home with his theory. He is going over old ground and not now breaking new ground. But this ready and orderly delivery of simple and complex indicative sentences is quite unlike those perplexed, tentative and laboured wrestlings and wrigglings which had constituted the probably protracted building of his theory. These were what had prepared and trained him to be able ultimately to give this ready delivery of the elements of his theory. So we ought to decide whether the required acts of conceiving, making judgments and drawing conclusions from premisses are to be looked for in the theorist's earlier exploratory, or in his resultant expository, activities, in his acquiring knowledge, or in his telling what he knows. Is it in the detective's reports, or in his investigations, that we are supposed to find his judgments and his inferences?

I say that we ought to pose this question, but in fact epistemologists tend not to realise that such a question exists. What they commonly do is to classify the elements of doctrines didactically expounded by theorists already at home in them, and to postulate that counterpart elements must have occurred as episodes in the work of building those theories. Finding premisses and conclusions among the elements of published theories, they postulate separate, antecedent, 'cognitive acts' of judging; and finding arguments among the elements of published theories, they postulate separate antecedent processes of moving to the 'cognising' of conclusions from the 'cognising' of premisses. I hope to show that these separate intellectual processes postulated by epistemologists are para-mechanical dramatisations of the classified elements of achieved and expounded theories.

It is not being denied that our theorising labours do incorporate a lot of soliloquy and colloquy, a lot of calculating and miscalculating on paper and in our heads, a lot of diagram-sketching and erasing on the blackboard and in our minds' eyes, a lot of interrogating, cross-examining, debating and experimental asseverating; and certainly some of these pieces of expression-using operate, not as self-addressed interim reports of sub-theories already built or grasped, but as parts of the exercises by which we prepare ourselves for getting theories which we have not yet got. I say, for example, a lot of things tentatively; I roll them on my tongue and, if there seems any promise in them, I repeat them again and again in a rehearsing frame of mind, so as to get myself used to the ideas; thus I prepare myself by practice to work with them later on, if they turn out well, or else to wean myself from them for good, if they turn out ill. I give myself tutorial behests, reproaches, commendations and encouragements, and I put to myself searching and leading questions in a magisterial tone of voice to keep myself from shirking dull or difficult problems. But expressions like these, used in these ways, cannot be described as expressing judgments or inferences, in the sense of being didactic expositions of conclusions reached, or arguments mastered. They will not, for the most part, appear in the publication of the theory, when and if this is arrived at; any more than the teacher's blue- and red-pencilled scorings, ticks, exclamation-marks, queries and reminders in the margins of his pupils' essays will be reproduced in the pupils' final statements of the theory. They are parts of the scaffolding which theorising uses, not parts of the edifice in which successful theorising results. Nor are recruit drill orders shouted aloud, or said in their heads, by trained soldiers on the battlefield.

(4) *The Application and Misapplication of Epistemological Terms.*

The glossary of terms in which intellectual powers and operations are traditionally described contains such words and phrases as 'judgment', 'reasoning', 'conception', 'idea', 'abstract idea', 'concept', 'making judgments', 'inferring', 'drawing conclusions from premises', 'considering propositions', 'subsuming', 'generalising', 'inducing', 'cognition', 'apprehension', 'intuition', 'intellection' and 'discursive thinking'. Such expressions are employed, not indeed by the laity but by theorists, as if with their aid, and not easily without it, correct descriptions can be given of what has at a particular moment been occupying a particular person; as if, for example, John Doe could and should sometimes be described as having woken up and started to do some judging, conceiving, subsuming or abstracting; as spending more than three seconds in entertaining a proposition, or in moving from some premises to a conclusion; or as sitting on a fence, alternately whistling and deducing; or as having had an intuition of something a moment before he coughed.

Probably most people feel vaguely that there is a tinge of unreality attaching to such recommended biographical anecdotes. John Doe's own stories about himself are not expressed in such terms, or in terms easily translatable into them. How many cognitive acts did he perform before breakfast, and what did it feel like to do them? Were they tiring? Did he enjoy his passage from his premises to his conclusion, and did he make it cautiously or recklessly? Did the breakfast bell make him stop short halfway between his premises and his conclusion? Just when did he last make a judgment, or form an abstract idea, what happened to it when he had made or formed it and who taught him how to do it? Is conceiving a quick or a gradual process, an easy or difficult one, and can he dawdle over it or shirk doing it? About how long did it take him to consider the proposition and was the spectacle in the later stages of the consideration like or unlike that in the initial stages? Was it rather like gazing blankly at something, or more like detailed scrutiny? He does not know how to begin to answer such questions. These questions which he answers easily and confidently about the incidents in his life which he does report, he cannot answer at all about the sorts of incidents which epistemologists suggest that he must be able to report.

Moreover these postulated cognitive acts and processes are said to take place behind locked doors. We cannot witness them taking place in John Doe's life. He alone could report their occurrence, though unfortunately he never does divulge any such things. Nor, however well indoctrinated, do we ourselves ever divulge any such things. And the reason why such episodes never are divulged is clear. Biographical anecdotes told in these idioms are myths, which means that these idioms, or some of them, have their proper applications, but are being misapplied, when used in anecdotes about what people are at a particular moment doing or undergoing. So what is their proper application? And what is wrong with their employment in descriptions of what people do and undergo?

If we read a scientist's printed treatise, or a detective's typewritten report, or listen to an historian's lecture on a campaign, we are indeed presented with arguments, which can be called 'inferences' or 'reasonings', with conclusions, which can be called 'verdicts', 'findings' or 'judgments', with abstract terms, which can be said to signify 'abstract ideas' or 'concepts', with class-membership statements, which can be said to be or signify 'subsumptions', and so on. The comparative anatomy of the limbs, joints and nerves of the statements of built theories is a proper and necessary branch of study, and the terms in which it classifies these elements are indispensable for the discussion of the truth and consistency of particular theories and for the comparison of the methods of different sciences.

But then we shall be asked, 'Why, if it is legitimate to characterise pieces of published theories in such idioms, is it not also legitimate to describe in corresponding idioms corresponding pieces of theorising? If the printed statement of a theory embodies the printed statements of some premisses and conclusions, why should we not say that the thinking out of the theory embodied corresponding premiss-cognising and conclusion-cognising acts? If there is an argument in a book, must there not have been a corresponding piece of implication-cognising in the biography of the thinker who discovered what the book tells? If a detective's report contains an abstract term like 'alibi', must there not have taken place in the course of his investigations an internal episode of having the corresponding abstract idea of Alibi? Surely theories printed in books, or delivered in lecture-halls, are like the footprints left by the previous tread of a foot. It is legitimate to apply directly some of the predicates of a footprint to the foot that printed it, and to infer from some of the other predicates of the footprint to some different but co-ordinate predicates of the foot; so why should we not in the same way characterise the theorising operations of the theorist by predicates transferred or inferred from those of his handiwork? From what other causes could these effects have come?'

This last question, which I have tendentiously put into the mouths of the champions of the tradition that I am criticising, shows, I think, the nature of the myth. It is a variant of the old causal myth that we have already considered and rejected. It is the para-mechanical hypothesis applied specifically to the separable slices of didactic prose which enter into the statements of theories.

There must occur, so the argument might run, special internal processes of abstraction, subsumption and judgment, for of what else could the abstract terms of published theories, their class-membership phrases and their conclusions be the effects? There must occur private operations of discursive thinking, for what else could cause passages of significant prose to appear in public lectures or in print? Or, to put this para-mechanical point in terms of the favoured verb 'to express', there must be mental acts of passing from premisses to conclusions, since the 'because' and 'so' sentences which feature in the statements of theories are significant and therefore express counterpart cogitative operations in the theorist's mind. Every significant expression has a meaning, so when an expression is actually used, the meaning of it must have been occurring somewhere, and it can have been occurring only in the form of a thought that took place in the speaker's or writer's private stream of consciousness. Presumably, if epistemologists had paid as much attention to arithmetical and algebraical reckonings as they have to geometrical demonstrations, they would, in consistency, have used analogous arguments to prove the occurrence, behind our postulated Iron Curtains, of mental processes of adding, subtracting, multiplying and dividing, and we should have been told that, besides such mental acts as conception, judgment and inference, there are also the cognitive acts of adding, subtracting and equating. We might even have been credited with one Faculty of Long Division and another of Quadratic Equations. Of the exercises of what other mental powers could our pencilled long-division sums and our dictated quadratic equations be the outward expressions?

With the general defects of the para-mechanical hypothesis we need no longer concern ourselves. But we should attend to certain specific points that arise in its application to intellectual operations. First, while it is certainly true, because tautologous, to say that properly used significant expressions have their particular meanings, this does not warrant us in asking, 'When and where do these meanings occur?' A bear may be now being led about by a bear-leader, and a footprint must once have been imprinted by a particular foot, but to say that an expression has a meaning is not to say that the expression is on a lead held by a ghostly leader called a 'meaning' or a 'thought', or that the expression is a public trace left behind by an unheard and invisible step. To understand an expression is not to infer an unwitnessable cause. The very fact that an expression is made to be understood by anyone shows that the meaning of the expression is not to be described as being, or belonging to, an event that at most one person could know anything about. The phrase 'what such and such an expression means' does not describe a thing or happening at all, and *a fortiori* not an occult thing or happening.

Next, the suggestion that, for a person wittingly to use a significant word, phrase or sentence, there must antecedently or concomitantly occur inside him a momentary something, some-times called 'the thought that corresponds with the word, phrase or sentence', leads us to expect that this supposed internal occurrence will be described to us. But when descriptions are proffered, they seem to be descriptions of ghostly doubles of the words, phrases or sentences themselves. The 'thought' is described as if it were just another more shadowy naming, asserting or arguing. The thought that is supposed to bear-lead the overt announcement 'tomorrow cannot be Sunday, unless today is Saturday' turns out to be just the announcement to oneself that tomorrow cannot be Sunday without today being Saturday, i.e. just a soliloquised or muttered rehearsal of the overt statement itself. We certainly can, and often do, rehearse in our heads or *sotto voce* what we are then going to tell the audience, or write down on foolscap. But this makes no theoretical difference, as the same supposed question again arises, 'In what does the significance of this soliloquised or muttered expression consist? In yet another 'thought to correspond' going on in yet another still more twilit studio? And would this in its turn be just another rehearsed announcement?' To say something significant, in awareness of its significance, is not to do two things, namely to say something aloud or in one's head and at the same time, or shortly before, to go through some other shadowy move. It is to do one thing with a certain drill and in a certain frame of mind, not by rote, chattily, recklessly, histrionically, absent-mindedly or deliriously, but on purpose, with a method, carefully, seriously and on the *qui vive*. Saying something in this specific frame of mind, whether aloud or in one's head, *is* thinking the thought. It is not an after-effect of thinking the thought, such that the author might conceivably have thought the thought, but shirked saying the thing to himself, or to the world. But, of course, he might have thought the same thought, saying a different thing, since he might have uttered a sentence to the same effect in a different language, or in a different form of words in the same language. Knocking in a nail is not doing two things, one with a hammer and another without a hammer, for all that just brandishing a hammer unskilfully, carelessly or aimlessly does not get nails knocked in, and for all that the carpenter could have knocked in his nail with another hammer instead of with this one.

So when a person has, or is at home· with, a theory and is, therefore, prepared, among many other things, to deliver to himself or to others a didactic statement of it, he is *ipso facto* prepared to deliver the required premiss-sentences, conclusion-sentences, narrative-sentences and arguments, together with the required abstract nouns, equations, diagrams, imaginary illustrations and so forth. And when called on to give such an exposition, he will at particular moments be actually in process of deploying these expressions, in his head, or *viva voce*, or on his typewriter, and he may and should be doing this with his mind on his job, i.e. purposefully, with method, carefully, seriously and on the *qui vive*. He will be talking or writing, heeding what he is saying. So we can say, if we like, that since he is at particular moments heedfully deploying his abstract terms, premiss-sentences, conclusion-sentences, arguments, graphs, equations, etc., he is then and there 'thinking' what they mean. To say this is perfectly legitimate, but it is slightly hazardous, since the present participle 'thinking' is liable to tempt us to suppose that he is being the author of two processes, one probably overt process of saying or typing concatenated phrases and sentences, and another, necessarily covert shadow-process of having or producing some ghostly harbingers of those sayings and writings, namely some 'ideas' or 'judgments' or 'inferences' or 'thoughts', 'cognitive acts' of which his vocal and manual acts of saying and writing are the mere 'expressions' or 'footprints'. And this is just the temptation that is yielded to by those who describe theorising activities as internal foreshadowings of the prose-moves made in the didactic telling of an achieved theory.

This brings us back to our earlier question, whether we are supposed to look for the supposed acts of 'judging', 'having abstract ideas', 'inferring' and the rest in the theorist's exploratory, or in his expository operations. Are they supposed to be manifested in his saying things, when he knows what to say, or in his travailings, when he does not yet know what to say, since he is still trying to get this knowledge? When he is exercising acquired facilities, or when he is still in difficulties? When teaching *how* or when learning *how*? I think it is clear, without much more argument, that didactic expositions of arguments with their conclusions and their premisses, of abstract ideas, of equations, etc., belong to the stage after arrival and not to any of the stages of travelling thither. The theorist can impart his lessons, because he has finished learning them. He can use his equipment, because he is at last equipped. It is just because the pathmaking is over that he is able to saunter on the paths that he had laboured to construct for that purpose; or it is just because the arduous weapon-training is at last completed that he can now without any difficulties handle his weapons. His 'thoughts' are what he has now got; they are not the toils without which he would not have got them.

If we are to use at all the odd expression 'making a judgment', we must say that the detective makes the judgment that the game-keeper killed the squire, only when he is putting into indicative prose a piece of the theory that he now has, and that he keeps on making this judgment as often as he is called upon to tell this part of his theory, whether to himself, to the reporters or to Scotland Yard. And then we shall refrain from talking as if a separate antecedent act of making this judgment had occurred as a part of his investigations.

So if we like to reserve the word 'thinking', in the sense of 'thinking out', for some of the preparatory pondering labours without which he would not have got his theory, then that thinking cannot be described as consisting of, or containing, the making of any judgments, save in so far as he may have settled some sub-theories *en route*, which he was accordingly prepared to deliver to himself, to the reporters, or to Scotland Yard in interim reports. Travelling to London does not consist of jobs done in London, or of rehearsals of the interviews which may be held there.

Doubtless in the course of his inquiries the detective may have spurred on and directed his efforts by putting to himself the interrogation 'Was it the gamekeeper who killed the squire?' But an interrogative sentence, so used, is not a conclusion-teaching sentence but a conclusion-hunting directive. He asks it, because there is something he has not established, not because there is something that he is prepared to tell, because he has established it.

Doubtless, again, he may tentatively announce to himself or to Scotland Yard 'It might have been the gamekeeper'. But not only would this not pass for an act of making the judgment, or reporting that the gamekeeper did kill the squire, but, anyhow in certain junctures, it would have to be taken as the interim report of a sub-theory already built and occupied, and therefore no longer under construction.

'Well', it may be conceded, 'perhaps there is something wrong with the idea that theorising ought to be described as consisting of, or containing, 'acts of judging'. Certainly a theorist cannot tell things, before he can tell them; he cannot declare his findings, while still investigating. Trials terminate in verdicts; they do not consist of them. But what about inferring? Surely it is part of the very notion of a rational being that his thoughts sometimes progress by passages from premises to conclusions? It must therefore sometimes be true of any rational being, John Doe, say, that he is at a particular moment moving to a conclusion from some premises, even though he is strangely embarrassed at being asked whether he enjoyed his trips the last three times he made such passages, how long they took him, whether he dawdled over them, whether he inferred hard or idly and whether he ever stopped halfway between premises and conclusions.'

It is certainly true that John Doe may, on finding or being told certain things, then tell himself and us consequential truths which had not occurred to him before. Discoveries are often made by inference. But not all arguing is discovering. The same argument can be used by the same person time and time again, but we should not say that he repeatedly made the same discovery. The detective was, perhaps, given certain clues on Tuesday and at some moment on Wednesday he says to himself for the first time 'it could not have been the poacher, so it was the gamekeeper who killed the squire'. But when reporting his results to his superiors he need not say in the past tense 'On Wednesday afternoon I argued that the gamekeeper killed the squire'; he may say 'From these clues I conclude that the gamekeeper killed the squire', or 'From these clues it follows that he was the murderer', or 'The poacher did not, so the gamekeeper did kill the squire'. He may say this several times to his slow-witted superior, and later say it again several times in Court. Each time he is using his argument, drawing his conclusion, or making his inference. These descriptions are not reserved for the one occasion when the light burst upon him.

Nor need there have been any occasion on which the light burst upon him. It might well be that the idea that the gamekeeper was the murderer had already occurred to him and that the new clues seemed at first to have only a slight pertinence to the case. Perhaps during some minutes or days he considered and reconsidered these clues, and found that the loopholes they seemed to leave became gradually smaller and smaller until, at no specifiable moment, they dwindled away altogether. In such a situation, which was the situation of all of us when we began to study the proof of Euclid's first theorem, the force of the argument does not flash, but only dawn, upon the thinker, much as the meaning of a stiff piece of Latin unseen does not flash, but only dawns, upon the translator. Here we cannot say that at such and such a moment the thinker first drew his conclusion, but only that, after such and such a period of chewing and digesting, he was at last ready to draw it in the knowledge that he was entitled to do so. His mastery of the argument came gradually, like all masteries which involve learning by practice; but when it was achieved, he was then ready to state the whole argument without hesitation or qualms, to state it as often as might be necessary and to state it in a variety of alternative phrasings.

This familiar fact that before we can use an argument readily we have to acquire mastery of it by more or less gradual practice is apt to be obscured by the logicians' habit of adducing for their examples specimens of completely hackneyed arguments. An argument is hackneyed, when practice with it or its kin has long since prepared us to use it unhesitatingly and without qualms. The force of a hackneyed argument is immediately obvious for the same reason that the meaning of a Latin sentence is immediately obvious when we are quite used both to its vocabulary and to its syntax. They leap to the eye or flash upon us now, but it was not so once. Nor is it so now, when we are confronted by arguments, or Latin sentences, of which we have never met even the brothers or the cousins.

So far from it being true that 'inference' denotes an operation in which a discovery is made, an operation, therefore which could not be repeated, we mean by 'inference' an operation which the thinker must be able to repeat. He has not got hold of an argument, unless he can wield it and its brothers on all sorts of occasions and in various formulations. It is not enough that a new and true idea should once occur to him on once receiving a piece of information. If he is to merit the description of having deduced a consequence from premisses, he must know that acceptance of those premisses gives him the right to accept that conclusion; and the tests of whether he does know this would be other applications of the principle of the argument, though he would not, of course, be expected to name or to formulate that principle *in abstracto*.

We must, therefore, distinguish learning to use a particular argument, or to use any arguments of a certain family, from learning new truths by using such an argument. The more prompt the latter is the better, probably, is our mastery of the argument. But our acquisition of this mastery may well have been gradual and perhaps all the more sure for having been gradual. If a person shows that he can use the argument by actually using it properly in the discovery of a new truth, he shows also that he can use this same argument for a variety of ends other than that of solving his own momentary queries. Having an argument, like having a pen, a theory or a plan, is different both from getting it and from using it. Using it entails having it and having it involves having got, and not lost, it. But, unlike some sorts of theories and plans, arguments are not mastered merely by absorbing information, nor is mastery of them lost through shortness of memory. They are more like skills. Practice is necessary for mastering them and even long desuetude is seldom sufficient for forgetting how to work them. By 'practice' I refer not to the special exercises given to the few by instructors in logic, but to the ordinary exercises taken by everyone in everyday discussion and reading, as well as to the more academic exercises given to nearly everyone in the classroom.

An argument is used, or a conclusion drawn, when a person says or writes, for private or public consumption, 'this, so that', or 'because this, therefore that', or 'this involves that', provided that he says or writes it knowing that he is licensed to do so. This saying or writing in this frame of mind is, of course, a mental, indeed an intellectual act, since it is an exercise of one of those competences which are properly ranked as 'intellectual'. But this is not to say that it is a 'mental act' in the sense that it is performed behind the scenes. It may be done in silent soliloquy, but it may just as well be done aloud, or in ink. Indeed we expect to find a thinker's most subtle and most careful arguments, where we expect to find a mathematician's best calculations and demonstrations, namely in what he submits in print for the criticism of his colleagues. We know what to suspect if a thinker boasts that he has a good argument which he will not or cannot publish.

This brings us to another point. We saw that there was some sort of incongruity in describing someone as being at a time and for a period engaged in passing from premises to a conclusion. 'Inferring' is not used to denote either a slowish or a quickish process. 'I began to deduce, but had no time to finish' is not the sort of thing that can significantly be said. In recognition of this sort of incongruity, some theorists like to describe inferring as an instantaneous operation, one which, like a glimpse or a flash, is completed as soon as it is begun. But this is the wrong sort of story. The reason why we cannot describe drawing a conclusion as a slowish or quickish passage is not that it is a 'Hey, presto' passage, but that it is not a passage at all. A person may be quick or slow to reach London, solve an anagram or checkmate the opposing king; but reaching a conclusion, like arriving in London, solving an anagram and checkmating the king, is not the sort of thing that can be described as gradual, quick or instantaneous. We can ask how long it took to run a race, but not how long it took to win it. Up to a certain moment the race was still in progress; from that moment the race was over and someone was the victor. But it was not a long or short moment. Coming into possession of a piece of property is another instance of the same kind. The preliminary negotiations may take a long or a short time, but the passage from not yet owning the article to being its owner is neither as quick as a lightning flash nor as protracted as the dawn. 'Passage' was a misleading metaphor. It is equally misleading when used to describe the change that occurs when a person comes into possession of a truth for which he has been for a long or a short time negotiating.

When a person has got an argument, his first or his fiftieth deployment of it in speech or writing certainly takes time. He may gabble it very fast to himself and drawl it rather slowly over the telephone. The delivery of an argument may take seconds or hours. Often we use the verb 'argue', though seldom the verbs 'infer', 'deduce' or 'draw conclusions', for the process of delivering an argument. In this use we can say that the speaker was interrupted half-way between stating his premisses and stating his conclusions, or that he got from his premisses to his conclusions much faster today than he did yesterday. Similarly a stammerer may take a long time telling a joke. But we do not ask how long it took him to make the joke. Nor do we ask how long a thinker spent in arriving at, as distinct from travelling towards, his conclusion. 'Conclude', 'deduce' and 'prove', like 'checkmate', 'score', 'invent' and 'arrive', are, in their primary uses, what I have called 'got it' verbs, and while a person's publications, or other exploitations of what he has got, may take much or little time, his transition from not yet having got it to having now got it cannot be qualified by epithets of rapidity. When a person uses these verbs in the timeless present tense, as in 'I conclude', 'he deduces' or 'we prove', he is using them in a sense derivative from their primary sense. They do not directly report gettings, but something nearer akin to possession.

The traditional assumption that inference-verbs denote processes or operations required its makers to say, first, that the processes or operations were of lightning rapidity and, second, that their occurrence was the impenetrable secret of their author. The arguments he produced in discussions, or in print, were mere 'expressions' of his own privy operations and mere spurs to kindred privy operations on the part of their recipients. Misconstruing referees' verbs as biographers' verbs leads inevitably to demanding double-life biographies.

The epistemology of ratiocination has, with many other branches of epistemology, been handicapped by allegiance to a special superstition, the superstition that the theorising operations which it is trying to describe ought to be described by analogies with seeing. It takes as its standard model the prompt, effortless and correct visual recognition of what is familiar, expected and sunlit, and makes no mention of the belated and hesitant recognition, or mis-recognition, of what is strange, unexpected or moonlit. Furthermore, it takes as its model what is denoted by the visual achievement verb 'see', and not what is denoted by the visual task words 'peer', 'scrutinise' and 'watch'. Thinking things out is described as consisting, at least partly, of consecutive 'seeings' of implications. But this is to describe theorising work by analogies with what is not work but achievement; or it is to describe what are actually more or less difficult self-schoolings by analogies with achievements, which are effortless, just because a long run of previous efforts has long since inculcated complete facility in making them. It is like describing a journey as constituted by arrivals, searching as constituted by findings, studying as constituted by examination triumphs, or, in a word, trying as constituted by successes.

It is true that quite often implications are immediately obvious, in something like the ways in which jokes and cows are often immediately obvious. Just as we do not, in ordinary favourable circumstances, have to study at all in order to make out that the creature in the meadow is a cow, so, in favourable circumstances, we do not have now to study at all in order to be ready to say, for example, 'then tomorrow is Boxing Day' on being reminded that today is Christmas Day. Here we already enjoy full familiarity, either with the particular argument, or with a lot of its brothers and sisters. When an argument is itself hackneyed, or of a hackneyed sort, no present studying is needed, since those former encounters with it or its kin, which made it hackneyed, have already given us this preparation. Nor do we now have to cudgel our brains, when required to give the English for *mensa*.

The same is true of seeing cows. Our recognition of them is nowadays effortless and instantaneous, just because the necessary preparatory studies which we went through in our infancy have long since made hackneyed the ordinary appearances of cows. So these favourite specimens of the effortless and instantaneous act of 'seeing' that one truth follows from another show nothing about the process of learning how to use or follow arguments, since they are nothing but further instances of things done with complete facility by people who have already got by practice the knack of doing them.

It is a curious fact that, though we make this metaphorical use of the verb 'to see' even more commonly in speaking of our instantaneous appreciation of jokes than we do in speaking of our instantaneous acceptance of arguments, no epistemologist has supposed that joking entails the prefatory occurrence of 'mental acts' of cognising the points of jokes, as they commonly do suppose that using arguments presupposes prefatory 'mental acts' of 'seeing' implications. Perhaps this is only because Euclid's 'Elements' do not contain any jokes. But perhaps the reason is that it is patent that a piece of joke-seeing could not be a causal antecedent of joke-telling, i.e. that telling a joke is not 'expressing' an antecedent piece of joke-seeing.

I now want to show that using an argument does not 'express' an antecedent and 'internal' piece of implication-seeing. If someone tells a joke, it follows that he has got a joke to tell, and he can not only tell it over and over again, but also see its point, when someone else tells it. Similarly, if he uses an argument, it follows that he has got an argument to use and may not only produce it over and over again, but can also acknowledge its force, when someone else uses it. But the fact that ability to use an argument carries with it the ability to 'see' the implication, when someone else presents the argument to him, does not require that he is causally bound to do such a piece of 'seeing' just before, or just while, he himself uses the argument. The contemplative metaphor of 'seeing' implications or jokes, which is perfectly appropriate to certain special situations is, for that very reason, inappropriate to others. The jester's audience has indeed not made any jokes; it has only appreciated, or failed to appreciate, the jokes made by him. The audience has been receptive or unreceptive, discerning or undiscerning, quick or slow in the uptake; but it has not been either original or unoriginal, inventive or uninventive. It has found something funny, found it unfunny, or failed to find it funny; but it has not said or done anything funny or unfunny. Seeing jokes is the role of the audience, whereas making them is the job of the jester. The audience can be described in contemplative metaphors, but the jester must be described in executive terms. If no jokes were made, there would exist no jokes to be seen. For a repartee to be found amusing, a repartee must have been made. The jester himself cannot 'see' the humour of his repartee, until he has made it, though he can 'see' it, before he tells it to a larger audience. Seeing jokes presupposes the making of jokes, as art galleries presuppose easels and consumers presuppose producers. If the idioms of construction, execution, invention and production were not applicable to jesters, painters and farmers, the idioms of seeing jokes, appreciating pictures and consuming farm produce would be left without application.

The same holds good in matters of theory. If proofs were not given, proofs could not be accepted; if conclusions were not drawn, there could be no allowing or disallowing of inferences; if statements were not made, there could be no acquiescing in statements. For one judge to concur in a verdict, another judge must have given a verdict. Only constructed and delivered arguments can be examined and only when an inference has been at least mooted, can an implication be seen or missed. We do not first see an implication and then go on to draw a conclusion, any more than we first accept the solution of an anagram and then go on to solve it. Multiplications have to be done before they can be marked 'correct'.

This contrast between the uses of the contemplative and of the executive or constructive idioms in the description of intellectual work may be illustrated in another way. When children are given their elementary instruction in geometry, the proofs of the theorems are commonly presented to them printed in books, or written on the blackboard. The task of the pupils is to study, follow and acquiesce in those proofs. They learn by concurring. But when they are given their elementary instruction in arithmetic and algebra, they are set to work in quite a different way. They have to do their own adding, subtracting, multiplying and dividing. Nor do they study classical solutions of equations; they have to solve their own equations. They learn by operating. Consequently, while the contemplative idiom belongs naturally to the instruction and description of learners of geometry, it is the executive idioms which belong to the instruction and description of learners of arithmetic and algebra. Pupils are criticised for not being able to 'see' or 'follow' demonstrations, whereas they are criticised for not being able to 'do' long division or 'solve' quadratic equations. Similarly we talk of translations rather as being made or given, than as being allowed or adopted.

Formal logic was, unfortunately, taught from the start in the esteemed geometrical manner, with the result that the epistemology of ratiocination and of intellectual work in general continues to be told chiefly in the contemplative idiom, that is, in terms appropriate to classrooms furnished with blackboard, but no pens or paper, instead of in terms appropriate to classrooms furnished with pens and paper, but no blackboard. We are given to understand that to 'cognise' is not to work something out, but to be shown something. Had arithmetic and chess been brought into the curriculum before geometry and formal logic, theorising work might have been likened to the execution of calculations and gambits instead of to the struggle for a bench from which the blackboard can be clearly seen. We might have formed the habit of talking of inference in the vocabulary of the football field, instead of in that of the grandstand, and we should have thought of the rules of logic rather as licenses to make inferences than as licenses to concur in them. It would not then have occurred to us that an act of internally 'seeing' an implication must be a prelude of using any argument; it would have been obvious, as is true, that a person can be described as 'seeing' that one truth follows from another only when he hears or reads, perhaps in his head, the promulgated argument 'this, so that', 'because this, therefore that', or the statement 'if this, then that'.

I shall discuss briefly one more instance of terminological malversation. There are certain kinds of expressions in regular use by both theorists and laymen which are properly and conveniently classified as 'abstract'. A mile is an abstraction, so are the National Debt, the Equator, the average taxpayer, the square root of 169, and Cricket. Every moderately educated person knows how to make intelligent use of a good many abstract terms and how to follow their use by others; he wields them, for the most part, unperplexedly, consistently and appropriately in general statements, homilies, questions and arguments. In certain junctures he recognises the utility of classifying such terms as 'abstract'. When his child asks him why the Equator is marked on the map, yet is invisible to the people who cross it, or how it is that cricket has been played in England for many years, though no cricket matches last more than three or four days, he is ready to answer or divert the question by saying that the Equator and Cricket are only abstract ideas. Saying this is to say, though the layman is unlikely to put it in this way, that statements, questions and arguments which incorporate abstract terms like 'the Equator', 'the average taxpayer' and 'Cricket' are on a higher level of generality than their syntax would suggest. They read as if they contained mentions of individual things, persons and matches, when in fact they refer, in different ways, to ranges of individually unmentioned things, persons and matches.

If a person is at a particular moment using an abstract term, using it significantly and using it knowing its significance, he can be said to be using an abstract idea, or even thinking an abstract thought, notion or concept. And from these innocuous, if infelicitous expressions, it has been easy to move to making such seemingly more profound and diagnostic statements as that his abstract term 'expresses' the abstract idea that he is there and then having. Exciting questions then raise their heads. How and when did he form this abstract idea? Where has it been and what has it been doing in the period between his last and his present use of it? Is it somewhat like a badly blurred picture in the mind's eye, or is it more like a pack of clear mental pictures, each one of which differs slightly from its neighbours? That minds are the only warehouses which could possibly store such precious, if ethereal, articles would naturally not be in question.

In real life no one ever tells this sort of story. No one refuses to join a game on the score that he is busy forming an abstract idea, or says that he finds conceiving concepts a harder or longer job than doing long division. No one says that he has just found an abstract idea, after having mislaid it for some weeks, or that his idea of the average taxpayer is not blurred enough, or, alternatively, not photographic enough, to do its job. No teacher bids his pupils to sit down and do some abstracting, or gives them good or bad marks for their exercises in such a task. No novelist depicts his hero as pluckily, briskly or half-heartedly abstracting. The verb 'to abstract' is clearly not a genuine biographical verb; it is therefore not a verb appropriate even to shadow biographies.

Consider a new example. Geographical contours are certainly abstractions. The soldier finds nothing on the hillside answering to the 300-feet contour line on his map, in the way in which he does find rivers and roads answering to the map-symbols for rivers and roads. But though contour lines are abstract symbols, in a way in which symbols for rivers are not abstract, the soldier may know quite well how to read and use them. Identifying his coppice with a coppice marked on his map, he can tell how high above sea level he is, how high he must climb to reach the summit and whether he will be able to see the bridge over the railway when the fog lifts. He can draw a map with roughly judged contours, he can fix and keep rendezvous at points on given contours and he can talk sense about contours. So, startled though he would be by the allegation, he has the abstract idea of Contour.

But in saying that he has this idea we are not saying that there exists an impalpable something which he and he alone can find if he turns his attention inwards. We are saying that he can execute, regularly executes, or is now executing, some of the tasks just described, together with an indefinite variety of kindred tasks.

The question, 'How did he form this abstract idea?' becomes the question, 'How did he acquire this specific knack or competence?' To this question he himself can provide the answer. He was given lectures in map reading and map drawing; he was sent out over strange country with a compass and a map; he was told to notice how the wrack left behind by a recent flood had formed a line along the hillside twelve feet above the lake; he was asked what would be obscured and what would be left visible, if the flat-bottomed cloud sank to 300 feet above sea-level; he was ridiculed when he drew a map in which the contour lines were crossed or broken. It had taken him three weeks before he really knew the ropes. We could paraphrase this by saying that he was for three weeks forming the abstract idea of Contour. But it would be safer and more natural to say that it took him three weeks to learn how contour lines are read and used and how the word 'Contour' is used. The other description tempts one to suppose that throughout the period of three weeks something was being slowly distilled or concocted in his metaphorical insides, or that something rather like a negative was being gradually developed in a metaphorical dark room, even while he himself was occupied in football, eating and sleeping.

'Contours are abstractions', or 'Contour lines are abstract map-symbols' is a proper and useful instruction for a map-referee to give to would-be readers and makers of maps. 'Contour lines are the outward expressions of the mapmakers' mental acts of conceiving heights (in feet) above sea-level' suggests that reading a map entails penetrating the impenetrable shadow-life of some anonymous surveyor.

(5) *Saying and Teaching.*

In this chapter, as well as elsewhere in this book, I have been at pains to distinguish different sorts of talk, the sociable, unstudied chat of slippered conversation, the guarded conversational talk of the reticent and insincere, and the studied, unconversational, shod talk of the instructor. In this chapter we have been particularly concerned with this last, namely the didactic discourse, written or spoken, published or self-addressed, in which a person teaches what he has to teach. The main reason for harping here upon the methods, ends and even tones of voice of didactic discourse is that it is in terms of didactic discourse that the concept of the intellect is being elucidated. At least an important part of what we mean by 'intellectual powers' is those specific capacities which are originally inculcated and developed predominantly by didactic discourse, and are themselves exercised, *inter alia*, in teaching the same lessons or adaptations and expansions of them in further allocutions. Didactic discourse is the vehicle for the transmission of knowledge.

But there is also a more general reason for discussing the different sorts of talk. Epistemologists have always been aware that there are some close connections between thought and speech, but their elucidations of these connections have been retarded by the tacit supposal that there exists some nuclear and homogeneous activity of saying things. They have used, without apparent qualms, verbs like 'state', 'propound', 'enunciate', 'declare', 'describe', 'assert', 'express', 'tell', 'say' and 'discourse', as if they provided both a full and an unambiguous account of what a person is about, when he is described as doing one or other of these things. But there is no single-track or nuclear activity of just saying things. What is said is said either conversationally, or coaxingly, or reassuringly, or peremptorily, or entertainingly, or reproachfully, and so forth. Talking in a bargaining way is different from talking in a confessional way, and both are different from talking anecdotally, menacingly or provokingly. Even what we write is meant to be read in a special tone of voice, and what we say to ourselves in our heads is not 'said' in a monotone.

Didactic speaking and writing is the species with which we are here concerned. It is talk in which, unlike most of the others, what we tell is intended to be kept in mind. Talk of most of the other kinds is not intended to be kept in mind, but responded to, or otherwise acted on straightway. Didactic talk, unlike most of the others, is meant to better the mind of the recipient, that is, to improve its equipment or strengthen its powers. Teaching is teaching someone to do, which includes to say, things, and what a pupil has been taught to do, he is expected to continue to be able to do for at least a fair time afterwards. Lessons are meant to be learned and not forgotten. In a word, teaching is deliberate equipping. Of course, not all teaching is done by talking didactically. Infants learn things by following examples which may, or may not, be deliberately set for their imitation. Some lessons are taught by deliberately setting examples and giving demonstrations. Some are taught by sheer drill, some by ridicule and so forth.

Now didactic discourse, like other sorts of lessons, but unlike most of the other sorts of talk, is intended to be remembered, imitated and rehearsed by the recipient. It can be repeated without losing its point, and it is suitable for retransmission by word of mouth or in writing. Lessons so taught can be preserved, as lessons taught by demonstrations and examples cannot be preserved; they can therefore be accumulated, assembled, compared, sifted and criticised. Thus we can learn both what our grandfathers taught to our fathers and what our fathers added to, or modified, in the lessons they had been taught. The original discoveries by which they bettered their instructions can be embodied in the schooling of their sons, for it does not take genius to learn what it has taken genius to invent. Intellectual progress is possible just because the immature can be taught what only the mature could have found out. The sciences grow because the undergraduate can by suitable schooling be trained to start where Euclid, Harvey and Newton left off.

Furthermore, didactic discourse is impersonal and untopical, in the sense that the lessons it delivers could be delivered by any suitably trained teacher to any suitably prepared recipient; and the occasions of delivering it are not fixed, as the occasions of delivering conversational, bargaining, reassuring, or prosecuting remarks are fixed, by non-recurrent situations. If a repartee, a traffic-signal or a promise is not made by a particular person to a particular person at a particular juncture, the opportunity for making it has gone for ever; but if John Doe missed yesterday's lesson on the Latin subjunctive, or failed to finish the chapter on the size and distance of the moon, there may be the same point as before in his reception tomorrow or next week of those same lessons. It will not escape those who are familiar with the philosophical discussions of the nature and status of what are called 'propositions', that the predicates by which propositions are described are just those which do belong *ex officio* to the jobs of didactic discourse and do not belong to repartees, limericks, queries, interjections, condolences, accusations, vows, behests, complaints, or any of the countless other sorts of non-didactic saying. It is no accident that some theorists like to define 'intellectual operations' as operations with propositions, or that other theorists like to define 'propositions' as the products or implements of intellectual operations. Both are implicitly referring to our lesson giving, lesson taking and lesson using activities and powers, without, of course, explicitly mentioning such vulgar matters.

All talk is meant to exert some specific influence. A question is meant to be heard, understood and answered; an offer is meant to be considered and accepted; a threat is meant to deter; and a condolence is meant to give comfort. Didactic talk is meant to instruct. The swimming instructor says things to his pupils, but he is not primarily intending to get the pupil to say those same things. He intends him now to make the required strokes with his arms and legs and later to make strokes like these without the accompaniment of spoken or silent instructions. Ultimately, perhaps, the pupil will teach other novices to swim, or at least teach himself to make new strokes and to make the old strokes in more difficult conditions. Learning the imparted lesson is becoming competent, not merely or primarily to parrot it, but to do a systematic variety of other things. The same holds good of more academic lessons, like lessons in pronunciation, geography, grammar, style, botany, calculation and ratiocination. We learn from these lessons how to say and do things, most of which are not echoes of the words of the lessons.

Didactic influence can be exerted not only by one person upon another but also by one person upon himself. He can coach himself to say and do things which are not echoes of the words in which that coaching is given. Just as he can give himself orders, which he then complies with in manual evolutions, so he can tell himself things which he then turns to account in new didactic moves. Having told himself that in the garage there are seven tins each containing two gallons of petrol, he can then tell himself that there are fourteen gallons of petrol in the garage. The activities which we call 'thinking things out', 'pondering', 'considering', 'debating' and 'excogitating' are notoriously capable of being progressive. They can achieve new results. The answers to some, but not all, questions can be found out merely by private or inter-personal talking, provided that the talking is the right sort of talking and is carried on with some skill, industry and care. Jocose talking does not solve algebraical problems nor yet does a helter-skelter spate of algebraical expressions.

When we comment on a person's intellectual proficiencies and limitations, the main things we have in mind are his efficiency and keenness in making such advances. It may be thought that in referring to the achievement of new results by intellectual work I am talking simply of deduction, or more generally of inference. But this, though an important species, is not the sole species of progressive thinking. In multiplying and dividing we arrive by thinking at the previously unknown answers to questions, but we do not call those answers 'conclusions'; nor do we call misreckonings 'fallacies'. The historian, having assembled a mass of relevant facts, has to think before he can give a coherent account of a campaign; but the coherence of his final account is a unity of quite a different kind from that of a chain of theorems. His account will contain a lot of inferences and it must be free from inconsistencies; but, to be good history, it must have other intellectual merits as well. Excellence in translation also requires careful thinking, but the rules and canons that have to be observed are not only rules of inference. Clumsiness in translation shows faulty, but not fallacious, thinking. No questions are begged nor middle terms undistributed, in the composition of a metrically incorrect sonnet.

Thinking things out involves saying things to oneself, or to one's other companions, with an instructive intent. The assertion of each proposition is intended to equip or prepare the recipient to turn what he is told to further accounts, to use it, for example, as a premiss, or as a procedure maxim. As in the classroom, so in inter-personal discussion and in private excogitation, neither the teacher nor the learner is ever absolutely proficient, patient, energetic, alert or concentrated. The instruction may have to be repeated, rephrased, postponed or withdrawn; the recipient's responses may be wrong, off the track, faltering and perfunctory. Progress made on one day may on the next day seem to have been completely lost, and protracted bafflement may give place in a moment to forward strides which make the thinker wonder how a task so difficult yesterday was so easy today. Tomorrow, perhaps, he will complain that the results achieved have done nothing but set him further tasks as tough as any that he has yet overcome. He has, perhaps, found out a way of using yesterday's proposition as a premiss; but the conclusion got today must in its turn be turned to some further premissory account. His results are always usable as lessons from which, with skill, work and luck, further results can be got

We see then that the well-known fact that pondering can be progressive, despite its consisting only in the serial production of seemingly inert sentences, is not inexplicable. Certain sorts of sentences, properly delivered and properly received, have an instructive effect. They teach us to do and say things which were not said or done in their delivery. Some thinkers have been puzzled by the question, 'How can a person get to know new things by dint of merely telling himself what he knows already?' They would not be puzzled by the question, 'How can a novice learn to make new and correct swimming strokes from listening to words from the instructor on the bank?' or even by the question, 'How can a novice learn to make new and correct swimming strokes from listening to words which he impresses on himself?' The question, 'How can a person learn to make new didactic strokes from listening to instructively intended pronouncements from his tutor, his colleague or himself?' is no more mysterious.

## (6) *The Primacy of the Intellect.*

It is now easy to distinguish the sense in which intellectual operations are higher than, and do 'govern', the exercises of other mental capacities, from the sense in which I have denied that the occurrence of intellectual operations is implied in all those descriptions we give of people's actions and reactions which embody mental concepts.

Intellectual work has a cultural primacy, since it is the work of those who have received and can give a higher education, education, namely, by didactic discourse. It is what constitutes, or is a *sine qua non* of, culture. To put it crudely, barbarians and infants do not do intellectual work, since, if they did, we should describe them instead as at least part-civilised and near to school age. There is a sort of contradiction in speaking of a quite unschooled intellect, unless one is referring to someone's capacity to profit by such schooling, but there is no contradiction in speaking of a quite unschooled mind, The schooling of a person requires that he has already acquired the capacity to receive that schooling. Lectures cannot be followed, much less delivered, by persons who cannot yet use or follow artless talk.

It is therefore absurd to speak as if such things as attending, trying, wanting, fearing, being amused, perceiving, bearing in mind, recollecting, purposing, learning, pretending, playing and chatting could occur only in obedience to didactically given instructions, whether from an internal or an external lecturer. This is, however, quite compatible with saying that some degree of intellectual accomplishment is a *sine qua non* of, for example, wanting to be a patent-lawyer, being amused at a witticism by Voltaire, bearing in mind the rules of Greek conditional sentences, or identifying a magneto, or a dividend warrant. Even so, to describe someone as doing something which he could not have done without formerly having had a certain education does not entail saying that he must have recited all or any of those early lessons just before he acted. I could not now read a Greek sentence, if I had not formerly learned Greek grammar, but I do not ordinarily have to remind myself of any rules of Greek grammar, before I construe a Greek sentence. I construe according to those rules, but I do not think of them. I bear them in mind, but I do not appeal to them, unless I get into difficulties.

There is a tendency among epistemologists and moralists to pretend that to have a mind is to have inside one, not merely potentially but actually, either one or two lecturers, Reason and Conscience. Sometimes Conscience is held to be just Reason talking in its sabbatical tone of voice. These internal lecturers are supposed already to know, since they are competent to teach, the things which their audience does not yet know. My Reason is, what I myself am not yet, perfectly rational and my Conscience is, what I am not yet, perfectly conscientious. They have not anything to learn. And if we asked, 'Who taught my Reason and who taught my Conscience the things that they have learned and not forgotten?' we should perhaps be told of corresponding instructors lodged inside their bosoms. There is, of course, a serious intention behind this nursery myth, just as there is a serious intention behind my flippant extension of it. It is quite true that when a child has part-learned something and learned it partly from the didactic discourses of his parents and schoolmasters, he has acquired some capacity and inclination to deliver refresher-lessons to himself in their magisterial tones of voice. He does not, in the stock situations, have to wonder what they would tell him, or what he should tell himself. He knows the hackneyed parts of his lessons well enough to deliver them unhesitatingly, appropriately and with the right gravity. And, when he does this, he does, if you like, 'hear the voice of Reason', or 'of Conscience', speaking authoritatively in accents which are a queer blend of, say, his father's and his own. He can easily give himself the instructions which he still finds it difficult to observe. His preaching is necessarily ahead of his practice, since the object of delivering didactic talks to him is to inculcate better practices in him by doing so. So at this stage he may have learned quite well how and when to tell himself to do things, though he has not yet learned very well how and when to do them. The corresponding thing may occur when he is wrestling with a piece of Latin prose. Experiencing difficulties with the syntax of his sentence, he may 'listen for' and 'hear' the appropriate rule of syntax being dictated to him in a tone of voice which is half his own and half that of his schoolmaster. This voice might then be picturesquely described as 'the Voice of Latin Grammar'. But in this case the provenance of the 'voice' would be too obvious for anyone to talk seriously of the original source of his grammatical scruples being the dictates of an angelic, internal philologist.

This mention of conscience and of the knowledge of Latin grammar brings us back to a matter already mentioned but not yet discussed, namely to intellectual activities other than those of theorising. Grammatical knowledge is, for example, knowing how to compose and construe Latin sentences, and moral knowledge, if the strained phrase is to be used at all, is knowing how to behave in certain sorts of situations in which the problems are neither merely theoretical nor merely technical. Knowledge of chess or bridge is an intellectual accomplishment which is exercised in trying to win games; strategy is one which is exercised in trying to win battles and campaigns; the engineer's schooling and workshop experience teach him to design bridges and not, save *per accidens*, to build or expound theories.

The reason why we call such games and work 'intellectual' is not far to seek. Not only the education necessary for mastering the arts, but also many of the operations necessary in the practice of them are homogeneous with those required for, and in, tasks of building, expounding and applying theories. The ability to compose and construe Latin sentences is an art, while the philology of the Latin tongue is a science; but the teaching and practising of the one coincides with a part of the teaching and applying of the other. Engineering does not advance physics, chemistry or economics; but competence at engineering is not compatible with complete innocence of those branches of theory. If not the calculation, at least some estimation, of probabilities is an integral part of playing the more intellectual card games, and this is part of our reason for describing them as 'intellectual'.

It is easy to see that intellectual development is a condition of the existence of all but the most primitive occupations and interests. Every advanced craft, game, project, amusement, organisation or industry is necessarily above the heads of untutored savages and infants, or else we could not call it 'advanced'. We do not have to be scientists in order to solve anagrams, or play whist. But we have to be literate and be able to add and subtract.

## (7) *Epistemology.*

Before concluding this chapter, we must consider an academic and departmental matter. A part of philosophy is traditionally called 'theory of knowledge', or 'epistemology'. Our present question is, 'What sorts of theories about knowledge should epistemologists try to build, given that we have found something radically wrong with important parts of the theories which they have hitherto offered? If the whole imposing apparatus of terms like 'idea', 'conception', 'judgment', 'inference' and the rest has been wrongly transferred from the functional descriptions of the elements of published theories to the description of acts and processes of building theories, what is left of the theory of knowledge? If these terms do not denote the hidden wires and pulleys by which intellectual operations were wrongly supposed to work, what is the proper subject matter of the theory of knowledge?'

The phrase 'theory of knowledge' could be used to stand for either of two things. (1) It might be used to stand for the theory of the sciences, i.e. the systematic study of the structures of built theories. (2) Or it might be used to stand for the theory of learning, discovery and invention.

(1) The philosophical theory of the sciences or, more generally, of built theories, gives a functional account of the terms, statements and arguments as well as of the numerous other kinds of expressions which enter into the formulation of the theories. It could be called 'the Logic of Science' or, metaphorically, 'the Grammar of Science'. (But 'science' should not be used so parochially as to exclude theories unpatronised by the Royal Society.) This sort of account does not describe or allude to episodes in the lives of individual scientists. It does not therefore describe or allude to any supposed

private episodes in those lives. It describes in a special manner what is, or might be, found in print.

(2) As there do exist the practice and the profession of teaching, there could exist a branch of philosophical theory concerned with the concepts of learning, teaching and examining. This might be called 'the philosophy of learning', 'the methodology of education' or, more grandly, 'the Grammar of Pedagogy'. This would be the theory of knowledge in the sense of being the theory of getting to know. This study would be concerned with the terms in which certain episodes in the lives of individuals are described and prescribed for by teachers and examiners.

Now the great epistemologists, Locke, Hume and Kant, were in the main advancing the Grammar of Science, when they thought that they were discussing parts of the occult life-story of persons acquiring knowledge. They were discussing the credentials of sorts of theories, but they were doing this in para-physiological allegories. The recommended restoration of the trade-names of traditional epistemology to their proper place in the anatomy of built theories would have a salutary influence upon our theories about minds. One of the strongest forces making for belief in the doctrine that a mind is a private stage is the ingrained habit of assuming that there must exist the 'cognitive acts' and 'cognitive processes' which these trade-names have been perverted to signify. So, since none of the things which we could witness John Doe doing were the required acts of having ideas, abstracting, making judgments or passing from premisses to conclusions, it seemed necessary to locate these acts on the boards of a stage to which only he had access. The wealth of convincing biographical detail given in the epistemologists' allegories has been, at least in my own case, what gave one of the two strongest motives for adhering to the myth of the ghost in the machine. The imputed episodes seemed to be impenetrably 'internal' because they were genuinely unwitnessable. But they were genuinely unwitnessable because they were mythical. They were causal hypotheses substituted for functional descriptions of the elements of published theories.

CHAPTER X

PSYCHOLOGY

(1) *The Programme of Psychology*.

IN the course of this book I have said very little about the science of psychology. This omission will have appeared particularly perverse, since the entire book could properly be described as an essay, not indeed in scientific but in philosophical psychology. Part of the explanation of the omission is this. I have been examining the logical behaviour of a set of concepts all of which are regularly employed by everyone. The concepts of learning, practice, trying, heeding, pretending, wanting, pondering, arguing, shirking, watching, seeing and being perturbed are not technical concepts. Everyone has to learn, and does learn, how to use them. Their use by psychologists is not different from their use by novelists, biographers, historians, teachers, magistrates, coastguards, politicians, detectives or men in the street. But this is not the whole story.

When we think of the science or sciences of psychology, we are apt, and often encouraged, to equate the official programmes of psychology with the researches that psychologists actually carry on, their public promises with their laboratory performances. Now when the word 'psychology' was coined, two hundred years ago, it was supposed that the two-worlds legend was true. It was supposed, in consequence, that since Newtonian science explains (it was erroneously thought) everything that exists and occurs in the physical world, there could and should be just one other counterpart science explaining what exists and occurs in the postulated non-physical world. As Newtonian scientists studied the phenomena of the one field, so there ought to be scientists studying the phenomena of the other field. 'Psychology' was supposed to be the title of the one empirical study of 'mental phenomena'. Moreover, as Newtonian scientists found and examined their data in visual, auditory and tactual perception, so psychologists would find and examine their counterpart data by counterpart, non-visual, non-auditory, non-tactual perception.

It was not, of course, denied that there existed and could exist plenty of other systematic and unsystematic studies of specifically human behaviour. Historians had for two thousand years been studying the deeds and words, opinions and projects of men and groups of men. Philologists, literary critics and scholars had been studying men's speech and writing, their poetry and drama, their religion and philosophy. Even dramatists and novelists, in depicting ways in which the creatures of their fancy acted and reacted, were showing in fable how they thought that real people do or might behave. Economists study the actual and hypothetical dealings and expectations of men in markets; strategists study the actual and possible perplexities and decisions of generals; teachers study the performances of their pupils; detectives and chess-players study the manoeuvres, habits, weaknesses and strengths of their adversaries. But, according to the para-Newtonian programme, psychologists would study human beings in a completely different way. They would find and examine data inaccessible to teachers, detectives, biographers or friends; data, too, which could not be represented on the stage or in the pages of novels. These other studies of man were restricted to the inspection of the mere tents and houses in which the real men dwelt. The psychological study of man would use direct access to the residents themselves. Indeed, not until psychologists had found and turned the key, could the other students of human thought and behaviour hope to do more than batter vainly on locked doors. The visible deeds and the audible words of human beings were not themselves exercises of the qualities of their characters or intellects, but only external symptoms or expressions of their real but privy exercises.

Abandonment of the two-worlds legend involves the abandonment of the idea that there is a locked door and a still to be discovered key. Those human actions and reactions, those spoken and unspoken utterances, those tones of voice, facial expressions and gestures, which have always been the data of all the other students of men, have, after all, been the right and the only manifestations to study. They and they alone have merited, but fortunately not received, the grandiose title 'mental phenomena'.

But though the official programme of psychology promised that the subject matter of its investigations would consist of happenings differing in kind from, and lying 'behind', those bits of human conduct which alone were accessible to the other studies of man, the experimental psychologists in their daily practice had perforce to break this promise. A researcher's day cannot be satisfactorily occupied in observing nonentities and describing the mythical. Practising psychologists found themselves examining the actions, grimaces and utterances of lunatics and idiots, of persons under the influence of alcohol, fatigue, terror and hypnosis, and of the victims of brain injuries. They studied sense perception as ophthalmologists, for example, study sense perception, partly by making and applying physiological experiments and partly by analysing the reactions and verbal responses of the subjects of their experiments. They studied the wits of children by collecting and comparing their failures and successes in various kinds of standardised tests. They counted the blunders made by typists at different stages of their day's work, and they examined people's differing liabilities to forget different kinds of memorised syllables and phrases by recording their successes and failures in recitations after the lapse of different periods of time. They studied the behaviour of animals in mazes and of chickens in incubators. Even the spell-binding, because so promisingly 'chemical', principle of the Association of Ideas found its chief practical application in the prompt word-responses voiced aloud by subjects to whom test words were spoken by the experimenter.

There is nothing peculiar in such a disparity between programme and performance. We ought to expect wisdom about questions and methods to come after the event. The descriptions given by philosophers of their own objectives and their own procedures have seldom squared with their actual results or their actual manners of working. They have promised, for example, to give an account of the World as a Whole, and to arrive at this account by some process of synoptic contemplation. In fact they have practised a highly proprietary brand of haggling, and their results, though much more valuable than the promised Darien-panorama could have been, have not been in any obvious respects like such a panorama.

Chemists once tried hard to find out the properties of phlogiston, but, as they never captured any phlogiston, they reconciled themselves to studying instead its influences and outward manifestations. They examined, in fact, the phenomena of combustion and soon abandoned the postulate of an uninspectable heat-stuff. The postulation of it had been a will-o'-the-wisp, the sort of will-o'-the-wisp that encourages the adventurous to explore uncharted thickets and then, ungratefully, to chart the thickets in maps that make no further mention of those false beacons. Psychological research work will not have been wasted, if the postulate of a special mind-stuff goes the same way.

However, the question 'What should be the programme of psychology?' has still to be answered. Attempts to answer it would now be faced by the following difficulty. I have argued that the workings of men's minds are studied from the same sorts of data by practising psychologists and by economists, criminologists, anthropologists, political scientists and sociologists, by teachers, examiners, detectives, biographers, historians and players of games, by strategists, statesmen, employers, confessors, parents, lovers and novelists. How then are certain inquiries to be selected, while all the rest are to be rejected, as 'psychological'? By what criteria are we to say that the statistical results of Schools Examination Boards are not, while the results of intelligence tests are, the products of psychological investigations? Why is the historian's examination of Napoleon's motives, intentions, talents and stupidities not, when that of Sally Beauchamp's is, a psychological study? If we give up the idea that psychology is about something that the other human studies are not about, and if we give up, therewith, the idea that psychologists work on data from which the other studies are debarred, what is the *differentia* between psychology and these other studies?

Part of the answer might be given thus. The country postman knows a district like the back of his hand; he knows all the roads, lanes, streams, hills and coppices; he can find his way about it in all weathers, lights and seasons. Yet he is not a geographer. He cannot construct a map of the district, or tell how it links on to adjoining districts; he does not know the exact compass-bearings, distances or heights above sea-level of any of the places that, in another way, he knows so well. He has no classification of the types of terrain that his district contains, and he can make no inferences from its features to features of neighbouring districts. In discussing the district he mentions all the features that the geographer might mention, but he does not say the same sorts of things about them. He applies no geographical generalisations, uses no geographical methods of mensuration, and employs no general explanatory or predictive theories. Similarly, it might be suggested, the detective, the confessor, the examiner and the novelist may be thoroughly conversant, in a rule of thumb way, with the kinds of data which the psychologist would collect, but their handling of them would be unscientific, where the psychologist's handling of them would be scientific. Theirs would correspond to the shepherd's weather-lore; his to the meteorologist's science.

But this answer would not establish any difference between psychology and the other scientific or would-be scientific studies of human behaviour, like economics, sociology, anthropology, criminology and philology. Even public librarians study popular tastes by statistical methods, yet, though tastes in books are indubitably characteristics of minds, this sort of study of them would not be allowed to rank as psychology.

The right answer to the question seems to be that the abandonment of the dream of psychology as a counterpart to Newtonian science, as this was piously misrepresented, involves abandonment of the notion that 'psychology' is the name of a unitary inquiry or tree of inquiries. Much as 'Medicine' is the name of a somewhat arbitrary consortium of more or less loosely connected inquiries and techniques, a consortium which neither has, nor needs, a logically trim statement of programme, so 'psychology' can quite conveniently be used to denote a partly fortuitous federation of inquiries and techniques. After all, not only was the dream of a para-Newtonian science derived from a myth, but it was also an empty dream that there was or would be one unitary, because Newtonian, science of the 'external world'. The erroneous doctrine that there was a segregated field of 'mental phenomena' was based on a principle which also implied that there was no room for the biological sciences. Newtonian physics was proclaimed as the all-embracing science of what exists in space. The Cartesian picture left no place for Mendel or Darwin. The two-worlds legend was also a two-sciences legend, and the recognition that there are many sciences should remove the sting from the suggestion that 'psychology' is not the name of a single homogeneous theory. Few of the names of sciences do denote such unitary theories, or show any promise of doing so. Nor is 'cards' the name either of a single game, or of a 'tree' of games.

The analogy suggested above between psychology and medicine was misleading in one important respect, namely that several of the most progressive and useful psychological researches have themselves been in a broad sense of the adjective, medical researches. Among others, and above all others, the researches of psychology's one man of genius, Freud, must not be classed as belonging to a family of inquiries analogous to the family of medical inquiries; they belong to this family. Indeed, so deservedly profound has been the influence of Freud's teaching and so damagingly popular have its allegories become, that there is now evident a strong tendency to use the word 'psychologists' as if it stood only for those who investigate and treat mental disabilities. 'Mental' is commonly used, from the same motives. to mean 'mentally disordered'. Perhaps it would have been a terminological convenience, had the word 'psychology' been originally given this restricted sense; but the academic world is now too well accustomed to the more hospitable and undiscriminating use of the word to make such a reform possible or desirable.

Probably some people will be inclined to protest that there does exist some general and formulable distinction between psychological inquiries and all the other inquiries that are concerned with the wits and characters of human beings. Even if psychologists enjoy no proprietary data on which to found their theories, still their theories themselves are different in kind from those of philologists, camouflage-experts, anthropologists or detectives. Psychological theories provide, or will provide, causal explanations of human conduct. Granted that there are hosts of different ways in which the workings of men's minds are studied, psychology differs from all the other studies in trying to find out the causes of these workings.

The word 'cause' and the phrase 'causal explanation' are, of course, very solemn expressions. They remind us at once of those unheard impacts of those little invisible billiard-balls which we learned to fancy, erroneously, were the truly scientific explanation of everything that goes on in the world. So when we hear the promise of a new scientific explanation of what we say and do, we expect to hear of some counterparts to these impacts, some forces or agencies of which we should never ourselves have dreamed and which we shall certainly never witness at their subterranean work. But when we are in a less impressionable frame of mind, we find something unplausible in the promise of discoveries yet to be made of the hidden causes of our own actions and reactions. We know quite well what caused the farmer to return from the market with his pigs unsold. He found that the prices were lower than he had expected. We know quite well why John Doe scowled and slammed the door. He had been insulted. We know quite well why the heroine took one of her morning letters to read in solitude, for the novelist gives us the required causal explanation. The heroine recognised her lover's handwriting on the envelope. The schoolboy knows quite well what made him write down the answer '225' when asked for the square of 15. Each of the operations he performed had put him on the track to its successor.

There are, as will be seen in a moment, a lot of other sorts of actions, fidgets and utterances, the author of which cannot say what made him produce them. But the actions and reactions which their authors can explain are not in need of an ulterior and disparate kind of explanation. Where their causes are well known to the agent and to all of his acquaintances, the promise of surprising news about their real but hidden causes is not merely like the promise, but is a special case of the promise of news about the occult causes of mechanical happenings whose ordinary causes are notorious. The cyclist knows what makes the back wheel of his cycle go round, namely, pressure on the pedals communicated by the tension of the chain. The questions, 'What makes the pressure on the pedals make the chain taut?' and, 'What makes the tautening of the chain make the back wheel go round?' would strike him as unreal questions. So would the question, 'What makes him try to make the back wheel go round by pressing on the pedals?'

In this everyday sense in which we can all give 'causal explanations' for many of our actions and reactions, mention of these causes is not the perquisite of psychologists. The economist, in talking of 'sellers' strikes', is talking in general terms about such episodes as that of the farmer taking his pigs back to the farm because he found that the prices were too low. The literary critic, in discussing why the poet used a new rhythm in a particular line of his verse, is considering what composition worry was affecting the poet at that particular juncture. Nor does the teacher want to hear about any back-stage incidents, in order to understand what made the boy get to the correct answer of his multiplication problem; for he has himself witnessed the front-stage incidents which got him there.

On the other hand, there are plenty of kinds of behaviour of which we can give no such explanations. I do not know why I was so tongue-tied in the presence of a certain acquaintance; why I dreamed a certain dream last night; why I suddenly saw in my mind's eye an uninteresting street corner of a town that I hardly know; why I chatter more rapidly after the air-raid siren is heard; or how I came to address a friend by the wrong Christian name. We recognise that questions of these kinds are genuine psychological questions. I should, very likely, not even know why gardening is unusually attractive when a piece of disagreeable letter-writing awaits me in my study, if I had not learned a modicum of psychology. The question why the farmer will not sell his pigs at certain prices is not a psychological but an economic question; but the question why he will not sell his pigs at any price to a customer with a certain look in his eye might be a psychological question. Even in the field of sense perception and memory the corresponding thing seems to hold. We cannot, from our own knowledge, tell why a straight line cutting through certain cross-hatchings looks bent, or why conversations in foreign languages seem to be spoken much more rapidly than conversations in our own, and we recognise these for psychological questions. Yet we feel that the wrong sort of promise is being made when we are offered corresponding psychological explanations of our correct estimations of shape, size, illumination and speed. Let the psychologist tell us why we are deceived; but we can tell ourselves and him why we are not deceived.

The classification and diagnosis of exhibitions of our mental impotences require specialised research methods. The explanation of the exhibitions of our mental competences often requires nothing but ordinary good sense, or it may require the specialised methods of economists, scholars, strategists and examiners. But their explanations are not cheques drawn on the accounts of some yet more fundamental diagnoses. So not all, or even most, causal explanations of human actions and reactions are to be ranked as psychological. But, furthermore, not all psychological researches are searches for causal explanations. Many psychologists are occupied, with greater or less profit, in devising methods of mensuration and in making collections of the measurements so achieved. Certainly the hope is that their measurements will one day subserve the establishment of precise functional correlations or causal laws, but their own work is at best only preparatory to this ulterior task. So, as it must be styled 'psychological research', 'psychological research' cannot be defined as the search for causal explanations.

It will now be realised why I have said so little about psychology in the body of this book. Part of the purpose of the book has been to argue against the false notion that psychology is the sole empirical study of people's mental powers, propensities and performances, together with its implied false corollary that 'the mind' is what is properly describable only in the technical terms proprietary to psychological research. England cannot be described solely in seismological terms.

(2) *Behaviourism.*

The general trend of this book will undoubtedly, and harmlessly be stigmatised as 'behaviourist'. So it is pertinent to say something about Behaviourism. Behaviourism was, in the beginning, a theory about the proper methods of scientific psychology. It held that the example of the other progressive sciences ought to be followed, as it had not previously been followed, by psychologists; their theories should be based upon repeatable and publicly checkable observations and experiments. But the reputed deliverances of consciousness and introspection are not publicly checkable. Only people's overt behaviour can be observed by several witnesses, measured and mechanically recorded. The early adherents of this methodological programme seem to have been in two minds whether to assert that the data of consciousness and introspection were myths, or to assert merely that they were insusceptible of scientific examination. It was not clear whether they were espousing a not very sophisticated mechanistic doctrine, like that of Hobbes and Gassendi, or whether they were still cleaving to the Cartesian para-mechanical theory, but restricting their research procedures to those that we have inherited from Galileo; whether, for example, they held that thinking just consists in making certain complex noises and movements or whether they held that though these movements and noises were connected with 'inner life' processes, the movements and noises alone were laboratory phenomena.

However it does not matter whether the early Behaviourists accepted a mechanist or a para-mechanist theory. They were in error in either case. The important thing is that the practice of describing specifically human doings according to the recommended methodology quickly made it apparent to psychologists how shadowy were the supposed 'inner-life' occurrences which the Behaviourists were at first reproached for ignoring or denying. Psychological theories which made no mention of the deliverances of 'inner perception' were at first likened to 'Hamlet' without the Prince of Denmark. But the extruded hero soon came to seem so bloodless and spineless a being that even the opponents of these theories began to feel shy of imposing heavy theoretical burdens upon his spectral shoulders.

Novelists, dramatists and biographers had always been satisfied to exhibit people's motives, thoughts, perturbations and habits by describing their doings, sayings, and imaginings, their grimaces, gestures and tones of voice. In concentrating on what Jane Austen concentrated on, psychologists began to find that these were, after all, the stuff and not the mere trappings of their subjects. They have, of course, continued to suffer unnecessary qualms of anxiety, lest this diversion of psychology from the task of describing the ghostly might not commit it to tasks of describing the merely mechanical. But the influence of the bogy of mechanism has for a century been dwindling because, among other reasons, during this period the biological sciences have established their title of 'sciences'. The Newtonian system is no longer the sole paradigm of natural science. Man need not be degraded to a machine by being denied to be a ghost in a machine. He might, after all, be a sort of animal, namely, a higher mammal. There has yet to be ventured the hazardous leap to the hypothesis that perhaps he is a man.

The Behaviourists' methodological programme has been of revolutionary importance to the programme of psychology. But more, it has been one of the main sources of the philosophical suspicion that the two-worlds story is a myth. It is a matter of relatively slight importance that the champions of this methodological principle have tended to espouse as well a kind of Hobbist theory, and even to imagine that the truth of mechanism is entailed by the truth of their theory of scientific research method in psychology.

It is not for me to say to what extent the concrete research procedures of practising psychologists have been affected by their long adherence to the two-worlds story, or to what extent the Behaviourist revolt has led to modifications of their methods. For all that I know, the ill effects of the myth may, on balance, have been outweighed by the good, and the Behaviourist revolt against it may have led to reforms more nominal than real. Myths are not always detrimental to the progress of theories. Indeed, in their youth they are often of inestimable value. Pioneers are, at the start, fortified by the dream that the New World is, behind its alien appearances, a sort of duplicate of the Old World, and the child is not so much baffled by a strange house if, wherever they may actually lead him, its bannisters feel to his hand like those he knew at home.

But it has not been a part of the object of this book to advance the methodology of psychology or to canvass the special hypotheses of this or that science. Its object has been to show that the two-worlds story is a philosophers' myth, though not a fable, and, by showing this, to begin to repair the damage that this myth has for some time been doing inside philosophy. I have tried to establish this point, not by adducing evidence from the troubles of psychologists, but by arguing that the cardinal mental concepts have been credited by philosophers themselves with the wrong sorts of logical behaviour. If my arguments have any force, then these concepts have been misallocated in the same general way, though in opposing particular ways, by both mechanists and para-mechanists, by Hobbes and by Descartes.

If, in conclusion, we try to compare the theoretical fruitfulness of the Hobbes-Gassendi story of the mind with that of the Cartesians, we must undoubtedly grant that the Cartesian story has been the more productive. We might describe their opposition in this picture. One company of a country's defenders instals itself in a fortress. The soldiers of the second company notice that the moat is dry, the gates are missing and the walls are in collapse. Scorning the protection of such a rickety fort, yet still ridden by the idea that only from forts like this can the country be defended, they take up their stand in the most fort-like thing they can see, namely, the shadow of the decrepit fort. Neither position is defensible; and obviously the shadow-stronghold has all the vulnerability of the stone fort, with some extra vulnerabilities of its own. Yet in one respect the occupants of the shadow-fort have shown themselves the better soldiers, since they have seen the weaknesses of the stone fort, even if they are silly to fancy themselves secure in a fort made of no stones at all. The omens are not good for their victory, but they have given some evidence of teachability. They have exercised some vicarious strategic sense; they have realised that a stone fort whose walls are broken is not a stronghold. That the shadow of such a fort is not a stronghold either is the next lesson that they may come to learn.

We may apply this picture to one of our own central issues. Thinking, on the one view, is identical with saying. The holders of the rival view rightly reject this identification, but they make this rejection, naturally but wrongly, in the form that saying is doing one thing and thinking is doing another. Thinking operations are numerically different from verbal operations, and they control these verbal operations from another place than the place in which these verbal operations occur. This, however, will not do either, and for the very same reasons as those which showed the vulnerability of the identification of thinking with mere saying. Just as undisciplined and heedless saying is not thinking but babbling, so, whatever shadow-operations may be postulated as occurring in the other place, these too might go on there in an undisciplined and heedless manner; and then they in their turn would not be thinking. But to offer even an erroneous description of what distinguishes heedless and undisciplined chattering from thinking is to recognise a cardinal distinction. The Cartesian myth does indeed repair the defects of the Hobbist myth only by duplicating it. But even doctrinal homeopathy involves the recognition of disorders.

INDEX

## A

Abstract terms, 120, 227, 293–4, 307–8
Achievements and Achievement words, 130–1, 149–53, 222–3, 238, 278, 301–304
Actions, 33, 65 ff., 74, 89
——Automatic, 110
——Causes of, 90, 113–14, 325
——Voluntary and involuntary, 67, 69 ff.
Agitations and Agitation words, 83, 93, 95, 97–8, 104, 107–8, 166, 180
    See Moods, Motives, Feelings.
Appraisals, 66–9, 73, 75, 80, 180
Argument, 47, 123, 299–304
Aristotle, 30, 48, 65, 112, 149
Attending, 164, and see Heeding.
Avowals, 102, 183–4

## B

Bearing in mind, see Serial Performances, and Remembering.
'Because,' see Explanation.
Behaviourism, 32, 84, 327–30
Believing, 28, 133–5
Biology, 117, 323
Bodies, see Physical World.

## C

'Can,' see Modal Sentences.
Care, see Heeding.
Category, 8, 22
Category-mistake, 16 ff., 33, 77–9, 94, 152, 168, 206
Causal Connexion, 122–3
    See Law Sentences.
Chatting, see Unstudied Talk.
Choice, 68
Cognition, 26, 62, 258

Competences and liabilities, 70, 79, 111, 130–3
Conscience, 159, 315
Consciousness, 12, 14, 83, 136, 154 ff., 199, 204, and see Heeding.
Conversing, see Unstudied Talk.
'Could,' see Modal Sentences.

## D

Descartes' Myth, 8, 11 ff., 33, 158, 201, 329
    See 'Ghost in the Machine.'
Determinable words, 44–5, 96, 118–19, 256–7
Didactic Talk, see Teaching, Propositions, Intellect, Theorizing, Studied Talk.
Dispositions and Disposition words, 33, 42, 43 ff., 51, 56, 71, 73, 85–6, 88, 91, 95, 112, 116 ff.
——Generic and specific, 118
Disposition sentences, 117–25
——Logic of, 117 ff., 138–9
——Not fact-reporting, 117–20, 123–125
——Not deduced from laws, 124

## E

Emotions, 83–4, 95, 104, 114
Enjoying, 107–9, 132
Episodes, see Occurrences.
Epistemological words, 185, 203, 265, 284, 292–309
Epistemology, 317
Ethical sentences, 128, 315
Exercises, 33, 51, 54–5, 60, 70, 86, 97, 104
    See Dispositions.
Expecting, 226 ff., and see Serial Performances.

331

Law, Open hypotheticals, 120–1, 142
  *See* Mongrel-categoricals.
Learning, 42, 49, 56, 59, 60, 129, 146–8,
  231, 232, 272, 284, 306
——and didactic discourse, 284–7, 309–
  314
Liabilities, *see* Competences.
Locke, 159, 318

M

Matter, *see* Physical World, *etc.*
Mechanism, 75 ff., 328
Memory, *see* Remembering
'Mental,' 34, 199, 245, 280, 324
Mental conduct words, 7, 15–16, 19,
  21, 25–6, 62
Mental operations, 7–8, 15, 22, 48, 61,
  63 ff., 67, 81, 90–1, 105, 244
——Connexion with physical events,
  12, 19, 58, 63 ff., 81, 90–1, 105,
  135, 168, 222–3, 231–2, 240
——Unconscious, 14, 157, 162
Mind, 36, 40, 46, 51, 168 ff., 199–200
——and body, 22–3, 52, 63–4, 84, 105,
  168–9, 189, 199–200, 242
Minding, *see* Heed.
'Mind's Eye, in the,' *see* Imagining *and*
  'Head, in the.'
Misunderstanding, 51–61
Modal sentences, 126 ff.
——'Can,' 'could,' 'would,' *etc.*, 46, 71,
  119, 120, 126–31, 202, 220, 261
——'Would,' 93, 141–2
——Compared with hypotheticals,
  127–8, 140
'Mongrel-categoricals,' 47–8, 123 ff.,
  138–41, 145, 217, 229
Moods and Mood words, 83, 93, 95–6,
  97–8, 100 ff., 109, 244
Motives and Motive words, 81–95,
  98–99, 104, 106, 110 ff., 133–4, 171
——Second-order inclinations, 112–13

O

Observation and Observation words,
  151, 199 ff., 201–4, 207, 214, 222

Observation, Perception recipes, 218–
  19, 228–34
——Problems of perception, 208, 224
Occurrences and Occurrence words, 15,
  46–7, 83, 85, 117–18, 135, 142, 149 ff.
Optical metaphors, 136–7, 159–62, 174,
  178, 303–5
Other minds, 14, 21, 51 ff., 61, 66, 90,
  114, 155, 169, 179 ff. 205 *see* Solipsism.

P

Pain, 102, 105, 108, 203, 244
Para-mechanical hypotheses, 19–23, 64,
  68, 114, 117, 186, 222, 243, 251, 272,
  291–5, 323, 327
Para-political myth, 23
Perception, *see* Observation.
Phenomenalism, 234–40
Physical world, *etc.*, 11 ff., 76 ff., 198,
  319
Pleasure, *see* Enjoying.
Preparation, *see* Teaching.
Pretending, 102, 133, 172, 181, 191, 256–
  64, 267, 270–1
——Higher order activity, 259–64
Privileged access, 11–14, 25 ff., 33–4,
  45, 51, 54, 57, 61, 66, 83, 115, 119,
  154, 163, 165, 167, 179, 181, 207, 209,
  211, 216, 219, 247 ff., 293–5, 304–5
  *See* 'Ghost in the Machine.'
Propositions, 185, 311
Psychology, 22, 53–4, 76, 165, 242,
  319 ff.
——Programme of, 322
——Two worlds myth of, 319–22

R

Readiness, *see* Heeding *and* Prepara-
  tion.
Reason, 47, 280–1, 284, 288, 315
Remembering, 178, 288, 272 ff.
——Not a source of knowledge, 274–6
——and recalling, 272–3
Retrospection, 159–60, 166–7